DO YOU WANNA PLAY SOME MAGIC?

EMERSON, LAKE AND PALMER
IN CONCERT 1970–1979

CW01496559

This edition published in Great Britain in 2012 by Soundcheck Books LLP, 88 Northchurch Road, London, N1 3NY, under licence from Helter Skelter Publishing Limited of PO Box 50497, London, W8 9FA

ISBN: 978-0-9566420-8-0

Every effort has been made to contact copyright holders of photographic and other resource material used in this book. Some were unreachable. If they contact the publishers we will endeavour to credit them in reprints and future editions.

A CIP record for this book is available from the British Library

Book design: Benn Linfield (www.bennlinfield.com)
Printed and Bound in Great Britain by CPI Group, Eastbourne

Contents

Acknowledgements

Gudrun Friedrich for the limitless supply of resource material and advice on any matters relating to ELP: this book could not have been completed without her help. Extra special mention to Tony Ortiz, ELP's archivist, for supplying so many photographic, written and picture resources, and for his generous help. Dirk Uther and Attila Sik for their help and reviews. Simon Fetherston (ELP Downunder), Neil Corsatea/Air C Images and Todd Benson for their help with resource material of all kinds. Special thanks to Jane Thresher, Michael Richards, Ian Laycock and everyone from the ELP online discussion group for their limitless, unconditional support and never-failing humour. Linda Heath, Mary Ann Burns and Craig Fenton for offering tremendous amounts of information about the ELP live act; Craig is the supreme archivist. Graham Kennedy for some superb photos of the Tarkus models used during the UK tour of 1972.

Bruce Pilato and Will Alexander, ELP's management, for paving the way; Keith Emerson, Greg Lake and Carl Palmer for their unswerving support and encouragement throughout. Martin Darvill and QEDG. Martyn Hanson, George Forrester and Frank Askew for allowing me to use references from their work, *Emerson, Lake and Palmer: The Show That Never Ends*. Frank was also a mine of information about Carl's kits, particularly which kit was used when. John Blake Publishing Ltd for allowing me to use references from Keith's autobiography, *Pictures Of An Exhibitionist*. The BBC for allowing me to use a transcription of Keith's appearance on *The John Dankworth And Cleo Laine Show*. Chris Welch for some great original quotes, notwithstanding the fact that no-one knows where he is now.

Particular thanks to;

Keith for telling me a joke I couldn't possibly repeat in these pages and for clarifying some technical specifications.

Greg for being able to identify guitars from grainy, still images and for a superb interview that in a sense kick-started the book.

Carl for remembering some details about the very first gig that I just couldn't get anywhere else, and for his encouragement of the project.

You all converted Elliott Freeman to the music of ELP at the tender age of 7.

Foreword

My life became better when I heard the first few bars of *'The Barbarian'*. This was Emerson, Lake and Palmer and they were to become a great part of my life.

They were my band, much like one's football team. I played their stuff to everybody and became an ELP bore. I once went through the bins outside their offices in the hope of finding a souvenir.

I first saw them at the Oval in the early seventies and was blown away. The next time was at Wembley and I think I went into shock. The shock that three blokes were able to make that huge sound; the sound that was made just for me it seemed.

Later when I became a 'celebrity' I always tried to be cutting edge, like my heroes and to leave an audience thinking, "That was special." This is chiefly down to ELP and their ability to make all other groups sound like pub bands to me.

I've since met and become friends with them and it is a privilege. Carl once called me the fourth member of the band. I had a 'woodie' for weeks!

So enjoy this book and remember days of ribbon controllers and perfection.

Emerson, Lake and Palmer ... The best little ol' rock band there ever was, don't you worry 'bout that!

Jim Davidson OBE (One Band's Enough)

Introduction

The seeds of the idea for this book were sown in 2000 when I first began researching *The Bootleg Guide* and realized just how many Emerson, Lake and Palmer shows are out there. The ELP connection came when I invited Carl Palmer to come to St Bede's in Bradford (where I was teaching at the time), to run one of his Drum Circles for hearing-impaired children and a master class for St Bede's students.

This became a regular event and Carl's reaction towards a live guide book was positive. Contact with Bruce Pilato, Will Alexander and Tony Ortiz paved the way for interviews with Greg and Keith, both of whom were only too happy to support the project with information, technical and otherwise.

"You'll never get the co-operation of the band," is what someone warned me. Wrong! All three guys have been true gentlemen of rock, always answering emails and phone calls, no matter how busy with recording or touring schedules.

More than a few of the reviews in this book are courtesy of the efforts of the online ELP discussion group, with a special mention for Gudrun Friedrich, Dirk Uther and Attila Sik. The internet has brought together so many of the tape (and now CD) collecting community to exchange shows and their thoughts.

Some of the shows in this book are so rare that even the collectors mentioned above don't have them. They rest in the hands of a tiny number of über fans who were willing to help me by providing copies of the rarest for review. Gudrun's site, for example, lists recordings that exist but are as rare as hen's teeth. I managed to listen to almost all of them, realizing just how generous to a fault their owners were.

When you look at just how many shows ELP played between 1970 and 1978, it's sad that so many of them have never appeared, and will never appear, on tape or CD. This book has allowed us to trace the development of songs, epic or otherwise, across the years and tours. Songs like "Take A Pebble" and "Tarkus" changed dramatically, but each kept a kernel that remained a focal jumping-off point for superb improvisations and add-ons.

Improvisation? ELP? Surely not? Oh yes! Some people say that all their improvs were annotated. When you've listened to as many shows as I have, you realize that this is just impossible. Carl once said that at least 40% of ELP on-stage material was totally improvised. In my view, there were many nights where that was an understatement.

A friend said to me, in all sincerity, during the course of the year I spent on the project, "How can you review all those shows? They played the same things every night." Nominally yes, they did. In reality, they were probably the only one of the big progressive rock bands that did not go out and replicate on stage what they'd just laid down on vinyl. "Pictures At An Exhibition", "Tarkus", "Hoedown", "Nutrocker", "Take A Pebble", "Fanfare For The Common Man", all core elements of the live act over the years, are noticeably different each and every night.

The best thing about writing this book? Listening to over 150 shows and never hearing a duff one.

The worst thing? Worrying about getting the equipment and technical specs correct. Keith, Greg and Carl always did, and still do, pride themselves on the quality of the on-stage equipment. Deciphering which keyboard or guitar made which sound was a learning curve for me. As for identifying drum kits, thank goodness for such things as the engravings on the stainless steel kit!

Do I have a favourite ELP live track? In fairness, there are so many that make me play air drums or air keyboards that it's difficult to choose. I do have favourite tours. I have a distinct soft spot, for the *Trilogy* UK tour of autumn 1972 because, at St George's Hall in Bradford, England, I saw the band live for the first time (and you never forget your first time!). One of my all-time favourite tracks, "The Endless Enigma", was only ever played in the UK on that tour, and it was then also I noticed the light-hearted humour in ELP, with the addition to the set-list of the theme from *The Alan Freeman Show*.

My other favourite tour is the final North American outing of winter 1977-1978. The signs were already there that the band wouldn't be together much longer, but what they delivered on that tour was amazing. The energy, the quality of the improvisations, the humour, the sheer verve in each show was remarkable.

Critics took them to task for including numbers such as "Tiger In A Spotlight", "Watching Over You" (another of my lasting favourites), "Maple Leaf Rag" and "Peter Gunn", but what came across with each performance was the determination of Keith, Greg and Carl to put on a varied, dynamic, attention-demanding and, above all, entertaining set.

If ever there was a rock band that really was the sum of its parts, that band was Emerson, Lake and Palmer: perfectionists to a man, with a complete mastery of their instruments, a keen sense of what worked on a stage, and what constituted a successful show. It's obvious from listening to so many tapes that the guys did like poking fun at each other but that the humour had a cathartic effect, which fans lapped up.

Equally, they took each show seriously enough to recognize that the punters had paid their money and wanted the very best that ELP could deliver. There are a number of occasions in these pages when Keith or Greg took members of the audience to task for being too noisy, for throwing things onto the stage, or for doing something downright dangerous. They knew that they had to get it right every night to meet the high expectations of the faithful.

In total, between Sunday 23 August 1970 and Monday 13 March 1978, Emerson, Lake and Palmer played 494 shows. Over 150 of those gigs are reviewed in this book; every one is a gem. Regrettably, few of the recordings on which this book is based have been released officially, more's the pity.

Maybe some more of them should be officially released as follow-ups to the famous *Manticore* boxed sets. Let the fans hear just how professional ELP were, night after night, tour after tour. Let them experience ELP's greatest hits in the format they should be heard – live on stage.

I have also included, for your delight and delectation, a transcript of Keith's appearance on the *John Dankworth And Cleo Laine Show* from BBC 2 TV in 1973.

It has been a privilege to listen to so many ELP shows whilst researching this book. Now it's the turn of their legion of fans worldwide to be reminded just how good they were – and still are.

THE SHOWS

1. *The Brightest Hope Of 1970?*

23 AUGUST – 12 DECEMBER 1970: FIRST EUROPEAN TOUR
(INCLUDING UK)
35 SHOWS PLUS AN APPEARANCE ON *BEAT CLUB* FOR GERMAN TV

Typical set list:	"Pictures At An Exhibition", "The Barbarian", "Take A Pebble", Greg Lake acoustic solo, piano improvisations, "Take A Pebble" reprise, "Knife Edge", "Rondo"/"America"/drum solo, "Nutrocker".
Keith:	Hammond C3, Hammond L100, grand piano, Modular Moog Synthesizer 1C with pre-set boxes, Electric Clavinet.
Greg:	Gibson JT100 custom acoustic and a Fender Jazz bass with fuzz and wah-wah foot pedals.
Carl:	Gretsch kit, (complete with Enid Blyton's Noddy painted on the bass drum), Paiste cymbals and hi-hat, Paiste gongs, woodblocks, cowbells.
PA system:	WEM: 2 Crown stereo amplifiers driving 2,000 watts of speakers in 4 Loudmouth stacks. 20 channel stereo mixer.

This new band had spent much of the summer of 1970 rehearsing in a church hall in Shepherd's Bush, London, building up a set list of "Rondo"/"America", "21st Century Schizoid Man" (dropped when they begin gigging; a verse from "Epitaph" shoe-horned into "Tarkus" is the only thing Greg Lake took from the Crimson King), "Pictures At An Exhibition", "The Barbarian" and "Knife Edge". Keith and Carl were happy that the new band seemed to be picking up nicely where the Nice had left off, but Greg was wary that ELP would just be a "Nice Mark II".

This wariness helps explain why and how Greg would successfully take ELP in a new and different direction with his own brand of musical experimentations. The band soon began to gel in rehearsals: "I remember Greg and Keith smiling proudly when Carl launched into a drum solo at the speed of light. And the feeling was of quiet confidence and eager anticipation. ELP were going to have fun, play to the maximum and conquer the world" [1]

Expectations of this 'new' band were sky high, with sections of the music press dubbing them with the dreaded 'supergroup' moniker. As Carl said, "I'm dreaming of gigs man. It's like two months since I played in public and for Keith it's even longer. I don't think Greg has done a gig since last Christmas."[2] Keith, too, was optimistic, "I certainly hope we will live up to the expectations of all those who voted us brightest hope."[3]

Unlike the other two, laid-back Carl never had to fight to make a living as a musician and had been earning money from drumming since 1962. He told me he used to play working men's clubs at weekends. Keith and Greg, however, had known some tough times, which made them more assertive individuals and equipped them in the struggles for musical supremacy that lay ahead.

Control of the producer's chair also undoubtedly contributed to this, although Keith had told the others that they were all equals. Greg had the most experience in studio production and so it made sense for him to lead in these duties. It was never openly stated, but Keith seemed relieved to give up some of the musical power; after all, he had really felt the pressure of being just about the only truly creative force within the Nice.

ELP's first album had all the winning components that were to power their career for so many years: fierce riffs, battling solos, iron-hard discipline, with lyrics that were, by turns, gentle, thoughtful and tortured. The new material was distinctive, unusual and well-crafted, which was to become the band's trademark.

★|★|★

On Friday 21 August the band played a three number dress rehearsal, including "Pictures At An Exhibition" at London's Lyceum in London, in front of music moguls Robert Stigwood, Ahmet Ertegun, and their roadies. Keith's Moog was one of four custom-built models created by Dr Robert Moog in the summer of 1970 for New York's Jazz In The Garden festival. It was a modular synthesizer with pre-set boxes specially created for live performance, so Keith could just push a button and bring up a new pre-set sound. It cost a hefty £4,000, but still went out of tune with annoying regularity! From the earliest days of rehearsal, it was Keith stage left, with Carl centre stage and Greg over on the right.

The band's first gig proper was not the Isle of Wight Festival on 29 August, as many fans believe, but at the 800 seater Plymouth Guildhall on 23 August 1970. After these two shows, a British tour was organized for September-October, with European dates in the run up to Christmas. Back-drops and lighting were basic at best but the band went down a storm with fans and most of the music press, both in the UK and in Europe. Everywhere they played to packed, or almost packed, houses. The *Beat Club* appearance was recorded for Radio Bremen (at that time also a TV station) sometime in late November/early December, and aired on New Year's Eve 1970.

Recordings from this era are few and far between – and the audience ones that exist suffer from the unsophisticated tape machines around at the time.

1971 would be the year when ELP established themselves as members of rock's aristocracy, but it was 1970 when they proved themselves on stage and their reputation started to go before them. From the word go their music divided people: like Marmite, you either loved or hated them. John Peel uncharitably described them as "A tragic waste of talent and electricity" and their music as "A load of bollocks". The band however quickly established themselves as favourites with the punters, and that's what counted.

An interesting point: check out the dates towards the end of the tour as the band, and Keith in particular, tried out new riffs during the "Take A Pebble" improvisation.

SUNDAY, 23 AUGUST 1970

The Guildhall, Plymouth, England

Tickets: 10, 12 and 15 shillings (50p, 60p and 75p)

A debut show in front of 800 people, for which the band was, reputedly, paid the princely sum of £400.

Plymouth is chosen for the first, warm-up show because of its distance from London and the sharpened pens of the rock press. Keith's introduction, "This is what we sound like"[4], shows a nervousness that we're not really going to see again until the first reunion show at the Tower Theater, Philadelphia in July 1992. Greg's bass launches them into "The Barbarian" and the capacity audience are very quickly on their side. They're under-rehearsed and they know it, but they seem to be carried along by the sheer wild enthusiasm of the fans.

Once they've warmed up there's no stopping them: "Take A Pebble" and the full length version of "Pictures At An Exhibition" are played to the max, with the former staying pretty close to what will become the album version (with the addition of Greg's acoustic break).

Although they stick quite closely to the studio version of "Knife Edge", it is played slightly faster and by this point the band are clearly enjoying themselves. After what sounds like the closing chords, Carl plays a ten second snare drum break and Keith throws himself (and the L100) into 50 seconds of organ gymnastics before Carl counts them into the closing chords proper.

Even then, with the applause starting, Keith is already playing the 'train' sounds of "Rondo"; his interpretation of Dave Brubeck's "Blue Rondo A La Turk". As Carl bangs the gongs, Keith begins to build up the opening crescendo and we're off with Greg and Carl laying down a solid beat – to the obvious delight of one fan in particular, who can be heard clearly on the brief recording that exists of this debut show.

"Rondo"/"America" is the only Nice number featured by the band and it has been re-arranged to suit the new trio. It's fast, furious and definitely brings out the showman in Keith, but this is not the Nice Mark II! Less than four minutes in and Carl tears into a speed of light solo – a blur of hair and drumsticks. At no point do his fingers ever leave his hands, as the old joke goes. His work on the snare, toms and hi-hat is very tight, precise and incredibly fast. He then moves onto the cowbell and blocks before getting the crowd involved with bass drum patterns and handclaps. It's rolls on the gongs next and then off comes the shirt before he lays down the pounding beat again.

Greg and Keith come back on, the crowd go wild with applause and we're into "America". It's hard to believe that Carl holds all those fans in the palm of his hand with a solo that lasts nearly eleven minutes; such was the silence during most of his first-ever solo with the new band that you can almost visualize the crowd open-mouthed in admiration.

"America" is the vehicle for Keith throwing the L100 around the stage, vaulting over it and sticking his knives into the speaker cabinets, before bringing the others back to the finale of "Rondo". Carl proves his worth with a powerful snare drum break before the final crashing chords.

Encores? The crowd demands them, which they get with two more versions of "Rondo" before ending with their version of B. Bumble And The Stingers' "Nutrocker". They get a fifteen minute standing ovation at the end of their first ever gig.

This is a major new force in rock!

SATURDAY, 29 AUGUST 1970

The Third Isle of Wight Festival, East Afton Farm, Freshwater, West Wight, England.

Tickets: Weekend £3, Saturday 35 shillings (£1.75)

In a later interview, Keith confessed, "I wasn't very happy with the Isle of Wight performance. I felt there was a tired atmosphere in the audience."[5]

They're under-rehearsed, but contrary to what Keith and the others feel, their performance that Saturday evening is top-notch. Against the backdrop of Keith's Moog, the band are introduced by the MC: "Ladies and Gentlemen please welcome for their first debut performance ever, Emerson, Lake and Palmer!" They stride on and take control from the off.

The downright 'in yer face' aggression of the still-unreleased "The Barbarian" is such a potent force that it grabs the crowd and shakes them out of their torpor. All three are giving their all but for once the sheer power of Greg and Carl seems to outshine even Keith, resplendent as he is in silvery-blue glitter outfit and brown leather hat. Carl looks very '1970' in his bright green waistcoat with silver edging, whilst Greg is looking the business in a dark shirt; his involuntary shouts of "Yeah!" adding to the feeling that this is a band with a point to prove.

"We'd like to do a number for you now which will be on an album coming out pretty shortly. This is a number called 'Take A Pebble'," Keith announces. The first part sticks almost rigidly to what will become the recorded version, with more perfect brushwork from Carl. Greg's acoustic break is still at the embryonic stage, but helps builds the melodic effect of the whole number. A superbly played piano improvisation takes the piece to almost twelve sublime minutes.

"This is a thing called 'Pictures At An Exhibition' and features the Moog synthesizer," says Keith. "Which doesn't weigh three tons," retorts Greg. They launch into "Pictures ..." and it sounds huge – it's hard to believe the band is only a three piece. Keith works overtime and is visibly shattered by the end of it. "'Pictures ...' is a hard one to play because there's so much to remember"[6]

Each of them gets to showcase during this epic, which climaxes with first Keith, and then Greg, setting off two stage-side cannons. "Pictures ..." typifies a spectacular show and by now the applause is as loud as the cannon blasts. The two instrumentals of "Rondo" and "Nutrocker" close the set and by this time it's obvious they are going down a storm and proving themselves as the hungry hot shots of the festival. Keith's work on "Rondo" is tight and incredibly fast, underpinned by solid rhythm from Greg and Carl. A brief, lightning fast, drum solo works up the crowd into a further frenzy.

The MC asks "We're short of time but do you really want one more?" Dumb question. "Nutrocker" starts in a quite slow, measured way but picks up momentum, Greg doing overtime on the "Yeah" shouts again. As the shouts for "More" echo around, they leave the stage as one of the most theatrical bands of the whole festival; in retrospect, a landmark event in the history of ELP.

Karl Dallas of *The Times* wasn't terribly impressed, describing it as "... a performance in which visual excitement and special effects sometimes attracted rather more attention than what he [Keith] was doing musically."[7]

Let's leave the last word to Keith himself though: "Our intention was to blow every other band off the stage with eccentricity."[8] They succeeded.

THURSDAY, 24 SEPTEMBER 1970

The Town Hall, Watford, England.

Tickets: 18 shillings (90p). Advertised as their "First Home Counties appearance"

Reputedly only their fourth gig and, for many, the one that saw them prove themselves beyond reasonable doubt.

A capacity crowd is stamping and cheering from the word go even though the band themselves seemed to take a while to warm up.

"Pictures ..." is beginning to show what the Moog is really capable of in the right hands and includes all the elements that are establishing the band as the innovative force they are evolving into: wah-wah work on the bass, duelling between the rhythm section and Keith, and acoustic playing that's both slick and tasteful, topped off with Greg's dramatic vocals. Keith's use of the Hammond's higher register drawbars [these increase or decrease the sound depending on whether they are pushed in or pulled out, as well as giving thousands of different sound combinations] creates the haunting, almost unearthly, chime-like sounds in "The Great Gates of Kiev". "The Barbarian" is greeted, deservedly, with a loud cheer and, again, Carl and Greg if anything outshine Keith.

"Take A Pebble" is developing an improvised life all of its own with Keith's keyboard and Greg's acoustic solo. Carl's perfect brushwork reflects his feeling that "I'm pleased to be playing with brushes on the freed jazz thing".[9] "Knife Edge" shows the band at their heaviest, with the crowd clapping along to Greg's intro bass and vocals.

"Rondo" is really beginning to bring out the showman in Keith. Dressed in his glittery tail suit, he vaults over the L100 and throws the knives into the speaker cabinet – and the crowd go ballistic. Carl's solo has developed so much from the Plymouth debut and the Isle of Wight: even faster, crisper, determined as he is "that in future I'll play all the riffs I've worked out quickly, instead of spinning them out."[10] The encore was "Nutrocker" and the dancers are out in the aisles.

The band are growing in confidence with every gig and word is beginning to spread: there are three new sheriffs in town.

TUESDAY, 20 OCTOBER 1970

The Winter Gardens, Bournemouth, England.

Tickets: 17 shillings (85p), 15 shillings (75p), 13 shillings (65p) and 10 shillings (50p)

This gig has to get a mention because it takes place in Greg's home town. "I remember the *Bournemouth Echo* and, you know, it was just one of those things that just confirmed that you had done something with your life".[11]

SUNDAY, 25 OCTOBER 1970

The Royal Festival Hall, London, England.
(originally scheduled for Monday 26 October)

Tickets: from 14 shillings (70p)

Their reputation was beginning to precede them – and they lived up to it here, their first gig at a major London venue.

Again, there is an almost tangible feeling of "We have to prove ourselves here". Keith kicks off "Pictures ..." on the house organ and then runs back to his own keyboards for what can only be described as a powerful, inventive and inspiring version of this epic. In contrast to the sounds from Keith's corner of the stage, Greg's acoustic work is mellow, his Gibson sounding sweet, especially in "The Sage".

"The Barbarian", "Take A Pebble" and "Knife Edge" all receive rapturous applause but it is "Rondo", not surprisingly, that brings the crowd to its feet. It's played at a breathtaking pace, with Keith knifing the speaker cabinets and throwing the L100 round the stage. Cue Carl's unbelievably fast solo before a pounding last segment of "Rondo" that seems to shake the venue to its very foundations. The audience may have been anticipating a band to take over where the Nice left off. True, they get the exaggerated showmanship that Keith excels at, but they also hear a tasty new trio proving their competence, skill and sheer power.

"Nutrocker" follows at a breakneck pace and then, unusually for this band, a second encore of a twelve bar jam that has the crowd up and rocking.

An improvised jam at their first London gig? Is that confidence or is that confidence?

Michael Wale writing in The Times *wasn't entirely convinced though: "As an evening of human pyrotechnics it was engrossing. Who cares about the music? Certainly not the audience."*[12] *Ouch!*

SATURDAY, 29 NOVEMBER 1970

Circus Krone, Munich, Germany

Yes, this is a real circus and the band played on the centre stage, the real circus stage. Too many people are allowed into the tent, a riot ensues and the fire brigade are called. Water hoses are turned on the crowd from the back of the stage and the entire audience gets blasted outside like a clown's routine – only this one isn't funny. The band, who continue playing up to that point, have to call it a day but Greg has one abiding memory, "I'll never forget the smell of elephants which came up with the sawdust which was still on the floor ... the smell of elephants was on the gear for like weeks."[13]

MONDAY, 1 DECEMBER, 1970

Konzerthaus, Vienna, Austria
(some sources list this show at the Stadthalle)

Their fourth gig in a whistlestop European tour (before heading back to the UK for pre-Christmas shows), and their first in Austria.

The audience is treated to a 36 minute version of "Pictures ..." here with some very enthusiastic Moog improvisations in "The Gnome". Greg plays a note perfect "The Sage" to only polite applause from a reserved audience. Keith and Carl fight it out in a friendly duel at the beginning of "The Old Castle", before Greg rejoins and they race through, segueing nicely into "Blues Variation". For the first time in "Pictures ..." they really gel as the powerful energy of the piece, and Keith's Hammond solo, shines through.

A pounding "Promenade" opens the second half of "Pictures ..." and all three are on fire with confident, aggressive playing. They push things to the limits with more improvisation during "Baba Yaga" and a machine-gun like snare drum break from Carl. The drama and crescendo of "The Great Gates of Kiev", with the added spectacle of Keith's Hammond throwing, wins ecstatic applause from an audience that is, not before time, warming to the band.

A few words of German from Keith are followed by a brief introduction to "The Barbarian" by Greg. Carl's strong drum work carries the piece along to a powerful ending. "We're gonna take another song off the album. This is a thing by Greg Lake called 'Take ... A ... Pebble'," shouts Keith.

"Pebble" is now eighteen minutes long and, from the very beginning, Greg's rich vocals and Keith's stunning grand piano make this a memorable version. At one point, Keith throws in a couple of bars of what was to become the riff from "Eruption" at the beginning of "Tarkus", clearly using the free form of the solo to try out new things.

Carl's finger cymbal at the start of Greg's acoustic break is clearly audible and this audience are soon clapping along to Greg's singing – which now includes an adaptation of a verse of the Byrds' song, "Old Blue" – before the solo ends with another precise ping on the finger cymbal from Carl. Keith's piano solo and the jazz-style improvisations are full-on, much to the obvious delight of the crowd.

Keith moves to the clavinet and they play a few snatches from "Tank", before bursting into several more bars from Aaron Copland's "Hoedown".

Greg says a few words of introduction for "Knife Edge" and then asks "How many people here understand English?". Many of them seem to and so he relates the story of how, whilst listening to the supposedly finished first album, he realized it was five minutes short, and so came up with "Knife Edge". Keith counts them in and immediately the crowd are on their side, clapping along in time. Again, it's full on with powerful, resounding bass from Greg. This band enjoys playing heavy.

"Rondo" is, well ... "Rondo", and by now these once reserved Austrians are ecstatic. Keith can do no wrong.

"Nutrocker" follows at a breakneck pace, complete with improvised keyboard/drum break as a middle eight.

An outstanding, truly entertaining show and the band leave them wanting more: the only way to go.

TUESDAY, 2 DECEMBER 1970

Stadthalle, Stuttgart, Germany

Some sources believe this show took place at the Festhalle, Boblingen, about 30 kilometres from Stuttgart

A roar of applause greets Keith's "Promenade" as he launches into "Pictures ...". This version seems to be played with even more gusto than the previous night's. The Moog-inspired imagery of "The Gnome" is highly effective and Greg's "The Sage" is developing into a real *tour de force*. Keith overdoses on the ribbon controller [a manual device for controlling the sound of a synthesizer, where the finger is moved up and down a ribbon to produce interesting sounds] before producing two superb, aggressively-played solos in "The Old Castle" and "Blues Variation". Carl and Greg are laying down a pounding beat and the two movements zip along to the obvious delight of the crowd.

An extended snare roll from Carl leads into "Promenade", with all three playing their hearts out. The depth and force of Keith's keyboard work in the second half of "Pictures ..." is astonishing, with Carl, in particular, determined not to be outdone. Vocals seem lower than normal in the mix when all the band are playing and Greg has to put everything he's got into it just to be heard. But not a peep can be heard from the audience during the quieter bits of "Baba Yaga" and "The Great Gates ...".

The acoustics of the hall help the sound of the Hammond during this last movement, with Keith playing a fuzz bass effect reminiscent of "Rondo" from the latter days of the Nice. As "Pictures ..." fades, the applause is deafening.

Greg announces a short break, after which Keith introduces the new songs: "We're gonna do some tracks off our album now. This is the first one on Side 1, dedicated to [the recently deceased] Jimi Hendrix, called 'The Barbarian'." It's played majestically and heavily but doesn't win the rapturous applause that "Pictures ..." did.

Keith then takes introduction duties again: "We'd like to do a Greg Lake composition for you now. This is a thing with the piano called 'Take A Pebble'."

German single. Courtesy of Gudrun Friedrich

Applause is polite, with some cheering as Keith plays the intro on the strings of the piano not the keys! This number is getting better all the time. Vocals are now higher in the mix with Greg sounding his best so far in the show, accompanied by delicate work from Carl on the cymbals and hi-hat. Greg's acoustic break goes down a treat judging by the applause and the whistles, before Keith charges into his piano piece, which this time includes a lengthy coda from the Nice's "Five Bridges" but speeded up, of course. Then it's the clavinet section again, much loved by the audience who, by this point in the show, are right behind the band. At one point, they go into one of the riffs from "Hoedown" with the others in close attendance. Keith credits Greg as the applause fades on this twenty-minute version.

A little banter between Greg and the crowd precedes a prime version of "Knife Edge", Keith's soaring Hammond towards the end of each verse has a particularly sinister effect and encourages Greg to put even more gusto into the vocals than normal. It builds to almost a wall of sound before Keith marches into his synthesizer and organ solos. Carl, meantime, is playing like a man possessed.

"Rondo" kicks off to wild applause and whistles. Keith sounds like he is determined to outplay every other version of this he's ever played. Turning up the heat he dares the others to catch him if they can. Carl and Greg won't be outdone and we end up with an almost surreally fast piece, full of attacking organ and pounding rhythm (and a couple of stray chords from Keith too: it happens to the best of 'em!).

Six minutes in and Carl launches into a hectic, incredibly accurate assault on the drums. His hi-hat and cymbal solo gets a wave of applause and cheers in its own right. Yet again, he doesn't miss a beat on the bass drum or the gongs as he removes his shirt. This section of the solo in particular gets a huge round of applause, as he sets up a series of note-perfect drum patterns.

The pace doesn't let up as Keith and Greg come back in, and Carl finishes this mighty piece, and the set, with yet another perfect drum break. The audience aren't up on their feet for long before the guys are back with a roaring, heavier than normal version of "Nutrocker".

A fine show, which must surely have added to their reputation in Germany.

THURSDAY, 4 DECEMBER 1970

Limathaus, Zurich, Switzerland.

The guys performed an impromptu 'show' in a local restaurant the afternoon before the gig, having gone there after the soundcheck in search of tea and cakes, but they ended up with a jam! Off-the-cuff and breakneck versions of "Rondo" and "Nutrocker" brought in the punters and the boys were offered a residency on the spot. This had to be declined due to prior commitments!

Their first Swiss gig, on the final lap of this short European tour, and so far the crowds have loved them. Not the biggest of venues but still over a thousand fans sitting patiently on the floor – and the band treats them to one of the first performances of a new song as an encore!

Another full-on version of "Pictures ..." opens the show and the guys are working overtime to win applause but, of course, it isn't familiar material to the audience as the live album is still a few months away.

As Keith and Greg expertly create a thoughtful, evocative mood with the second "Promenade" and "The Sage", with Greg's vocals resonating, the reserved Swiss still offer only polite applause. Keith strays from the script with Moog improvisations at the start of "The Old Castle" but Carl keeps up with him as only he can. The solos in "The Old Castle" and "Blues Variation" sound fantastic, with Greg's bass soaring above even the Hammond at times – with still scarcely a ripple of applause as Keith gets back into "Promenade" with the others not far behind.

Classic versions of "Baba Yaga" and "The Great Gates ..." build to a stunning crescendo. Keith's playing seems to have a harder edge to it and Carl puts in some interesting improvised fills on both snare and bass drum. It's almost like they're leaving the script behind so as to get a reaction from the audience. Keith almost completely skips the Hammond throwing as Greg's "No beginning to my death" phrase from "The Great Gates ..." seems to take on a literal meaning at this quiet gig.

Loud, albeit brief, applause is followed by Greg talking to the crowd for a few moments: "We'd like to play you some tracks off the album. First of all one dedicated to Jimi Hendrix." The audience seem to appreciate this as the applause gets distinctly louder and some cheers are heard. "The Barbarian" itself is heavy and gutsy, Carl is smoking and the whole thing goes down a stormer. This audience is now warming up as Keith steps up to the mic: "We'd like to carry on with a Greg Lake composition, a thing called 'Take A Pebble'."

It's definitely tear-up-the-script night as both Carl and Keith play some extra fills and change drum and keyboard runs. Once again, Keith tries out the "Eruption" riff. As Greg starts his guitar break you can hear a pin drop, but by the end of it he's won them over, the crowd goes wild (in a reserved Swiss way!). Interesting that the synching of Greg's last acoustic note and the finger cymbal from Carl is by now becoming a fun item each night, with bets being exchanged between the two of them about who's going to miss the beat.

There's free rein literally on the jazz section, with one or two members of the audience cheering them on, as Keith and Carl dominate the number, even playing a couple of bars of "Nutrocker" at one point. They're enjoying this now! Extended polite applause leads Greg into his introduction for "Knife Edge". A crack performance and Keith really hits the mark with his Moog solo.

A wave of applause and roars of approval takes us straight into "Rondo", with Keith this time building the opening sounds of the Hammond more slowly to get the crowd clapping in time – and they do! Cheers and whistles abound (not before time) encouraging Keith to attack the keys with even more venom than usual, and then the whole thing erupts. Keith goes to town with more improvisations over a thumping bass beat from Greg.

Some serious Hammond throwing takes us into Carl's furiously fast solo. A more than usual amount of the solo centres on snare, bass drum and hi-hat and the crowd love it. Quiet, evocative rolls on the gongs distinguish this, before he's back to the snare, building patterns that allow Keith and Greg to re-enter the fray and all hell breaks loose. Carl's final drum break brings this towering piece to a close as the audience at last shouts for "More".

The first encore is a raggedy but competent romp through "Nutrocker" but it has the punters up and dancing. The guys come back for a second number, with the theatre allegedly so hot they all strip off to their underwear on stage, launching unexpectedly into a brand new song for them, "Preacher Blues", that gets the biggest cheer of the night with Keith taking the lead on clavinet and Hammond. All three sound like they're having the time of their lives and Greg's clearly going for broke with his vocals and powerful bass chords, before they suddenly zap back into the last eight bars of "Nutrocker".

A stunning testimony to the professionalism of the band, taking a quiet audience by the scruff of the neck and winning them over.

TUESDAY, 9 DECEMBER 1970

The Lyceum, London, England.

Tickets: 18 shillings (90p)

Lindsey Clennell filmed this show for Visual And Musical Entertainments, the same company that recorded their Newcastle show in March 1971 for the album release of **Pictures At An Exhibition.** *The film got a cinematic release in February 1971, on a triple bill with films by the Strawbs and Scaffold.*

A power cut threatens to disrupt the show, but TV generators provide the electricity. What the cameras capture is a vital document from an important phase in the band's career. They are wearing their 'normal uniform': Keith looking cool in his silvery-blue glitter suit; Carl in a brown velveteen top and Greg in jeans and an off-white patterned shirt.

Keith sets the scene: "We're gonna start off with a descriptive piece of music. The scene is an art gallery. The pictures on display – some are Mussorgsky's, some are our own – which goes to make up 'Pictures at an Exhibition'".

For sheer passion, musicianship and enjoyment this version is unbeatable. In "The Gnome", we see just how much the band relies on visual cues and nods: Carl and Greg taking theirs from Keith as he looks in their direction and jumps up so that he's visible over the top of the drums. At one point, Keith ducks down before a cue and Carl laughingly sticks his tongue out at him.

With incredibly fast and fluid work on the cymbal and hi-hat from Carl, and Keith getting some astonishing noises out of his Moog they take us into "The Sage", where Greg delivers another strong performance. As Greg switches guitars, Keith and Carl provide the entertainment. Out comes the ribbon controller with weird and wonderful noises, which no doubt makes things interesting for any members of the audience who are tripping. Keith's all over the stage (and off it), and Carl matches his every sound on cymbals and snare. Keith then flies through the solos in "The Old Castle" and "Blues Variation", the others providing strong bottom-end rhythm. Both Carl and Greg have heads rocking and swaying, hair flailing like a prototype Status Quo, obviously loving every minute. They turn in an all-round superb version of "Pictures..." with Keith giving Carl's playing special credit as the applause fades. They then put their all into "The Barbarian" with Keith offering some brief improvisation in his solo.

"Since we recorded this one, it's changed quite a bit," Keith admits. "It's a Greg Lake composition called 'Take A Pebble', and it's on the album." Greg takes a sip of his drink and they're off. This is an exemplary version of the number and for the first time we can see the delicate interplay between Carl and Keith, and Carl and Greg. By this stage, the audience involvement during Greg's solo break is really taking off as both Keith and Carl jump to their feet and clap along in time. "My Dog Blue" is now a song within a song, laying the foundation for later ballads such as "Lucky Man" and "Still ... You Turn Me On".

"This bit's incredibly difficult," says Greg as he launches into the *arpeggio* at the end of his solo. A signal nod of the head to Carl, and his final guitar note and Palmer's finger cymbal coincide perfectly. The end of "Pebble" is a stunningly beautiful and dramatic piece of music, Keith's piano perfectly complementing Greg's vocals.

As the guys catch their breath, what's noticeable is the complete lack of any back-drop or real attempt at presentation on a very crowded stage. Keith's set-up occupies almost half the space, Carl takes up most of the rest and Greg is relegated to far stage right.

"Thank you very much indeed. You're very kind," Greg tells the audience.

Straight into "Knife Edge" and Carl immediately gets the crowd clapping along. Greg is seriously on the case with strong, almost menacing vocals against a backdrop of archetypal rock. Keith throws in some free-form synth for his solo. All hell threatens to break loose on stage as the ending gets the applause it deserves.

"Rondo" kicks in before the cheers have died down and crowns a winning performance from the band. A magnificent rendition, full of aggression and some very hot drumming. Keith taking an almost demonic stance, hovering over his keyboards, and Carl is ... well ... Carl! He must be one of the few rock drummers who can truly entertain a crowd with a solo. Often drum solos are an excuse for the punters to switch off or grab a swift one at the bar, but not when Carl is on skins. His pedal work on the bass drum is perfect before he sets up his usual patterns on cymbals and snare drum. The man's skill on the snare has to be seen to be believed. At a little over six minutes, he counts the others back in, opening the way for Keith to attack the L100 as he stands astride it.

Carl ends the piece with a furiously played drum break and the band leave the stage to wild applause, cheering and foot-stomping.

WEDNESDAY, 31 DECEMBER 1970

Beat Club, **Radio Bremen, Germany.**

(Probably recorded late November/early December)

This was the first chance that most Germans had to see Emerson, Lake and Palmer play live. What they got was akin to two different bands: one camera-shy and staid, the other rocking, extrovert and lords of all they survey.

They open with a version of "Take A Pebble" that is so close to the album original that they could be miming; but they're not. A professional performance for sure, but they look stiff and shy. The unusually bright stage lights don't help either as they dampen the atmosphere, but it's clear the guys are trying to entertain as best they can. It's skilful in the extreme with masterly piano and clear clips of Keith playing the *ostinatos* [a musical phrase repeated throughout a piece] with his left hand while casually looking round the hall and doing nothing in particular with the right. Carl sits patiently as Keith delivers a solo to die for, paving the way for Greg's acoustic break. This is still at the instrumental stage – no "My Dog Blue" just yet – played slowly, deliberately and with real feeling right up to the last note with Carl on the finger cymbal.

Keith's long piano solo is where he really begins to visibly loosen up, repeatedly glancing over at Carl and Greg and, yes, smiling! He's beginning to enjoy himself, which rubs off on the others as they come in, and the free rein of the jazz improvisation ends up lively and fairly bouncing along.

As they go into "Knife Edge", relaxation and enjoyment kick in; Greg's almost bare-chested with his shirt open to the waist, and Carl starts to drive things forward. The rocking, hard-edged feel to "Knife Edge" has just the right effect: all three of them are bouncing up and down, picking up the cues as they should, and putting 100% into the song. Keith lets rip, soloing first with the Moog, then the ribbon controller, as they build nicely, and loudly, towards a strong climax – where Keith throws the L100 around, vaults over it, hauls it on top of himself and plays the final chords from the wrong side of the keyboard, back to front (don't try this at home!).

They're just nicely warming up when it's time to stop. Another 60 or 70 minutes and they would really be cooking.

2. *Clear The Battlefield And Let Me See ...*

4 MARCH – 9 APRIL 1971: SECOND UK TOUR
23 SHOWS, PRECEDED BY A WARM-UP GIG IN SOUTHAMPTON ON
4 FEBRUARY.

Typical set list:	"The Barbarian", "Tarkus", "Jeremy Bender" (from Sheffield 24 March), "Take A Pebble", Greg Lake acoustic solo, piano improvisations, "Take A Pebble" reprise, "Knife Edge", "Pictures At An Exhibition", "Rondo", "Nutrocker".
Keith:	Hammond C3, Hammond L100, Bechstein grand piano, Modular Moog synthesizer 1C with pre-set boxes, Mini-Moog, Hohner 'L' Electric Clavinet.
Greg:	Gibson J200 custom acoustic, Fender Jazz bass, modified Telecaster, fuzz and wah-wah foot pedals.
Carl:	Gretsch kit, 7 Paiste cymbals and hi-hat, 2 Paiste gongs, set of woodblocks, 3 cowbells and a Swiss cowbell (bought from a farmer for £18).
PA system:	WEM: 2 Crown stereo amplifiers driving 2,000 watts of speakers in 4 Loudmouth stacks, 11 Quad amplifiers, 20 channel stereo mixer.

This was the debut tour for *Tarkus* material. The band had only recently recorded the album over two weeks in January 1971 and they didn't all seem convinced that it would go down well on stage.

"Greg wasn't too sure about it from the beginning. It was too weird. But he agreed to try it, and afterwards he loved it,"[14] commented Keith.

Very few recordings from this tour (of any kind) exist. Before it got underway, the band did a warm up gig at the Guildhall in Southampton on Thursday, 4 February followed by a promotional appearance on Belgian TV, recorded at The Theatre 140 in Brussels over two nights – 6 and 7 February. The subsequent appearance of *Masters From The Vaults*, a compilation film from both nights, sees instantaneous costume changes and terrible edits in some tracks, notably "Knife Edge" resulting in Greg singing the opening verse twice – once from each night!

This tour saw the recording of the *Pictures At An Exhibition* album at Newcastle City Hall and the band playing some venues that weren't normally on the tour schedules for big groups, such as the ABC in Wigan and the Big Apple in Brighton.

One feature of their act that became established during this tour was Keith's technique of switching on the Moog as the lights go down so that the crowd got treated to weird rippling, water-like noises to slowly build the atmosphere.

SATURDAY, 6 AND SUNDAY, 7 FEBRUARY 1971

Theatre 140, Brussels, Belgium.

Recorded for broadcast on Belgian TV and later issued as **Masters From The Vaults,** *this was clearly intended as a showcase for the band's talents and it showed them at their early best, with flair, abandon, abrasion and lots of humour.*

The record of these shows is a composite one – with some continuity-defying costume changes as they go through their sets. They're in top form and with a strong performance of "The Barbarian", we're treated again to the intricate system of cues and nods used by the band. Greg takes off with a prolonged fuzz bass after the piano break, much to the amusement of Keith – who then launches into his own improvisation.

Carl gets a credit for some superbly powerful, 'let it rip' drumming. Greg's rich baritone shines throughout "Take A Pebble" as both he and Keith improvise during their solo spots. They're enjoying this one so much that Greg loses track of the words in "My Dog Blue" and messes up the lyrics. But he gets the cheers anyway!

Then we see just how much humour there is in this band as Carl comes out stage front with Greg so they can synchronize the finger cymbal with the last note of the *arpeggio*. And … they get it wrong! Keith's improvisation has the crowd cheering, including a few bars from "La Marseillaise" before he brings the others back in. The usual excerpts from "Tank" and "Hoedown" on the clavinet see some top intricate free-form jazz playing, before climaxing with beautifully rich vocals from Greg.

"Knife Edge" is a full-on rocker as Keith improvises yet again during his solo on Hammond and Moog. "Rondo" by now has the definite stamp of ELP on it, being much tighter and more aggressive than the Nice's interpretation. Greg is mostly hunched over his bass and Carl watches Keith for the cues. Solo time: Carl cocks his head slightly forward to the snare and races round the kit, never missing a beat. Building to a crescendo with rolls on the gongs and furiously attacking the snare, this solo showcases the man's extraordinary ability. After he counts Keith and Greg back in, the Hammond throwing and knife antics are on cue, crowning a magnificent rendition of what's by now an ELP standard. Interestingly, during his solo Keith plays a few bars from "Toccata" that will re-surface on 1974's *Brain Salad Surgery.*

As they return for the encore, a grinning Keith launches into the by now customary "Nutrocker", a number that's becoming tighter all the time. The snare beats have become machine gun rolls in themselves and even Greg, with his shouts of "Yeah, yeah, yeah" seems to enjoy the piece – contrary to what he'd said to

Keith in the dressing room after the gig at The Winter Gardens in Watford the previous September: "I'm not playing that crap again".[15]

Some nice tempo changes towards the end take us into the riff that later becomes "Tiger In A Spotlight", and then into a second encore of "Preacher Blues" before reprising "Nutrocker" to close the show.

FRIDAY, 12 MARCH 1971

The ABC Theatre, Plymouth, England.

The sixth show of the tour and, as Keith says, "It's good to be back where we started from."

A few seconds of Moog tuning is followed by Keith saying: "We're gonna give you some old ones and some new ones, starting off with an old one." Scarcely have the cheers died down when Greg's bass powers into "The Barbarian". Yet again, Carl's drumming sets out his stall for the night: flair, abrasion and always the right texture for the piece.

There are whistles and jubilant applause as Greg steps forward to explain the concept of the *Tarkus* album. To the background of still more Moog tuning, he introduces the title track: "We're gonna play the first side of the album, 'Tarkus'." This first marathon of the night is a real workout for Keith's keyboards – including some clever improvisation in "Stones Of Years" – with Greg and Carl in close attendance. "Tarkus" is amazingly tight and precision-played as all the tempo changes work perfectly. Greg handles the vocals with aplomb, making apparently easy switches from bass to Fender Telecaster and back again.

"Mass" becomes a real showcase for Keith's ribbon controller solo, but what is becoming obvious is that he is no longer the superstar; simply one third of a very talented trio. The majestic intro to "Battlefield" is handled with consummate ease and Greg's embellishments in the solo stand out well against the backdrop of Hammond and drums. The last verse of "Battlefield" is played by Greg alone with his guitar – incredibly atmospheric when we bear in mind the lyrical content about surveying the aftermath of a bloody battle. As the Moog extravaganza that is "Aquatarkus" brings the piece to a close, the audience response is ecstatic.

As a general rule, this band doesn't waste time on elaborate stories between songs: it's the music that's all-important. Keith says it all: "We'd like to do 'Knife Edge' for you." It's shorter than usual and the band takes an enforced break, after which they return to loud cheers for the second set. Keith explains why: "Sorry to keep you waiting, but in the heat the Moog synthesizer goes out of tune and it needs everything to get together. Yeah, happens all the time."

At which point Greg and Carl provide a few seconds of impromptu backing and then back to Keith, who recalls: "When we played in Plymouth at the beginning, one of the things we did was 'Pictures At An Exhibition'." Ecstatic applause sees Keith take us on the first "Promenade" from "Pictures ..." (which in total lasts a full 41 minutes) and is worth every penny of the ticket price on its own.

Greg plays the first wah-wah bass of "The Gnome" for laughs and it's not lost on the audience. Keith copes well with a temperamental Moog and they turn in a classic performance. After coming in late for some reason on the vocal "Promenade", forcing Keith to play the opening notes twice over, Greg's vocals and acoustic work on the Gibson are a real delight as he captivates everyone with "The Sage".

The second half of "Pictures ..." gives each of them their own chance to really shine, as Keith attacks the Hammond in more ways than one, Greg takes on the vocals with relish, and Carl drives the whole thing. With the Moog continuing to play up, Keith still gets some truly innovative improvisational solos out of it, proving his growing confidence with the instrument. "Baba Yaga" and "The Great Gates ..." are as strong as ever, with the solo sections being particularly aggressive.

"We'd like to continue with something off the first album ... this is 'Take A Pebble'," Keith tells the fans. Clocking in at almost eighteen minutes, "Pebble" is now Keith's second *magnum opus* of the night with some inspired piano playing.

There have been shouts for old Nice numbers and Keith resists everything (well ok, apart from a few bars from *Five Bridges* in his "Pebble" solo) until the time comes for the old train whistle to blow the roof off the ABC as "Rondo" powers in. This second UK tour really sees this number emerging as the classic ELP piece it is, no longer simply a carryover from a bygone life.

Carl's solo is yet another example of his stunning ability, met with long and wild applause from the crowd, before Keith and Greg join him for the finale of "Rondo".

The crowd go bananas in its appreciation. One of their best ever shows in their short career ... so far.

WEDNESDAY, 24 MARCH 1971

The City Hall, Sheffield, England.

Tickets: Up to 17 shillings (85p)

Almost exactly the mid-point of the tour and they were well into their stride with the new material.

After a short winter break, ELP are again on tour in Britain warming up before crossing the pond to America to promote their new album which will be released shortly. Two days before the famous Newcastle gig where the *Pictures At An Exhibition* album will be recorded, the guys are presenting a modified set list.

Instead of opening with the calm before the storm of "Pictures ..." the boys go straight for the jugular with a loud and powerful version of "The Barbarian". The audience is so excited that many don't hear Greg announcing "Tarkus". As with all these early 1971 shows, "Tarkus" closely follows the studio recording with only a few keyboard improvisations, mainly in "Iconoclast" and "Aquatarkus". During "Eruption" and "Aquatarkus" the Moog shows its temper with a slightly detuned sound – Keith isn't very happy with it and tries his best to teach it some manners – but he fails! So the solid, workmanlike "Knife Edge" includes only a few riffs on the detuned Moog.

It seems that Keith wants to cock a snook at the Moog by delivering a splendid piano performance in "Take A Pebble". The audience thankfully applaud three times during Keith's breaks and give Greg clapping rhythm support in the now country sounding "My Dog Blue". With "Jeremy Bender" comes the second new song and with it, possibly, the live debut of ELP's brand of so called 'humorous' songs. It proves so popular with the audience that Keith has to play two short reprises. So much for this band being overly serious!

What follows is ELP's classic live act, a 39 minutes "Pictures ..." opened on City Hall's pipe organ to the obvious surprise of the audience. To give Keith the chance to hurry back to his keyboards, Carl and Greg play a long *intermezzo* before starting "The Gnome". At the end of "The Gnome" Keith tries again to defeat the Moog, successfully on this occasion. Greg seems relieved to hear that and repays with quality guitar and vocal performances on "Promenade" and "The Sage". Keith is happy too and proves it with a perfectly played "Blues Variation".

The second half of "Pictures ..." makes clear why ELP are the cream of the Progressive Rock movement: virtuosity, perfect interaction and inventiveness presented in a totally live environment. Of course the audience wants more, and more is what they jolly well get! The compulsory encore of "Rondo" is different every night, but always an exciting platform for Keith's Hammond riding and Carl's ten minute drum solo.[16]

This must have really got them in the mood to record the* Pictures At An Exhibition *album in Newcastle two days later

FRIDAY, 26 MARCH 1971

The City Hall, Newcastle, England.

The scene of the recording of Pictures At An Exhibition, *an album that caused so many disagreements between band and management and wasn't released until November 1971. Keith was only allowed to use the Hall's pipe organ after promising not to stick knives into it! The mixing and recording desk was upstairs in the circle, manned by Eddie Offord of "Are You Ready Eddie?" fame.*

The sheer range and power of the sounds produced at this show is mind-boggling, but it gives a fair indication of how Keith in particular is mastering the Moog. The beauty of this show, and the recording, is that we see and hear just how well they handle the furious playing and complex time changes. They really hold things together and never seem to succumb to the adrenalin rush that can lead to uneven tempos in live recordings which make the whole thing sound messy.

Keith plays the opening "Promenade" from the pipe organ console and, as he runs back to the keyboards, Carl fills in the seconds with a perfect left-handed single press roll. The soloing is spot on; the duels – especially keyboards and drums in "The Gnome" – are sharp and well-balanced, producing the perfect showcase for the band.

One of the highlights of the show is Greg's acoustic and vocal solo spot in "The Sage", the perfect foil to the electronic wizardry that dominates much of the set, and proving (if anyone needed to be convinced) that Greg is a musician of the highest calibre.

Keith, noticeably on "The Gnome" and "The Old Castle", explores the Moog's capabilities – using it not only to create but also to amuse and entertain. "The Great Gates of Kiev" stands out as not only the climax of the whole piece, but as a magnificent example of how this band goes from shattering crescendos to delicately quiet pieces in an instant.

Fitting also that they include "Nutrocker", a tune guaranteed to get everyone on their feet, cheering and dancing as the guys bring this show to a close.

You've all got the album, so you know this was a show to savour.

THURSDAY, 1 APRIL 1971

The ABC Theatre, Wigan, England.

Show number eighteen of this UK tour and ELP were one of the very few bands to hit the road to Wigan. There hadn't been a rock concert there for over three years before the group rolled into town.

In the darkness before the band comes on, the Moogs are sending out gentle ripples of sound: the calm before the storm. ELP walk on to 2,000 ecstatic fans going wild. "The Barbarian", "Tarkus" and "Knife Edge" are all played with the polish you'd expect from tunes that have been road tested for some time. Keith, during the ribbon controller solo in "Tarkus", wanders out into the audience and for a while even disappears into the Gents toilet!

Greg's voice and guitar on this song are sublime, befitting this dramatic grand piece, and his "Battlefield" acoustic break in particular provides a poignant contrast to the sheer force of the rest of the number.

"Pictures ..." follows after the now mandatory break but the highlight of the second set must be "Rondo", with Keith and Carl sharing the spotlight. The crowd go crazy as Keith, ever the showman, hauls the Hammond around, jumping over it, stabbing it and then pulling it on top of him as he played the keys from the wrong side. Carl has now acquired his own following: three girls in the circle are "standing on their seats to display identical red hot pants embroidered with the words 'Carl The Greatest' ".[17]

3. *All The Profits From Our Victory ...*

21 APRIL – 30 MAY 1971: FIRST NORTH AMERICAN TOUR
13 SHOWS

Typical set list:	"The Barbarian", "Tarkus", "Take A Pebble", Greg Lake acoustic solo, piano improvisations, "Take A Pebble" reprise, "Knife Edge", "Rondo", "Nutrocker" (very soon replaced with "A Time And A Place").
Keith:	Hammond C3, Hammond L100, Bechstein grand piano, Modular Moog Synthesizer 1C with pre-set boxes, Mini Moog, Hohner 'L' Electric Clavinet.
Greg:	Gibson J300 custom acoustic, Fender Jazz bass, modified Fender Telecaster, fuzz and wah-wah foot pedals.
Carl:	Gretsch kit, 7 Paiste cymbals and hi-hat, 2 Paiste gongs, set of woodblocks, 3 cowbells and a Swiss cowbell
PA system:	WEM: 2 Crown stereo amplifiers driving 2,000 watts of speakers in 4 Loudmouth stacks, 11 Quad amplifiers, 20 channel stereo mixer.

They crossed the pond to conquer the New World in April 1971 after claiming the UK and swathes of Europe. The expectation was tremendous. As fans in the Old World already knew, this band's natural home was the stage. ELP's first studio album had already hit the record stores and needed a big push to sell well in North America.

They played "Pictures ..." just once – at Carnegie Hall. Again, very few recordings from this tour have survived the test of time.

WEDNESDAY, 21 APRIL 1971

Theil College, Greenville, PA, USA.

The band's US debut was at a small Lutheran college in Greenville, PA, and as Keith later said: "The first one was in the outback somewhere – very informal – so we felt at ease."[18]

To gain entry to the gig, you have to be either a student or a guest of one, so the band plays to a select lucky few.

Such is the band's power they repeatedly blow out circuit breakers in the gymnasium where the show is held. They very nearly don't appear at all: the band's management reputedly tries to get the gig cancelled as such a small venue, with album sales in the USA starting to take off, it is a lost opportunity to promote the band to a large audience.

They fail and, by all accounts, it's a typically strong ELP show.

FRIDAY, 23 APRIL or SATURDAY, 24 1971

Easttown Theater, Detroit, MI, USA.

The home of Motown was their first major performance in the USA. "Our act is a little shorter than it is in England and we're not doing 'Pictures At An Exhibition'" [19]

The audience applauds politely, but no more than that, as the band start to warm up (quick riffs on the Hammond, short drum solo, tickling of the bass guitar and a little humming by Greg). Fittingly they open with a song by an American, Aaron Copland's "Hoedown" – the first time that anyone is aware of the band playing it in its entirety. The band take it slow and careful: the first part is very close to the version that will surface on *Trilogy* next year, and is played at a relatively slow tempo, when compared to the frenetic speed experienced in later years. Or is it jetlag?

In the middle of the song Keith can't resist improvising a nice little jazzy solo using the Hammond and the Moog. His roots in the Nice are obvious: similar chords, but the progressive nature is there for all to see too. The Moog produces fat analogue sounds, akin to those he uses in the famous "Lucky Man" solo.

After Keith's short introduction about an armadillo called Tarkus, the band start to play, again at a relatively slow tempo, what will become a prog rock classic. It is the perfect vehicle for Keith to show off his talents as a virtuoso by improvising first on the Hammond and later on the Moog. Greg kicks in during "Battlefield" with a melodic ballad-like guitar solo. The highlight for Keith is "Aquatarkus" where he puts the Moog through its paces. He's really mastered this instrument and even dares to experiment on stage. Imagine, almost four minutes of pure analogue synthesizer sound! The crowd's ecstatic reaction says it all. And throughout this twenty-minute piece, Carl never lets up, revelling in the sudden changes in time signature and different tempos.

Almost without a break, they launch straight into "Take A Pebble". Again Keith's fingers float over the keys and Greg, who accompanies the keyboard solo by drumming on the body of the guitar, later takes the spotlight in "My Dog Blue". At the end of the show they play "Rondo", a piece never knowingly played the same way twice: a few chords are taken from Bach's "Toccata" and "Fugue" on the Hammond; Keith's white-handled knives, and a nine minute drum solo by Carl as icing on the cake. What else the fans could wish for?

An encore!

Not the usual "Nutrocker" because US audiences aren't as familiar with the piece as those in the UK and Europe (even though B. Bumble And The Stingers are American), so instead it's another *Tarkus* number, "A Time And A Place", a routine and competent version to send the fans home happy.

It's obvious from the audience reaction as the show progressed, that American fans are already recognizing the importance of this band and the thrill of their live performance.[20]

SATURDAY, 1 MAY 1971

Fillmore East, New York, NY, USA.

Tickets: $5.50

The biggest gigs of their career so far at a venue that has gone down in rock folklore.

The legendary Bill Graham introduces the band for the last of four gigs in two days at the Fillmore East: "It's a pleasure for me to present three exceptional musicians: on bass Mr Greg Lake, on drums Mr Carl Palmer, on electricity Mr Keith Emerson."

Keith let the audience immediately hear what "electricity" means – bubbling and shrieking sounds of the Moog are the intro for an extremely powerful version of "The Barbarian". The audience are knocked back in their seats as Keith moves from one keyboard to another in his shiny blue glitter suit.

On this, their first US Tour, ELP share the bill with other bands such as Yes, Edgar Winter and Curved Air and so can only play a truncated set without "Pictures ..." (the only known exception on this tour being May 26 at Carnegie Hall).

After "The Barbarian", follows "a track off the next album ... a story of an armadillo ... It's called 'Tarkus'," Keith tells the assembled. This show gives us the first chance to see and hear how the piece has been improved and re-worked. Having been camped out for two days at the Fillmore, the equipment is perfectly tuned and the musicians can concentrate on the essential point: the music.

"Tarkus" is played much faster with improvisations and Moog riffs, Carl's melodic drumming comes through to perfection and even Greg seems to love this new piece now. This seems to have been the first time that Greg sings the lyrics to "Tarkus" exactly as they are on the album: as with so many other pieces, he's changed the words at previous shows.

The audience show their appreciation for "Tarkus" with generous applause and yells (as one young fan says, "Christ, they're brilliant!")[21] as ELP ascend to the next height with "Take A Pebble". There have been shouts for this all evening because of the airplay it's been getting on FM stations. The classic piece – wonderfully played in its piano parts, overlaid with Greg's smooth, rich voice – is rapidly developing into a marathon in its own right as it flows through its different phases.

The band is in high humour with Carl and Greg clowning around with the audience at the beginning of "My Dog Blue". As is usual in this era, the piano improvisation closes with "Tank" (featuring intricate interaction between Keith and Greg with electric piano and bass) and snippets of "Hoedown". Keith even manages at one point to include a few choruses of "Lady Madonna".

"Pebble" brings the audience to their feet, where they stay for the rest of the night, and the menace of what follows, in "Knife Edge", blows a few minds. The band plays very aggressively, laying the foundations for the cataclysmic grand finale that is "Rondo". The audience can't believe what they see. Keith and the L100 give of their best and Carl shows just how damn good he is in his solo.

Of course the audience demands an encore so back they come to try "Nutrocker" with "Preacher Blues" in the middle section.

Another fantastic show is over, Greg thanks the audience and says farewell with "See you in Carnegie Hall".[22] Veni, Vidi, Vici.

However, the critics aren't always so enthusiastic. Mike John, of **The New York Times** *agreed that "The audience loved it ... ", but went on to add "My first reaction was disbelief followed by amusement; then disbelief again and finally headache."* [23]

SUNDAY, MAY 2 1971

Shea Theater, Buffalo, NY, USA.

This show opens with an 'arrangement' of "The Barbarian". Uncharacteristically, Keith throws in a short improvisation on the Hammond in the middle of this warm up piece, before jumping into "Take A Pebble".

Both Keith and Greg have opportunities to play solo here: after Keith's grand piano outing, Greg starts his "My Dog Blue" on the acoustic, but obviously has some technical difficulties and finishes it after playing a couple of chords without singing. Keith helps him out by starting his improvisation for which he gets thanks from Greg. A perfect example of how members of a band who are on the same wavelength can help each other out and step in if something goes awry.

Since the ball's in Keith's court already, he runs his left hand over the ivories playing very fast *ostinatos* to accompany the right hand melody. What an impressive improvisation! In the same spirit the whole band continues in a very jazzy jam containing parts from "Tank" and "Tiger In The Spotlight".

Another classy performance, but these tracks are sadly all that survives from this show. [24]

WEDNESDAY, 26 MAY 1971

Carnegie Hall, New York, NY, USA.

Tickets: $4 - $6

This show sees the debut performance of "Pictures..." in North America, and the only venue on the tour to see it given the full treatment.

After a very slow, deliberate and decidedly typical Carnegie Hall introduction, there are shouts of "Hello!" from the stage and "Pictures ..." gets under way with a well-paced, heavy "Promenade" from Keith. There's an almost tangible air of "We're at Carnegie Hall and we just have to get this right!". The whole epic piece is taken at a steady tempo, nothing rushed, everything carefully weighed. Greg misses his cue in "The Gnome" but it still sounds right, the audience laughing and applauding at the way Keith tries to catch out the others in the stop-start section.

They're very tight on this number and as they go into the swirling, swishing Moog section, Carl is manic on the hi-hat and cymbals, followed by the ever-so-quiet organ intro to the vocal "Promenade" where you can hear a pin drop. Greg turns in a strong vocal and acoustic performance, handing the baton next to Keith before it's returned for "The Sage". His guitar work is faultless and the applause comes readily. "The Old Castle" and "Blues Variation" are excellent examples of trio work, with a band improvising and melding together well.

There's real depth and force to the playing throughout the second half of "Pictures ...", kicking off with a thundering "Promenade", before moving into a weird and wonderful "Baba Yaga". Greg sings his heart out as they charge headlong into "The Great Gates Of Kiev" with that majestic opening. The Hammond just hangs there and fills the hall. It's ELP at their best, determined to impress and succeeding.

All three excel in the bell section, Keith working the stops, Carl on the tubular bells and Greg in particular playing a simple but effective bass line. The Hammond throwing – to polite, restrained applause – and the grand finale top a magnificent piece and close the first part of the show. Keith treats the audience to some whooping and gurgling sounds from the Moog and then introduces "The Barbarian". This crowd get a taste of real Brit Prog.

Keith also does his stand-up comedy act: "This here is the Moog synthesizer. Well as you can see by the size of it, it doesn't weigh 4,000 pounds as you've got in your programme – it's 4,000 English pounds in money. It's still very weighty. It's got diarrhoea at the moment! Very temperamental machine. By the way, since its invention, several tunes and things have been written for it by notable people. You may remember 'Shine On Harvest Moog' (audible groans from the audience and a drum roll from Carl), 'I'm in the Moog for love'... this is 'Barbarian'!"

It's played much faster than normal and gets a terrific response from the New Yorkers. A wave of applause greets the piano break, with a number of voices calling out "Wow", and more clapping signals the return of the Hammond as the guys go hell for leather towards the end.

It's Greg's turn to talk as he introduces everyone's favourite armadillo: "We'd like to play you something off the next album, which should be released not so long away. It's a story about an armadillo and his trials and tribulations. He's got tank tracks and guns and things. So, we'd like to play it for you, it's called 'Tarkus'."

As at the Fillmore, this epic is now played faster and more confidently than on the spring UK tour. As Keith moves from one break (and one solo) to another, Carl and Greg lay down a never-faltering beat. Extended improvisations are beginning to appear throughout "Tarkus", grabbing the crowd's attention in "Stones Of Years" and hitting them right between the eyes in "Mass".

Keith's machine-gun ribbon controller antics go down a storm, evidenced by the huge applause, as Carl counts Greg back into the vocals. A stunning guitar solo from Greg, aided by the powerhouse of Keith's Hammond, takes us through "Battlefield" to his quiet solo spot. This movement of "Tarkus" is fast becoming a real showcase for Greg as his delicate, and increasingly improvised, use of the Telecaster creates the right mood for what is, after all, a very sombre and thought-provoking piece.

If Greg takes the honours in "Battlefield", Keith trumps him in "Aquatarkus": Carl's drumming is the perfect backdrop as we march with the Moog through this post-apocalyptic world.

"This is written by Greg. This is 'Take A Pebble'," says Keith. After the noise and sheer power of "Tarkus", there is a real sea change with "Pebble". Keith adds extra piano licks everywhere, over the top of some jazzy playing by the others, and superb bass parts in particular from Greg. Between the piano break and Greg's spot, Keith is now playing a whole new section on the piano strings which wins tremendous applause.

As Greg gently strums, the whole feeling of the show seeming to change from rock to country and back again, with the Carl and Greg 'feature' on the finger cymbal and Keith's piano improvisations stealing the show in the second half of the song. A by now very appreciative crowd applaud wildly at the end.

The still popular "Knife Edge" is competently played, with some eerily menacing Hammond from Keith underlying Greg's voice in the opening verses.

The new Moog solo in the middle is so reminiscent of "Mass", but from that point on sticks to the album version.

"What the hell is he doing? Must be a train!" shouts one excited member of the audience. Train? No, it's the opening whistles of "Rondo". More screeching from the Hammond as Carl thunders into his solo, more than a few echoes of "Wow!" are heard, and loud cheers greet a whole new section on the cowbells. After the now obligatory "One, two, three, four!" shouts from Carl, the others are back; Greg's powerful yet snappy bass stands out for the rest of the number, with Keith producing chain saw noises from the trusty L100.

Long, sustained shouts for more bring them back. Keith is trying to work this very obliging and lively crowd even further: "Stand up in your seats, it's 'Nutrocker!'". Nifty keys from Keith and shouts of "Yeah" from Greg precede the segue into "Preacher Blues", only this time Greg throws in some old fashioned rock'n'roll screams and shouts of "Yeah, yeah" to get the crowd going – not that they need it. The final reprise of "Nutrocker" sends them home happy; ELP have done it again.

"The real highlight of that tour was playing Carnegie Hall because at that time, if you played Carnegie Hall, you were SOMEBODY!"[25]

"I felt very proud after that concert"[26]

SATURDAY, 29 MAY 1971

The Hatch Memorial Shell, Boston, MA, USA.

This penultimate show of the short US tour was a free concert. The contrast with Carnegie Hall couldn't be greater.

Keith opens with "OK, this is 'The Barbarian'!". A bit lacklustre at first until they seem to get a second wind during the piano section – and then normal service is resumed. They receive loud, but hardly ecstatic, applause from this New England audience.

Greg introduces the next track, "Thank you. We'd like to play for you now something that you probably haven't heard before. It's off the next album and takes up one side. It's a story about an armadillo and it's called 'Tarkus'."

The unfamiliarity of the piece results, for once, in considerable background audience noise throughout which, you sense, dampens the band's enthusiasm for a track they have begun to excel at playing. Keith goes to town with the ribbon controller, machine gunning the audience and, by the end of his solo in "Mass", appears to be winning them over.

By the time they reach "Battlefield", they've proved they aren't a band that rests on its laurels and refuse to write off the show because of poor audience reaction.

Keith throws in an extra low register Moog solo at the start before Greg weighs in with some emotively sung vocals. Carl's drums and the Hammond power this section along until Greg launches into a typically tasteful solo, underpinned by yet more fuzzy Hammond and Moog. "Aquatarkus" marches along to a dramatic conclusion and this crowd are starting to warm up.

No record of any other tracks at this concert exists but we have to assume they played the full American show of "Take A Pebble", "Knife Edge", "Rondo" and "Nutrocker".

4. *Just A Step ...*

5 – 17 JUNE 1971: SECOND EUROPEAN TOUR
12 SHOWS PLUS AN APPEARANCE AT THE THEATRE ROYAL, DRURY
LANE, LONDON.

Typical set list:	"Pictures At An Exhibition", "The Barbarian", "Tarkus", "Jeremy Bender" (only sometimes played), "Take A Pebble", Greg Lake acoustic solo, piano improvisations, "Take A Pebble" reprise, "Knife Edge", "Rondo", "Nutrocker". Usually played in two sets with a break in the middle.
Band equipment:	As for the previous American tour.

The US tour lasted longer than originally planned so this short European tour, due to start on 1 June at the Schwarzwaldhalle in Karlsruhe, Germany, was put back to 5 June at the Sporthaus, Zoffingen in Switzerland. Initially set at eleven shows, an additional show in Offenbach was added for 15 June.

They returned to England for their one-off Drury Lane show on 20 June before a short break with rehearsals for the US tour, which began on 17 July (officially described in a press statement as 'resting'). The Drury Lane show itself was a landmark moment in retrospect: the final performance ever of the complete "Pictures At An Exhibition".

In Europe, the hard work they put in on their few European dates in late 1970 paid dividends and every night was sold out. Like any other tour this one had its highs and low: the highs were plenty, and most of the lows seemed to come at once in Oldenburg on 14 June. However this gig was noteworthy because it featured the band's longest ever version of "Rondo" along with, possibly, Carl's longest-ever solo.

SATURDAY, 5 JUNE 1971

The Sporthaus, Zoffingen, Switzerland

We know they played "Pictures ..." at this gig, the opening night of the tour, but no record of it exists.

Weird sounds from the Moog, as if straight out of a science fiction movie, gets the second set under way. After a minute or so, Keith, keeping it simple, announces "The Barbarian". What's clear already is how they've loosened up on the arrangements. Keith plays some nifty Hammond improvisations and Carl powers his way through the piece. All hell's let loose on the coda as Keith races up and down the keys, Greg and Carl play like men possessed, and the applause is anything but restrained.

Keith introduces "Tarkus" in the usual way, but with an amusing *caveat*: "We're gonna play you something now you haven't heard before and it's the story of an armadillo. He travels on tank tracks. It takes up the whole side of an album, it's a bit long so if anybody wants to go to the toilet you'd better go now."

The whole pace of "Tarkus" has quickened, Greg's phrasing in "Stones Of Years" is different, adding a touch of interest – with a few shouts of "Yeah" thrown in – before Keith plays a free-form solo. As Carl pointed out: "On stage we're getting looser and pieces like 'Tarkus' have changed considerably. We adlib about forty per cent on stage and the rest is arranged."[27]

The ribbon controller gets the usual run out in "Mass" with Greg and Carl providing a pounding back beat. Keith plays a few wayward notes for once in "Manticore" but by this point they've built up a head of steam as we come to the drama of "Battlefield". Some tasteful extra guitar licks and *arpeggio* from Greg add to the mood as he takes centre stage with his vocal/acoustic solo, one that shows he's in top form tonight.

Tremendous applause precedes the shortest piece of the evening. "This is a quickie, about one minute long," says Greg and then Keith cuts in "It's called Jeremy Bender." It's a competent version, dominated by the electric piano, and cut short, but it still wins loud applause.

The opening and close of "Take A Pebble" sees a different arrangement from Keith, almost as if the whole number has been lowered by an octave, but he still does a solid job decorating the foundation laid down by the others. He even throws in a few bars of "The Harry Lime Theme" from the Orson Welles movie *The Third Man*, played on the piano strings to ease us into Greg's solo.

Country and western night takes over as the audience claps along with him, the vocal adlibs showing how much he's enjoying this. Riotous applause greets the 'finger cymbal' clowning and then Keith's return, where he announces "Ok, we're gonna give you 'Knife Edge'." The classic bass line is a killer on this one, the organ sounds just perfect, and this is definitely one of the strongest versions.

The usual noises of the Emerson Express herald the start of a breakneck "Rondo", which strangely seems more tightly controlled because of its speed. Keith hits a few wrong notes here and there but with everyone on their feet who notices? The Hammond throwing is right on cue, leading as it does into a feast of histrionics before the final reprise of the riff – oddly enough no solo from Carl tonight.

The encore of "Nutrocker" still sticks quite closely to the live album version from Newcastle and it brings the house down.

MONDAY, 7 JUNE 1971

Konzerthaus, Vienna, Austria.

The third stop on the tour and a return to the scene of last December's triumph.

Several minutes of un-ELP like tuning and twiddling precede Keith's introduction to what's now become the first set of the evening: "Pictures ...". "Promenade" is played on the house pipe-organ and sounds magnificent, setting the tone for an epic 39-minute version of this opus. Keith and Carl dominate "The Gnome", as does Greg with "The Sage". Unusually the vocal "Promenade" is cut so short that it's just a few seconds of Keith on his own leading the band into Greg's acoustic spot, a feature which is itself growing in stature.

"The Old Castle" and "Blues Variation" fly by in a hail of keyboard solos, firstly Moog and then Hammond. Both movements give everyone a chance to do their stuff. With the addition of Carl and Greg, the "Promenade" that opens the second half of "Pictures ..." sounds even grander than the first.

"Baba Yaga" fair rocks along. Greg's definitely having an 'in your face' night with booming bass almost dominating this movement and also the "The Great Gates ...", the whole thing sounding better for it. Keith's work on the Hammond, against the backdrop of the bells in "The Great Gates ..." is wonderful.

Greg introduces "The Barbarian" which opens the second set. The arrangement for this one has loosened up before, during and after the piano break, as if they're giving it some new blood and a kick up the backside, and it's well executed – despite a few duff notes on the Hammond.

At this point, they must have played "Tarkus" but no record exists.

Keith steps up to introduce "Take A Pebble" in the same, slow, deliberate voice he did the last time they played Vienna. Greg's introduction to his acoustic solo is now well-paced with the crowd clapping along and the vocals quite laid back.

Variations on themes is the only way to describe Keith's long piano solo, some choice lines with titbits of old Nice pieces, a theme or two from *Tarkus* – before the others come back in. The different moods of the song, from country and western through jazz to melodic prog, really win over the crowd with loud applause at several points, especially at the end.

A super version of "Knife Edge" follows, Greg's vocals are almost screamed at times over Keith's ballsy Hammond and Carl's frenetic playing. At nearly nine minutes, it benefits from a long improvised Moog solo in the middle and the most powerful ending of any song in the show: Carl's playing driving it along.

Crashing gongs and the L100 train herald the start to "Rondo" – greeted with shattering applause. Even with Carl and Greg pounding away, heads down and swaying, Keith reigns supreme on this one as he takes us quite slowly into what becomes the frantic middle section of the piece. Inventiveness is his watchword for this show. Carl is on top form again: his solo, at almost eight minutes, sees him working his way round every part of the kit with the snare drum particularly noteworthy.

Keith introduces "Nutrocker" as the usual encore, which gets off to a poor start due to some wrong chords, but then he picks it up at breakneck speed as only Keith can. Carl gets the crowd clapping along with his drum break, Greg whistles for all he's worth and Keith gives the Hammond absolute hell.

With applause reverberating around the hall, it's a fitting end to another successful Viennese whirl.

WEDNESDAY, 9 JUNE 1971

Circus Krone, Munich, Germany.

The fourth gig of the tour, and their first of the year in Germany, sees a return to the scene of the riot in November 1970 when hoses were turned on the crowd. Fate decides that this show isn't without incident either.

A bit of tuning and a few words from Greg asking for "a modicum of quiet", and we're off with "Pictures ..."

An enthusiastic crowd warms to Keith's powerful "Promenade", the first movement of a version every bit the equal of the Newcastle recording in spite of a few missed notes on the Hammond. The second "Promenade" and "The Sage" are, as usual, Greg's showpieces, with vocals high in the mix.

It's at this point that Greg, clearly fed up with a heckler firstly and then the security people in the hall, departs from the script but keeps his professionalism intact. During his acoustic solo, he calls "shut up!" to the heckler – to ecstatic applause from a grateful audience – and then stops playing altogether as obviously the security people have incurred his ire.

"Come here, come here. Listen, listen, hang on. I know these people do wanna hear, and even if they took a lot of trouble getting in here, just let the people hear you know. It's easy." [28]

He resumes playing the *arpeggio* to massive applause and never once loses his stride. Warm applause again as Keith and Carl come back in and briefly duel into "The Old Castle" and "Blues Variation"

The band seems to realize that they've got the crowd on their side and they go for it, no holds barred.

An announcement in German excites the crowd: "Es besteht immer noch die Möglichkeit, dass dies das beste Konzert der Saison wird. Bitte setzten Sie sich hin, damit alle etwas sehen können", which translates to: "There is still the possibility, that this show will become the best one of this tour. So please sit down, to give everybody here the chance to enjoy the show."[29]

There are a few klaxons, plenty more tuning and they give a spot-on version of "The Barbarian": the renditions on this tour are following a pattern of being generally faster than previously, more fluid and heavier.

The by now customary speech from Greg introduces "Tarkus" as they waste no time getting into it – again to loud applause that spurs them to play a truly powerful version and tonight they keep an expert grip on the ever-changing time signatures. Some nice funky drumming in "Stones Of Years" backs up Keith's Hammond improvisation that is, if anything, a little overdone.

This second movement of the epic is fast developing its own identity after the speedy but routine "Eruption", with the rest of the piece mesmerizing the audience into silence until the very last echoes of the very last note of "Aquatarkus" reverberates around the hall.

"Take A Pebble" is slightly shorter than on other nights on the tour but is nonetheless well-received as usual except for a few idiots who insist on calling out all the way through Keith's delicate opening on the piano strings. This is one of the few occasions when Keith doesn't get instant applause for his rendition of the "The Harry Lime Theme" but the crowd make up for it with their support for Greg's "My Dog Blue". As Greg approaches the end of his solo, Keith throws in a rippling water effect on the Moog, so similar to the recorded version on the first album. The whole middle section belongs to Keith, who takes off with some superb clavinet and piano work that fills the hall, and it seems that Greg and Carl have difficulty keeping up with him or holding him back. They even jazz up the closing section tonight and the applause becomes ecstatic.

"Knife Edge" is atmospheric, heavy and surprisingly fast: Keith playing with real mcnace; Greg screaming the lyrics in places, and Carl powering it along with hard aggressive work on toms and snare.

The version of "Rondo" typifies the longer and longer introduction that's creeping in, and the others burst a blood vessel trying to keep up with Keith.

Klaxons, cheers and shouts for more bring the guys back to play "Nutrocker" at supersonic speed to wrap things up nicely.

THURSDAY, 10 JUNE 1971

Festhalle (Stadthalle), Offenbach, Germany.

Show five of a twelve date European tour saw ELP at their best in 1971. After mainly favourable press reviews of the band's gigs in Germany last year the concert halls were packed .

An enthusiastic audience applauds fanatically but during the songs it's so quiet the silence is eerie. All three men are on top form and their equipment works perfectly (which was the exception on the previous tour).

A calm "Promenade" opens the show, so calm you still can't imagine the storm to follow. Keith and Carl spur on "Pictures ..." with a perfect duel in "The Gnome". Greg plays his part (both vocals and guitar) impeccably and "The Sage" is presented very atmospherically – interrupted by the first Moog solo. In "The Old Castle"/"Blues Variation" Keith is demonstrating his and the modular Moog's abilities: fast and full of improvisational ideas on the well-tempered Moog and the C3.

The second half of "Pictures ..." shows the guys in perfect interaction, powerful and aggressive. You have to take pity on the poor L100 in "The Great Gates ..." which would be waving a white flag if it had one. Little wonder that everyone – band, audience and equipment – need a break, announced by Keith in German.

The second set is opened by a long Moog intro going straight into "The Barbarian". Carl drives the band at a gallop and Greg shows incredible bass-work. Then Greg announces a new piece from the just released new album "... in fact it has been released today or yesterday". It will last the whole side of an album, so ... if anybody wants to go to the toilet you better go now!" The first half of "Tarkus" is played a little clumsily, the band finding it difficult to manage the multiple changes of tempo and keys. We get a solid performance of "Iconoclast" with excellent keyboard and guitar solos and end up with a short but sweet "Aquatarkus". "Take A Pebble" is an outstanding performance. Keith again introduces Greg's "My Dog Blue" with the "Harry Lime Theme" played on the piano strings and well recognized by the audience.

At the end of "Blue", Greg and Carl are clowning around and Keith starts with a stunning piano solo followed by "Tank" on the electric piano. "Knife Edge", with some mighty Moog riffs, closes the show. They encore with "Rondo" which starts in the usual way before taking on a life of its own.

"Don't we all wish we'd been at this one!"[30]

FRIDAY, 11 JUNE 1971

Meistersingerhalle, Nuremberg, Germany.

For the first time, "Rondo" exceeded "Take A Pebble" in length.

Keith opens proceedings with a businesslike, "Ok, we'd like to start off with "Pictures At An Exhibition". If you could sit down at the front, it will be very helpful."

This version sets the scene for another top-notch performance: it's gutsier, heavier and Keith adds so many extra licks on the Moog to add texture and atmosphere. In "The Gnome" there's even a whole new synth-driven section in 4/4 time and the resulting applause shows it's not lost on the knowledgeable crowd.

Greg's crystal clear vocals lead us into Keith's solo, which itself provides a smooth path into the acoustic break in "The Sage". This whole section of "Pictures ..." is now so accomplished, one of the main highlights being Greg's *arpeggio* work on the Gibson, perfectly complemented by outstanding vocals. As Carl duels with him, Keith machine-guns the crowd with the ubiquitous ribbon controller before we hear the introduction to "The Old Castle". Other than the final bridging section with "Blues Variation", the Moog solo is almost completely re-worked, much more free-form than normal. Improvisation is again the order of the day as Keith thunders through the solo, the rhythm section doing their job with vigour.

The second half of "Pictures ..." opens with a "Promenade" that has 'grandeur' stamped all over it. Movements are played confidently, even aggressively, as they stretch the pieces as far as they will go: "Baba Yaga" sees yet more Moog improvisation from Keith. "The Great Gates...", by this stage of its evolution, is definitely a "Pictures ..." highlight: building to a crescendo as Keith throws the L100 around. Greg sings his heart out, but the crowd give, surprisingly, only polite applause.

"Thank you very much... we're gonna take a short break, Funfzehn minuten, funfzehn minuten, ja?" commands Keith in his best German.

The second half starts, to the accompaniment of plenty of Moog and bass tuning, with Keith's Moog sounding suspiciously like a variation on the intro to "Space Oddity". It's an uninspiring version of "The Barbarian" notwithstanding some colourful licks on the Hammond – maybe they felt let down by the lack of applause after "Pictures ..."?

By way of contrast, "Tarkus" – still the new boy of the set – is played with precision and vigour. This is a masterful performance of what is fast becoming another ELP epic – all 23 minutes of it. Greg's new phrasing of some lyrics is still there and Carl is adding some nice fills on toms and hi-hat in "Stones Of Years". In "Mass", they tear up the script and throw it out the window with some lovely embellishments on the bass and what sounds like a beautifully improvised middle section, before a short solo on the ribbon controller.

Greg's six string playing in "Battlefield" is distinctive and his vocals fill the hall, as he launches into a well-crafted extended lead solo, backed to perfection by Keith's Hammond and Carl's metronomic time-keeping, before they bow out and leave centre stage to Greg. Loud applause follows this emotional section of "Tarkus" and then it's over to the post-apocalyptic world of "Aquatarkus" – complete with some noticeably apocalyptic faulty chords from Keith.

A short pause and Keith plays that beautiful intro to "Take A Pebble" to sustained applause from the crowd and, at almost twenty minutes, this version deserves the plaudits; classic ELP at their best. Greg is so high in the mix that we can really appreciate his rich tones even though most of the piece is Keith-driven, laying down as he does a note-perfect solo for Greg to come in on with the acoustic guitar. "My Dog Blue" goes down well as usual, with some extra licks towards the end winning an ovation. A passionately played solo from Keith, hammering on the keys, before the main theme brings in Greg and Carl for a classic jazz improvisation.

"Knife Edge" is fast and furious, with a hard-edged aggression to both the Hammond and the vocals. The Moog solo is completely improvised, the whole thing showcasing Keith's incredible dexterity.

"Rondo" now clocks in at 23 minutes – and what a version!

Repeated cries for "More" bring them back: "You're the best audience in Germany that we've played to yet!" says Keith, flattering the faithful. Well, after that, it's hardly surprising that "Nutrocker" gets one of the loudest cheers of the night – even more so as all three ham it up in style, rightly believing that they can do no wrong.

Greg sings the lyrics to "Preacher Blues" as Keith carries on playing the riff to "Nutrocker", the result being an encore that has everyone up and dancing.

SATURDAY, 12 JUNE 1971

Concertgebouw, Amsterdam, the Netherlands.

The seventh night of the tour, their first ever show in the Netherlands and they were clearly determined to impress.

Greg starts by telling the audience that "We'd like to play you tonight, to start with, a piece called 'Pictures At An Exhibition'."

Keith plays "Promenade" on the Concertgebouw's pipe organ – incredibly quietly at first, then thundering in to shake the hall to its rafters, thus setting the scene for the rest of this epic with Carl, in particular, playing for all he's worth. Keyboards are high in the mix and they stay there all night.

The Moog's rippling water effect in "The Gnome", and Greg's solo break are both stunning, as he weaves his spell on the audience. All the instrumental sections of this epic are played full-on, in your face as only this band can, and applause, when it comes, is lengthy.

In "Blues Variation", Keith attacks the almost funky groove laid down by the others, throwing in plenty of improvised stuff. "Baba Yaga" is ... well ... frenetic as usual and as we go into "The Great Gates...", Greg's voice soars above everything with a magical effect as Keith drives the melody on the trusty Hammond.

The Dutch crowd don't seem too sure how to respond to Keith's organ-throwing but he gives them the full works anyway, coaxing so many unnatural sounds out of the L100. For once, "Pictures ..." comes to a very abrupt end, catching the crowd by surprise but they respond positively anyway.

"The Barbarian" opens the second half as usual, a slower and more ponderous version than earlier dates on the tour, with Keith still very high in the mix. It comes alive during the closing section as Carl hammers the snare, and, almost immediately, a short intro from Greg heralds "Take A Pebble", almost three minutes shorter than the previous night. It's a revelation in contrast to "The Barbarian" – sharp, precise, with beautiful phrasing.

As the crowd gets into the mood for Greg's "My Dog Blue" break, he extends both the intro and the *arpeggio* close by several bars. Carl's antics with the finger cymbal are much appreciated, followed by Keith's blisteringly impressive solo, fast and note-perfect.

There's not much in the way of spoken introductions to songs and Greg curtails the usual intro to "Tarkus" as the band launch into their second epic of the show. After a fairly straight-laced "Eruption", "Stones Of Years" sees Keith adding new lines on the Hammond and Carl throwing in some fresh jazzy fills on the small toms.

"Battlefield" is immaculate, with Keith and Carl this time providing a tight, precise rhythm, over which Greg lays down a solo so full of feeling, you can almost see the expression on his face as he plays it. He improvises with such a light touch, fading out tastefully as Keith plays the opening chords to "Aquatarkus"; a true vehicle for the Moog.

"We're gonna give you 'Knife Edge'," says Keith in keeping with the mood for short intros to the songs tonight. More than competent but not a classic version, with Keith's rough Hammond sound leading the way, underpinned by Carl's hi-hat and snare.

The crowd are still applauding wildly as Keith gives us what must surely be one of the most recognizable keyboard intros in the history of prog with "Rondo". It starts at breakneck speed, but seems to slow down slightly moving into the long improvised keyboard solo. Carl puts an end to all thoughts of slowing down with one of his best solos of the tour that includes the longest gong section yet as he plays rolls on them, both quiet and loud. Ten minutes now seems the standard for his solos.

"Nutrocker" starts slowly and deliberately and in contrast to "Rondo", speeds up as they get the crowd going.

No "Preacher Blues" tonight but what the heck – they go down a storm anyway.

SUNDAY, 13 JUNE 1971

Philipshalle, Dusseldorf, Germany.
Tickets: DM 10,-

The band's fame in Germany was constantly growing by the time of this gig, and so German television decided to record it for broadcast four days later (with a little mixing of the set list) as part of the **Supergroups In Concert** *show.*

They almost certainly play "Pictures..." at this show but we have no definite record of it. They start what was probably the second set with "The Barbarian" – Greg's heavily distorted bass accompanied by Keith's percussive Hammond sound. ELP indeed do catch the essence of this very dynamic and rhythmic piece. Being the "warm up" song for the band it's not surprising that Keith played a few wrong notes, but he seems to instinctively know that playing the right ones cleanly isn't the most important part of the performance.

Coming up with a sensible running order is always one of the main strengths of this band. They continue with "Take A Pebble", a number that has developed so much recently, allowing each of them to show their skills as soloist and also as team members. Keith's playing on the strings of the grand piano complements Greg's alto bass voice; a treat for the fans' ears.

In the middle of "Pebble", Greg starts his own acoustic solo – which even sees him laughing and cursing as Carl deliberately disturbs "My Dog Blue" and dares to play a note or two on Greg's guitar. The audience love this clowning around, after which Keith jumps on the grand piano, improvising from well-known melodies with accompaniment from his left hand *ostinatos*. After almost wearing out the grand piano with his aggressive style of playing, he finds his next victim: the electric piano on which he continues his improvisation including themes from "Hoedown" and "Tank".

After the solo performances, all three work together in the jazz improvisation to satisfy the prog fans' appetite. The song comes to a calm but spectacular finish with Greg's magnificent voice. The audience really appreciate this professional performance, but what would you expect after hearing a sixteen minute gem?

Without any interruption the band jumps into "Knife Edge". A faithful rendition of this song with very telling keyboard solos: Keith is quite gentle with the Moog but the Hammond is not so fortunate. For the desired effect, Keith starts to torture it, as if getting ready for what will happen later.

One of the all time favourites, "Tarkus", follows, played at greater speed than the studio recording. As usual this piece is unlike any other "Tarkus" performance: each night seems so distinctive and individual. "Mass" was left out from the suite, replaced with a variant on "Manticore". During "Battlefield", Greg shows that he can also do variations on a theme by playing chords gently on his Telecaster. In "Aquatarkus", Keith squeezes out so many effects and interesting melodies from the Moog during his long solo. The audience show their appreciation of this giant performance with a long and loud ovation.

The speeding locomotive-like sound emerging from the Hammond announces "Rondo", becoming more and more an ELP number. The poor Hammond organ, modified to withstand the abuse, just screams like an ancient giant reptile under Keith's hands. Carl interrupts all of this with a spunky seven minute drum solo using the whole enchilada of percussion including gongs. Then the real agony of the Hammond begins as Keith squeezes out sound effects which no one ever expects from the organ. So much so that it's not the melody but rather the sheer texture of the sound that increases the adrenaline level of the audience.

"Nutrocker" follows. It's noticeable how Greg doesn't need to expend energy to get the audience involved: they clap and sing, dancing in the aisles spontaneously.

As they segue into "Preacher Blues", they work in themes from "Tiger In The Spotlight", which won't be released for another six years, and then reprise "Nutrocker" for the grand finale.[31]

With the TV broadcast, this performance can only enhance the band's growing reputation.

THURSDAY, 17 JUNE, 1971

Schwarzwaldhalle, Karlsruhe, Germany.

The final show of this short European tour would become the major component in a bootleg triple album. Since equipment failures at Oldenburg, they played two more shows in Offenbach and Hamburg and tonight's gig in Karlsruhe was a killer – their last in Germany for almost exactly a year.

This version of "Pictures ..." is played well and as tight as they come, especially in the rhythm section. Everything is timed exactly, all three players excelling themselves. Greg's lyrical sections shine through with the clarity and tone of his voice so well suited to each of the relevant 'Pictures', especially complemented tonight by Keith's Moog.

For some reason, Keith plays "The Old Castle" solo partly on the Hammond, only coming in towards the end with a delicately-pitched Moog section.

Keith reverts to playing the opening of "Take A Pebble" pretty much as it is on the album and as Greg plays the *arpeggio* in his acoustic solo, he actually stops playing and talks to the crowd. "Sounds great doesn't it?" he asks, as well as commenting on how hard it is to play.

Carl throws in a bit of levity with the finger cymbal, to much applause, and then Keith's off and on fire. The others pile in and the jazz improvisation takes off, until just before the final verse of the song when Keith leads the way into a simple but effective little boogie-woogie number.

Everyone claps along almost as soon as Greg touches his bass strings for "Knife Edge". It's generally a solid version, but they all try to charge along just a little too fast during Keith's Moog solo until Carl brings them back to rock reality.

A tight version of "Rondo" follows, with first class timing – most importantly with the train whistle-meets-gong introduction and some nice syncopated touches from Carl. The crowd want an encore and they get "Nutrocker" of course; Keith improvises all over the place, Carl gets the audience clapping along again, and Greg lets go of a few "Yeah-yeah"s.

People went home very happy – audience and band!

SUNDAY, 20 JUNE 1971

Theatre Royal, Drury Lane, London, England.
Tickets: £1.50 – 50p.

Described in Melody Maker *as "a special one night concert"[32], there was no supporting act at a show, which turned into a strange affair. Greg described the atmosphere as "tense".[33] "The trouble with their kind of music is that it requires to be played at full tilt … consequently, when perhaps the musicians are tired … neurotic energy replaces meaningful high spirits."[34]*

This gig is also memorable because it is the final time that ELP play "Pictures At An Exhibition" in its entirety anywhere, ever.

The beauty of "Pictures …" is in the detail: Greg's gentle acoustic work and vocals are faultless, the audience listen in absolute silence to his every note and word in "The Sage". Keith's "Promenade" and "The Great Gates of Kiev" are his *chef d'oeuvre*, whilst Carl is as forceful, driving and precise as ever. That's the end of "Pictures At An Exhibition" as we have come to know it and therefore the closing of a chapter in the ELP story.

"Take A Pebble" works beautifully. This crowd are so appreciatively quiet that the band could have been in a studio, apart from the loud applause for the "The Harry Lime Theme" and Greg's solo spot. It's now become a nightly feature that Greg stops playing before the *arpeggio*, telling the crowd that he's going to do something that he usually doesn't do, after which he and Carl get the laughs with the finger cymbal bit.

"Tarkus" is the second suite of the evening, which the guys now have off pat. As well as throwing in some new Hammond lines in "Stones Of Years", Keith plays very much in the background to allow Greg's vocals to shine through, something he then repeats in "Mass" and "Battlefield". During the ribbon controller solo in "Mass", Keith actually climbs up some of the boxes at his side of the stage whilst machine-gunning the crowd, and they love it

No introduction to "Knife Edge" as Greg goes straight into one of the most famous bass lines in prog, and receives rapturous applause. Vintage ELP this as Greg shouts "Yeeeeeaaaaaaaah" to the accompaniment of the Hammond, and for once the final verse sounds just like the album version. With a version as tasty as this one, Keith's antics on the L100, as the others stop playing, detract from the effect created.

"Rondo" again suffers from speed over style, Carl frantically creating sounds akin to ploughing his way through a minefield and Keith providing the spectacle, leaping from one keyboard to another, attacking the poor old L100 one moment and wriggling beneath it the next.

"Nutrocker", as usual, has them dancing in the aisles, the house lights are on and that's it, the last gig from this inventive and entertaining band for almost a month.

Technically and musically a first-rate performance but the signs are there that they need a break.

5. *I Carry The Dust Of A Journey ...*

17 JULY – 25 NOVEMBER 1971: SECOND NORTH AMERICAN TOUR
35 SHOWS (FIRST LEG: 27, SECOND LEG: 8) ACROSS THE USA AND
CANADA, WITH A 2 MONTH BREAK DURING SEPTEMBER AND
OCTOBER.

Typical set list: "The Barbarian", "Tarkus", "Take A Pebble", Greg Lake acoustic solo, piano improvisations, "Take A Pebble" reprise, "Knife Edge", "Rondo", "Nutrocker" (sometimes with "A Time And A Place" as an extra encore).

Keith: Hammond C3, Hammond L100, Bechstein grand piano, Modular Moog Synthesizer 1C with pre-set boxes, Mini Moog, Hohner 'L' Electric Clavinet.

Greg: Gibson J300 custom acoustic, Fender Jazz bass, Gibson stereo 6 string lead (replacing the Fender Telecaster part way through the tour), fuzz and wah-wah foot pedals.

Carl: Gretsch kit, 7 Paiste cymbals and hi-hat, 2 Paiste gongs, set of woodblocks, 3 cowbells and the Swiss cowbell.
Note: During the second leg, Carl acquired a custom-made Ludwig Octaplus kit (to which 8 extra concert toms were added in Spring 1972), a triangle, a chain of small bells, and a set of whistles hung around his neck.

PA system: WEM: 2 Crown stereo amplifiers driving 2,000 watts of speakers in 4 Loudmouth stacks, 11 Quad amplifiers, 20 channel stereo mixer.

By now, the act was developing well. "Take A Pebble" was recognizably different, benefiting from long improvisations that took it (in Chicago on 14 November) to a touch under 26 minutes – the longest ever. Carl's solo in "Rondo" was growing too – edging up towards eleven minutes by the end of the tour. They also rang the changes in "Tarkus" to keep it fresh.

This tour bade *adieu* to "The Barbarian", played for the last time at Madison Square Garden. "A Time and A Place" consolidated itself into the act for the time being as a regular second encore and, on occasions, a replacement for "Nutrocker".

Again a real mixture of venues for ELP, from the pomp of the Hollywood Bowl and Madison Square Garden, to the down home Pirates' World leisure park in Florida, plus two free concerts in Boston in September and November.

MONDAY, 19 JULY 1971

The Hollywood Bowl, Los Angeles, CA, USA.

Tickets: $6.50 - $2.50

Another milestone for ELP – their first video-screen synchronized gig; very state-of-the-art for 1971. In fact, it may have been the first time in concert history that this was used.

Day three of the first leg of the tour and the M.C. does the introductions, Hollywood style, "Thank you for your patience. Three good friends from England, Three big pals. On drums Mr Carl Palmer, on bass guitar and vocals Mr Greg Lake, on electricity Mr Keith Emerson – Emerson, Lake and Palmer!"

Keith seems to have perfected the weird and wonderful siren sounds that come from the Moog as everyone gets ready, making the most of the stereo PA, and then he announces "We'd like to start off with 'The Barbarian'."

The fuzz on Greg's bass seems to last forever, so harsh and aggressive, yet this version is lighter and less ponderous than on the last European tour. It is noticeable how precise Carl's playing is on the closing section as they build to a crashing conclusion.

Keith introduces a much-changed "Take A Pebble", with the opening set against a back-drop of noisy fans, and Carl adding some snare during the verses. There are a few wrong notes on the piano. 'The Harry Lime Theme" is still there, but without the widespread recognition it had in Europe.

Greg's gone country for "My Dog Blue" before Keith, and then Carl, come crashing back in for a long improvisation with a nice light, jazzy feel to it. A lively crowd show their appreciation in no uncertain manner as they launch into "Tarkus".

The announcement of this track is greeted as if they'd introduced a new Hollywood blockbuster:

"'Tarkus' – Jeeeeesus, they're going to play 'Tarkus!'", says one happy camper in the crowd.[35]

Greg messes up the words in "Stones Of Years", with the second verse all over the shop. The Moog and ribbon controller are nothing less than rampant throughout. "Mass" soars over the top of machine-gun drumming and some snappy bass. "Battlefield" is the highlight of the piece, Greg's clear, intense vocals supported by increasingly funky drumming from Carl and soaring Hammond from Keith. A worthy lead solo from Greg and then he sings the final verse unaccompanied, full of emotion with a dramatic pause before Keith counts in "Aquatarkus".

The Moog fanfare that closes "Tarkus" is a hair's breadth from being out of tune, which possibly explains it being a shorter than usual version tonight.

"Knife Edge" is as wonderful as ever, but from the start falls a bit flat in the atmosphere stakes because this audience don't instantly clap along as do fans elsewhere. Keith throws himself into the heavy chords that power the piece along, but the out of tune Moog forces him to cut short his solo. The closing section raises the roof, metaphorically, at this open air gig – as Keith takes us straight into "Rondo", the crowd whistling and whooping loudly.

"Rondo" is executed with masterful precision as Keith races up and down the keys like a maniac. Carl's ten minute solo is tumultuous: one moment staccato snare work, the next a fast and furious section on rim and cow-bell, then an unparalleled symphony of cymbal and hi-hat. He risks serious injury as he bangs his head against the cowbell, whilst keeping the rhythm going on the bass drum and crashing the gongs.

Sustained calls for more bring them back for "Nutrocker", played slowly and deliberately at first and immediately picking up speed till it rocks along nicely to make sure everyone is up and dancing. As Carl furiously plays his break in the middle, Greg shouts "Everybody!", someone in the crowd shouts "Boogie!" and it's one hell of a party all round.

Keith thanks the audience, acknowledging "Greg Lake on bass, Carl Palmer on drums", and that's it.

It was at this show that Keith fell down the boarded-over fountain on the edge of the stage into the orchestra pit during a ribbon controller solo and broke a rib – not that it stopped his antics, nor could anyone tell he was in pain.

SATURDAY, 7 AUGUST 1971

Pirates' World, Dania, FL, USA.

Tickets: $4.00 in advance, $5.00 at the door.

The second of two nights at the venue and nearly the midway point of the first part of the tour. Hollywood was a long way behind them and they were playing an amusement park where the rides were still going until 10.00p.m. – well after show time.

Tuning up seems to take forever but then we have to remember that it has a purpose – to introduce the audience to the superb stereo PA system the band have. "Wow, it's stereo!" as one perceptive member of the crowd comments.

"The Barbarian" starts the show, all growling Hammond and fuzzy bass, powerful with Carl driving it along and followed by "Take A Pebble", though we have no record of the latter.

Greg introduces "Tarkus" as a lengthy piece "so if you need to go and urinate ..." This version sounds more muscular, more confidently played, than at the start of the tour, with Carl in particular playing the syncopated fills we'd heard during the previous European dates. The two bridging movements of "Iconoclast" and "Manticore" are now, by this stage in the development of "Tarkus", doing their job perfectly as the band regularly throw in impromptu sections to take us respectively into "Mass" and "Battlefield". Greg's solo in the latter is full of feeling and the whole movement is played a little more slowly now to add to the dramatic effect.

For such a relatively short piece, "Knife Edge" has plenty of light and shade, aided tonight by this enthusiastic crowd. Greg's ad-libs on the vocals suit the mood of this piece and Carl shows off with some extra fills before Keith takes centre stage with a simple, effective and much-applauded Moog solo.

The punters are amazed at the beginning of "Rondo", all train whistles and crashing gongs. Keith even goes as far as to repeat the whistle sounds in different keys to get the crowd going and, as the Emerson Express starts its journey, everyone's clapping along. The lengthy middle section is frantic, all three let loose in the mayhem and Keith seems to use every impromptu line he knows, together with still more whistle sounds that send this Florida crowd wild.

There's no doubt that, with the way the guys had this audience eating out of their hands, they must have played at least one encore – but we have no record of it.

THURSDAY, 12 AUGUST 1971

Stanley Park, Toronto, Canada.

Only their third ever show in Canada, following stops in Montreal and Vancouver immediately after the Hollywood Bowl gig, and there was very much a feeling that the audience appreciated the 'live' side to ELP compared to the recorded output. For this enthusiastic audience, every song was a crowd-pleaser.

Some interesting, and very different, stabbing left hand lines from Keith as "The Barbarian" gets under way, greeted by instant applause. They go wild again at the jazz middle section, and the ending fair raises the roof with Keith and Greg having to work hard to keep up with Carl's demonic pace.

"Pebble" is shorter on this tour, the opening section sticking closely to the album version. As he goes into "My Dog Blue", Greg cries "It's a string!" as one breaks, and Keith and Carl come to the rescue with a wonderfully improvised boogie-woogie/jazz section. With Greg still busy on the broken string front, Keith charges off into his solo improvisation, shorter and played more dramatically than the norm – except that is when he goes off into the riff from "Preacher Blues" and the others charge after him. Order is restored for the pro-forma ending, greeted with loud applause from this very vocal audience.

"Tarkus" is masterfully played, both Keith's lead lines and Greg's vocals soaring above everything else, Greg indulges himself again with "Yeahs" and "Oooohs" and why not? Keith's frantic Moog solo in "Mass" flies through the air like a pilot machine-gunning the foot soldiers, coming back to earth with Carl's cowbell intro to the last verse.

The lead solo from Greg in "Battlefield", played tastefully and quite slowly over the top of some bass Moog from Keith, gives this piece its identity, even more so as he goes into the vocal/guitar break, his voice almost breaking with emotion.

"Aquatarkus" is different every time it's played, and tonight is no exception, rising to its final crashing chords. A manic crowd show their appreciation and it's almost straight into "Knife Edge". This version is loud, played at frantic speed, with Greg going overboard a bit on the screamed vocals to the point where he fails to hit a note or two. The overall impression of this piece tonight is that it's a bit messy, especially in the middle solos, but it's doubtful if anyone in this adoring crowd even notices or cares.

As with the previous gigs in America, Keith extends the train intro to "Rondo" to build the excitement and anticipation. Tonight's audience are so worked up that if he rearranged his stamp collection on stage they'd be screaming their heads off. "Rondo" by now has such an ELP-identity about it, but every so often Keith throws in phrases from way-back-when with the Nice. Carl's solo has stabilized at about ten minutes, stunning the crowd into a silenced admiration broken only by applause for the super-fast snare work and the gongs/Swiss cowbell bit.

The audience go wild with shouts of "Wow" and "Yeah" as Keith throws and drags the L100 around the stage, before bringing "Rondo" to its all-guns-blazing conclusion.

They demand an encore and they get "A Time And A Place", a bit of an untidy, loud and very raw version. It's short with a very abrupt ending and this crowd go wild for just one more time, but nothing doing.

The guys leave the stage, heading off towards Montreal for the next show.

FRIDAY, 13 AUGUST 1971

Place des Nations, Montreal, Canada.

Sadly, what record exists of this, their fourth Canadian show, lacks the entire first half: "The Barbarian", "Take A Pebble" and "Tarkus". What we can assume, given the audience reaction to the other tracks played, is that tonight is yet another blinder from ELP.

"Knife Edge" is much more bass-heavy than usual and the dramatic pauses between the verses have gone, the aggressive Hammond sound providing the bridge between Greg's lyrics. The audience are still going wild as Keith takes the band into the show-stopper.

"Rondo" is long tonight at a touch over 23 minutes, Keith slowly and so effectively building the speed of the chuff-chuff noises on the Hammond as the train picks up speed out of the station. After eleven minutes of what has to be the most stunning and entertaining drum solo in rock, Keith takes over, torturing the poor L100 before the whole express train crashes to a halt with the usual mighty power chords.

"Nutrocker" is the first encore. Extra drum fills from Carl, improvisations from Keith, and Greg's shouts of "Alright!" and "Yeah!" work up this crowd into a frenzy.

Loud chants for "more" bring back the guys for a second encore of "A Time And A Place", a version that rocks along without any of the subtleties of the original.

"Thank you, you've been really great," shouts Greg as the outro music kicks in.

SATURDAY, 21 AUGUST 1971

Transit Auditorium, Chicago, IL, USA.

Show twenty of the first leg of the tour and the band's first visit to Chicago.

Tonight, the opening of "The Barbarian" sounds even more heavy rock than usual before going into the piano section – to resounding applause from this crowd who are behind the band from the off. Thundering bass and Hammond close the piece and for once it seems like Carl is having to keep pace with the others.

Funny that here we have another example of ELP returning to a textbook-like version of "Take A Pebble" for the North American audiences, so unlike the European performances that were full of improvisations all round. This one lacks sparkle – competent, professional, entertaining but it wins no cigar. Instead it's now just the "The Harry Lime Theme" (Keith's piano free-for-all) and Greg's acoustic solo that stray from the script. The last of these is routine to say the least, the jazz improvisation a tad messy and a bit too loose.

Again, they play the riff from "Preacher Blues" but with nothing like the fervour it had when played as an encore at the European shows.

"Ok, we're gonna play for you now – 'Tarkus'," announces Greg in an unbelievably low-key voice, with nothing like the long sometimes humorous introductions he has recently been doing.

This epic is in stark contrast to "Pebble": fresh, dynamic with lots of extra fills from Carl and loud, punchy bass from Greg. There is a wonderfully improvised Moog solo in "Mass" that begins with pure genius staccato Hammond, viciously punched on the keys by Keith, and some lovely interplay between him and Carl. The applause for this alone lasts almost the entire next verse, before a fast and furious "Manticore" leads us to "Battlefield", the only movement of "Tarkus" written by Greg.

Loads of Hammond and Moog lines from Keith provide an atmospheric, inspirational basis for strong vocals but the guitar solo is disappointing. Greg misses his cue, comes in late and the Telecaster sounds completely out of tune – a real rarity. Keith goes into auto-pilot and compensates well with the Hammond, playing some blockbusting power chords, but it's obvious that the guitar is out for the count – for tonight at least.

"Aquatarkus" is now all about variations on a theme, all skilfully highlighted by Keith and perfectly matched by Carl's snare. The imagery created by the ripples on the Moog, Carl's increasingly military drumming and some uncanny bagpipe-like sounds suits the piece well and it gets the applause it deserves.

A particularly commendable version of "Knife Edge" follows, powerful throughout with a real storming ending. As one rabble-rouser ends, and the crowd go wild, another starts and we go almost immediately into a full tilt "Rondo". Keith's long improvisation sounds so different tonight, played with so much controlled restraint you feel it's about to explode at any moment, with tons of two-handed stabbing at the keys.

As Carl's turn in the relay comes round, he knocks seven bells out of the kit, the snare in particular suffering from a stupendously fast solo. After only four minutes, Carl counts the others back in and Keith persecutes the L100, dragging it around up to the backline and then away again, to a slightly discordant backing from the bass.

Keith bids everyone goodnight at the end of another powerful show, lots of highs and the people of Illinois can take home some wonderful memories.

SATURDAY, 28 AUGUST 1971

The Public Auditorium, Cleveland, OH, USA.

Worthy of mention as the show where, for once, crowd noise almost stopped the spectacle in its tracks. In full flow during his acoustic break in "Take A Pebble", Greg stops playing and says, "Either you fucking shut up and let us fucking play or we will pack up our fucking instruments and fucking go home."[36] Not eloquent, but effective.

Carl and Keith look absolutely stunned, but everyone shuts up, they resume playing and deliver an outstanding show.

WEDNESDAY, 1 SEPTEMBER 1971

Gaelic Park, Riverdale, NY, USA.

This last show of the first leg of the second US tour in 1971 was noteworthy for ELP fans from a number of perspectives. This tour established ELP as the supergroup de jour of the early 1970s – only Led Zeppelin attracted more people to concerts.

Tarkus and the impending release of the new album Trilogy would in future give the guys the chance to present a wider set list on their return to the continent for the second leg of the tour in November.

Bob Moog (who sadly died in 2005), the inventor and design engineer of the Moog synthesizer, is invited by Keith to join the show. Finding the venue, a soccer field in the Bronx, causes him a few problems, but he reaches it in time for the band's soundcheck.

The chugging Moog introduces a powerful and speedy rendition of "The Barbarian", which is making its swansong as an opening number at a ticketed gig. Tonight Keith's using different stops on the Hammond which makes it sound in the style of the late Jon Lord of Deep Purple, which may be accidental or prophetic depending on your viewpoint given the California Jam [which we will cover later] in 1974.

A keep-it-steady-play-it-smoothly "Take A Pebble", interrupted only by extra applause after "The Harry Lime Theme" and Greg's "My Dog Blue", tranquilizes the frenetic New York audience. Keith gives us a modified piano improvisation with the first rudiments of Gulda's *Fugue* and the standard "Little Rock Getaway".

The themes of "Tank" and "Hoedown" are now played on the grand piano too – not really surprising as Keith has never made a secret of hating the electric piano he used at that time.

Greg announces "Tarkus" and realizes that Keith has major trouble with his "electricity". The Moog is detuned and the Hammond still sounds 'Lordish'. After the experience of a long tour, Greg thinks he knows the reason: "It's cold here!" Later on this problem was solved by separate heaters behind the Moog to keep the sensitive valves at a constant temperature.

So the beginning of "Tarkus" doesn't sound too healthy as Keith needs until the ribbon controller solo in "Mass" to tune the stubborn Moog. The man must be related to an octopus to manage all this, multi-tasking and still performing new improvisations in "Iconoclast" and "Mass".

Greg's happy now too, and gives us an atmospheric solo on electric guitar, preparing the ground for "Aquatarkus".

The Moog rewards Keith's huge efforts with an excellent sound. He modifies the dramaturgic structure of the piece with new riffs, powerful bass sounds and picks out a tune in the rhythm of a military march interrupted by far out sounds like a siren wailing, rippling of water and a short circuit

Keith seems exhausted now. He recovers in a slyly presented "Knife Edge" finished with excessive war-like noises.

The skirling and stomping of a steam locomotive produced on the L100 introduces "Rondo". By this stage of its life, the L100 is apparently damaged. Missing or inhibited keys cause heavy discords – but who really cares when it's presented with such extraordinary showmanship?

After Bach's "Toccata In D Minor" at demonic speed, Keith passes the baton to Carl for his eleven minute drum solo. Today it's much more aggressive than usual but nevertheless still very melodic. This man really is one of the best musical drummers in rock, bar none. Every section of his drum kit (tom toms, cymbals, snare drum, cow bells, gongs, bass drum and the detuned church bell) is played in several small solos, climaxed by a finale on the full kit, with Carl calling out the count back into "Rondo".

Greg gets his sixpence worth in with the staccato bass line but the L100 is only able to produce pathetic clusters of yowling and screaming sounds. Some hard work being lined up here for Rocky Morley, the long suffering roadie, and the Hammond mechanics.

But the audience like the show and demand an encore. The band comes back on stage. Greg thanks the audience, announcing their return to the USA in November, which is given a massive thumbs up.

"A Time And A Place" isn't the hymn that it is on the album, but played loud and aggressively. More like a heavy rock piece with hymnal bits thrown in for extra emphasis. But this interpretation gives Greg the opportunity to show the complete range of his voice crying out the lyrics akin to (at the risk of taking the Deep Purple analogies in this section further than one perhaps should) Ian Gillan.

So what did Bob Moog make of it all? "And in front, here's this guy throwing an organ around, making keys fly off, and making the instruments scream. That was the most incredible experience I've ever had! Maybe we could design a special instrument for you". [37]

Keith repaid the compliment years later: "His respect means more to me than an ill-informed critic. [38]"

After this event Bob and Keith started their collaboration to improve the modular Moog and to develop the Polymoog.[39]

WEDNESDAY, 15 SEPTEMBER 1971.

The Hatch Memorial Shell, Boston, MA, USA.

A bit of an oddity this one, a free show before the big "lay-off" until November. They played the full set, still opening with "The Barbarian" and although no record of it exists it was, by all accounts, a stunner.

FRIDAY, 12 NOVEMBER 1971

The Music Hall, Boston, MA, USA.

Another free concert and the opening night of the second, shorter leg of the tour which comprised just eight dates.

It's a typical first-nighter with the band confident but still very cautious, too much so at times, though they get better as the night progresses. Introductions are now generally, unlike earlier American dates, done by Keith, such as: "We've been recording a new album in England. One of the tracks on it is something we'd like to start off with. It's called 'Hoedown'."

This version is a bit of a mixed bag: cautiously adventurous is the best description. Very slightly faster than the studio version but sticking pretty close overall, although now and again Keith strains at the leash with Hammond and Moog improvisations. It's powerful, no doubt about it, and a suitable replacement for "The Barbarian" as an opener, but the band still need to get their collective heads round it to give it identity as a live piece.

Keith had to remove a paper aeroplane from his keyboards before they could continue, describing "Tarkus" as a "fantasia" piece. With a laid back introduction, "It's all about an armadillo you see," Keith wins loud applause for what turns out to be a very long and very skilled 29 minute version of the classic, but it lacks the controlled aggression of earlier versions. "Eruption" and "Stones Of Years" are faultless, Keith giving us an inspired improvised solo, which leads into a surprise bass solo backed by well-syncopated drumming from Carl. This is brought about by a power cut on all Keith's keyboards. Greg realizes what's happened and extemporizes for a few bars He even plays some of Keith's lead lines, making a fine fist of it too. They then stop completely before Keith announces "... a power cut on the organ. Bear with us a second and we'll carry on where we left off."

Carl, ever the light-hearted one, cracks a joke at Keith's expense, and then these consummate professionals pick up almost exactly where the keyboards had packed up.

Keith plays a low-key Moog solo in "Aquatarkus" set against a steady military beat from Carl and Greg. They've changed and developed this last movement so dramatically that there is now a long section of dripping water Moog sounds, with everything hushed in the theatre so we can hear each bass note and percussive stroke.

As Greg sings the opening lines to "Take A Pebble", he gets instant applause. They're still sticking unbelievably close to the original: the phrasing of lyrics, the licks on the grand piano and even Carl's jazzy fills and brush strokes on the hi-hat are taken straight from the first album.

But then comes a surprise: a simple, beautifully-played improvisation from Keith on the piano featuring themes from "Fugue" and "The Sheriff", both recently laid-down in the studio, and this time accompanied by Carl on hand-played toms. Another surprise occurs as Keith pauses in his solo, Greg sings the first verse to "Oh Susannah", a strange choice of a southern song here in the heart of New England.

After "My Dog Blue", Keith is well on top of his solo improvisations, and they all get gold stars for the closing six riveting minutes. The audience are up for anything now, cheering and clapping to the rhythm of "Knife Edge" as the band play what must surely be one of the best ever versions of this track. The applause nearly drowns out the band as they bring it to a close. This kind of playing is the stuff ELP legends are made of.

The fuzzier Hammond sound is still there for "Rondo", producing an inspired solo from Keith both before and after Carl's spotlight, all eleven mind-blowing minutes of it. This is one of those rare versions of "Rondo" when we can hear Keith calling out as he goes through the different phases of throwing around the L100 and lying underneath it whilst still playing.

Welcome back my friends to the tour that never ends.

SUNDAY, 14 NOVEMBER 1971

Transit Auditorium, Chicago, IL, USA.

Some sources gave this show's venue as the Arie Crown Theater in Chicago. Either way, they were back in the Windy City for the second time in three months.

Overall, a notable gig with Carl and Greg high in the mix, giving the whole concert a real solid, rocking feel to it. And it has one of the longest ever performances of "Take A Pebble" at just under 26 minutes.

They're growing in confidence with the opener, "Hoedown", as Carl and Greg seem to be restraining Keith to the more moderate tempo of the early versions. Some nifty Hammond soloing here, full of improvisations, and they're still very much feeling their way to see what goes down well with the audiences.

The crowd love it as Keith says a few words about the opener coming from the new album, and then back to more familiar ground with what he describes as "a suite ... we gave you last time, called 'Tarkus'." Loud cheers greet the start of this epic. Carl is up there at the front of the mix, whilst Keith is scuttling from one keyboard to another, without the faintest suggestion he may make an error. They canter into "Mass", slow to a trot and then gallop at full pelt into the improvised ribbon controller solo with Keith attacking everyone and everything in sight

As Greg sings the next verse, we literally cannot hear the band for the applause ringing round the hall. His showpiece in "Tarkus" is so obviously "Battlefield", but the clarity and power of his bass work throughout the song grows each night.

The pulsating, quieter section in the middle of "Aquatarkus" doesn't spoil the mood of the piece as Keith produces plenty of sharp, haunting sounds before building to its more normal crashing close to tumultuous applause.

Back to even more familiar ground with "Take A Pebble", and a nice, well-polished version this is. The hand-played toms are out again during Keith's solo before "My Dog Blue", something that appears to be a tasteful addition to the song. Greg chats to the audience during his spot, explaining how he sometimes changes the way he plays the acoustic solo so that it's harder one night, easier the next, and then it's into the final section – jazz, boogie-woogie and melodic prog all rolled into one.

The opening of "Knife Edge" is carried along by Greg's bass and the clapping crowd before Keith's chords come crashing in and the whole thing bounces along at a rocking pace. The middle section, with its oh-so-many-notes-on-both-hands from Keith, is mesmerizing and the ending deserves the credit the faithful give it.

With the reception they're getting from this crowd, the band go for broke with "Rondo". Screams, whistles and generous applause greet Keith and Carl as train sounds and gong crashes rule. The bass slams in, hitting right in the solar plexus and we're off.

A fitting show-closer, "Rondo" winds everyone up and, although it's by far the oldest piece in the set, with only a six minute drum solo tonight, it still kicks prog rock butt.

MONDAY, 15 NOVEMBER 1971

Eastown Theater, Detroit, MI, USA.

Some doubt exists as to whether the band played Detroit on the 15 or 16 November – but either way it was a great show in true ELP style.

It also bears witness to what was a typically low-key start to an ELP show. They wander on, a bit of tuning here and there, although rarely a drum is heard because

Carl is all revved up and ready to go. Then Keith strolls up the mic and almost apologetically introduces the opener. The days of taped intros, TV screens and proscenium arches are still a long way off.

Tonight's "Hoedown" is even slower than usual, note-perfect in every sense, but sticking like glue to the original except for the middle solo. It's very laid-back and jazzy in style, with subtle Moog licks thrown in towards the end.

"Tarkus", all 28 minutes and 30 seconds of it, belies its quiet introduction. From the crowd reaction, we all know what's coming. "Stones Of Years", "Mass" and "Battlefield" are all just so atmospheric, with the guitar and keyboard solos befitting well the mood of each section. Carl's playing, too, is full of sensitivity. The middle of "Mass" has become a well-ordered, restrained *mêlée* with Keith leading the way into true prog near-excess that never quite goes over the top. Greg has the audience in the palm of his hand in "Battlefield", then Keith and Carl crash in with "Aquatarkus" that takes us to the roof-shaking close.

Some jubilant members of the audience show their welcome for "Take A Pebble" but then all settles down quietly as Greg sings the opening lines and the crowd react again. After a breathtaking solo from Keith with some deft touches from his left hand, Greg steps up in the old denim jacket he has taken to wearing for this part of the concert and entertains with "My Dog Blue", extending the *arpeggio* bit, which is warmly appreciated by the crowd. They may have played "Knife Edge" but we'll never know for certain.

"Rondo" sounds a little subdued compared to some recent versions, a little shorter, a little slower but for once the clarity of Carl's snare work can clearly be heard. We reach the drum solo earlier than normal and, as usual, no-one can see Carl's face because of his swirling, dripping-wet hair.

Noisy demands for more bring them back for "A Time And A Place", driven along by the fuzzy, soaring Hammond with more than a few wobbles in Greg's voice as he aims for, but doesn't always hit, the high notes. Still, it sends them away happy as the outro music kicks in.

Another triumphant visit to the heart of Motown.

THURSDAY, 25 NOVEMBER 1971

Madison Square Garden, New York, NY, USA.

The curtain came down on another classic at this show, as this was the last call for "The Barbarian".

This is the last gig of the second leg of the second US tour in 1971, on the bill too are the J. Geils Band. After a barrel-organ tape intro, ELP take to the stage and do a little soundcheck. They want to start but there is still a fairground-like atmosphere, very amusing for everybody especially Greg, who is tickled pink and shouts to the sound engineer "Turn that thing off now!". Nothing happens at first but finally the sound engineer succeeds.

Greg introduces "Hoedown": "We would like to give you some that rock more too". Keith shows the fairground music is over with ultra-fast Hammond playing.

A powerful "Eruption" preludes "Tarkus". Perfect in time and key, screaming Moog sounds aplenty, wonderful melodic drumming, opulent Hammond improvisations, fantastic bass lines and Greg's unique voice make this a performance of epic proportions. An over-the-top ribbon controller solo in "Mass" drives the audience really crazy and the band deserve the extra applause they receive. "Battlefield", sentimentally played with some lovely Moog riffs and an almost lyrical guitar solo, cools things down, preparing the way for a short but vigorous "Aquatarkus". This evening Keith drops the "Peer Gynt Suite" phrases he used earlier in the tour; instead we get lots of new, stunning sounds combined with witty variations on the Moog.

A speedy, precise and atmospheric "Take A Pebble" follows. After the first piano solo Greg plays a nice traditional break on acoustic guitar before treating everyone to his last ever Stateside outing for "Old Blue". The piano improvisation only uses tantalizing snippets of the well known milestones, like Gulda's "Fugue" and "Little Rock Getaway", to build new improvisations. As Christmas is near, Keith also throws in "Jingle Bells", to the audience's delight.

With a loud and fast "Knife Edge" the audience is led back to rock. The skirling of the L100 locomotive signals the departure of the grand finale. The train accelerates to a tremendous speed, and after a last triumphant skirl Keith starts with the "Rondo" theme at demonic speed with the left hand as well as with the right.

Bach's "Toccata in D Minor" is followed by some random phrases and then Keith introduces Carl for his drum solo, which is heavy on the cow bells and the duck-call whistle: perhaps Carl has discovered a passion for hunting? Then it's a long lasting Hammond ride with knife attacks galore: the Garden is beside itself with joy and the audience wants more.

For this enthusiastic and appreciative audience the guys have tonight's special: "The Barbarian". To celebrate a dignified send-off for this classic ELP piece, the guys play it very loud and aggressively, especially Greg with heavily distorted bass sounds. Some suitably loud Moog fanfares highlight the crashing end of this old warhorse.

"A memorable end to a memorable gig marking the end of the second US tour." [40] *Don Heckman of* The New York Times *was positive about the music, but less sure about the theatrics: "... Emerson, Lake and Palmer have less need of such absurdities than do many rock groups. All three musicians play exceptionally well ..."* [41]

6. *That Cannot Be Shaken Away ...*

8 - 19 DECEMBER 1971: THIRD UK TOUR.
20 SHOWS OVER 11 DAYS.

Typical set list:	"Hoedown", "Tarkus", "Take A Pebble", Greg Lake acoustic solo, piano improvisations, "Take A Pebble" reprise, "Knife Edge", "Rondo", "Nutrocker" and/or "A Time And A Place" as encore.
Keith:	Hammond C3, Hammond L100, Bechstein grand piano, Modular Moog Synthesizer 1C with pre-set boxes, Mini Moog, Hohner 'L' Electric Clavinet.
Greg:	Gibson J300 custom acoustic, Fender Jazz bass, Gibson stereo 6 string lead, fuzz and wah-wah foot pedals.
Carl:	Ludwig Octaplus kit, 7 Paiste cymbals and hi-hat, 2 Paiste gongs, set of woodblocks, triangle, chain of small bells, set of whistles, 3 cowbells and the Swiss cowbell.
PA system:	WEM: 2 Crown stereo amplifiers driving 2,000 watts of speakers in 4 Loudmouth stacks, 11 Quad amplifiers, 20 channel stereo mixer.

1971 had been a year of extensive touring in Europe and North America, two album releases (*Tarkus* and *Pictures At An Exhibition*) plus live and studio rehearsals for their fourth album *Trilogy*. Still, they were up for this short and extremely demanding tour. On the closing night, they played two shows at Green's Playhouse in Glasgow; both performances opened by the swirling bagpipes of the Red Hackle Pipes and Drums.

"This tour ended a year which laid the foundations for ELP as the most fascinating live act in the early 1970s."[42]

It also marked the first time when the pendulum swung in favour of "Hoedown" as the opener, to give a more dramatic and energetic feel to the start of the set.

Very few recordings of these shows survive and some accounts of them mention that the band played "Pictures ..." (presumably in truncated form since the final performance of the full piece is always acknowledged as Drury Lane on 20 June 1971). None of the recordings that exist have any mention of the piece being played.

THURSDAY, 9 DECEMBER 1971

The City Hall, Sheffield, UK.

Second venue of the tour and it's unclear whether the recording that exists was from the first or second show. It captured the band in top form, but whichever concert it was, this had to be one of the quietest audiences ELP ever played to, although they won them over in the end.

To his usual laid back introduction, Keith adds a short explanation about hassle with customs on their recent return from the States and how it's affected some of the equipment they have on stage. After that, the mention of "Hoedown" is almost a throw-away remark. As in North America, they take it slowly but forcefully as if they want to ensure they get the new material right for the UK tour. Hammond and Moog solos are played deliberately, at a stately pace and the new number goes down well.

"Tarkus" is well played: more slowly than on previous European and American dates, proving to the UK audiences that they have truly mastered the time shifts and intricacies of this epic. During "Stones Of Years" and "Mass", when the rhythm is as tight as can be and Keith piles into some first-rate solos, applause – unlike in America and Europe – is very slow to come and incredibly restrained. Even the majestic, rafter-lifting opening chords of "Battlefield" get no reaction.

You can almost see the expression on Greg's face as he kicks into the emotions of a stirring electric solo, the hall eerily silent except for him and Keith's bubbling Moog. The imagery of this piece is stunning but not even here, where American and European audiences went wild, does he get so much as a ripple of applause.

"Take A Pebble", surely one of their best ever songs, immediately dominates things as they replicate the original version so closely for the opening section. Beautiful, dreamy piano from Keith reverberates around the otherwise silent hall and again, as on some of the US dates, Greg quietly sings a verse from "Oh Susannah" before he picks the first notes on the acoustic, going into "My Dog Blue" and at last gets this audience to show some enthusiasm as they clap along.

The *arpeggio* sounds more classically-oriented than ever tonight. And then out steps Carl with the finger cymbal. Keith races through his improvisation to great effect, coming to a more subtle jazz free-form with superb syncopation from Carl in particular, before we return to the textbook ending.

"Knife Edge" is as stirring as usual, with Keith belting out the Hammond chords and solo, then everyone scrums back in for the shattering ending and, for once, this crowd are out of their seats and clapping before the last notes have died away.

"Rondo" has been changed for these UK dates, the opening is much shorter than they played for the European and North American audiences with the train sounds and gongs hardly in evidence. They quickly settle into the rhythm as Keith delivers one of his shortest but sweetest "Rondo" solos for a long time. Carl wins long and loud applause with a five minute solo, much shorter than recently and taken at a much faster pace because of it, before he hands over to Keith, who is on top, underneath and all over the poor old L100 and this crowd, having at long last woken up, love it. The outro music is already playing as the cheers and demands for more grow louder, and back they come for "A Time And A Place".

A punchy version of this *Tarkus* track ensues; Greg is still keen to impress but unable to stretch to those highest notes.

This was only their third or fourth UK show in almost six months, both band and audience more than a bit cagey about what was going to happen. All's well that ends well though.

SATURDAY, 11 DECEMBER 1971

The Odeon, Birmingham, UK.

Not much of a record exists of this show, but what there is gives a fascinating insight into the wicked sense of humour in this band. At one point, Greg put his foot clean through one of his acoustic guitars, wrecking the instrument.

They walk on, start a bit of tuning up and after a few runs up and down the keys, Keith pops up with "And now for the second number ...". Loud applause and laughter as Carl then picks up a ragtime rhythm on the cymbals, blocks and cowbells. Keith sees the opportunity, joins in on the piano and, before we know where we are, the two of them are playing full-on ragtime. They pause and Keith plucks from somewhere in the back of his brain theme after archetypal theme from the days of the silent cinema, and the hall erupts with laughter again. Carl does the whole Arthur Rank gong thing and Keith canters through the "Fugue" from "Endless Enigma", note-perfect, probably the first time this piece is played as such.

All this and as yet they haven't properly opened the show. Greg, who must have been standing watching all this, comes up with the killer quote of the night: "OK and now back to work." After all that, "Hoedown" is passable but not up to the standard of other nights on this tour, with a lacklustre solo. Keith introduces it as a track from their new album, to be released hopefully in February 1972;

Before we go any further, it's sort of ... we heard a lot of things about *Pictures At An Exhibition* being released at full price. The price we released it out at is £1.49 and if any record shops try and con you then let us know about it and don't buy it, don't buy it. It's as cheap as we can get it at, and there's no reason why people in record shops should be making extra bread, ok? This is a thing which was on our last album and is different to when we recorded it. If we played it the same every night we'd get fucking pissed off with it (some banter from Greg) ... It's a thing called "Tarkus".

It's as strong as ever with the rhythm particularly aggressive, providing a fitting background for Keith's, and later Greg's, solos. This is the fourth tour they've played it on, developing it all the time, tonight ringing the changes more than ever in "Mass". Greg plays the intro on bass in lead guitar style, and Keith runs riot on the Hammond and ribbon controller, allowing feedback to give a whole new dimension to the sound.

"Battlefield" is bass-heavy with a few stray notes on the Moog, sounding as if it's going out of tune again. If anything, Greg rescues it and earns his keep with his six string solo but then sings the first verse all over again instead of the "Every blade is sharp ..." stanza, killing the mood a little. As we move through "Aquatarkus" Carl, the engine room, rattles out that beat, Keith revels in his dripping water Moog solo, moving then into various classical themes. His improvised, spaced-out Moog section impedes the atmosphere of this part of the epic but then they all return to the main "Tarkus" theme and give it a powerful close.

Such a pity there isn't more of this concert showing the band in playful mood.

MONDAY, TUESDAY AND WEDNESDAY, 13, 14 AND 15 DECEMBER 1971

The Pavilion, London, UK.

The cover picture for this book has been adapted from a picture of this theatre with a billboard poster advertising that ELP were playing the Pavilion during this run of gigs (ably supported by Michael Chapman). It is now part of the Trocadero complex which, believe it or not, is home to a Ripley's Believe It Or Not.

Six shows over three days at London's Pavilion give us a deep and long lasting impression of what is probably ELP's most productive era. Astoundingly, this band are showing absolutely no signs of exhaustion after such a gruelling year. What's even more amazing is that they play two shows at nine of the eleven venues on this short UK tour: twenty full shows over just eleven days with only one day off for travelling between London and Dundee.

The recording that exists is from one of the six London shows, but it's unclear as to exactly which one. It's a small, intimate venue seating fewer than 1,000 people, a cinema that hadn't seen a live performance of any kind since 1935, and no live 'show' since 1908. The acoustics are surprisingly good (reputedly the best in London) as is the Pavilion's position in Piccadilly Circus, so the band could have their name and pictures on the billboard above the gig.

I was surprised to learn how this venue was chosen, as it wasn't a usual place for a rock band to play. Carl explained to me that it was his idea as he remembered it as a young boy of 12 years coming down to London for his drum lessons and the effect Piccadilly Circus had on him. He still loves Piccadilly Circus today as it made such an impression on him and he saw this theatre every time he came to London. With ELP he was then in a position to be able to get the band to play in this same theatre. No one had played a concert in it for over 35 years so it was unusual but apt for him as he had always wanted to play there.

Since the second US tour in November, "Hoedown", from the yet-to-be-released *Trilogy* album, replaces "The Barbarian" as the opener, with the beginning near to the later studio release. In the middle section Keith doesn't know how to go on, so he starts a nice little Hammond improvisation instead. It's very interesting to listen to this early version as we know that "Hoedown" is played later at a downright demonic tempo.

After welcoming the audience, Greg announces the release of *Trilogy* for February 1972 and then the band continues with the title track from *Tarkus*. The incredibly difficult change of key and tempo is now managed perfectly – the guys play it with obvious pleasure. The track is driven along by Carl's powerful drumming and Greg's unique voice; Keith plays the keys much more aggressively than in the earlier 1971 performances, adding stunning Hammond and Moog improvisations in "Stones Of Years and "Mass". "Aquatarkus" develops more and more into a lesson for keyboard players on how to handle a modular Moog on stage. During its ten minutes, Keith treats the crowd to amazing improvisations and snippets of "Peer Gynt" in a large spectrum of sounds alternating with noises this audience has never heard before, like water rippling and sirens wailing.

A very atmospheric "Take A Pebble" follows, again in a modified arrangement. Now the first piano part is played in a minimalistic jazzy style, reminiscent of Herbie Hancock, supported by Carl playing the tom toms with his hands, and by Greg's floating bass lines. After Greg's country style break, Keith's piano solo already shows some of the new aspects he will extend later to his legendary piano improvisations in 1973 and 1974, like Gulda's "Fugue", "Little Rock Getaway" and the main theme of the band jam.

"Knife Edge" comes very slickly finished with excessive L100 war-like noises. But the L100 is also able to imitate the sounds of the old steam locomotive – if Keith Emerson is driving! Everybody knows by now that this is the prelude to "Rondo" and the platform for a twelve minute drum solo. Carl plays it very melodically and in a perfect dramaturgic structure using gongs, cow bells and the old detuned church bell. Even during the quiet parts the audience listens in devoted silence. As Carl comes to his finale, instead of beating the time for "Rondo" as he

Ticket stub and signed photos from Dundee, Scotland. © Graham Kennedy.

usually does, he plays another rhythm. Keith and Greg seem confused for a couple of bars but then they know how Carl wants to continue – with "America", their take on Leonard Bernstein's *West Side Story* classic!

That's very surprising, especially here in London, because we know that Keith and his former band the Nice were banned for life from performing in the Royal Albert Hall, because Keith burned the US flag during the piece. The audience seem surprised but pleased to be part of such an ultra-rare performance of this piece. But after two minutes of "America" the L100 torture rings in the "Rondo" finale: it's always astonishing what sounds can be produced on this instrument as Keith drags it around the stage, holding it up the amps to get feedback.

"A clamouring audience demands an encore and it gets a very fast, rocking 'A Time And A Place' with lovely little additional Moog riffs." [43]

7. *There Might Have Been Things I Missed ...*

21 MARCH – 29 APRIL 1972: THIRD NORTH AMERICAN TOUR.
37 SHOWS PLUS A WARM-UP GIG AT THE CAPITOL THEATRE, CARDIFF, WALES, UK ON 10 MARCH 1972.

Typical set list:	"Hoedown", "Tarkus", "Trilogy" (sometimes), "Abaddon's Bolero" (sometimes), "The Endless Enigma", "The Sheriff" (both towards the end of the tour), "Take A Pebble", "Lucky Man", piano improvisations, "Take A Pebble" reprise, "Pictures At An Exhibition" (short version), "Rondo" (usually first encore) with "Nutrocker" as a second encore.
Band equipment:	As for previous UK tour plus 8 concert toms, a set of tubular bells, bongos and congas for Carl, both a Mellotron for "Abaddon's Bolero" and a custom Les Paul Gibson for Greg, and the mini-Moog for Keith.
PA system:	As for previous UK tour.

Surprisingly, very few recordings from this tour have ever seen the light of day, a pity as it was certainly a tour of "firsts", ranging from small-town venues to the bigger arenas so that "more fans in remote areas get to hear the band."[44] One of the best recordings to survive is that from the Mar Y Sol Festival in Puerto Rico, now officially released on the Shout label. However, the festival as a whole was overshadowed by tragedy when a 16-year-old was stabbed to death.

This outing saw the first real attempt to introduce audiences to tracks from the new album *Trilogy*, especially the complexity of "Abaddon's Bolero" and the album's title track. Keith always managed to mention the new album, "recorded back in England", before they played "Bolero", having already opened with "Hoedown".

Experimental it certainly was – the first time they ever used a tape backing track on stage because of the monophonic [only one note at a time can be played] nature of the Moog. Keith taught Greg how to play a Mellotron [a *de rigeur* for prog rockers, the Mellotron is a keyboard instrument where the depressed keys set off a pre-recorded tape sound thus allowing a band to simulate whatever is on the tape, for example, an orchestra or a choir] they adapted it so that Greg could play it by pedal. All worked well – until the tapes snapped.

By this stage of the band's touring, the ribbon controller was wearing down but instead of having it fixed, Keith left it because it sounded even more like the machine gun that audiences were becoming accustomed to. Just to stage right of Keith, Carl's new much-enhanced kit added a whole new dimension to the sound of the band, enriching the whole texture of the show.

Towards the end of the tour Greg begins to include a verse from the King Crimson classic "Epitaph" in his solo at the end of "Battlefield", as in "Confusion will be my epitaph".

These dates also saw the first performances of the now familiar shorter version of "Pictures ..." (to help make way for the *Trilogy* tracks), played towards the end of the show instead of its established position as the opener; and the first shows where Greg regularly played "Lucky Man" during his solo spot in "Take A Pebble", usually accompanied by both Carl and Keith. He had tried it out at Green's Playhouse in Glasgow at the end of the previous UK tour, after the Pavilion dates.

Technical upgrading to the band's rig was exemplified by a heavy investment in the state-of-the-art 'Super Trooper' lighting. Still, more often than not they were introduced by the M.C., wandered on, and launched into "Hoedown".

By the end of the year, things would be quite different.

WEDNESDAY, 22 MARCH 1972

The Arena, Long Beach, CA, USA.

Second night and a goodie in Long Beach! Having opened the tour the previous night at the Denver Coliseum, the ELP bandwagon hopped over to the West Coast for a series of shows kicking off with dates where they played the complex, multi-tracked pieces from their new album for the first time.

A very British voice (one of the crew perhaps?) announces "Emerson, Lake and Palmer!" and they're off ... but not just yet.

We get three minutes of keyboard runs, drum rolls and bass tuning, for which Keith apologizes at the end of "Hoedown", saying that "the bridge on Greg's guitar broke." The opening number itself is tight, determined but definitely played in a "start of the tour" fashion: almost exactly as the original apart from the Moog solo which has hints of "Aquatarkus" hidden away within it. Interesting!

After a laid back introduction from Keith, they deliver a stunning version of "Tarkus". Keith's left hand and Greg's powerful bass really drive things on and with Carl setting out his stall for the whole number, this audience listen in silent admiration. "Stones Of Years" is a really moody sounding piece, as Greg gives a mighty "Yeeeeeaaaah!" before the top-notch Hammond solo. One feature of this particular "Tarkus" is the sheer quality and variety of Carl's tom-tom fills and rolls, and the end of "Stones ..." going into "Mass" is just outstanding.

For some reason, the surviving recording then cuts to the start of "Battlefield", but what a "Battlefield"! It's moody, teeming with atmosphere and the "simple-is-better" guitar break is followed by outstanding Moog/Hammond work. This is Keith and Greg on the money.

"Every blade is sharp" is delivered to an absolutely silent auditorium; Greg earns loud applause for his *arpeggio* work on a soaring foundation of swirling Moog and growling Hammond. Carl gives the cue for "Aquatarkus", a wonderfully improvised piece with light and dark sections, two takes on the "Hall Of The Mountain King", and an impressively experimental – unaccompanied – Moog solo from Keith. The crowd go wild at the end of it, as well they might.

Experimental? "Trilogy" is up next, introduced at some length by Keith:

> Yeah, we'd like to try something now which we did for the first time last night. We've got a new album out – well not out yet, we're recording one in England. One of the tracks we'd like to try is something which is a bit difficult to do onstage. The Moog synthesizer, as you probably know, is a monophonic instrument which is to say that you can't play chords on it. You can play one note and if you try and play a chord, you still get one note (which he then demonstrates). So what we've done is put the backing track onto a tape recorder, just the backing track, and we're gonna try to play to that. This is a thing called "Trilogy".

Keith leads in gently on the grand piano, exactly as the album will sound, complemented by Greg's beautiful vocals; note-perfect and faultless. This highly appreciative audience again listen in silence. The upbeat second part is unsurpassed, driven by the Moog and Carl's powerful drumming, a nudge ahead of the beat and all the better for it. Keith improvises a nice, meandering solo towards the end, set against the background of the tapes and the rock-solid ELP rhythm section. Does it work?

Absolutely!

The irony is that Keith then tells the audience that the band couldn't hear what they were playing because the stage monitors had packed in, and Carl had been throwing drum sticks at the roadies throughout "Trilogy" to get the message across. When he asks the crowd if it sounded ok – he is left in on doubt that they've got a winner here.

"Take A Pebble" follows, a classic if ever there was one, with a first-rate opening section. Delicate playing by Keith opens an almost twenty minute version featuring confident, resonant vocals, powerful bass notes that hang in the air and perfectly-timed drum fills. Greg, enjoying himself, plays what sounds like the intro to "My Dog Blue", but then launches into a tremendous version of "Lucky Man", which the crowd listen to in reverential silence. However, as the last notes from the Moog reverberate, they applaud madly and Keith launches into a faultless, *ostinato*-fed keyboard solo with more than a few throwaway riffs from his time with the Nice.

Right on cue, Carl and Greg come back in to rapturous applause for a tight, jazzy, very free-form improvisation which has the crowd clapping along as Keith tries – with typical humour and unsuccessfully – to catch out the rhythm section with sudden key and tempo changes. Wonderful syncopation here. The last few bars of the song belong to Greg's powerfully clear baritone and the crowd love it! What's not to like?

Some Moog tuning takes us into the "Bolero", announced simply by Keith: "This is 'Bolona's Bolero'." By the way, I have no idea why Keith calls it "Bolona's Bolero" rather than "Abaddon's Bolero" as it is titled on *Trilogy*. More to the point, neither has Keith! I have asked him, but he honestly cannot recall why he gave it this title but, in the light of the recording from the show, accepts that he did.

There is no reaction at all from this up until now very vocal crowd as the piece builds and builds, becoming more powerful and dramatic. They seem stunned by the sheer splendour and majesty of the whole thing as sound fills the auditorium and, when the climax arrives, don't seem too sure how to react.

It gets politely loud applause, complemented by even more noise as Keith launches into "Promenade". This, when compared to the two previous tracks, is raw energy, driven along furiously by Carl, accompanied by deep, resonant bass and first-rate work on the keys. This is fast precision playing at its best as Keith throws wild improvisations into the mix in "The Curse of Baba Yaga". After an 'everybody-play-faster-than-everybody-else' phase, Greg's soaring vocals at the start of "The Great Gates ..." seem to rise heavenwards.

Keith's Hammond throwing antics are so reminiscent of his solo spot from "Intermezzo" on *Five Bridges*, a short-lived moment of mayhem before the mighty, dramatic ending that deserves every second of the wild, cheering applause and feet-stomping.

The encore "Rondo" is an absolute classic: heavy, driving, demonic at times and fast beyond belief. Shouts of "Wow!" can clearly be heard from this extra-appreciative audience. This sets the standard for encores on this tour – will they live up to it?

Keith's work is simply dazzling, set against the world-class rhythm section of Greg and Carl, before the latter takes us into a technically and musically impressive solo. His work on the snare, tom-toms and cymbals is just breath-taking, played to a totally awe-struck, silent crowd.

After he counts the others back in, the reprise is a cracker: they all go hell-for-leather and send these Californians home very, very happy.

THURSDAY, 23 MARCH 1972

The Civic Auditorium, Santa Monica, CA, USA.

Day three of the tour and a memorable gig in Santa Monica.

"Ladies and Gentlemen, from England: Emerson, Lake and Palmer!" Determined to make an impression, this is a lively, bouncy version of "Hoedown" full of snare and hi-hat as Carl drives it along.

"Tarkus" follows with Keith decorating the solid foundation laid down by Greg and Carl in "Eruption" and "Stones of Years". During the latter, Greg seems less than confident with the vocals to start with – but soon picks up and his baritone rings out clearly. The organ solo that follows is immaculate and the way Carl sets it up and powers it along is classic. They seem to pick up speed during "Mass", a killer in itself, with some superb fills on the toms from Carl, *that* organ/ Moog solo from Keith, and Greg in full flight on the bass. Long applause follows, then a wonderful "Manticore" leads into a stirring "Battlefield".

'Atmospheric' is an understatement with this one, there's real feeling in Greg's voice, the combination of Moog and Hammond sending tingles down the spine. The guitar solo is very laid back, even restrained and Greg is on super form for the "Every blade is sharp" solo – except that for some reason it's cut way short with no coda, so that they go straight into "Aquatarkus". There's an interesting and all-too-rare Moog/bass duel here, improvised to the last note before Keith takes them into the "Hall Of The Mountain King". His unaccompanied all-the-weird-noises-I-can-make busy Moog section goes down well, and the applause after that crashing ending is well-earned and sustained.

"Take A Pebble" is introduced as them "taking it down a bit". The playing is confident and the two focal points, Keith's solo and Greg's acoustic break, are worth mentioning. This California crowd go nuts as Greg steps up with the acoustic, strumming a theme and teasing them – before picking up the "Lucky Man" melody.

Keith silences the calls for various things as he introduces "Bolona's Bolero" by again explaining the shortcomings of the Moog and the need to use backing tapes.

Carl opens the two bar rhythm as the slow build-up, with piccolo-like Moog, which silences a very noisy crowd almost immediately. The theme is repeated and strengthened time and again with some of the independent synthesizer lines coming through half way through the piece. Brassy sounds, oboe-like lead and a number of voices combine to give a climactic finish that, if anything, takes this knowledgeable crowd by surprise – although they're not slow in showing their appreciation.

"Pictures ..." is greeted with barely a polite ripple of applause, a pity because it's well-handled, with not a fault in the tempo and mood changes. Maybe it's an 'old-timer' in Europe, but it's not so well-known this side of the pond.

All three take the spotlight at some point: Keith's Hammond theatrics is the most attention-grabbing, but Carl's beautifully-tuned bells at the start of "The Great Gates ...", together with Greg's soaring vocals throughout, earn every bit of the applause they receive.

They've dropped the extended intro to "Rondo" favoured on the last American tour. The crisper start seems more fitting to this audience, wild, noisy and impatient as they are. It's a classic with Keith taking flight on the Hammond as only he can before handing the reins over to Carl, who turns in a solo befitting his standing as the guv'nor of prog rock drummers.

It goes down a storm and rounds off an excellent performance.

THURSDAY, 30 MARCH 1972

The Bay Front Center, St.Petersburgh, FL, USA.

Tickets: $5.50

The tenth North American show of the tour and although we know they opened with "Hoedown", no record of it exists.

The crowd is noisy all the way through "Tarkus", the whole piece powered along by strong drumming and thumping bass. Plenty of percussive fills and aggressively played toms are in evidence, showing a drummer not content to sit back but always looking to improve and develop a piece.

Vocals are not as high in the mix as they could be and Greg throws in the odd improvised phrase or two in "Stones Of Years". "Mass", as usual, is one of the highlights with Keith machine-gunning the audience from the off at the end of every verse, and then charging through his manic solo, first on Hammond then on ribbon controller. Cheers, whooping and then loud applause greet him as he wanders out into the crowd before coming back to the organ.

The introduction to "Battlefield" again sees Carl playing some nice fills on his eight new concert toms as we go into Greg's mood-inspired six-string solo, so precisely backed all the time by Keith's Hammond and Moog. Carl misses his cue to stop playing at Greg's "Every blade is sharp" bit, but although this version is hampered by constant crowd calls for people to sit down, it still wins well-deserved applause as Keith leads them into the Moog showcase that "Aquatarkus" has become.

They've changed it again since the last UK tour: now it has a long improvisational duel between keyboards and drums, in which again Carl shows off the new toms. The themes from "Peer Gynt" are still there, especially "The Hall Of The Mountain King", but at just the point when they're motoring along nicely, and before they bring the epic to its crashing close, everything grinds to a halt for Keith to show off the new weird rippling sounds he extracts from the Moog.

Audience noise and calls continue through the beginning of "Take A Pebble" before the auditorium quietens. Keith plays so many variations on themes during his first piano solo, accompanied at times by Carl hand-playing the toms. Never a band to play by the book for long, Greg steps up and now starts his acoustic solo with the old closing *arpeggio* before he pauses and quietly picks the opening notes of "Lucky Man". Carl joins in and then Keith picks up the melody on the Moog to give us an excellent group rendition of one of the highlights from the first album.

Great stuff!

The improvised piano solo shows an expert at work, note perfect from start to finish, and clearly entertaining this crowd because it's almost the first time tonight that nearly everyone is silent – except to cheer on Keith during the more intricate phases. A very classy and tasteful jazz section precedes a perfect ending to a timeless song.

A touch of Moog tuning and Keith announces "Bolero", highlighting the shortcomings of the Moog and the need for a backing track.

The 4/4 beat from Carl begins very quietly, with Keith playing the melody, and almost immediately the crowd become very subdued. There are repeated loud audience calls for people to sit down and then the rest of the piece is played to a completely silent crowd, mesmerized by the novelty of this. The build-up from the band is suitably dramatic with the whole thing so well executed, the overall effect being as close to the original album as we're ever going to hear. By the mid-point, the synthesizer sounds are stronger and stronger, the distinct Mellotron sound washing over everything. It's a stunning piece of prog-rock with a crashing ending that drives the crowd mad, but still just seems to lack any real focal point compared to other ELP pieces.

After the opening notes of "Pictures ...", Carl and Greg crash in as a powerhouse rhythm section setting out their stall for the rest of this piece, much shortened but more effective as it really shows off their prowess and boils everything down to the essentials. Keith attacks the rhythm with vigour, laying down some very heavy Hammond and frighteningly accurate Moog solos. "Pictures ..." now sounds as if it has a real sense of purpose and doesn't get lost in its own length and improvisations. The ending is as majestic as ever, the crowd go wild and back they come for a rousing "Rondo".

This too is drastically re-worked, now featuring Moog as well as Hammond, with Keith exploring even further the limits of the former over the top of a solid foundation from Greg and Carl. His long solo is more laid back, yet so much more imaginative in its scope, using every conceivable facet of the Moog. Time and again, Carl uses the toms to match the highs and lows of the Moog before Keith hands over the baton to him. The solo that follows, all seven minutes of it, is intensely creative as Carl builds pattern after pattern around the toms and the snare, really working the audience to clap along with the bass drum pattern before the gong rolls, the snare solo, and the return of the "Rondo" rhythm.

A fanfare of Moog magic closes "Rondo"; a fitting end to an incredible show.

SUNDAY, 2 APRIL 1972

The Mar Y Sol Festival, Vega Baja, Puerto Rico.

Tickets: $15.00 (advance)

The band didn't get on stage until about 1.00a.m. but no matter: "Here they are, from England, Emerson, Lake and Palmer!"

No *portamento* [a musical term meaning an uninterrupted glide, which Keith uses as the 'whoop' at the start of "Hoedown" on *Trilogy* before the main theme kicks in] tonight on "Hoedown" – strange one that. Keith at times seems to be in a Highland fling mood as both the Moog and Hammond sound distinctly bagpipe-ish.

Right from the off, it's driven by bass and drums, especially the snare and kick. They're on fire in "Stones Of Years": incomparably-improvised Hammond, the vocals way up there, and Carl's fills develop the piece well. The solos in "Iconoclast" and "Mass" are wonderfully free-form, Keith soaring off into the blue yonder firstly on organ, then Moog, then ribbon controller, backed by a rock-solid rhythm that never falters. Improv rules!

"Manticore" is as tight as ever and" Battlefield" is up there with the best of them: fast and faultless. Greg is so on form for the vocal section, rich baritones delivering real emotion, plus a cracking lead solo. His "Every blade is sharp" vocal solo is sung against the backdrop of a silent crowd who then offer up their appreciation. "Aquatarkus" is a rich mix of quiet and rock sections around *Peer Gynt* and innovative improvisations on the Moog as Carl and Greg take a back seat.

After the classic ending to this monumental piece, it's straight into "Take A Pebble" after a quick intro by Keith to credit Greg. Very true to the original in the opening section, and the first piano solo, it's taken confidently and the quality shines through. Nicely improvised touches from Carl during Keith's solo precede Greg's spot where he goes, without preamble, straight into the chords to "Lucky Man". The audience signal their approval and it's a powerful version.

The others come in, Keith providing rich bass work on the synth. There's a couple of phrases from *that* solo just before a beautifully faded ending, segueing expertly into the long, entertaining solo from Keith that tonight draws heavily on old Nice numbers. [For the uninitiated, Garry is referring to the famous Moog solo at the end of the studio version of "Lucky Man" which Keith totally improvised in one amazing take]. Yet again, the precise *ostinato* work underpins the solo, ranging as it does from delicate to heavy in tone and texture. This is a master of his trade at work, ably backed by a rhythm section with some top-notch jazz syncopation and a bass line that's surely the best of the night.

It seems that the crowd, apart from a few calls of "Yeah" don't quite know what to make of the cut down "Pictures..." It's developing into a fifteen to twenty minute classic all on its own: the moods created by the music are so effective, the playing so delicate at times, so in-your-face at others, with each of the band taking the limelight at some point. The highlights from this piece? The organized chaos that is "Baba Yaga" and of course, "The Great Gates ...". Greg is obviously having fun tonight – would that we had a video recording of this performance!

The Hammond antics are different every night and those from this show echo the train sounds that usually heralds "Rondo", before Keith manhandles the organ around the stage, much to the delight of the crowd. On the final vocal lines, there's an interesting echo, intended or not, it's an amazingly sublime effect.

The crowd are left wanting more so back they come and they do play "Rondo". As the tumult mounts, Carl belts the gongs and Keith sets a pace that the others are determined to match – and do. Throughout the number there are the audible tilts and throws of the Hammond as it's played out at a truly breakneck pace that never lets up for an instant – and that includes the solo from Carl.

This evening, it's his tuneful ever-so-delicate work on the hi-hat and cymbals that wins the loudest applause from a crowd that may not have known ELP beforehand but loves them now. Cowbell and kick-drum are at machine-gun speed as Carl builds mesmerizing rhythms and patterns. Crashing gongs are the cue for the reprise as Carl counts them back in. "Rondo" is a fitting climax to a show that has typified Emerson, Lake and Palmer: stirring, innovative, and awesome.

It's goodnight from him and him and him. What a show! Don Heckman for **The New York Times** *reported that the band, in common with other acts, had power problems, as well as some out-of-tune instruments, but "... made up in drama what they lacked in musical excellence".*[45]

MONDAY, 10 APRIL 1972

The Academy Of Music, New York, NY, USA.

Tickets: $4.50 – $5.50

"Ladies and Gentlemen – We are proud to present Emerson, Lake and Palmer".

This is one of those shows where we ask the question, "Are the guys overawed by this announcement, or by the enthusiastic applause it caused, or are they just a little tired from last night's party? In any case, the show opener "Hoedown" is played much slower than usual. On the other hand, it's more accurate today and contains an exceptional Moog solo.

Greg then welcomes the audience and announces "Tarkus": "This piece has a meaning ... shown inside the album" Very cryptic. Is he hinting at the Vietnam War and the USA's role? Some people interpret "Tarkus" as an allegory of that conflict.

Either way, the beginning is bumpy with a couple of wrong notes. Greg seems to have forgotten some lyrics in "Stones Of Years" and the interaction, interplay, and hitting of cues is not as perfect as usual.

Problems in the monitors perhaps, but they are not themselves tonight. Keith hedges his bets, and gives us "Aquatarkus" with improvisations essentially built around the "Peer Gynt" theme, and only a few different Moog settings.

With "Take A Pebble", the guys turn things round with a striking performance. "Lucky Man" comes complete with drum and Moog support but without the Moog outro we've previously heard. A creative piano improvisation, followed by an equally together group jam bring the guys back to good humour and drive the audience crazy.

Calls for "Bolero" suggests the word has been spread about this piece, but Keith is already on the way up to the Academy's pipe organ to commence "Pictures ..." with "Promenade". A short drum *intermezzo* gives Keith the chance to return to his rig to continue the piece on his own keyboards. Any lingering disappointment by the audience about not hearing "Bolero" is blown away by long-lasting L100 torture in "Great Gates ...".

"Rondo" is the encore, opening with a short steam locomotive intro, followed by the theme on the Hammond at really demonic speed, and overlaid by a fantastic Moog solo that includes the "Rondo" theme and Bach's "Toccata in D Minor".

Carl delivers a ten minute drum solo, with tonight's speciality the drum Moog which replicates the sounds of a 'singing saw'. Five minutes of Hammond riding combined with Moog fanfares finish an eventful gig in New York.

"Plenty of highs and lows – but definitely ending on a series of highs!" [46]

THURSDAY, 13 APRIL 1972

F & M College, Lancaster, PA, USA.

Unfortunately, only three tracks survive from what must have been an excellent show.

Show 23 of the tour and we can hear Keith still tuning up and Carl testing the kit as the M.C. introduces them. Then it's all hands on deck and straight into a version of "Hoedown" that seriously rocks. For such a tight band, it's even more together than previously and gets long applause.

A few words from Keith, they dive into "Tarkus" and it's obvious that central Pennsylvania is the land of the whooping rock fan. Keith manages to get a dirtier sound than normal from the Hammond all the way through, and Carl and Greg both shine.

The highlight of this piece is "Aquatarkus", by now developed to a full nine minutes, a real showcase not only for Keith's skills on the Moog but also for this band's ability to improvise and play to each other's signals. All manner of rippling, dripping and crashing sounds emanate from Keith's side of the stage as the audience remain silent and spellbound before the textbook ending.

A strong performance of "Rondo" caps off the show, played at a hell-for-leather pace as Keith shines on both main keyboards, Carl and Greg never failing to keep up with him. For a short spell, they leave the Rondo rhythm behind and pick up a rock 4/4 time signature, but it's not for long as Carl brings them back and the others wander off for him to hold centre-stage. Shouts of "Alright!", screams and whoops greet every part of a blisteringly fast, inspired solo.

If only we had a record of the whole concert.

FRIDAY, 21 APRIL 1972

The Town Hall, Louisville, KY, USA.

The finishing line is in sight, with only six further dates remaining and they play a blinder at this one.

The M.C.'s simple introduction of "Emerson, Lake and Palmer!" is followed immediately by the now re-instated *portamento* 'whoops' of "Hoedown". The tempo of this one has quickened and the middle solo now has Keith's confidence stamped all over it, despite an out of tune Moog which results in it being shortened.

The applause has barely stopped when Keith steps up with an introduction to "Tarkus" that smacks a little of 'Oh well, here we go again': "Thank you. Hello. This next thing features a creature known as an armadillo. It has guns coming out the side of it and we call it 'Tarkus'."

Keith's introduction may have been perfunctory, but the epic that follows isn't. Faster than on previous tours, with nice touches from Keith in his solos during the first half and not a note missed by anyone. Extra tom fills from Carl add to the texture of both "Stones Of Years" and "Mass", but Keith dominates the latter with a fat, dirty Moog solo that has them applauding wildly.

An almost free-form solo in "Manticore" takes us into "Battlefield", Keith letting rip with bass on the Hammond and Moog as Greg takes up the six string. There's some nifty fretwork here foreshadowing as it does a smashing vocal that gets warm applause from this crowd. Carl's martial drumming is the backbone to "Aquatarkus", fleshed out by Keith's 'let's-go-where-no-one's-gone-before' Moog.

Tonight he can do no wrong as he stops and starts the piece with sounds reverential and futuristic, throwing in "The Hall Of The Mountain King", then leading the way back into the "Aquatarkus" theme and the crashing chords ending.

After all that, "Take A Pebble" seems quite restrained, delicate and melodic and is greeted with cheers, as is Keith's first stellar piano solo. The real star of this one though is Greg, who strums the opening to "Lucky Man", singing alone at first, then accompanied in a subtle, under-stated way by Keith and Carl.

Keith plays a flurry of notes for his second solo, as one of the audience can clearly be heard commenting, "His hands are huge you know!", and then the band swing through the improvisation in true jazz club style before closing the song to some rousing applause.

"'Knife Edge' I hope they do 'Knife Edge' now," pleads a fan. Afraid not. Keith tunes the Moog before introducing the real novelty of the evening, "Bolona's Abbadon's Bolero".

This one is by now so well played that it's difficult to tell where the tape ends and Keith begins among the delicately-constructed cascades, supported so skilfully by wonderfully simplistic but effective drumming and snappy bass.

The crowd listen in absolute silence, the texture and richness of the piece changes dramatically and Carl uses cymbal crashes for accentuation. Keith's got the closing *portamento* off to a tee and it ends massively as they seem to be getting their heads round this one as only ELP can.

The opening "Promenade" of "Pictures ..." is a truly dynamic version of the shortened suite, played with real fire in their bellies, plenty of improvisation and probably some of the fastest bass Greg has ever laid down

Everything about this one is masterful, from the sheer power of Carl's drum work, like he is using a Louisville Slugger baseball bat, and Keith on the Hammond, to the delicacy of the bells and the emotive vocals in "The Great Gates ...", the entire final section of which is almost drowned out by applause and cheers as the band bid goodnight.

First encore is an energetic "Nutrocker", followed by "Rondo" with all cylinders firing. Carl's first-rate solo is a whisper short of fourteen minutes, which the audience lap up. A piece that began life for many fans as a vehicle for Keith on the Hammond, has now changed to showcase Carl in particular and the whole band in general.

It sends everyone home with fond memories of a wonderful show.

FRIDAY, 28 APRIL 1972

The Forum, Montreal, Canada.

This must stand out as the show where Greg could do no wrong: cheers, whistles and loud applause mark everything he did and in so many ways he stole the show. No "Bolero" tonight but this is a not-to-be-forgotten show for all the right reasons.

The usual tuning up and Hammond runs, and then without any further ado "Hoedown" kicks in. There's no doubt this almost happy-go-lucky instrumental lifts the beginning of the show and gets the crowd up and dancing from the off.

Still no introduction – but a touch more tuning from Keith – and "Tarkus" is up and running. Loud applause greets the first vocals of the night from Greg in "Stones Of Years", where all three excel, and the crowd seem stunned into silence at a heavy and menacing "Iconoclast".

Greg's haunting lines in "Battlefield" weave amongst his delicate six string and Keith's Hammond to create the perfect mood for the piece, and again loud applause greets him as he steps up to the mic. There's a nice touch of echo on his Gibson for the main solo, Keith comes back in briefly with the theme and Greg takes centre stage, singing an emotive verse from "Epitaph" at the very end of the piece.

"Aquatarkus" begins as a looser, less rhythmical take on the original, and quickly goes into a long improvisational section with Keith playing "The Star Spangled Banner" to the Canadians as an extra theme before returning to the great crashing chords – and the plaudits.

Two new ones are up next: an early try-out for "The Endless Enigma" opens with Greg's bass and then the others smash in for the crescendo before the first verse. Yet again, loud cheers greet the vocals in a song full of mood and emotion on all levels; the Hammond complementing Greg's singing throughout. The middle "Fugue" is expertly played by Greg and Keith, written as it was for piano and bass. Exclamations and gasps of sheer admiration abound when Carl plays the tubular bell introduction to the closing verses, and they bring the piece to a majestic ending with some powerful chords.

A little ponderous on the whole, not quite as uplifting as the album version, but still very well received by this crowd.

"The Sheriff" is introduced low-key by Keith, and Carl beats hell out of the kit in his intro before they all roll along in a good-humoured, light-hearted effort that sticks closely to the studio version. Short, sweet and with a rollicking syncopated solo at the end, it has the crowd laughing as well as cheering.

24 minutes later, and a classic "Take A Pebble" ends. The opening chords and lines of "Lucky Man" are inaudible because of the ecstatic reception the song gets, then drums and Moog kick in to add to the effect.

Keith and Greg pull the strings on this one without a doubt, but all the time Carl is there as only he can be with spot-on time keeping, jazzy fills and particularly creative cymbals that add so much. His is the perfect example of understated playing, the 'it's what you don't play that counts' school of drumming.

The jazz-inspired section that leads to the closing verses is one of their finest hours: it's all there, a heady brew of Thelonius Monk, Fats Waller, some Jerry Lee Lewis, touches of the Nice and a few bars of slow boogie-woogie that have the crowd clapping along. With his rich baritone the only sound filling the stadium, Greg goes for broke at the end as he slightly changes the phrasing of the last line and pulls it off with true style. The crowd go wild.

By this stage, the shortened "Pictures …" needs no introduction other than the opening notes of "Promenade" – surely one of the most recognizable intros in prog. More gold stars all round for this one, which they all sound like they're really getting into, one dramatic piece following another as they build towards the climax of "The Great Gates …". This one-time opening epic now fits better as a show-closer, working up the audience to the point where they demand more – and in this well-crafted show, that's where "Rondo" comes in.

As tonight shows, this band are experts at building tension and atmosphere, and they don't let up just because it's the encore. Gong rolls, the train whistles, that driving beat and it seems like the entire arena is up and dancing. All three pile into this version, played with as much Moog as Hammond with Keith seems to use every dance and jig theme he knows; it sounds fantastic and the crowd love it.

Did Keith just fancy a change? Who cares!

8. *Maybe I Might Have Changed ...*

4 – 27 JUNE 1972: THIRD EUROPEAN TOUR
13 SHOWS FOLLOWED BY AN APPEARANCE AT THE POCONO INTERNATIONAL RACEWAY FESTIVAL, LONG POND, PA, USA (WITH HUMBLE PIE AND ROD STEWART AND THE FACES AMONGST OTHERS ON THE BILL) AND 2 SHOWS IN JAPAN, IN TOKYO AND OSAKA (THE JAPANESE TOUR).

Typical set list:	"Hoedown", "Tarkus", "The Endless Enigma", "Take A Pebble"," Lucky Man", piano improvisations, "Take A Pebble" reprise, "Pictures At An Exhibition", "Rondo".
Band equipment:	As for previous UK tour with addition of a Hollywood tuneable tom-tom with foot pedal for Carl.
PA system:	5,000 watt custom built system.

A kind of 'mini' European tour, their first for a year, where larger halls and arenas were becoming the norm. They were supposed to play a one-off at Crystal Palace in London on 17 June but it didn't materialize.

Stage and lighting equipment were becoming more sophisticated, with an ever-bigger entourage to take care of it on a nightly basis.

The new tracks from *Trilogy*, except for "Bolona's (Abaddon's) Bolero", remained in the act, and were being aired for the first time in Europe. What we hear is a well-crafted set list integrating the newbies and old favourites.

An interesting point: at one of the six German shows, they were reputed to have made their one and only European attempt at playing the title track from *Trilogy*, an exceptionally difficult piece to reproduce live because of the multi-tracking in the original.

At the Pocono festival, the band didn't get onstage until 4.00a.m. in a thick fog. Glamorous life eh?

The two Japanese dates developed a 'fame' all of their own, for entirely non-musical reasons: the weather in Tokyo and the riot in Osaka.

SUNDAY, 4 JUNE 1972

The Gruga Halle, Essen, Germany.

Tickets: DM 12,-

The opening night of the tour saw them in spanking form with some notable changes in both the new and the older material. They pulled off a superb performance, boding well for the rest of the tour.

"Hoedown" is its usual infectious self: an excellent choice for a regular opener, as it gives the audience a chance to focus on the instrumental skills of the band from the word go and it's well-received.

Keith does the introduction: "We're gonna give you something that we played to you last time we were over here. This is a thing called 'Tarkus'." A more percussive-sounding version of the classic follows.

An atmospheric "Stones Of Years", if anything an underrated staple of the show with its poetic lyrics, is now a touch shorter, with a less improvised solo. Carl makes full use of the concert toms towards the end of "Iconoclast", followed by a lively, inspired "Mass" and Keith's long solo arrives in a flurry of notes.

Cheers and whistles are the backdrop to Greg's closing verse and, before we know it, we're into a stunning "Battlefield". All the main elements are there with some pretty heavy drumming from Carl, Keith's bass pedals and the best guitar work of the night from Greg. Some thoughtful improvisation, vocal and guitar in the last verse but alas, no "Epitaph" on this tour.

The variations-on-a-theme "Aquatarkus" is the perfect contrast to the previous piece, full of changing moods and signatures, and Keith's unaccompanied solo on Moog, Moog and more Moog. Fifteen crashing chords mark the end of a memorable version.

"We'd like to debut a new number," Keith informs the faithful. "We've got an album coming out round about the 16 June. It's gonna be released over here a week later. This is a thing which we call 'The Endless Enigma'."

This one now sounds much livelier than on its early outings and Greg's vocals, so high and clear in the mix, fit like a glove into the song's structure. Carl does his usual thorough job of driving the instrumental sections and Keith's Hammond sounds sweet; the whole band are complementing each other.

An injection of fresh life into the middle "Prelude" and "Fugue" coupled with Greg's bass part, and Carl's show-stopping tubular bells, gives the whole thing another lift in terms of the reception it gets. The final section provides a fitting crescendo. A real pity this song never made it past the end of the year in the set list.

A return to more familiar ground with "Take A Pebble". After the much-welcomed opening verses, Keith grooves through his solo, leaving a nicely dramatic pause before Greg picks out the opening notes and chords of "Lucky Man". Carl and Keith come in after two verses, both a little heavy-handedly for such a thoughtful, meaningful, and ultimately sad song, but no matter because the jammed-out section makes up for it tenfold. They rely so much on cues in pieces like this and it's obvious from the playing and the applause that everyone is spot-on tonight, resulting in a very dramatic ending; classic ELP.

Another loud cheer greets "Promenade" as it opens another excellent version of the shorter "Pictures ..." Keith rips into the Hammond parts of "Baba Yaga", Greg's bass in "The Curse ..." sounds downright malevolent, after which they rock along with a vengeance and Carl, in particular, kicks some serious ass, making full use of his new toms.

"The Great Gates ..." does what it says on the tin and is ... great! After the *mêlée* of "Baba Yaga", the hovering Hammond that introduces "The Great Gates ..." sets the mood just nicely. Greg's soaring vocals, the tubular bells and the subtle use of the drawbars by Keith also help create the drama of the piece. As Greg sings "Death is life", Keith holds the chords, Carl smashes the gongs: what a finish!

Chants for "more" bring them back for "Rondo", which is becoming the standard show closer. This one is as strong as ever, played at a charge rather than a gallop and it rocks like crazy. Keith races up and down the keys, playing *arpeggios* at the speed of light, with Carl keeping time for once on the cowbell instead of the ride cymbal. There's some groovy Moog on this one too, as well as some real fuzzy, late 1960s-style Hammond: the improvisations at this point in the show are sounding better and better. After eleven minutes of a solo that has to be seen and heard to be believed, Carl gives the others their cue to come back on and they bring a truly class performance to a close.

What a statement of intent for the rest of the tour.

THURSDAY, 8 JUNE 1972

The Falkonerteatret, Copenhagen, Denmark.

Tickets: Kr. 36.00

Fifth night on the road and, with the band's second anniversary approaching, this was their first gig in Denmark. Sadly, only four tracks survive from this show.

Keith has Moog problems again before the things can get under way, so much so that the band get a slow hand-clap from the audience. Not the best of starts but they soon pick it up as only they can.

"From England, Emerson, Lake and Palmer!" and Keith begins a lively but routine version of "Hoedown". Unfortunately half way through the number the

Moog is misbehaving again; it's so out of tune that the scope of Keith's solo is curtailed, and he has to rely on his trusty Hammond for much of it.

Keith explains: "This thing here, the twiddly bit, is a Moog synthesizer and it goes out of tune quite frequently as it did in that number there ... by the way, it's really good to be in Denmark for the first time, to see you all."

A few seconds of tuning later and it's "Tarkus" time. Keen to win over any doubters in the audience, they all get the chance to showboat on this one, notwithstanding Keith audibly walking on eggshells with his temperamental Moog. Several times he starts a Moog part, only to quickly switch to organ when the synthesizer plays up. The organ work in "Tarkus" is magnificent with Keith on top form, although to keep up with the standard Greg and Carl are setting, he has to be. The staccato duelling in "Mass" is perfect, as is the ribbon controller solo and there are so many audible "Wow!"s and bouts of applause from the audience that it seems earlier Moog misdemeanours are forgiven.

Carl powers them into "Battlefield" with Greg's lead guitar high up in the mix, as he plays a confident solo before breaking into the "Every blade is sharp" verse; evocative and moody as ever. A ripple of applause follows, then it's "Aquatarkus" – played with an understated intro, through an inspired improvisation, to the pounding finale.

Applause is still fading as Carl begins "The Endless Enigma", another new one which is not as well known to this audience, but which they clearly love. The boys are thoroughly deserving of the loud cheers as the last notes fade. "The Fugue" in particular, written as it was for the three voices of pianos and bass, is a treasure, a real treat in this version.

By now, the hand-claps are back between the songs, but only as a sign of the crowd's frustration and impatience for more and, as the claps get louder, Keith strums the piano strings and an excellent "Take A Pebble" begins. The delicate handover from Keith to Greg, before "Lucky Man", gets a round of applause all on its own. The strummed intro to this one is changing almost imperceptibly on a nightly basis but surprisingly, it isn't greeted with the huge wave of cheers it usually gets as soon as Greg sings the opening line.

Things are warming up nicely but no record exists of any other tracks played that night

SATURDAY, 10 JUNE 1972

The Festhalle, Frankfurt, Germany.

Tickets: DM 14,-

After a rest day, spent travelling, a real cracker of a show with the Moog behaving itself for a change.

A lively version of "Hoedown" opens proceedings. Greg's bass is as high in the mix as the Hammond and for once, as bass complements organ to perfection, we can hear just how well-crafted the whole thing is.

"Tarkus" is up next and everything is right with this one tonight. As they play "Eruption", with the famous Moog fanfares, everything is hunky dory with the Moog. Keith produces a particularly swirling sound in "Stones Of Years", over which Greg's vocals sound sublime. The Hammond solo wins applause in its own right and some tight, aggressively-played organ in "Iconoclast" and "Manticore" give the piece a real sharp edge.

Greg's inventiveness with the bass at the beginning of "Mass" is apparent, making it sound so snappy and it fits well with the Moog introduction that's replaced the guitar on the original. The initiative rubs off on Keith to excellent effect and the famous organ/Moog solos are improvised from the first note to the last, fluid, enjoyable, and deserving of the loud applause.

Keith's bass pedals and Carl's drumming provide the backdrop to Greg's vocals and guitar work for a stirring "Battlefield". The lead solo grabs your attention from the first notes, and Keith plays some wonderfully understated runs on the organ. The hall's echo adds resonance to Greg's "Every blade is sharp" section, the haunting vocals floating around the arena.

Keith's Moog drifts quietly in as Greg plays out on the Gibson, to very loud applause, and then we're into "Aquatarkus", brim full of time and mood changes that rely so much on the Moog.

Claps and cheers interrupt the band several times and you can sense the guys are in high spirits as Keith launches enthusiastically into "The Hall Of The Mountain King".

"The Endless Enigma" is slightly faster than usual and all the more uplifting because of it, the Hammond sounding downright church-like at times. Again, the venue's acoustics cause Greg's line "You never spoke a word of truth" to hang in the air like never before. The first vocal part is quite heavy but at the same time restrained, although Carl must be impatient to come in with the cymbal and bass drum near the end of verse two because he pre-empts his cue by a full bar.

Keith twice fluffs a bit of the quiet organ section before each of the last two verses of Part 1 but, professional as ever, brings them back well and his "Prelude" is note-perfect. Fluffs aside (and, let's face it, every band makes them sometimes), it's definitely a strong version.

Without further ado, Keith strums the introduction to "Take A Pebble" with more applause as Greg sings the opening line. "Lucky Man" is as moving as ever with drums and Moog tellingly understated, and Greg's play-out of the last line "And so he laid down ... and he died" pulls at the heart strings.

Some very strong *ostinato* underpins Keith's piano solo, ranging as it does from delicate, near honky tonk lines to heavy chords. Textbooks go out of the window with the improvisation, a fact appreciated by this crowd, and the echoing vocals dominate the final verses before they end with a last strum from Keith.

No introduction to "Pictures ..." either, not that it's needed, as the fans recognize it instantly and act accordingly. This is powerful with a capital P. Keith changes the chord structure in "The Hut of Baba Yaga" which works, throwing in a Moog solo that sounds like he's auditioning for Bagpiper Of The Year. The others keep up with him and they pull the whole thing off well, handling the tricky sections in this and "The Curse ..." with ease.

"The Great Gates ..." is stately yet haunting, as this time it's the Hammond that sounds better with the hall's acoustics. Keith's organ-throwing sets the scene nicely for the build-up to the crashing close and the crowd go wild again, cheering and clapping wildly.

They're back for a thundering "Rondo", and this live staple rounds off another classy show.

THURSDAY, 15 JUNE 1972

Palazzo dello Sport, Genoa, Italy.

Tickets: L 1,500 (L 1,200 in advance)

The first of three Italian shows on this tour

A really upbeat "Hoedown", with a few shouts of 'Yeah' from Greg, shows that the guys are up for it from the word go. This gig sees the band in fine fettle in front of a very enthusiastic crowd.

Greg announces "OK, we'd like to play for you now, 'Tarkus'!" as Keith is still tuning up, but then it's into a very strong version, with applause breaking out for the Moog fanfares in "Eruption". There's a very percussive feel to the piece tonight, spell-binding instrumentals throughout and Greg's voice holding it all together. The mood seems to darken with "Iconoclast", but then the opening notes of "Mass" grab you by the throat.

Loud applause continues throughout the last verse, they power through "Manticore", and the drama of "Clear the battlefield and let me see" takes over. Greg steals the show in this one. The six string solo reminds us Greg used to play lead, and play it very well, before taking up the bass in King Crimson.

The softly spoken ad libs "Aaaah, aaah" and "Yeah, yeah" towards the end suit the piece, the guitar fading nicely before "Aquatarkus" takes over and Keith conjures up yet another inventive, improvised solo.

Wild applause from this enthusiastic crowd before the last notes have faded, and then Keith does the by now obligatory quickie introduction to mini epic "The Endless Enigma". The quick drum and bass intro is prolonged by a few bars as Keith gets everything set right, before coming in on the Hammond with a cathedral organ-like sound.

The line "Please, please, please open your eyes" is delivered with such force that it's a wonder Greg has any voice left after it. The honours for precision and sheer professionalism in "Prelude" and "Fugue" are evenly shared between Keith and Greg, Carl providing some wonderfully understated backing.

The delicately quiet section, followed by the loud crashing close, brings a terrific performance of a new song to an end. For a number that is unknown to this audience, it receives rapturous applause as it does most, if not all, nights. If only they had kept it in the set for longer …

"Take A Pebble" brings us back to the more established material, dominated by strong solos from Keith and a delicious acoustic break from Greg, with such a quiet beginning that some members of the audience audibly shush others.

"Lucky Man" is a classic, interrupted several times by applause, but this band version is starting to sound a little out of place, placed as it is in the middle of such a melodic, quiet and largely acoustic number. The power with which Carl and Keith come in changes every night too, as if they aren't quite sure how to take it.

Keith cues the others back in for a jazz section that sounds as if it's straight out of Ronnie Scott's, Carl in particular audibly enjoying himself, as all three show a real spirit of adventure. Keith goes for broke and quite noticeably changes the piano part of the closing section, sometimes playing in a different key, sometimes an octave higher or lower, but Greg or Carl aren't fazed and just get on with the job.

There's no introduction to "Pictures …", but the crowd go loco anyway for almost the whole of "Promenade". Such adulation lifts them and spurs them on and the second mini epic of the show, all sixteen minutes of it, is a real crowd-winner that paves the way for the only encore that could possibly fit the bill.

Sustained cheering and foot-stomping bring them back for a "Rondo" that rocks, raising the rafters and confirming what an inspired choice it is for a 22-minute encore. The lengthy introduction builds the tension, Keith plays a solo that's more Moog than Hammond – complete with bagpipes – a rendition of "Oh Susannah" that oddly gets a round of applause here in the heart of Italy, and touches of Bowie's "Space Oddity" – before stepping aside for Carl's eleven-minute showcase.

Magic!

SATURDAY, 24 JUNE 1972

The Mehrzweckhalle, Wetzikon, Switzerland.

Tickets: Sw. Fr. 17,-

This concert demonstrated how the band could often get better as they powered their way through the course of a set.

The tenth night of the tour in this relatively out-of-the-way place sees an incredibly vocal, supportive crowd.

The band are introduced individually by the M.C. but then it's another two minutes waiting for the roadies to put right what seems to be a problem with the Moog before "Hoedown" gets things going. Keith seems to be having some difficulty with the Moog, but things pick up as he charges into the middle solo and by the end of it they're firing on all cylinders.

The announcement of "Tarkus" is as well-received as expected. They're all on top of their game as they hit "Mass", the opening to which knocks the audience back into their seats. They love the machine-gun solo but it's "Battlefield" that's the real hero of the piece. The drumming and the Hammond are so sharp, the opening chords so dramatic, that the mood is beautifully set for Greg's lead and vocals. The essence of this, and "Aquatarkus", as the finale to the whole piece, is that together they put the spotlight on what each of the three does so well.

"The Endless Enigma" is downright lively, full of crashing chords, snare and cymbals, and Greg is right up there in the mix, in magnificent voice, loving every minute of it judging by the number of vocal improvisations. Wild applause as Part 1 ends, followed by a delicately and confidently played "Prelude" and "Fugue".

"Take A Pebble" has the perfect sound balance which is so telling on a largely acoustic number like this. The intro to "Lucky Man" is different again, as if Greg's trying to disguise what he's playing, and by now he manages to get as far as the opening "He had white horses" line every night before the crowd realize what's in store and go wild. "I'll name that tune in ...".

Keith revs up and weighs in with a superb piano solo, full of changing moods and gimmicks. Tonight's improvisation includes a honky tonk section with Carl on the temple blocks, touches of silent movie music, and a climax that brings everyone to their feet, whistling and cheering.

No sooner does the applause start, than it gets still louder as the familiar opening notes of "Promenade" ring out and Carl powers the whole thing along, filling in with toms and cymbal wherever he can. His speed around the toms in "Baba Yaga" is unbelievable, as is the spine-tingling opening to "The Curse ..." on bass and Moog. Moog improvisations abound, and they climax with a breathtaking (and madly applauded) "Great Gates ...".

This closing movement to "Pictures..." is pure musical theatre: soaring vocals, burning snare, clanging bells, and dramatic organ, all capped by Keith's Hammond throwing and a rousing finish.

No record of any encore, though they must have done "Rondo", but still ELP at their best.

MONDAY, 26 JUNE 1972

Palazzo dello Sport, Rome (also known as the PalaEur).

As audiences go, on this second of three Italian shows, this Roman crowd were warm, polite but hardly enthusiastic until the band won them over.

The group get off to a cracking start with a "Hoedown" that is both lively and dramatic, fast and furious, but sadly only receives a ripple of applause. In keeping with the now usual pattern, between-song raps are kept to a bare minimum.

26 minutes of musical theatre follows in the shape of "Tarkus", something they're now so confident with that they take it all in their stride, but still develop each part of it with every show so as never to get complacent. Carl's fills on the toms and bass drum are a case in point as he lays down a superb rhythm. Greg's vocals are very much in evidence as he throws in a number of rock'n'roll improvisations in "Stones Of Years", and Keith fair runs riot with the Hammond/Moog combination in "Mass", demanding all of your attention as usual.

"Battlefield" is moving, the opening powerful chords stirring the emotions from the outset, Keith nearly losing himself in the bass pedal/Moog combination as Greg steps up for the lead solos. The delicacy of the vocal/guitar quiet section, the richness of the baritone spellbinds the crowd, and the usual pause for effect before Keith leads in "Aquatarkus" is filled with applause.

Keith pulls off a winning solo in the closing section, one full of mood changes, tempo changes, using every facet of the Moog's capabilities. "The Hall Of The Mountain King" is now pretty much the cue for the main theme, with Carl's gong-smash leading to the final, roof-raising chords.

At this point in the proceedings, the crowd are beginning to liven up nicely: a subtle touch of stagecraft now to introduce the new mini epic, and it seems to work night after night. Keith and Greg play the "Prelude" and "Fugue" to perfection, and then as Carl comes in with the tubular bells a few people start to clap, then a wave of applause hits as Greg starts the last verses. It has been difficult to reproduce on stage to the band's satisfaction, but "The Endless Enigma", like a vintage wine, improves with age and is well received again tonight.

Keith Emerson

Above: Keith always liked to fully engage with his keyboards!
Tarkus tour 1971. Courtesy of Gudrun Friedrich.

Below: Signed publicity photo of a cool looking Keith.

Above: "It's behind you!"
Greg with Tarkus model in the background on the 3rd UK tour.

Opposite above: Those black and gold tom-toms were custom made
for Carl (3rd UK tour).

Opposite below: Keith at the Oval concert with his "armadillo suit".
The bottle of brandy is purely for medicinal purposes!

Belkin Productions Presents In Person

EMERSON LAKE & PALMER

SUNDAY • APRIL 9 — 3 P.M.
COLLEGE OF WOOSTER GYM

Routes 3 & 5. Wooster 0.

TICKETS 4.50 ADVANCE / 5.50 DOOR

Tickets on sale now at all Cleveland Fox Shops. Ward's Folly - Coventry. Sartorium - Euclid Ave.
Recordland - Richmond Mall. Mansfield Warehouse - Ashland. Threads Liberated - Wooster
Lowry Center - College Of Wooster. Mayflower Travel - Akron.

Opposite Top: Two keyboard maestros playing within two days of one another. Lucky old Tulsa! © Richard Galbraith

Opposite Left: Wish you were there? Courtesy of Neil Corsatea/Air C Images.

Opposite Right: "Fire regs? What fire regs?" Keith with legendary ribbon controller. © Richard Galbraith.

Above: Poster for the band's February 1978 gig at Expo Square Pavilion, Tulsa. © Richard Galbraith.

It pays never to leave a gig early. Absolutely fascinating shots of an ELP show being dismantled at the Assembly Center, Tulsa, 1977 © All photos, Richard Galbraith.

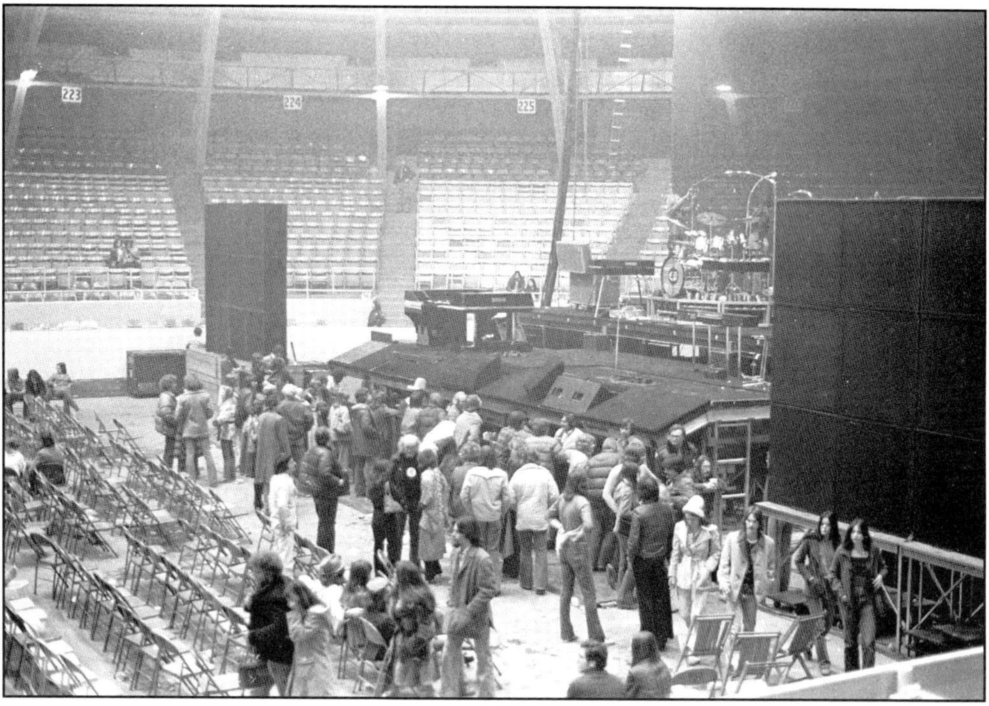
223
224
225

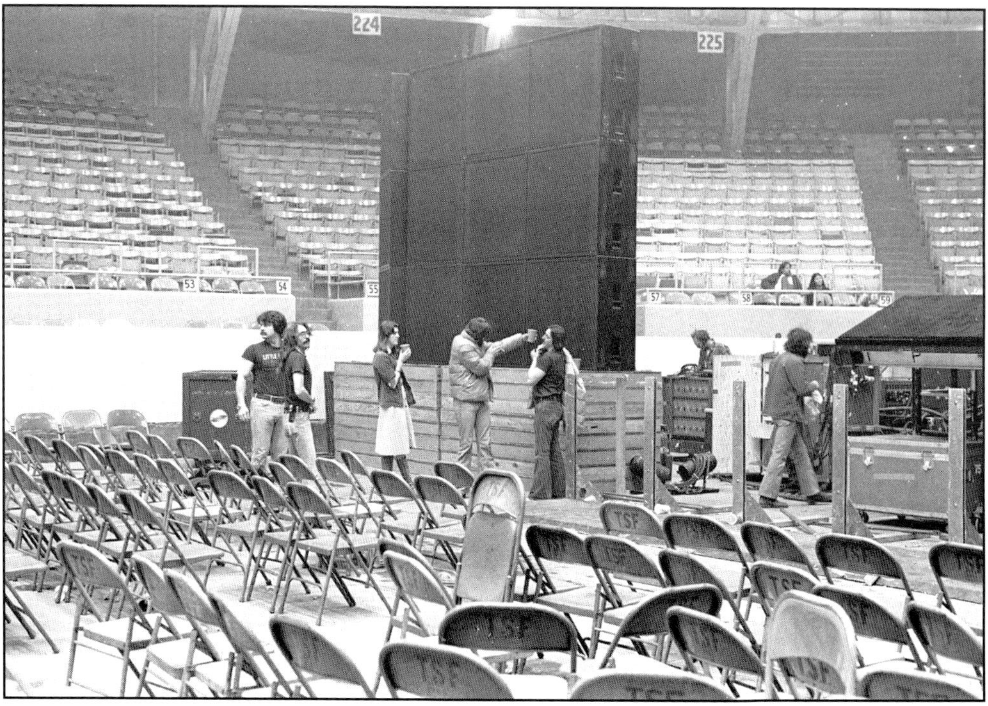
224
225
53
54
55
57
58
59
TSF

EMERSON LAKE & PALMER

ATLANTIC

The haircuts are shorter, so it must be the late 1970s. Publicity shot from 1977

Greg's vocals at the outset of "Take A Pebble" are, again, the prompt for some loud applause from this increasingly keen crowd. Just as they're settling to Keith's first solo, it's over, and out steps Greg with the acoustic, delicately picking at the strings, and sings the opening line to "Lucky Man"; he is drowned out by the cheers.

The longer, improvised piano and group section has a real laid back, swing feel to it. Keith pinches a few bars from Bach before pausing for that dramatic cascade down the piano keyboard that signals the final verses of the song; a majestic ending if ever there was one.

As the familiar strains of "Promenade" waft over the auditorium, even this crowd respond with cheers, shouts and wild applause, soon to be repeated at the start of "Baba Yaga". As they launch into a storming "Great Gates ..." a stately piece of pure prog theatre if ever there was one, more applause shakes the place to its foundations.

This is a real cracker, the highs and the lows of keyboards and vocals working even more effectively than usual above the precision playing from Carl. Keith tries some embellishments, playing a theme or two with the Hammond throwing, before the wailing sirens, and then the pounding rhythm from the others, signals the mounting climax to this show.

A shorter than usual intro to "Rondo", Greg and Carl making their entry like a Sherman tank smashing through a wall, the percussion all snare and toms. The highland fling bit goes down well for some reason, as does the space age Moog, and then the rest builds well, through a magnificent eleven minute drum solo, to the climax of another fantastic show as the express crashes to a halt.

A perfect example of how the band works a quiet audience around to their way of thinking.

TUESDAY, 27 JUNE 1972

Stadthalle, Vienna, Austria

The final show of this tour and what a show! The guys went from great to glorious, and the fans were no slackers when it came to showing their appreciation.

Always sure of a hearty reception from Austrian audiences, the crowd are still applauding several bars into a rip-roaring "Hoedown". They're tight, precise and in your face, with frantic solos from Keith.

The briefest of introductions, tonight from Greg, sees them play a truly stunning version of dear old "Tarkus", full of light and dark, highs and lows. In "Mass", all three are on blistering form but Keith undoubtedly steals the show with a rip-roaring Moog solo. "Manticore" heralds the mood change that goes with "Battlefield", the piece that Greg steals with simple but effective guitar, atmospheric, almost plaintive vocals and to die for phrasing.

In "Aquatarkus", Keith's soloing is faultless, on top of a rhythm section that's razor-sharp and inspired; both Greg and Carl match him at every turn. In the quiet section, they instinctively know just when to come in and drop out again, improvisation at its best. Shouts, cheers and deafening applause greet the end of the piece – classic song, classic performance.

"We've already played one track off the new album," states Keith. "The number we started off with was called 'Hoedown'. This other track is written by Greg and myself, and it's on the album called *Trilogy* which we hope will be out in three weeks time in this country. This track is called 'The Endless Enigma' and it's in two parts."

Before the applause fades, Greg and Carl have already begun. Part 1 announces itself loudly, and the song turns out to be one of the best versions of a number that's always played well; the organ and the vocals are particularly noteworthy. Keith and Greg are seriously on the case in the middle section, the bells/organ bridge to Part 2 sounds as good as ever and the whole thing comes to a majestic halt.

Piano and organ tuning follows for a while and then, without any introduction, Keith plucks his way into "Take A Pebble" and they're all cooking. Greg sings so well on this one that he threatens to steal the limelight from the instrumental sections, a touch of echo in the hall adding to the effect.

"Lucky Man" gets rapturous applause and Keith supports the tune with Moog pretty close to the album original. Even more rapturous cheers and claps follows the closing *arpeggio*, then it's hand-over-to-Keith time for a solo that gets ever more varied, pre-empting the jazz section where Carl shines with the improvised phrasing.

This is one of the few shows where the crowd clap along to the jazz bit and the whole section swings like an elephant's dick. You can almost see the grin on Keith's face as he plays the top-end notes in a devil-may-care, impish way.

The applause for "Pictures ..." raises the roof, a large number of the crowd clapping to "Promenade" with its stately chords and driving percussion. "The Great Gates ..." is nothing if not magnificent, Greg's vocals standing head and shoulders above everything, as they build a massive crescendo after what must be one of the most innovative Hammond breaks Keith has ever done

Long calls of "We want more" (in English) bring them back. A crashing roll on the gongs from Carl, the pounding rhythm from Greg, and Keith launches into a no frills "Rondo" without any of the normal build up.

What a way to say "Goodnight Vienna". Next up it's the Land of the Rising Sun.

SATURDAY, 22 JULY 1972

The Kourakuen Kyuiyo Suidoubashi, Tokyo, Japan.

Tickets: from Y1,700

"To call our performance that night a nightmare would be an insult to night, except that night itself hadn't yet fallen. The rain stopped and started like someone turning a tap in the sky as we hit the stage," recalled Keith.[47]

The tail-end of Typhoon Phyllis hit with a vengeance. ELP hired a Boeing 707 to fly everyone and everything, including a bunch of journalists and seven tons of equipment, out to Japan for their first ever shows there. "We want to play places where the fans don't get much of a chance to see so many groups. We've added some new numbers, cut out some old things ... but I don't think 'Bolero' is a stage number," Keith remembers.[48]

The band are driven on stage in a car, all three of them dressed in kimonos, three guys turning Japanese. Their appearance, in every sense of the word, earns them huge cheers.

As they kick off with "Hoedown", the Moog's *portamento* 'whoop' doesn't really happen, it sounds awful, and Keith has to keep switching the synthesizer on and off all night to get the sounds he needs. The number, with its infectious beat, is a vote-winner anyway, and after a short "hello" from Greg and an introduction from Keith, Carl counts in "Tarkus" and a wave of applause hits the stage as soon as the crowd realize what they're listening to.

They're visibly enjoying themselves, despite the rain, as the crowd cheers them on with huge rounds of applause every time they play an instrumental section, or Greg sings: actually, they clap and whoop all the time really. Never mind the out of tune Moog, Keith plays an unbelievable solo in "Mass" against a driving backdrop of Greg, head held back, the neck of his bass almost vertical, and Carl hunched over the kit, all sweat and drumsticks. The crowd love the ribbon controller as Keith machine guns everyone, and smashes it against the back line stack.

More applause deservedly greets the opening of an impressive "Battlefield", Greg stepping into the limelight with a well-phrased Gibson solo. The icing on the cake for this one? *The* verse from "Epitaph" that he's brought back into the song after the European tour, sung with real emotion on his face.

"Aquatarkus" is a Moog fanfare where, for once, the real focus is on Carl's inspired work on snare and cymbals, as he seems to match Keith note for note. As the final chords fade, the cheers get louder and Keith, strumming the grand, takes them straight into "Take A Pebble".

From the first line of "Just take a pebble ...", they're onto a winner as the crowd cheer and then fall silent, allowing this masterful version to build. A classic piano lead from Keith, with a groovy jazz backing from the others, then more strumming of piano strings, takes us into an acoustic solo from Greg that must be unique: he does both "Old Blue" and "Lucky Man" – probably the only time he has ever played both in one show.

As Greg steps forward, Keith walks out from behind the keyboards, obviously in a light-hearted mood, and gets the crowd clapping along. It's country and western night in Tokyo and everybody, especially the guys on stage, is having a high old time! As he goes into "Lucky Man", applause breaks out again and it's a powerful version, more so when he nods the cue to Carl and Keith to come in. Keith's aggressively-played solo, and the band improvisations, are faultless: jazz at its best when only a few minutes ago they were wrapped up in the Moog extravaganza that is "Aquatarkus": this is versatility.

Down comes the rain again as Greg takes a drink and, stepping up to the mic, gives a quick rendition of "Raindrops Keep Falling On My Head". Carl joins in, Greg breaks into a huge smile and the crowd cheer them on.

Next up is the shortened "Pictures ...". This version is dramatic, big, and well-played, with the intense concentration showing on the faces of all three. Keith rattles off the solos, with Greg and Carl keeping the whole thing nailed down. As they hit "The Great Gates ...", Keith jumps into the air to provide the cue for Greg and Carl to power things along.

When it comes to the Hammond throwing, he uses the switches on the amps to set up a new rhythm that Carl matches immediately, before another unique thing happens. Keith puts down the Hammond, Greg and Carl thunder into the "Rondo" beat, and for a full two minutes we have the mind-boggling sounds of "Rondo" being played in the middle of "The Great Gates ...". At the magnificent climax, once they've all come back into Mussorgsky, the applause is deafening.

"Rondo" is a crowd-pleaser. As he is in Japan, Keith takes a Samurai sword to the poor Hammond, Carl turns in a cracking solo, the 'watch-me-play-this-bell-with-a-rope-in-my-mouth' routine winning huge applause, as does the fact that with every stroke water showers him from the drum skins. Storm or no storm, this was a hell of a show, by the end of which it was still 90 degrees and all three guys were soaked to the skin.

30,000 people go home happy despite the pouring rain. Next stop is Osaka.

MONDAY, 24 JULY 1972

The Koshien Stadium, Osaka, Japan.

Tickets: from Y1,000

Musically, another show to be proud of but not without its share of problems.

The reception in Osaka is even louder than in Tokyo, if that's possible, but before they take the stage there seem to be Moog problems and delays set in. Keith helps things with shouts of 'Hello!' and a few runs up and down the keys as Greg tunes the bass.

Keith tries the *portamento* to see if the Moog's in tune, it is (almost) and bang! – off we go into a "Hoedown" that's very nearly drowned out by the sheer volume of clapping as this crowd quickly gets in the mood. The middle solo gets rapturous applause despite being cut short on account of the Moog sounding hideous.

Always focused on the music, Keith doesn't dwell on synth problems but gives "Tarkus" a quick introduction; Carl counts them in and we get nearly 26 minutes of prog magic. The rhythm section are spot on all the way through, giving first Keith and then Greg a rock solid foundation for some stunning solos. Keith does his thing on the Hammond in "Stones Of Years", having changed the solo around quite a bit, after which "Iconoclast" is a powerhouse.

The opening of "Mass" casts its usual spell, winning huge cheers, before Keith takes charge with a ribbon controller solo that has them all on their feet, whistling and cheering.

"Battlefield" is grandiose, organ and lead guitar in turn soaring above everything, with Greg's vocals reminding everyone that, live, this song belongs to him. He plays a masterful solo, backed so well by Carl, and by Keith on the bass pedals. For once, the "Every blade is sharp" section is performed as a band piece, after which Keith and Carl take a back seat for Greg to hold the spotlight with "Confusion will be my epitaph" as a solo piece, played and sung with real emotion, poise and drama.

This crowd are into clapping along and they do so energetically for the first few minutes of "Aquatarkus", before Keith takes the band up another level, with stop-start breaks, weird sounds and improvisation galore from Carl and Greg. The military beat reappears and the tension builds towards a typically rousing climax – even with a hopelessly out of tune Moog, this is the stuff that legendary shows are made of.

"Take A Pebble" brings a change in tone, the opening bars slowly subduing the noisy crowd into near-silence. A delicately-played intro on the Gibson turns into one of the best live versions of "Lucky Man" he's ever played, completely solo, setting the pattern for his future spots. For effect, he repeats the last verse and, as the guitar fades and the applause starts, Keith's already picking up the baton for the long improvisation.

After the jazz section it's "Pictures ..." time, which is played with a little more edge than normal. This crowd is clapping along again.

Nothing if not lively, the audience go nuts over Keith's Hammond throwing and stay noisy right to the intense, powerful end, breaking into a frenzy of applause even as Greg sings the final words.

"Rondo" almost lifts the roof off this stadium, as cheers, hand-clapping and wild shouts become the norm. Every move Keith makes is followed by more frenzy and as they sweep through "Rondo", hundreds, if not thousands, of fans charge the stage, some of them climbing up and grabbing Greg, who has to be rescued by security men.

The power goes dead, police began clubbing fans, and Carl carries on with a superb drum solo, until finally he is forced to throw down his sticks, jump into a car and get out fast. Keith and Greg have already been bundled into a limo by security people and driven off at speed. "There just wasn't enough security, we couldn't play anymore,"[49] Greg recalls.

As Keith and Greg drove away from the stadium, with no PA to amplify him, they could still hear Carl thrashing away. "Two miles down the freeway we wound down the windows. We could still hear Carl playing. 'You know, he's a fucking good drummer', said Greg 'Listen to that! No PA, we're two miles away and you can still hear the fucker'."[50]

Carl puts it more succinctly: "You bastards! I kept giving the cue for you to come back on and here you are frothing away in a fuckin' Jacuzzi!"[51]

A bizarre ending to an excellent show, but it proves what a phenomenon this band are everywhere they play.

9. *The Dawn Will Break Another Day ...*

27 JULY – 21 AUGUST 1972: FOURTH NORTH AMERICAN TOUR
17 SHOWS, INCLUDING 2 ON 1 DAY AT THE CONVENTION HALL, ASBURY PARK, NJ.

Typical set list:	"Hoedown", "Tarkus", "The Endless Enigma", "The Sheriff", "Take A Pebble", "Lucky Man", piano improvisations, "Take A Pebble" reprise, "Pictures At An Exhibition", "Rondo".
Band equipment:	As for previous tour.
PA system:	5,000 watt custom built system.

Barely a break from the traumatic Japanese dates, with only two 'rest days' to cross the Pacific with the entourage and the gear. They land in California the very next day after the Osaka traumas.

"The Endless Enigma" and "The Sheriff", one a mini epic, the other a light-hearted comedic piece, were in the set list, the latter for the first time. Both added enormously to the texture of the shows.

THURSDAY, 27 JULY 1972

The Civic Auditorium, San Francisco, CA, USA.

The first gig after riotous Japan and, by all accounts, an absolute stunner. Keith's wearing a full-length flaming red kimono that changes colour under the lights and Carl has the specially made karate outfit with his initials on the back. Playing was immaculate throughout the full set, building to a rousing "Rondo" for the encore. Wild cheers greet Keith's knives as he lays into the beleaguered L100.

FRIDAY, 28 JULY 1972

The Arena, Long Beach, CA, USA.

Second show of this short tour and another sterling show in Long Beach, which was always a popular place for the trio to play.

A minute or so for tuning up, then in kicks the Moog, off goes "Hoedown" and we are treated to one of the best ever versions of this piece. An enthusiastic crowd are up for it from the very beginning and this rubs off on the band. This number in particular shows off the musical tones of Carl's drums as he matches Keith note for note, blow for blow, with Greg belting along all the time as solidly as ever.

A wave of applause heralds 26 minutes of "Tarkus", the opening section attacked with real fire and power. The way this band gels is best exemplified in "Stones Of Years", Keith playing some stunning lines, Carl using every part of the kit, and Greg enjoying his vocal duties. The pace seems to quicken by the time they reach "Manticore", which takes us into a fearsome, emotional "Battlefield", the eerie Hammond setting just the right tone for the vocals. Carl shines here too, throwing in some nifty hi-hat work. Greg plays that beautiful solo on the Gibson and has the audience transfixed for his solo vocal spot.

The verse from "Epitaph" is there, sung to perfection, with precision timing for maximum dramatic effect. He earns every bit of his applause!

"Aquatarkus" brings the piece to a close, the intricacies of this movement really to the fore tonight as Carl adds some syncopation on hi-hat, cowbell and snare. It brings the house down.

They've really got hold of the intro to "The Endless Enigma"; to say it's tight is an understatement, and it sounds so impressive. Keith scuttles along the upper manual on the Hammond, pauses for the drama and Part 1 is stirring stuff, winning well-earned applause as Greg belts out the lyrics and Carl makes full use of the small toms and cymbals.

The duet that is the "Prelude" works every time, Carl adding some nice finger cymbal at just the right moments, and it leads smoothly into "Fugue". Tubular bells announce Part 2 and it's a classic.

Keith takes the mic: "We'd like to go on and play another track from *Trilogy*. This is something we haven't tried out on stage yet. This is 'The Sheriff'."

First time or not, Carl's drum intro is spot on as Greg comes in to tell the light-hearted story of Big Kid Josie. The whole thing rolls along well, and captures pretty closely the feel and mood of the original. The ending of the last verse is a bit messy but the syncopated piano solo at the end more than makes up for that and it gets polite applause.

Return to an old favourite next with "Take A Pebble". Light, delicate trio work opens the instrumental section, before Keith takes off into the piano solo. Greg thoroughly deserves his applause as he steps forward for a heartfelt acoustic introduction to "Lucky Man", even though at the beginning he has to tune the guitar as he plays it, describing the sound as "drastic".

Keith turns in a super solo, picking out phrases from the back of his mind, with the *ostinato* bubbling away underneath. You can almost see the concentration and sweat on Keith's face. Carl and Greg pick up their cues, the jazz improvisation is as free-form and as fresh as ever, real toe-tapping stuff.

"Promenade" is awash with stabbing Hammond chords, crashing cymbals and thumping bass. As Greg does the bass intro to "The Curse ...", Keith provides the organ backing and then the whole thing just takes off, fast, and full of controlled chaos. Again, having the concert toms gives Carl the chance to stamp his mark firmly on the rhythm, and he and Greg seem to go ballistic as Keith takes off with the solo.

They build firstly towards the Hammond throwing, which goes down a treat with this audience, and then reach a cymbal-crashing, soaring climax with Greg singing his heart out.

They come back for a "Rondo" with what must be the longest-ever intro, synthesizer, gongs and cymbals gone wild. Keith gives out the train sounds to alert everyone to what's coming, and in come Carl and Greg with the rhythm – and tonight, in particular, what a rhythm!

The keyboards are aggressive, swirling up and down, before Keith passes the baton to Carl for a strident nine minute solo. Carl has eight new toms – four black, four gold, arranged, alternately around his kit.

A truly magnificent show, quite possibly one of their best ever.

FRIDAY, 11 AUGUST 1972

Milwaukee Arena, Milwaukee, WI, USA.

The shows on the second US leg in 1972 were what could only be described as high level. The guys were fully au fait with the new Trilogy material and the old-timers were developing well from gig to gig.

The show kicks off with a now ultra fast "Hoedown". This musical sophistication is smoothly pursued into "Tarkus" – Keith's platform to strut his stuff. Technical expertise, joined with his flair for improvisations every night, gives the audience a true insight into what's possible on keyboards.

This epic just wouldn't be there without Carl's melodic drumming and Greg's guitar and vocal work. Greg plays tasty guitar solo in "Battlefield", and conjures up an atmospheric "Epitaph", to take extra applause before Keith goes into a speedy, seven minute "Aquatarkus". It's characterized by lots of new Moog phrases and by the use of the new sequencer.

In honour of Jimi Hendrix, Keith throws in some licks from the legendary "Star Spangled Banner" before "Peer Gynt" rings in the finale.

"The Endless Enigma" which follows is breathtaking, with some canny variations in the fugue. Then Carl preludes the next *Trilogy* tune with a drum upbeat and we're into "The Sheriff", which is faithful to the studio version. This leads nicely to the acoustic section of the evening with "Take A Pebble". Keith conjures up a new piano solo, then hands the baton over to Greg for "Lucky Man", again with full drum and Moog accompaniment, but without *that* Moog solo. The fabulous piano improvisation gives the audience some of the classic ragtime chords with which Keith occasionally indulges himself.

A vital, speedy and perfectly played "Pictures ..." continues the show. It's a real pleasure to hear how the guys 'pass the ball' to each other. Spiced with the "Bolero" theme on the Moog in "Baba Yaga", and a long lasting L100 feedback sound, it really whips up the fans.

The show is crowned by a twenty minute "Rondo". After a slow beginning with the steam locomotive sound, Keith continues with the really, really fast "Rondo" theme segueing from L100 into the Moog. It seems he's even trying to outdo himself today. Carl gives us an impressive eight minute drum solo with the "Singing Saw" inset.

"What a show!"[52]

SUNDAY, 13 AUGUST 1972

The Performing Arts Center, Saratoga, NY, USA.

Runs up and down the keys from Keith, "Hello" and some tuning from Greg, bit of practising on the concert toms from Carl and they were off with a very confidently played "Hoedown".

Without further ado, straight into "Tarkus" and this vocal, friendly crowd is right with them. Shouts of "Yeah" from Greg in "Stones Of Years" show that all is well, with his velvet voice well to the fore.

The solo is imaginative and creative, as is the bass work behind it, and the overall feel of this track is right. They give their all in "Mass", some stabbing embellishments on the Moog winning approval, before Keith takes the place by storm with the ribbon controller.

Unexpected improvisations by Keith during "Manticore" and at the beginning of "Battlefield" work well before he and Carl take something of a back seat, and Greg steps to the fore. Nice bass synth work from Keith, together with razor-sharp snare from Carl, underpins Greg's solo. "Every blade is sharp" is sung with hit-'em-in-the-face emotion, as is the increasingly used "Epitaph" verse. The silence in the hall for Greg's solo guitar is amazing – followed by a wave of applause as the others come back in.

Keith leads them into the "Aquatarkus" march, and the Moog fanfare causes much excitement. The supporting work by Carl is magical: another example of how musical a drummer he was and is. The truly solo bit is improvisation at its prog best as Keith throws in a few bars from the "Star Spangled Banner" and "The Hall Of The Mountain King", and then gives the cue for the return to the main theme and the grand finish.

"The Endless Enigma" is powerful, majestic and, as with most shows now, the approbation comes thick and fast as the guys reach the first verses. Barely have Keith and Greg got into the "Prelude" when Greg comments on an inordinate amount of noise coming from further back in the crowd: "What's the problem? What's the problem up there? Can't you see? Could all these people here just ease down so they can see?"

"I'm sorry, carry on, " he says to Keith before realizing that yet more people have the same problem:

"And on that side too, could you just sit down so those people could see?"

Keith and Greg, ever the consummate professionals, pick up exactly where they left off and when Carl comes in, they all play to perfection. In Part 2, Keith adds a few frills to the Moog lines before the final, crashing fanfare.

"Thank you!" yells Keith. "You probably know that one as a track off the *Trilogy* album inspired by a Salvador Dali painting, called *The Endless Enigma*. This next one – I don't know quite what it's inspired by but Greg's gonna sing it to you. It's called 'The Sheriff', also off the same album."

Carl's drum intro is slightly different each night and it's clear all three appreciate the humour of the piece. Keith does a couple of gun-shots on the Moog as Carl's temple blocks signal the nicely silly syncopated bit towards the end. The crowd fall for the false ending, applauding madly; Keith calls out "Thank you very much, excuse me ..." as they play another two bars to the real ending.

It's back to a serious piece of classic ELP as Keith strums the intro to "Take A Pebble". Rich vocals, delicate piano *glissandos* and faultless cymbal work are the trademarks of the first part, before Keith turns in a beautiful solo, jazzily underpinned by Carl and Greg.

Greg's solo spot, "Lucky Man", has a longer than usual intro, and Carl's drums and Keith's bass Moog work give the whole thing a touch more drama than usual. They string out the acoustic/Moog middle section, bringing the whole thing down in volume to add to the effect of the last verse – and it works. Greg strums the last chords and shouts "The end" to deafening applause.

The next piano solo is dangerously fast, but with not a duff note in sight. Toe-tapping *ostinato*, with melodies ranging from "Daisy Daisy" to "La Marseillaise" and some brand new licks, underpin the whole thing.

Lengthy applause, whistles and cheers precede a sock-it-to-em "Promenade", the opening to a cracking version of "Pictures ..." that grabs everyone by the scruff of the neck and doesn't let go.

The encore has to be "Rondo" – this time with over two minutes of Moog and organ train noises before Greg and Carl crash in with *that* rhythm.

A superbly played instrumental that leaves this lucky audience cheering all the way home.

FRIDAY, 18 AUGUST 1972

The War Memorial Auditorium, Rochester, NY, USA.

This animated audience was up for it from the get-go; so much so that, before the band play a note, Keith had to appeal to them not to push forward because they were crushing those at the front. It's not the best of starts and it seemed to unsettle the guys for a fair part of the show.

The *portamento* of "Hoedown" gets them cheering, a competent version but it doesn't raise the rafters. If anything it's subdued, with a few duff notes and a missed cue.

Applause is polite, after which a quick "Thank you" from Keith precedes the leap into 24 minutes of *Tarkus*. From the highs of Greg's lead guitar solo to the emotional calm of "Every blade is sharp", the effect is simply stunning. The timing on the vocals is drama itself, the "Confusion will be my epitaph" line thoroughly deserving the applause it receives.

"Aquatarkus" starts at a blistering pace, maintained by Carl almost the whole way through. Between Carl's aggressive drumming and Keith's attacking style, this part of the epic fair grabs your attention before taking you back into the "Tarkus" theme and those famous final chords. The crowd love it and are on their feet, applauding wildly long before the music dies away.

"The Endless Enigma" starts quietly, without any introduction, and develops forcefully in Part 1 as Keith's Hammond chords and Greg's vocals are both at full tilt. "Prelude" and "Fugue" are delivered with consummate ease, the more delicate parts of Keith's work shining through. Part 2 builds nicely to the climax – but the fire that usually accompanies this one just isn't there tonight.

"The Sheriff" too lacks a certain something. On previous nights, Keith has introduced it with a touch of irony and humour, setting the scene for the mood of the piece – but not tonight. It's routine, entertaining, but no more and even with two deliberately false endings it falls a bit flat.

After that, "Take A Pebble" needs to step up to the plate, and it does. The phrasing of the vocals, the piano solo, the delicately-played cymbals, it's all inspired stuff and the fans give it their full attention.

As Keith strums the piano strings one more time, Greg takes up the baton and picks his way through the opening of "Lucky Man". The song itself is beginning to sound a little tired as a band number, perhaps the reason why it soon becomes an entirely solo spot for Greg alone.

This is one of those audiences that clap along to "Promenade", and the playing gets better because of it. This version of "Pictures ..." is given a very serious workout. If anything, Keith and Carl seem a little subdued, giving Greg's vocals the run of the place, and the piece really shines because of it.

The "Rondo" encore, at almost 26 and a half minutes, stakes its claim as the longest the band ever play. The crowd are clapping along as soon as the express leaves the station. Keith sets the place alight with classic Moog and organ solos, putting the ending to this show right up there in the enjoyment stakes. Carl delivers a twelve minute solo breathtaking in its complexity and use of the tonal qualities of the kit, before the others come back and they all lift the roof off with the climactic ending.

A spellbound audience demands more but that's it for tonight.

SATURDAY, 19 AUGUST 1972

The Convention Hall, Asbury Park, NJ, USA.

Tickets: $6.00

The band played two shows at Asbury Park and the recording that exists features just three tracks, but we don't know from which gig. The audience are well up for it, giving the band warm greetings from Asbury Park, NJ.

Only the second half of "Take A Pebble" has survived and it has all the hallmarks of a version to be proud of. The piano playing is superb, with Greg and Carl really perking up the jazz section, but it's the closing verses that stand out and put the icing on the cake of this one. Perfect *glissandos*, powerful toms and cymbals, and beautifully rich vocals win applause well before the song's over and it's so well deserved.

This lively audience go wild at the opening notes of "Promenade", lifting the performance still further.

The fast, rocking sections stand out, the whole thing played at breakneck speed with still not a wrong note in sight. The pace of what's gone before means that the dramatic pause at the start of "Great Gates ..." is all the more effective in its simplicity: less means more and the crowd show their appreciation with rapturous cheering.

They encore with a fast and furious "Rondo". So fast, in fact, it's amazing that at this point in the show they can keep up this pace for almost 22 minutes. Carl maintains the excitement throughout his solo, cues Keith and Greg back in, and we have an ending to end all endings – organ, crashing gongs and thumping bass provide a fitting climax.

Shame that more doesn't survive from what sounds like a great show.

10. *The Dawn Opened The Play ...*

10 NOVEMBER – 1 DECEMBER 1972: FOURTH UK TOUR
22 SHOWS, PRECEDED BY THE *MELODY MAKER* POLL WINNERS SHOW
AT THE OVAL CRICKET GROUND, LONDON ON 30 SEPTEMBER 1972.

Typical set list:	"Hoedown", "Tarkus", "The Endless Enigma", "The Sheriff", "Take A Pebble", "Lucky Man", piano improvisations, "Take A Pebble" reprise, "Pictures At An Exhibition", "Rondo".
Band equipment:	As for previous tour.
PA system:	5,000 watt custom built system.

In the annual *Melody Maker* Readers' Pop Poll ELP scooped seven awards: for keyboards, producer, arranger (the whole band), composer (Keith and Greg), and drums, but the icing on the cake was winning best group in both the International and British sections. That led to them topping the bill in the Poll Winners show at the Kennington Park Oval Cricket ground in London, although Wishbone Ash actually closed the show. Also playing were Focus, Genesis, Argent, Jack Bruce and a band called Fudd (though nobody seems to remember which award they won).

The event marked the beginning of another successful touring season for ELP as they prepared for only their third UK tour proper in November and December. At five venues (Glasgow, Cardiff, Birmingham, London and Newcastle) they played two shows, early and late evening – a tremendous work-rate – with the second show usually ending around midnight.

This tour saw them debut the *Trilogy* tracks for British audiences and, as it progressed, they threw in another comedy number: the theme from *The Alan Freeman Show*. This was the band's thank you to Alan for the unswerving support he proffered them.

Theatrics to complement the music saw a model Tarkus, on either side of the stage, belching smoke (or other things!), firing cannons and throwing out strobe lights at the appropriate time. Stage production was upgraded to eight colour screens, four either side, flashing images in time with the introductory music of "Abaddon's Bolero", with the stage otherwise in complete darkness. The structure and shape of the stage show were so well-crafted, to the point where the short "Pictures ..." proved an inspired choice as a climax, and the set list remained static throughout the main tour.

SATURDAY, 30 SEPTEMBER 1972

The Oval Cricket Ground, London, UK.

Tickets: £1.00 in advance, £1.25 on the day.

"You can't charge people a lot of money just to say thank you to them,"[53] *Keith reasoned. And this was ELP's way of thanking* Melody Maker *readers.*

They play a barnstorming show – a harbinger of things to come on the main part of the UK tour in November and December.

Martin Walker writing in *The Guardian* noted, "There were two superpigs [sic] flanking the stage, breathing smoke through little snouts and firing big bang cannon and orange smoke-bombs and moog sounds like machine guns and wicked knives being thrown into the amplifiers and stabbed into the synthesizer."[54]

It is intended to be the debut for the Moog drum but fate has other plans: "Me Moog drum's bust and we promised everybody we'd use it ... it got shipped over from the States and like there were pedals missing and wires cut – inside!"[55] a saddened Carl reveals.

Keith explains that, "Since I last used my synthesizer in Britain I have added a complete new stack of modules and it now produces lots of new sounds. I just hope it will be warm enough to play it."[56]

Introduced on stage by arguably their biggest fan, DJ Alan Freeman, they kick off with "Hoedown", infectious and superbly-played – if a little slower than on the last tour across the States. A quick "thank you" from Keith, resplendent in an armadillo-type outfit, and as they move into "Tarkus", two massive armadillo tank-like, smoke-spewing creatures appear at either side of the stage in a breathtaking stunt of showmanship.

A dependable version of the epic follows, with the guys going for maximum impact on this excitable, and excited, crowd. Keith moves to stage front to whip up the audience with the ribbon controller in "Mass", machine-gunning everyone in sight, before an expertly-delivered tempo change in "Manticore". The beginning of "Battlefield" is pure musical theatre and Greg's guitar playing is sheer class, adding so much to the overall dimension of the band's sound as he delivers the lead solo. The "Confusion will be my epitaph" verse has a magical effect on this audience.

How do you follow that? "Aquatarkus" is the crowning glory of the suite with a Moog fanfare that builds on the theme over and over again, each time taking it off in a slightly different direction. The crowd are not slow to show their appreciation.

The UK debut of "The Endless Enigma" is next up – and a damn good version too. A little slow to come in, but Keith is so effective when he does, and Part 1 really gets going. There's more than a little edge to the keyboards in this one. "Fugue" wins applause in its own right as, despite the complexity of piano and bass parts,

Keith and Greg play it perfectly. The crowd have hardly stopped cheering at the end of Part 2 when Keith announces, in true short, sweet and to-the-point ELP style: "We'll do you another number off the *Trilogy* album. This is 'The Sheriff'!"

Vocals suddenly seem lower in the mix, but it's a punchy rendition given a real kick start with Carl's drum introduction. Keith plays some nice, light-hearted tongue-in-cheek phrases in the solo and yet again they throw the crowd with the false ending. As expected, it goes down a treat.

Well-honed classic follows light relief, and "Take A Pebble" deservedly gets loud cheers as soon as Keith touches the piano strings. True to form, Greg keeps up the standard with the acoustic break. "Lucky Man" sees him holding the last two lines longer than usual and finishing with some light touch *arpeggio*.

This audience loves the jazz section, Carl's crisp snare and cymbal sound perfect complementing as they do Greg's stunning bass, and providing a rhythm that Keith can attack with finesse – which he does.

Not to be outdone, "Pictures ..." gets the loudest cheer of the night and, in return, the audience get a spellbinding, thundering sixteen minutes of ELP-meets-Mussorgsky. A tremendous performance, Keith's opening statement in "Promenade" rings around Kennington like the bells of Kiev themselves. Keith changes the entire solo in "Curse of Baba Yaga" as he goes to town on the Moog and, given the eeriness and mood of the piece, it works well. The close of "Baba Yaga" is unbelievably fast and undeniably note-perfect, before Keith's hovering Hammond takes us into "The Great Gates..." This part of the classic has it all: mystical bells, soaring vocals, crashing chords, and a serious bout of Hammond throwing that has the London crowd clapping along in time.

The instantly recognizable train sounds of "Rondo" silence the calls for "Nutrocker" and, as Greg and Carl set up the groove, Keith wades in with a deafening solo.

Cannon reports from the Tarkus tanks and fireworks bring this one-off, dynamic show to a deafening close as Emerson, Lake and Palmer prove beyond all doubt just why they won seven awards.

The band wanted to thank the fans who voted for them ... and they did it in style.

FRIDAY, 10 NOVEMBER 1972

The Winter Gardens, Bournemouth, UK.

A return visit to Greg's home town and, so soon after his birthday, Carl and Keith have a surprise for him.

During the show, Carl steps up front and announces that it's been "Gregory's birthday" and everyone, to the accompaniment of Keith on the grand, sings "Happy Birthday".

SATURDAY, 11 NOVEMBER 1972

The Gaumont Theatre, Southampton, UK.

Tickets: £1.50

After opening the tour the previous night in Bournemouth, Greg's home town, they moved a little way along the south coast of England to the port of Southampton.

The lights go down and, as "Bolero" builds slowly and quietly, with Tarkus images on the screens at either side of the stage, tension and excitement builds. The traditional intro "Hoedown" comes fast and powerful with new Moog variations in the middle section.

Instead of the malfunctioning Tarkus replicas – they're actually supposed to produce roaring sounds and shoot confetti into the audience – Keith gives us some Moog fanfares as an intro and Greg counts them in.

Aggressively played with many new Hammond riffs, the epic is pushed onwards and upwards by the rhythm section. A fine Moog/guitar duet follows in "Battlefield" – and astonishingly tonight Greg wins no extra applause with his "Epitaph" quote. Was the audience taken aback – they must know it is gleaned from his King Crimson stint, surely?

Anyway, Keith isn't put off his stride and he goes straight into a nine minute version of "Aquatarkus". A very fast first section on both Moogs with lots of new settings, is followed by an atonal middle section. Far-out sounds emanate from the Sequencer which twice causes spasmodic extra applause before "Aquatarkus" is brought to its usual conclusion.

The Endless Enigma is now – after the "live rehearsals" on the previous gigs in US and Europe – a perfect performance with live features typical of ELP: variation and improvisation. It gets long lasting and warm applause. Then Greg creates an 'Instant Enigma' all of his own and asks the audience to solve a riddle: "Do you know what "ELP" stands for?". Nobody knows so mischievous Greg explains that "It stands for Extremely Large Parts."

After the laughter has died down, Greg introduces "The Sheriff". Still virtually identical to the studio version, this piece is just fit and proper to complement the good vibe in the Gaumont. So the guys give us three reprises of the last couple of bars, the 'ragtime express', winning big laughter and extra applause.

"Take A Pebble" comes with a wonderful first piano solo. Greg's "Lucky Man" is again modified, now backed by piano and Moog. The well-tried closing number of so many 1972 gigs, "Pictures ...", is another highlight.

The Southampton audience is beside itself and makes emphatic demands for more. Keith accelerates the L100 locomotive – push-started by the rhythmic support of the audience. After a short prelude of the "Rondo" theme on the

Hammond, Keith turns to the Moog. His phrases from Bach's "Toccata" are today embellished for the first time with notes from a Scottish jig.

Carl offers the audience something new too: he's connected most of his tom toms with the Moog and garnishes his drum solo with lots of electronic sounds.

"Unbelievable for the audience! As if that's not enough, Keith's knife attack on the Hammond and the organ riding finish a really remarkable show."[57]

MONDAY, 13 NOVEMBER 1972

The Free Trade Hall, Manchester, UK.

Tickets: £1

"Every accolade bestowed in their direction is well aimed."[58]

On only the third gig of the tour, they play a colourful set that delights a packed house. Keith throws himself into the Hammond with "Hoedown", whilst Carl and Greg set up a sheer wall of sound behind him.

As they move into "Tarkus", Keith pulls out all the stops and it becomes a real showpiece as first he, then Greg, step into the limelight, pulling off solo after solo. All the time, Carl works harder than anyone, relentlessly switching time signatures and keeping the beat.

Before "The Endless Enigma", Keith and Greg chat a little to the crowd, doing the 'Extra Large Parts' routine, and even giving a few at the front a sip or two of Keith's brandy. The bells at the start of Part 2 get a huge round of applause, and the piece as a whole goes down well.

The humour that is "The Sheriff" isn't lost on anyone, and as he comes to the last solo in true Mrs Mills [a famous London TV pianist from the 1960s] style, Keith grabs the limelight again.

The real masterpiece of the whole show though is "Take A Pebble". After a stunning introduction on the piano, Greg steps up into the spotlight on an otherwise darkened stage and delivers a tremendous version of "Lucky Man", helped along by Carl on tambourine.

"Pictures ..." is wide-reaching in its drama, poise and colour and as the band come off stage the crowd demand more, which they get with an impressive "Rondo". Out come the knives, up jumps Keith, on goes that pounding rhythm and we get musical theatre at its best.

The next night, they play a second Manc gig, this time at the Hard Rock. A special long, thin stage extends out into the audience, and at the end of this is placed one of the Tarkus models. At the appropriate time, it growls at the crowd and, during "Tarkus", Keith runs along the stage and fights the model with the ribbon controller. Who needs a light sabre?

Reputedly, ELP did three more encores, the last one after the lights had gone up, and in their dressing gowns, but no record of any material after the first "Rondo" exists.

Or does it – somewhere? Let me know.

WEDNESDAY, 15 NOVEMBER 1972

St George's Hall, Bradford, UK.

Tickets: £1.50

Only the fifth of 22 concerts, but already they were in full swing and it was another spectacular.

Down go the lights, on come the screens at either side of the stage, images flashing in time to the introductory music of "Abaddon's Bolero". The audience is already wound up and ready to rock. In perfect unison, as the last chord of the "Bolero" sounds, on come the spots and Keith hits the "Hoedown" *portamento* to wild cheers.

This Yorkshire crowd go bonkers even before the final notes have been played and then listen in almost complete silence as the Tarkus tanks roar and bellow smoke. No introduction tonight as they tear into this one at full pelt. 24 minutes of this epic is a real highlight of the show with everyone firing on all cylinders: powerful drums and bass, rich vocals and that gutsy Hammond sound, all combining in "Stones of Years". It's during the short movements, "Eruption", "Iconoclast" and "Manticore" that we can hear Greg hammering the bass, staying right up there in the mix, highlighting the one thing he often gets too little credit for.

"Aquatarkus" is a showcase for the Moog in the truest sense, and really takes off as the crowd start clapping in time. Keith slows the whole thing right down for a touch of Moog-meets-the-blues, then Carl quickens the pace again as they drive into the "Hall Of The Mountain King". Back comes the theme, and they take it to a magnificent climax and the fierce roars from our friends the Tarkus tanks.

Still no introductions as Greg and Carl bounce along with the opening bars of "The Endless Enigma", which is a first-class version.

They're now almost 42 minutes into the show and at last they speak! A few "thank you's" from Greg, and Keith introduces the next one as "A Tribute to Alan Freeman". A 30-second snippet of Alan's theme music from his BBC Radio 2 show then follows.

"We're gonna play you the one he keeps plugging on the radio. This is "The Sheriff," jokes Keith.

In this light-hearted piece, Big Kid Josie proves to be a big hit with the Bradford crowd. With a touch of "Daisy, Daisy" and some dramatic silent movie music thrown in, the final solo entertains in every sense of the word.

From the world of silent comedy, ELP then take us back to more familiar territory as Keith strums the first bars of "Take A Pebble", in which he treats the audience to a lengthy solo strumming break and, as the sound desk mixes down the volume, up steps Greg, picking up the melody of "Lucky Man" on the acoustic.

He has hardly finished the opening line before a wave of applause breaks. Like "Tarkus", this one seems different every night as Keith adds a delicate touch of piano to the chorus and the middle eight, which is a real winner. The second part, revolving as it does around Keith's piano solo, the jazz improvisations and imaginative work from Carl, goes down equally well.

Amid the cheers, whistles and roars, Keith runs up the steps at the back and plays "Promenade" on the house organ, introducing sixteen magical minutes. Well, that's it – this crowd go bananas with delight, so that much of "Pictures ..." is barely audible.

Back they come for "Nutrocker" but after the classic intro, the clavinet stops working – that is until Keith bangs and kicks it a few times. This tough love must work, as the second attempt is copybook and what a version: everything they play tonight seems to get faster and faster. The middle solo is longer than normal and this crowd love it.

Carl shoots out a machine-gun-like snare break and it's then that Keith hits them with "Rondo", over twenty minutes of terrific Hammond and synth, a mesmerizing drum solo and faultless bass rhythm. Carl proves time and time again just why he deserves the accolade of top drummer in the recent *Melody Maker* polls as he takes us through fourteen minutes of a highly skilful solo, including a section with the Moog drum.

The outro music plays amid wild cheers and shouts for more: a show to remember for all the right reasons: superb lighting, ear-pleasing sound and top notch entertainment.

FRIDAY, 17 NOVEMBER 1972

Green's Playhouse, Glasgow, UK (2 shows).

Tickets: £1.25

By all accounts both shows were fantastic, and some tracks have survived, although it's unclear from which of the two performances. One thing stands out: a receptive, enthusiastic and very up-for-it audience lift the band to still new heights.

Riotous applause and cheers greets them onstage and within seconds a chant of "ELP, ELP" begins, only to be silenced by the opening of a killer "Hoedown", driven along skilfully by Carl and Greg. Every time the whoop of the *portamento* puts in an appearance, this crowd go wild and Keith has them hooked for the solo as he throws in some traditional Scottish themes to keep on the Glaswegians right side.

Applause starts even before the end of the piece and gets still louder as the Tarkus tanks roar and the guys kick off a copious 25 minutes of the second album's title track: one of the best-ever versions. "Eruption" bursts in with real power before an even better "Stones Of Years" where, for once, there's a sing-along as most of the audience join in with the opening verse.

To a huge round of applause (yet again), Carl drives them through "Mass", full of exceptional fills, snappy bass and aggressive, swirling Hammond. The ribbon controller solo sets the place alight – Keith's on fire tonight! He jumps down into the audience and runs amok, machine-gunning everyone but then found that the stage at the Playhouse is higher than elsewhere and he can't climb back on. So, for a minute he just stands there watching Carl and Greg while soloing away. Eventually, the security people realize what's going on and help him back on stage.

"The show that never ends very nearly did!"[59]

With "Battlefield", Greg delivers "Every blade is sharp" so soulfully and "Confusion will be my epitaph" gets loud applause and cheers. As the whoosh of the Moog builds underneath him, Greg delicately plays out the solo spot and then we get an "Aquatarkus" with the whole theatre clapping along in time for the first dozen bars or so.

A plain "Thank you!" from Keith and then it's the second 'newie' of the night. "The Endless Enigma" goes down a treat, despite some wild calling by sections of the crowd – who are promptly told to "Shut up!" by the rest.

The next two lighter comedy pieces – *The Alan Freeman Show* theme (tonight played on the Moog) and "The Sheriff" – are enjoyably done and deserve the recognition they get. For the latter, Keith invites the crowd to "sing along to this one" – and they do, providing a second rhythm section as they clap along to the story of Big Kid Josie. The ragtime solo at the end is the usual showstopper, the two false endings catching everyone by surprise but, when it does end, the noise lifts the roof.

The contrast continues with "Take A Pebble". The piano solos are the stuff Keith is made of, matched in every way by Greg's mastery of the acoustic guitar in the introduction to "Lucky Man"; a really classy piece of guitar playing. A nice, measured build-up teases the crowd and then suddenly Greg stops for a few seconds to inform the audience: "Gonna sing a song for you now. I'll tell you a story, the first time I did this song was in this very hall in Glasgow. Let's hope it's not the last time, eh?". It's not surprising that they go ballistic, almost drowning out the opening lines.

It's sing-along-a-Greg night in Glasgow, the guy can do no wrong. It's nearly a full half minute before Keith can pick up the solo, with plenty of stalwart work, and the group jazz section is fast-paced, wonderfully improvised and a delight to the ears. As the whole piece comes to a stunning close, *glissandos* and vocals echoing around the hall, the wild applause resumes.

As Keith opens "Pictures ...", it sounds like half of Glasgow are clapping along in time. It's a cracking version and seals what must surely be one of their best, if not *the* best performance of the tour.

Shouts, not surprisingly, of "We want more, we want more!" bring the guys back for a rip-roaring "Nutrocker", segueing into a fanfare of Moog and Hammond and then a hell-for-leather "Rondo "in a flurry of keyboards and drums.

Clearly, this is one of this band's favourite venues – and tonight it showed! Glasgow belongs to ELP.

THURSDAY, 23 NOVEMBER 1972

The Capitol Theatre, Cardiff, UK (2 shows).

The band's third consecutive show at the same venue in Wales and they were on a winner from the word go, although it's not clear from which show(s) this recording originates.

From the off, this crowd clap along to the taped intro of "Abaddon's Bolero" and they seem so up for it. The lights are down, the atmosphere palpably building and cheers-a-plenty as the guys creep on stage ready for the opener.

The whoop of the Moog, and the entrance of the Greg/Carl rhythm section is one of the tightest in prog circles, and tonight it sets up Keith for a first-rate version of "Hoedown" on both Hammond and Moog, as the middle solo just takes off into an inspired improvisation.

True to form for this tour, there are no introductions yet, just the Tarkus tanks roaring us into nearly 24 minutes of what is by now a classic. Well supported by the crowd, they turn in a slick performance, a touch slower than other nights on the tour, but with more poise and weight because of it. The vocal sections in particular benefit from a slightly slower delivery, Greg's rich tones hanging in the air that bit longer.

Keith's solo in "Stones Of Years" ups the pace a bit, but Carl reins back for the next verses. "Mass" and "Battlefield" are what really carry this one: tight interplay in "Mass" between Keith and Carl in particular leads to a wild, free-ranging ribbon controller solo, Greg and Carl playing furiously in the background. By this point, "Manticore" leading into "Battlefield", the pace has quickened, set very much by Carl.

The main lead solo from Greg is pure rock, before a change of mood and volume heralds in "Every blade is sharp", accompanied by some stunning and well-received *arpeggios*. Of all the seven movements, "Aquatarkus" has changed the most since it was first played in the spring of 1971, with huge variations in time and pace, together with very effective stop-start improvisations.

The crowd are on their feet, cheering and applauding long before the end comes, accompanied by the roar of the Tarkus tanks. Something of an anti-climax, Keith announces that he has a problem with the organ, and is instantly reassured by someone who shouts "Well, you're still a genius!"

A mighty cheer greets the repair of the offending instrument and Greg and Carl pick up the intro to "The Endless Enigma", by now a central feature of the act and one that never fails to go down well. This is the fourth tour it's featured on, and it's remained basically the same as on day one.

For some reason, 40 seconds of *The Alan Freeman Show* theme doesn't go down as well in Cardiff as it does elsewhere – but never mind. A quick introduction from Keith, and Carl tears into "The Sheriff". You can sense the smiles on their faces as they play this one, and there's no holding Keith and Carl in the ragtime ending: temple blocks, false ending, 'Daisy, Daisy', a touch of Laurel and Hardy – the whole shebang.

"Take A Pebble", the only original piece still in the show, gets the respect it deserves – and at 24 minutes it deserves plenty. At the end of the first part, Keith plays an extended watch-me-strum-the-piano-strings section, fading as Greg picks up the melody on the acoustic. "Lucky Man" brings the house down, accompanied by Keith on the grand piano. But, as a total contrast Keith plays it for laughs with "Chopsticks" in mock ham-fisted style.

"Pictures ..." is dynamic from the first to the very last note. There's intricate group work in "Baba Yaga", fast, accurate solos, and a "Great Gates ..." so full of majesty that it earns its place as the climax of the show, leaving this animated audience demanding more; which they get.

"Nutrocker" is so fast that Keith almost loses himself in a flurry of notes, before Carl steps up for the snare break and Keith wastes no time getting into "Rondo". They've judged the mood of this crowd perfectly, not bothering with the usual train and whistle sounds, but instead jumping straight into that pounding rhythm. Too often the forgotten one in this, Greg keeps the bass on a rock-steady beat as all hell breaks loose around him on the keyboards and drums.

As the by-now standard outro music plays, this crowd leave the hall a happy and satisfied bunch who have given ELP a welcome in the hillsides.

SUNDAY, 26 NOVEMBER 1972

The Hammersmith Odeon, London, UK (2 shows).

Tickets: £1.50 – 75p

Well, if ever there was a show where they wanted to prove themselves, this was it – their first indoor gig in London for almost a year.

By this part of their career, stage production is as polished as it will ever be, engineered to such a standard that they give one of the best performances of their lives.

With the stage in total darkness, and the eight screens flashing coloured images in time with "Abbadon's Bolero", the guys walk on and, exactly as the tape reaches the final deafening note, the stage lights come up and they charge into "Hoedown". It's fast, precise and as tight as a drum.

A deafening roar from the audience, another one from the Tarkus tanks, and we're off. Carl adds some strong accentuated fills in "Stones Of Years", the vocals rich, confident and clear. The "Confusion will be my epitaph" bit is set against an absolutely silent crowd. Keith and Carl step forward to drive along "Aquatarkus". Stop-start musical histrionics add to the drama, but slowly they build the tension, Keith winning a round of applause (or maybe they're clapping the Moog?) as he steps back and the synthesizer keeps on playing 'by itself'.

The live version of "The Endless Enigma" just keeps getting better and better with each outing, and tonight is no exception. They've mastered the intricacies of the piece and it's a delight to listen to.

It's so quiet during "Prelude" and "Fugue", they could be in a studio, ensuring that everyone can hear Carl's finger cymbals. The opening of Part 2, with the tubular bells, rivals "Great Gates ..." for sheer atmosphere. The applause is long and loud.

Lifted by that, the guys play a red-hot *Alan Freeman Show* theme and "Sheriff", tonight with a faster, different intro from Carl. The audience love the let's-have-a-laugh ragtime duet between Keith and Carl at the end.

Fun time is followed by the gravitas of "Take A Pebble", including an excellent rendition of "Lucky Man". The long duet between Greg on the acoustic and Keith on the piano strings is now well-established, delicately played and serving as the perfect intro to "Lucky Man". After the usual self-parody with "Chopsticks", Keith sweeps all before him with the solo, as does the whole band in the jazz section, set against a backdrop of a very respectful and appreciative audience.

Keith opens "Pictures ..." on the cinema's mighty Wurlitzer organ, having first played a few notes of typical silent-movie music, and this crowd love it. The shows where Keith can use the house organ really benefit from the added atmosphere, and the dramatic tension is also heightened as he charges back to the stage.

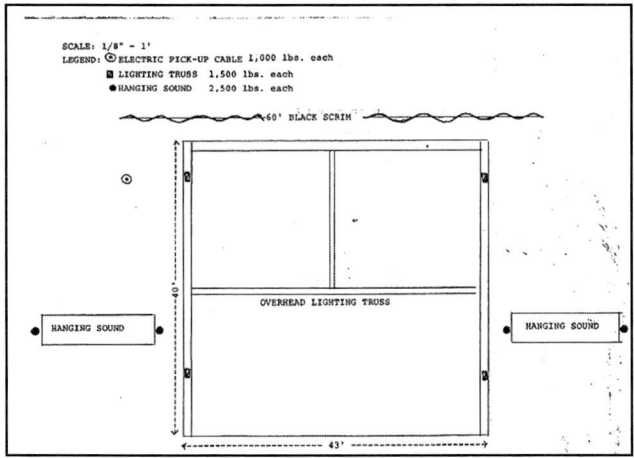

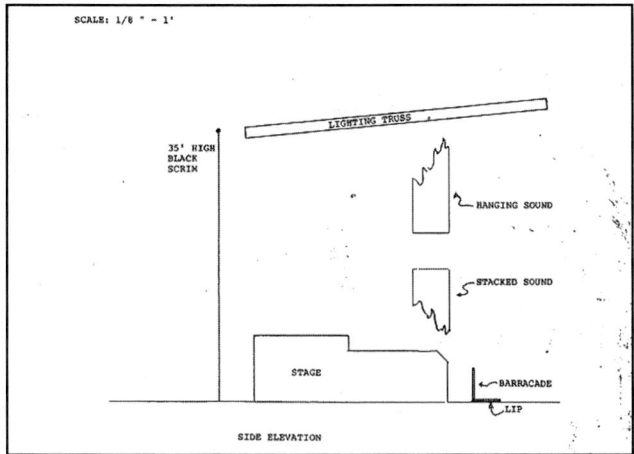

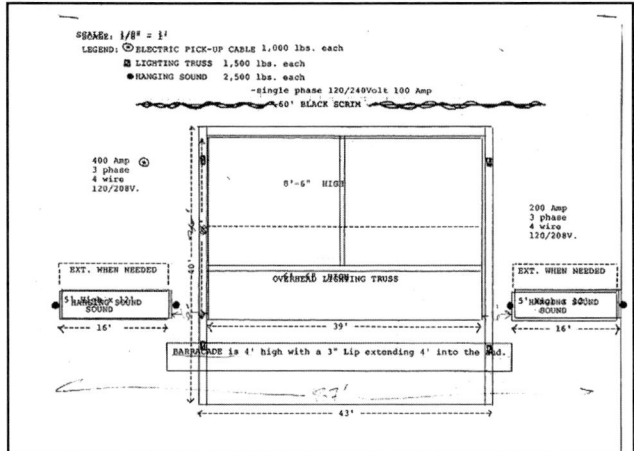

Now you can make your own ELP stage set at home! Courtesy of Tony Ortiz.

They tear into the encore of the "Nutrocker"/"Rondo" medley, a classic show-stopper if ever there was one, as Keith seems to build more and more Moog into the runs before handing over the baton to Carl, amid plenty of cheers and whistles, for his ten minute solo.

All in all, a slick, professional and fun performance at the Mecca of English rock music.

MONDAY, 27 NOVEMBER 1972

The Dome, Brighton, UK.

Here was a band in fine fettle in front of a very enthusiastic audience. The hall also had sympathetic acoustics that added to the atmosphere of the set.

Due to a shortage of stage space, one of the Tarkus models was positioned centre stage, right above the piano. The full nine minutes of the taped "Abaddon's Bolero" intro does its job well, setting up ELP to launch into "Hoedown" amid riotous applause, a tactic that now gets every show off to a lively start.

Oddly enough, no tank roars tonight, instead a quick count in from Keith and a powerful, rocking 26 minute "Tarkus" gets under way. The wind effects on the Moog during "Battlefield" as Greg plays out are atmospheric and prove that real thought has gone into this one.

Tonight's game for a laugh, *The Alan Freeman Show* theme, is on the Hammond, but over almost as soon as it starts, and gets a warm reception before Keith steps up to the mic: "I've got a present! It says, 'This dagger comes to you from the Knife Edge Appreciation Society'. Good one, yes, I'll hang it on my wall! Anyway, we'd like to dedicate this next one to Alan Freeman, who seems to insist on playing the ends of our records and never the beginnings (loud cheers). This is called 'The Sheriff'." During the ragtime ending Keith deliberately plays off key.

There is no record of "The Endless Enigma" being played tonight although doubtless it is.

"Take A Pebble" is up next, but as Keith takes up his place by the piano, he notices hundreds of the polystyrene balls fired by the Tarkus tanks have lodged inside the piano's workings and every key he presses remains stuck down! You won't believe the next bit: the roadies come onstage with vacuum cleaners, much to the delight of the Brighton audience as the band take a short, enforced break. The band return to play the song as if nothing has happened.

What is interesting about "Lucky Man" is that Greg can only get as far as the word "He" before the place erupts and then, just as quickly, lapses into silent admiration. With Keith on grand piano and Carl playing tambourine this is a probably the finest version of the song they will ever play.

As usual Keith lightens the mood with "Chopsticks" for a few seconds, and then really gets into the swing of his solo, first alone, then backed by the Lake-Palmer jazz combo. If we didn't know better, we would swear they are auditioning for a residency at Ronnie Scott's!

"Pictures ..." thunders by in grand style and the "Nutrocker"/"Rondo" encore is played with such energy considering it is the end of a long show that has seen Hoovering roadies, and Keith veers off into a few rock'n'roll phrases on the clavinet.

"Rondo" is nineteen minutes of pounding rock with aggressive keyboards, a magical drum solo, and a rock steady Greg bringing a memorable, spectacular show to a fitting close.

11. *We're So Glad You Could Attend ...*

30 MARCH – 4 MAY 1973: FOURTH EUROPEAN TOUR.
THE 'GET ME A LADDER TOUR'
22 SHOWS, PLUS 4 FRENCH SHOWS WHICH WERE CANCELLED

Typical set list:	"Abaddon's Bolero" (sometimes played later in the set), "Tarkus", "Karn Evil 9: 1st Impression", "Jeremy Bender"/"The Sheriff", "Take A Pebble", "Still ... You Turn Me On", "Lucky Man", piano improvisations, "Take A Pebble" reprise, "Hoedown", "Pictures At An Exhibition", "Toccata".
Band equipment:	As for previous tour, but with the four new guitars and Echoplex unit for Greg to replace existing ones. The new ones were all custom made by Tony Zemaitis: a metal-fronted electric, a six string acoustic inlaid with mother-of-pearl with a heart-shaped sound hole, a twin-necked electric and bass, and a twelve string acoustic.
PA system:	5,000 watt custom built system.

"The biggest mobile musical production ever staged ... The most ambitious production ever mobilized by a rock group."[60] In so many respects, this tour proves the turning point for ELP.

After a break from touring of almost four months, fifty personnel (so many roadies they reputedly even had a roadie to wake up the roadies!) and over twenty tons of equipment in two 40 feet long, articulated trucks brought the ELP extravaganza to Europe, which saw the debut performance for material that would later surface on *Brain Salad Surgery*.

Dropped from the team were "The Endless Enigma", "Nutrocker" and "Rondo" (as a discrete piece in its own right); in came new signings "Karn Evil 9: 1st Impression", "Toccata" (because Carl needed something for his drum solo with "Rondo" out) and "Still ... You Turn Me On". There was a recall for "Jeremy Bender".

The costs that came with the personnel and equipment meant that ELP now had to perform in arenas that could hold 10,000 punters or more – hence the development of the proscenium arch in an attempt to put a more intimate theatre setting into a big arena context.

The proscenium arch was a massive 60 feet wide and 30 feet high, 25 feet deep, equipped with 100 spotlights (at that time an unheard of quantity for a rock band), lasers and five sets of theatre curtains. "The arch is to create a sympathetic setting for our new musical concept," said ELP. "We feel the visual aspect is a natural development towards a portable ambience."[61] They gave the arch a pre-tour inspection at Shepperton Studios – and it got the thumbs up.

The band rehearsed material in the former London cinema that is now Manticore Studios. They had been so conscious, when playing material from *Trilogy*, that what had sounded right on record couldn't always be successfully transferred to a live situation. They were now adamant that what was recorded had to be capable of being reproduced live. A full four weeks' rehearsals with only roadies and management present paid dividends.

As Greg told me in a 2005 interview:

> The reason ELP was so successful was that a lot of what it did DID work, and that's the simple truth of it. That's why we bought Manticore, the theatre. We were determined not to make a record we couldn't play live. So this time, we made sure we could play the whole bloody thing live! We went in there, wrote it, rehearsed it and made sure we could play it.

Keith was still sporting the armadillo suit from Japan; Greg in the immaculate white suit, usually with a black shirt, and Carl bare-chested beneath his waistcoat, showing off his leather trousers every night when he came out to accompany Greg on tambourine on "Lucky Man". He looked rather natty in the black leather, decorated with a single curved white stripe down both pieces of the outfit.

"Still ... You Turn Me On" was so new that Greg sang different lyrics almost every night, adding an extra interest to his growing solo spot. That was all part of the ELP song development process whereby the lyrics came last.

This was also the first outing for the infamous £2,000 Persian carpet for Greg to stand on. Despite later assurances that it was to help prevent electric shocks, he was quite unabashed at the time: "Well, I used to have a bit of dirty old carpet to stand on, I used to drag it around the States, so I got a Persian rug. Playing has to do with being in the right frame of mind. It's the little things that make the gigs more pleasant and more familiar."[62]

The new guitars were custom-made by Tony Zemaitis, with a superb feel to them but the twin-necked guitar didn't last too long – it was simply too heavy. "I'd seen that I could change quickly across the guitars. With a flick of the switch I was into something else. However, sadly it still didn't overcome the main problem that when the bass stops ... the bass stops. And it was brutally heavy," Greg told me. Don't forget, Greg's double-neck was a bass and a guitar, rather than a six and twelve string guitar as used by Jimmy Page for example, which made it heavier.

The stage show was more of a production but with fewer theatrics and gimmicks than ever: not a flying bird in sight, much more of a polished presentation with the emphasis very much on the stunning music. As Greg explained to me:

The reality of it was that both elements were there from the beginning. The show was one thing. The music was one thing. Both of these things developed in a linear way right throughout the 70s and we tried to improve everything on both fronts. We tried to do the best we possibly could on all levels. The idea of the show was not to make it as big as we possibly could. We just had thoughts on the best possible layout, the best possible scenario. The idea was to try and perform every night in as similar an environment as possible. We got it so the only thing we had to change was the people out front. That's why it developed in the way it did. We tried not to have production effects, gratuitous things going on. We always tried to link production directly with the music.

They retained the two Tarkus models at either side of the stage – they growled at the start of "Tarkus" and had the added benefit of giving Keith an opponent to fight with his ribbon controller.

SATURDAY, 31 MARCH 1973

The Philipshalle, Dusseldorf, Germany.

Tickets: DM 13,00

Only the second outing for the show, the first known recording from the tour.

"The concept of the arch is to provide more of a West End theatre production as opposed to an effects production. And psychologically, although we will be playing in a different hall each night, we will feel we have the same facilities."[63]

Teething problems hit them before the gig, as Keith explains: "In Dusseldorf we couldn't get the equipment there on time, and thousands of kids had to wait from 8p.m. till midnight before we could start ... they were amazing kids. They sat and watched the roadies put up the proscenium arch. As each piece was lowered into place, they sent up a cheer."[64]

This is the one known to fans as "The long concert", because it didn't end until the early hours of the following morning, after it had taken the roadies almost six hours to erect the staging.

The set list is not that different but, with the order changed, the whole show has a different feel to it. As soon as they walk on, the model tanks start their growling and ELP launch into their new opening number "Tarkus". The 10/8 time signature of "Eruption" is, as ever, faultless and "Stones Of Years" sounds better for the extra keyboard and drum fills. After singing the first verse by the book, Greg changes most of the next two verses, followed by an incredibly fast Hammond solo, backed by Carl working as hard as ever. When they come back to the final verse, Greg is all over the place, lines from here, there and everywhere, but the effect is still magical ELP.

The ribbon controller solo is still there in "Mass", more manic than ever as Keith 'mows down' the crowd, and Greg changes the lyrics again.

For the rest of this epic, it's all honours to Greg: word-perfect vocals soaring above everything, strong bass and, in "Battlefield", a truly electric solo. The intro and coda to "Every blade is sharp" are both shortened, not quite so much solo Greg on this one, but still he carries all before him.

It seems strange listening to "Hoedown" at this point, but it's as lively and as upbeat as it ever was. As if to change the mood yet again, it's the return of "Abaddon's Bolero", this time introduced as such.

Compared to when ELP last played this one, it sounds beefier, more gutsy, with tons more bass and more Moog/Mellotron up front courtesy of Keith and Greg.

Having had the lively, dancing beat of "Hoedown", followed by the heavy drama of "Bolero", it's comedy time. The medley of "Jeremy Bender" and "The Sheriff" work well together: we go from the gay man who wants to become a nun, to the story of Big Kid Josie and, interestingly, it's the latter that gets bigger applause. Both are played on electric piano (even the ragtime duet with Carl at the end of "The Sheriff") and it gives them a lighter, more enjoyable feel.

Moving on again in terms of mood, "Take A Pebble" commands the same respect as ever and it too isn't exempt from the changes that have been rung: for the first time in ages, there is no "Lucky Man" to go with it.

Unknown at the time, this is possibly the first ever performance of "Still ... You Turn Me On". Interesting to hear the evolution of one of Greg's and ELP's loveliest ballads: the first two verses are as they will be on *Brain Salad Surgery* but from there on, it's quite different and the last verse he sings is in a different key and tempo to the finished version. This last verse[65] never made it to the album stage but goes down a treat tonight as Greg 'rocks it up' with wonderful vocals, the audience clap along, and a poetic, acoustic coda on his new twelve string brings it to a gentle conclusion. Tucked in there also is ... guess what? Possibly the earliest recognizable melody from "Closer To Believing", subtly played, but definitely there.

The last four verses of the final version clearly haven't been written yet, a fascinating example of a song developing in the muck and bullets of live performance.

Mild applause, then Keith picks up his solo, moving from slow to mid-tempo to faster, boogie-woogie phrases with consummate ease. The Emerson *glissandos* come thick and fast and the left hand works overtime keeping a pattern going. The close of this timeless song hasn't lost any of its drama but strange that as the last notes fade, Greg calls out "Rock'n'roll!".

Another epic rendition of "Pictures ..." is up next. Keith revs up during "Baba Yaga" and the pace never falters. Tonight's organ theatrics are more than just that: Keith conjures up all kinds of sounds with feedback and the Moog, complementing the usual siren-like noises and generating sporadic, but loud, applause. Keith again blasts out some killer chords as the song reaches its dramatic conclusion with "Death is life" and emphatic shouts of "Yeah" from Greg.

"Karn Evil 9: 1ˢᵗ Impression" is a stunner and well-received by this crowd. There are early differences but the instrumental framework is there as are most of the vocals. Greg takes over with the guitar solos, with Keith and Carl in close attendance, and then Carl produces an upbeat drum break to lead into the closing section. Shades of things to come when they will eventually play the entire "Karn Evil 9".

The final one tonight, a long night, is a medley of "Toccata"/"Rondo" and, as befits ELP, it's a classic with no sign of fatigue from either audience or band. It's recognizably close to the final album version, with the synthesizer playing the main melody while the organ and bass take the orchestral parts.

The percussion movement itself is magical: Carl plays some complex rhythmic figures on the tympani and tubular bells, highlighted by plenty of gong-bashing, and then it's back to the kit for a snare-based, fever-pitch, solo. He works his way round the entire kit: every block, cymbal, drum and the Moog drum, building rhythm after rhythm and winning some sincere applause. He even gets the audience clapping along to a random bass drum pattern – and they so obviously enjoy it. A crescendo of snare, tympani and gongs usher back the others, and bass Moog and guitar belt out the riff to "America", soon joined by Carl on the tympani.

What we then have are sporadic train sounds, a synthesizer playing the melody to "America" – and then suddenly it's back to the "Toccata" melody, a few minutes of "Rondo", and the closing music kicks in.

A long wait for the audience, but well worth it in the end.

TUESDAY, 10 APRIL 1973

Friedrich-Ebert-Halle, Ludswigshafen, Germany

Tickets: DM 14,00

According to adverts at the time, this was the first of two consecutive nights at this venue – although no other evidence exists that they played a second night.

A change of running order from Dusseldorf as "Abaddon's Bolero" opens, the tension building slowly yet effectively. It's heralded in, surprisingly, by some tympani and then Carl quickens the tempo as Keith and Greg come in on synthesizer and Mellotron.

Moving away from the recorded version helps enormously: it's shorter, punchier and the collective fanfares better suit ELP live. They've also changed the ending, with a pause and then a long, sustained chord.

"A lot of electrical problems tonight, one second," pleads Keith. He also admits: "These new numbers we play to you, they're so new we haven't even got titles for 'em yet, so … dunno … we'll have to make one up."

He then goes straight into the two-voice organ introduction to "Karn Evil 9: 1ˢᵗ Impression", played just as on the album, as is most of the piece. Greg's vocals are upfront, loud but unaccompanied for the first three verses and his bass playing provides some interesting counterpoints to the keyboards. A bit of bass drop-out as Greg takes over the lead guitar work but it's well worth it, the guitar solo is precise with a hint of broodiness, followed a few bars later by an equally tasteful Hammond solo. All in all, the playing here is fabulous and the crowd warm to it. Greg said to me about playing lead six string, "I tried to do it whenever I could get away with it … it wasn't an easy role to fill because every time I played the guitar the bass player went on holiday."

"Gonna play you some things we hope you're familiar with, off the last albums," Keith announces.

More problems with the electric piano before Keith finally gets the "Jeremy Bender"/"Sheriff" medley under way. It's meant as a light-hearted break but it's lost something because of the problems earlier, and both songs lack the punchy frivolity of the last show. Keith even fluffs a line or two in "The Sheriff" (the equipment again?) and it has to be rescued by the superb ragtime ending, a fact not missed by the warm reception it receives.

Roars from the armadillo tanks, the odd Moog note or two and they get 22 minutes of "Tarkus" under way, much to the delight of this lively crowd. "Aquatarkus" comes alive after the textbook introduction: inspired free-form soloing from Keith, and a section where Greg leads on bass and the keyboards imitate and follow him. Wonderful stuff!

As in some of the older shows, the opening lines of the vocals for "Pebble" get rapturous applause, as does Keith's and Carl's immaculate counterpoint playing on piano strings and cymbals. The initial piano solos are lively, furious left-handed *ostinatos* providing a deceptively easy basis for a solo where Keith wins loud applause and cheers.

Yet more applause as Greg steps up and delivers a first-rate "Still … You Turn Me On". He keeps the rocking section towards the end (that never makes it to the album), but before that changes a whole verse to try out new lines. No sooner has he finished this lovely new song, than he launches into "Lucky Man" with an extended "Heeeeeeeeeeeeee had white horses ..." that fair brings the house down. Carl on tambourine and Keith on dramatically-played grand add a nice touch and the song sweeps all before it.

Keith the soloist, and ELP the jazz trio, show everyone how it's done for the next thirteen minutes before picking up the song again. There may have been problems earlier, but not anymore.

The Moog isn't working properly for the whoop at the start of "Hoedown" and Keith tries out the usual 'Emerson solution' to any faulty keyboard: hitting and banging it very loudly, greeted with stentorian cheers from the audience. Suitably fixed, off they go with this lively and light-hearted instrumental.

"Pictures ..." is now well placed at the climax of the main set, and earns the respect and applause it generates.

Prolonged roars for more are silenced by a "Toccata" taken at a furious pace, full of drama. All three of them excel, and Carl shines on the tympani and bells in a thirteen-minute solo that seems to change and develop each night.

After that, it's heads down no-nonsense boogie for the headlong charge into the "Rondo" part of the double header: Moog and Hammond in equal amounts.

A fitting end to a typically mighty ELP show.

FRIDAY, 13 APRIL 1973

The Sporthalle, Cologne, Germany.

Tickets: DM 13, 00 in advance, 15, 00 on the night.

The guys came on stage, to what was by now the classic opener for this tour, *"Abaddon's Bolero".*

Carl starts the beat very slowly, very deliberately and gradually the pace quickens as Keith and Greg come in. Fanfares abound, a wall of sound hits the crowd – atmosphere and tension are built up well.

Having worked up the audience, ELP let 'em have it with "Karn Evil 9: 1st Impression", one of the new numbers that has benefited so much from being rehearsed for a month at Manticore studios.

The coda and Moog themes shine and it's well-received by the crowd as usual and, with no further ado, to loud roars, it's "Tarkus". "Mass" has its own special magic tonight, the stop-start bit at the front of the solo so well improvised, and Keith takes off like a warplane with the ribbon controller. Carl and Greg, as the super-fast rhythm section, hold their own and the cowbell heralds the arrival of "Manticore". "Battlefield" sees arguably the best Greg solo spot of the evening. He rules supreme with "Epitaph". As if that isn't enough, the guitar coda earns applause in its own right.

Carl at first quickens the pace in "Aquatarkus", Greg keeps right up there and Keith uses a much cleaner, purer sound on the Moog, especially when they slow things down and play the main theme in a very orthodox 4/4 time before returning to the textbook ending.

After that, "Jeremy Bender" and "The Sheriff" are downright light-hearted and tongue-in-cheek – but they lack sparkle until the ragtime ending, when Keith and Carl come into their own. Quotes from silent film music, Rachmaninov's "First Prelude" and what sounds like Laurel and Hardy's theme, work well.

"Take A Pebble": classic song, wonderful performance. Greg picks out the melody to "Still ... You Turn Me On", on the twelve string. It's another stunning solo spot, again he's still developing the lyrics in the second half of the song to test the lie of the land.[66]

The song's senior partner, "Lucky Man", quickly follows. The improvisation is played with a touch of levity, before we get the seriousness and richness of the final verse, with the guys pausing for several seconds as if daring the audience to hold the applause.

"Hoedown" is a cracker and, apart from the improvised solo, still tends on this tour to stick closely to the original.

They take "Pictures ..." at a stately pace compared to some recent performances, with Greg at full cry in the vocal sections, and it gives the piece a much heavier feel. Eeriness abounds in the slow bit of "Baba Yaga" and as they pick up the pace for the solo, every drum beat, every note on the bass and keyboards is clearly audible. They wind up with a superlative "Great Gates ..." featuring a heart-felt performance by Greg, and that foundation-shaking ending does just that – hardly surprising that the audience clamour for more.

The shows closing encore, "Toccata", is developing into a tight live piece, with tonight some changes in Keith's keyboard phrases in the first part. The main solo is typical Carl, and a show-stopper, giving the whole band the perfect opportunity to charge into "Rondo".

Just nine performances under their belt this time out, and already this show is setting the template for the next sixteen months.

SUNDAY, 15 APRIL 1973

The Hallenstadion, Zurich, Switzerland.

Tickets: Sw. Fr. 22,-

Only the band's fourth ever show in Switzerland, in an indoor sports arena with appalling acoustics, but 10,000 eager fans.

Opening with "Abbadon's Bolero" – starting slowly with tympani – as the front curtains part to reveal a shimmering ELP symbol changing in colour as the lights hit it; then a second curtain parts revealing the band.

Carl takes up the beat, emphasizing each one on the snare. Dry ice winds across the stage, falling over the edge like a waterfall. "Bolero" builds tension and pace well, but they have lost a certain something since giving up "Hoedown" as an instant, lively opener that sets out their stall for the evening,

"Nice to see you, glad you could all make it! We've got some new numbers to lay on you first. A few knobs to twiddle first. So if you twiddle your knobs while I twiddle mine ... should be pretty cool," jokes Keith.

Plenty of knob twiddling indeed and weird sounds but, with "Karn Evil 9: 1st Impression" an unknown quantity, as Keith starts the two organ voice intro he gets no reaction from the crowd.

Greg's way out there at the top of the mix and singing for all he's worth. The first solos see organ and guitar roar into action, a mood change in an instant as we head towards the circus with Greg as the ringmaster advertising his thrills and shocks. Plenty of Keith's trademark organ *glissandos* followed by an impressive lead guitar solo.

The "Welcome Back My Friends" second part is so close to the classic we've all come to know and love, but Greg fluffs the lyrics a couple of times, almost as if he isn't quite sure of what lines to sing.

"Tarkus" clearly enthralls this animated crowd. The only Lake composition of the epic, "Battlefield", is the star. Greg's solo playing and singing are simultaneously exciting and atmospheric, and his performance of "Epitaph" wipes the floor with just about everything else tonight.

Much of "Aquatarkus" is based on a nice, clean sound from the Moog, and the guys vary the tempo to telling effect, returning to a classic ending when it matters. Then it's Rocky Morley the roadie's turn.

"This is Rocky here. Tonight he's wearing a gold lamé jock strap and a feather up his bottom, and he's gonna stand on the piano and do his impersonation of the sinking of the Titanic. Thank you! We're gonna do two songs written by Rocky. They need no introduction so we're not gonna give them any," Keith announces cryptically.

It takes this audience a full four bars to realize what Keith's playing and they offer a ripple of applause. Both "Jeremy Bender" and "The Sheriff" are competently done as light relief, though Keith and Carl continue to make the ragtime coda their own as Keith quips "A little bit of jollity there!".

No introduction again for "Take A Pebble", with Keith adding more new phrases to the legendary piano solo leading up to Greg's spot. The counterpoint technique of Keith fading out on the strings as Greg comes in on the acoustic has an almost out of tune childish feel about it. The richness of Greg's voice is what makes "Still ... You Turn Me On" such a moving piece, even at this stage of its development with a different chord structure and experimental vocals every night; here, it's got an almost a Dylan-meets-the-Byrds feel about it, the crowd warm to it and he gets a genuine ovation before "Lucky Man", fusing into applause for the song itself, a true classic of its time.

In its strange place in the set list, "Hoedown" gets by far the biggest cheer of the night, played at the furious pace we will hear on future tours, and it further enlivens an already vocal audience as Keith begins "Pictures ..." They play like men possessed and they're loving it.

There is no record of "Toccata" being played, although they must have done it as an encore.

A competent show, not in the best of locations, but all the more successful for the way ELP seduce their audience by moving effortlessly between aggressive prog, ballad, and ragtime to switch the emphasis.

WEDNESDAY, 18 APRIL 1973

The Scandinavium, Gothenburg, Sweden.

Tickets: Kr.20,-

ELP's Swedish debut and so it's a pity that only a partial recording of this one has survived.

Keith tries out the Moog voice for the opener of "Karn Evil 9: 1st Impression" and tells everybody "That's disastrous!" and then "Got some new numbers to play for you. Haven't got titles for 'em yet!"

The usual organ intro to the "1st Impression" is so quiet but this number has changed. A cowbell beats time during each vocal line, drum fills aplenty, and Greg's voice is noticeably more aggressive, more dramatic: they've given the piece a bit more 'ooomph' and it's worked.

The whole thing is much more akin to the version that will end up on vinyl. That mind-boggling string of seventeen *glissandos* from Keith is there, adding to the thrills and shocks of the second half.

"Tarkus" is taken at full tilt, but more controlled and more effective for it: swirling organ melodies, clear, precise drum fills, and confidently-handled vocals make this a version they can be proud of.

The show-stopper tonight is "Aquatarkus", driven along by martial drumming and so close to the *Welcome Back My Friends To The Show That Never Ends* live album version. Even as Carl plays the 4/4 time slower middle section, he embellishes and fills with consummate skill, never a musician to sit back and play it by the book

"Jeremy Bender" fair bounces along after a lively opening on the electric piano from Keith, a much stronger version than of late and one of those where the humorous energy of the ragtime ending doesn't embarrass what's gone before. All in all, a nice medley, done to perfection, and obviously to the liking of this Swedish audience as they cheer and foot-stomp after it.

"Take A Pebble", apart from a bout of the terrible feedbacks, is a first-class version. Greg's vocals are richer than ever, warming, gentle and filling the arena. "Still ... You Turn Me On" is admirably well received and, although still not an officially recorded song, is clearly growing in stature in its own right as a live piece. In keeping with this tour, the melody and words are different again but fits well with the overall mood of the song.

Again, there's a whiff of "Closer To Believing" in its earliest developmental, instrumental form. We know that the piece was penned by Greg and Pete Sinfield [lyricist *par excellence* who wrote the words for *In The Court Of The Crimson King* on which Greg played bass and sang] around this time, and that ELP had a track record of trying out pieces long before they were recorded. It's a major success tonight as this crowd clap along enthusiastically.

They're in excellent form at this show and so appreciated by this audience: a real pity that no further tracks have survived.

SATURDAY, 21 APRIL 1973

Oude Rai, Amsterdam, The Netherlands.

Not too many power failures at ELP shows but today, the "Bolero" is played in total darkness, other than a few tiny red lights from the amps.

Before "Karn Evil 9: 1st Impression", Greg asked the inevitable question, "Anybody got a match?", and, as if by magic, all the hall lights come up. A brief interval to make sure the problem is fixed and the band continue the show in their inimitably professional way.

TUESDAY, 24 APRIL 1973

The Olympiahalle, Munich, Germany.

Tickets: DM 15,30

Although not the best of venues acoustically, it was another very commendable show. Yet again only a few of the tracks played have made it to the present day.

"Tarkus" bears evidence to one of the truisms of ELP: that familiarity never breeds contempt. It's creatively played and is the perfect showcase for the individual and collective skills of this band. Vocal ad-libs at the end show that Greg is grooving. In his solo acoustic spot, there's a nice pause before he starts the "Every blade is sharp" lines, setting the mood in just the right way. The verse from "Epitaph" and the guitar coda win applause and cheers, and justifiably so.

Some shouts of 'Yeah!' from Greg as they launch into "Aquatarkus". This section starts fast, slows down, then speeds up again, all the time coming back to repeats of the main "Tarkus" theme before reaching the inevitable climax.

"We've got some new stuff to play you. I don't know what the name of this one is," confesses Keith.

We, with hindsight, do. "Karn Evil 9: 1st Impression" begins quietly before the rhythm section give it the kick it needs and they're off into a rip-roaring version. Tonight's vocals are near-shouted, a combination of aggression and despair, given the subject nature of the lyrics.

"Welcome Back My Friends" gets some applause even though the crowd have never heard it before – a promising omen. The two main solos are all-powerful, uplifting and hopeful when compared to the mood of despair in the first part of the piece, and under-pinned by some simply stunning drumming. No wonder it's so well applauded.

Keith introduces the next thing: "Bringing on Rocky now. Tonight he's wearing reinforced concrete socks and a star-spangled jockstrap. He does a few numbers himself actually." (Keyboard fanfare)

The opening bars of "Jeremy Bender" earn applause and the rest of the medley is reasonably, if uninspiringly, played as the evening's light relief.

The segue into "The Sheriff" is messy, Greg completely misses the cue for the first verse and they have to do the rounds again so he can catch up. When the ragtime bit kicks in, however, Carl and Keith admirably salvage what they can and deserve every bit of the applause.

The sound gremlins are at work as the opening bars of "Take A Pebble" are marred by feedback. Not to be outdone by this, or the missed cue in the "The Sheriff", Greg is in his element and his vocals are spot on. This is surely one of the best-ever opening solos in "Pebble" from Keith, as he flies across the grand piano in a note-perfect solo, fading out nicely for Greg to step up with "Still … You Turn Me On".

As Greg plays a much shorter coda, the sheer quality of the piece goes down well, and with the crowd just about to cheer wildly, he plays the opening chords of "Lucky Man" and it brings the house down

Probably not their best performance on this tour, but everyone seems satisfied.

WEDNESDAY, 25 APRIL 1973

The Konzerthaus, Vienna, Austria

The first of two nights at the venue and again Vienna took the band to its heart

They have dropped "Abaddon's Bolero" altogether by this stage of the tour and they go straight in with a well-applauded and well-executed version of "Tarkus". Always a band that can be proud of their sound system, a prominent feature of this tour is the all-over quality of the sound in an increasingly technical set, and "Tarkus" is the perfect way to let the crowd know what they're in for as it shows off their equipment to best advantage.

"Aquatarkus" completes the piece and pretty much follows the formula with plenty of improvisation from all three, leading up to the big ending.

The unmistakeable (to us, now) organ counterpoint marks the beginning of "Karn Evil 9: 1ˢᵗ Impression", and the echo in this hall adds to the atmosphere of this new and increasingly epic piece. The level of excitement builds throughout with plenty of powerful playing by all of them, particularly some solid supportive bass from Greg behind Keith's strong solo flight on the Moog.

The guys seem happier with the "Jeremy Bender"/"Sheriff" medley tonight: it's tighter, better-played and everyone's on cue. The contrast with the epic qualities of "Karn Evil 9" couldn't be greater but it sits so well at this point in the set after the seriousness, despair, and then hope of the previous number. It's followed by long and loud applause, whistles and audible laughter. This version was rightly included on the official live album, *Welcome Back My Friends To The Show That Never Ends.*

By the time "Take A Pebble" gets going, the excitement of a few moments ago has died down and, apart from a few hecklers, the crowd are all ears as they begin the classic from the first album, which at 25 minutes is exactly double the length of the recorded version. This rendition is fluent and precise, taken at just the right pace for a beautiful piano solo from Keith that leads into a stunning "Still … You Turn Me On".

The mesmeric quality of this one holds sway as Greg sings to a completely silent audience, his voice filling the hall. He's dropped the final sing-and-clap-along section and the acoustic coda is just a four bar slow fade-out before he quietly picks up the "Lucky Man" melody – much to the delight of this crowd. As Keith comes in on the grand, tastefully and understated, the audience have quietened down and actually clap along in time with this one. There's a rarity!

Keith gives Greg a well-deserved credit before launching into the *portamento* whoops of "Hoedown"; one classic following another. They might have changed its place in the set, but Keith is still very much on top of his game with the Hammond solo.

An excellent run through of "Pictures ..." closes the main set, the changes in tempo, mood and atmosphere still enthralling the near-silent crowd. The organ throwing has barely an effect on this quiet-as-a-mouse audience as Keith forces weird and wonderful noises from the L100 and, as Greg and Carl come back in, the tension builds to its dramatic conclusion. A novel way to end both the piece and the set itself.

The encore of "Toccata" is so unfamiliar that, as is to be expected, it starts to almost complete silence from the crowd. Keith works expertly on the main theme, on both organ and Moog, leading into a work of art solo from Carl. Beginning on the tympani, bringing in first tubular bells, then gongs, then the rest of the kit, he builds a sound picture that's truly musical in its own right. The audience participation part goes down a treat, with first the bass drum patterns, and then the watch-me-play-the-bell-with-my-teeth bit, before he sets the pace for a resounding "Rondo", a true show-stopper if ever there was one.

It's fast, incredibly fast, heading for a crashing finale from a band that doesn't know what it means to pull its punches.

WEDNESDAY, 2 MAY 1973

Stadio Flaminio, Rome, Italy

Tickets: L 1,500 in advance; 2,000 on the night

"OK, it's not gonna rain any more. We've just telephoned the Vatican and it's cool," joked Keith.

An unusually hesitant start to the opener, "Tarkus", on this, the twentieth show of the tour, but they're soon in their stride with a version that goes down a storm, Carl driving things along like a man possessed.

The free improvisational synthesizer section of "Aquatarkus" is beginning to sound very like the version on *Welcome Back My Friends To The Show That Never Ends*, with the rhythm bubbling away underneath. The lengthy applause starts long before the final fanfare has even begun.

The impact of the opening to "Karn Evil 9: 1st Impression", is not lost on this crowd, who give an immediate round of applause and cheers. Once again, as so often with the *Brain Salad Surgery* material on this tour, Greg sings slightly different lyrics each night and is obviously having fun – the throw-away 'Woo, yeah, alright baby' appears several times. Carl? He just nails the whole thing down in a way that only he can.

Rocky gets his name-check (as he sets up the electric piano) from Keith before the comedy medley. Keith, sticking to English, explains all about Rocky tap-dancing to "We'll Keep A Welcome In The Hillsides", and introduces him actually playing four bars of "Nutrocker", much to the obvious delight of this crowd. The fact that most of what he says seems to be totally lost on them is ... well ... lost on Mr Emerson. The applause and cheers are for "Nutrocker".

The medley itself is a bit faster, and a bit livelier, than previously, but it goes down well despite Keith getting his fingers caught up during the solo parts. "The Sheriff" in particular is well received, the loudest applause reserved for the ragtime ending.

No introduction as such for "Take A Pebble" and only a polite ripple of applause greets Greg's opening lines. It's an excellent run-through, Keith coming up with a classic performance of his solo parts with more than a hint of older Nice material still there.

Greg's acoustic spot is just that: spot on, and he earns himself some generous applause, especially remembering that "Still ... You Turn Me On", as an unrecorded track, has to stand on its own merits. It's now much shorter than earlier on the tour, the extended clap-along and acoustic coda parts have been dropped. "Lucky Man" is quickly acquiring classic status and it's obvious from Greg's phrasing and vocal improvisations that he feels totally comfortable and confident with the piece, still accompanied quietly by Keith.

The final sections of this piece are as spell-binding as ever: variations on a theme, immaculately played and driven along by a mix of Keith's left hand *ostinato* rhythm and Carl's delicate drumming.

On this tour, "Hoedown" is taken at an increasingly manic speed as Keith and Greg keep up with a slave-driving Carl, powering his way through the piece. The solo is a true flight of improvisation on organ and Moog, shorter than on previous tours, but probably packing more of a punch because of it.

It's definitely the night of few words tonight as, yet again, another classic is played with no introduction as they give a stirring rendition of "Pictures ...", by this stage of the tour hovering around the seventeen or eighteen minute mark, consistently longer than when they first played the shortened version.

"Toccata" is fast becoming a live masterpiece, reserved for the encore but earning its soon-to-be promotion to a higher ranking in the set list. It's masterfully played, Keith shining on Hammond and Moog before handing over to Carl. From quiet bells and hi-hat to thunderous tympani and crashing gongs, Carl entertains musically as well as showing his skill, and again earns loud applause and calls of "Bravo!".

The return of Keith and Greg sees them hurtle into "Rondo" at an incredible speed like a bobsleigh run. It's now cut to a little over five minutes but what a five minutes! The keyboard solo starts on the synth, moves to the Hammond and is full of sweeping *glissandos*, siren wails and screeches.

"Thank you, goodnight! Carl Palmer... Greg Lake," shouts Keith crediting the others and, as the outro plays, that's it. The crowd are cheering for more but already the guys are back in the dressing room being helped out of sweat-soaked outfits, and ready for the off.

With or without help from the Vatican, a divine show.

THURSDAY, 3 MAY 1973

Stadio Comunale, Bologna, Italy

Tickets: L 1,500 in advance; 2,000 on the night

Another rescheduled gig after Greg's ill health, the penultimate show of the tour, which was surely one of the very best of this trip. Greg's recovery after his throat problems seemed to revitalize the whole band.

They've certainly cranked up the pace in "Tarkus" and it shows. There's plenty of bass from both Greg and Keith, helping to give it more of a powerful, heavy feel. Just how fast this is now played is more noticeable when Greg comes in on "Stones Of Years". Carl powers it along some more, Greg shouting 'Yeah!' in the background. For some reason, there is no "Epitaph" tonight, just a delicately-played coda leading into a magnificent "Aquatarkus".

The usual Moog tuning and then they launch into "Karn Evil 9: 1st Impression", Greg's vocals echoing round the stadium. In the 'thrills and shocks' bit, the echo on Greg's vocals gives it an even more authentic circus ringmaster feel, especially on the "Roll up, Roll up!" lines. The long electric solo is well delivered and leads into a Part 2 that benefits from some dominant, heavy bass power chords.

He then riffs away like mad on the twin-neck, behind a first-rate solo from Keith, before the two switch roles and Greg pulls off yet another showcase solo. From the first note to the last, Carl never lets up with drum work that proves why he is about to take yet another award in *Melody Maker*'s Polls.

After Rocky's nightly bars of "Nutrocker", Keith gives the comedy introduction to "Jeremy Bender"/"The Sheriff" but it goes down like a lead balloon: "We'd like to play you two numbers, one of which is called 'She sits among the cabbages and peas (pees)', and the other one is 'They call my sister biscuit because she's been away for (a wafer) so long'." Let's face it, English audiences might have trouble with those old music hall gags! The songs themselves get far more by way of cheers.

A 25 minute version of "Take A Pebble" then follows, taken at a stately pace. As Keith tinkles away quietly, Greg picks out the twelve string melody to "Still … You Turn Me On". This moving version gets no initial reaction at all from the crowd but a polite wave of applause at the end. Prolonged tuning up, then the first chords of "Lucky Man" prove what fine voice Greg's in tonight.

Keith's extended solo and the jazz interlude see new deviations to the regular format to keep the piece fresh. At times this crowd have seemed well up for it, but they are certainly sitting on their hands during this second half of a classic piece – a pity since all three work hard and produce some nifty playing. "The Sheriff" makes a welcome return to the jazz improvisation in the way Keith and Carl play off each other, and then the reprise benefits so much from the bassy feel to the sound, adding still more richness and texture to that superb voice.

From the magnificent ending of "Take A Pebble", they go straight into the frenetic liveliness of "Hoedown". For all its speed, every drum beat, every bass drum kick, every touch of the ivories and every guitar note is audible as Keith goes completely off-the-wall for the solo before Carl speeds things up yet more for the final headlong charge.

"Pictures ..." sees Keith in top form. The organ part at the beginning of "Great Gates ..." is totally different here, and the rest of it is taken at a faster pace than usual with the result that although there's nothing wrong with it, it doesn't quite have the usual 'finale' impact as they build towards the huge ending.

The encore, after lengthy cheers and calls for more, is a 25 minute version of "Toccata"/"Rondo" that seriously rocks. The first part is surprisingly close to the eventual album recording and Carl's solo, taking sixteen minutes of a nineteen minute number, which proves how fit this man is. It incorporates everything that worked from earlier solos with his newest interpretation of Ginastera's work.

As they close the whole thing with a rip-roaring, belting "Rondo", everyone seems to have got up off their hands and ELP leave the stage to loud cheers and demands for more.

FRIDAY, 4 MAY 1973

Velodromo Vigorelli, Milan, Italy

It's a case of third time lucky in playing this venue, as ELP needed to cancel on the 28 and 30 April because of poor weather and Greg's illness.

Tonight they come out to an audience of 50,000 – more than three times the promoter's prediction – and as the double curtains pull back, ELP go straight into "Tarkus", a stonking way to start what would be their last show for six months.

It might be the last night of the tour, but there are no signs of battle fatigue. Keith time and again throws in extra licks and phrases, Carl all the time pushing things onwards and upwards, Greg dominating vocally. The honours again go to

"Battlefield": it's restrained, dramatic and the swirling Hammond is the perfect backdrop to the message of the lyrics. "Epitaph" makes a welcome return and is well received.

After the impressive "Aquatarkus", it's over to Keith for some Moog twiddling and, as he plays the organ intro to "Karn Evil 9: 1ˢᵗ Impression", Greg shouts "here we go!". Interestingly, for the first time the lines of the opening verses are sung without any accompaniment, increasing the sense of despair and drama as Greg's voice reverberates around this cycle stadium. It's stirring stuff!

The echo on the vocals, because of the stadium's acoustics, again works to the advantage of the band in the "Roll up, Roll up!" circus section, followed by an uplifting solo from Greg on the twin-neck, and a "Whooo!" as the Moog takes us into Part 2.

Keith introduces Rocky and the "Bender"/"Sheriff" medley with the same *double entendre* lines as last night, and then it's into a slightly muddier version of the two light-hearted songs. True to form, "The Sheriff" is the one that takes the applause.

"Take A Pebble" is restrained, serious and dominated by Greg's vocals and Keith's piano work. "Still … You Turn Me On", on the twelve string, seems more beautiful and heartfelt every night, even if he does, as tonight, sing some of the verses twice.

Before he plays out the coda, Greg is obviously aware of some problem in the crowd and shouts: "You big noisy fucker!" winning immediate applause. "Lucky Man", on the wonderful sounding mother-of-pearl inlaid acoustic, is excellent and clearly whatever problems there are don't put him off his stride. The piano and tambourine backing are still there, understated as always and more effective for it.

"Hoedown", as an instrumental break between two classics, works well: it's so fast, really swings along and every note is crystal clear. After a quick "Thank you!" from Greg, it's into "Promenade" with gusto, although the cheers are so loud that at times the Hammond is barely audible. Keith uses the lower manual in particular to give the whole piece a kick with extra bass lines.

It's a pity that, as "Pictures …" unfolds, the noise from sections of the crowd gets louder and louder and very nearly disrupts the piece – until the organ throwing, where Keith makes sure the odds are even by forcing unheard-of noises from the Moog.

This unruly but appreciative crowd want more, and they get the final version of "Toccata" on this tour: a superb encore that demands and gets their attention from the off. Carl produces a no-holds-barred solo that's a fantastic showcase for his skills, using every part of the kit.

A perfect way to end a tour that will undoubtedly win them yet more support on the European circuit.

12. *We've Got Thrills And Shocks ...*

14 NOVEMBER – 18 DECEMBER 1973: FIFTH NORTH AMERICAN TOUR.
THE BRAIN SALAD SURGERY US TOUR.
31 SHOWS.

Typical set list:	"Tarkus", "Karn Evil 9: 1st Impression Part 2", "Benny The Bouncer", "Take A Pebble", "Still ... You Turn Me On", "Lucky Man", piano improvisations, "Take A Pebble" reprise, "Hoedown", "Pictures At An Exhibition".
Keith:	As for previous tour, plus the Constellation, consisting of the Apollo, the prototype of what was to become the Polymoog, a monophonic instrument known as the Lyra, and the Taurus bass pedals. Total now of eight custom built Moog keyboards.
Greg:	Zemaitis custom made guitars as on previous tour plus an Alembic bass.
Carl:	£4,000 stainless steel drum kit on an 11ft diameter, Perspex-sided, rotating riser operated with a motor with top speed of 50 mph. It consisted of: 28" bass drum; 6", 8", 10", 12", 13", 14", 15" and 16" single headed toms; 18" single headed floor tom; Ludwig 14" x 3.5" snare; 24" medium ride, 16" heavy ride, 20" crash/ride, 22" crash, 22" china type, 7.5" splash, and 7", 5", 4", 3" and 2" cymbals; 26" and 29" Ludwig symphonic tympani; octave and a half of tubular bells; 50" and 38" Paiste gongs; temple blocks; camel bells; vibraslap; ratchet; violin bow; large triangle; cymbal and chain in a bucket; 134lb church bell (initialled 'CP') suspended above his head; drum synthesizer (one of the first ever electronic drums).
PA system:	30 channel quadraphonic system with 32 speaker bins in the stacks. 36 tons of it in total.

The first part of a 'split' tour of North America that ran in its entirety from November 1973 to April 1974 saw ELP at the very peak of their success.

The stage show that hit North America in autumn 1973 featured a Shinto-style temple proscenium to frame the action. Above centre stage was a circular screen with the *Brain Salad Surgery* symbol on it.

The band hit the continent with at least 45 roadies each night – 30 of their own plus at least fifteen local union guys – to look after equipment worth an estimated $750,000.

The band were working with a new lighting company who would complement the music with special effects.

This tour was the big try-out tour for the *Brain Salad Surgery* material: "Jerusalem", the complete "Karn Evil 9", "Toccata" (now moved into the main set instead of being an encore), "Benny The Bouncer", and "Still … You Turn Me On" (no longer part of the acoustic break in "Take A Pebble") all featured in the 'new' part of the set.

However, the band were well aware of the need for a balanced set of new and old material, as Greg pointed out to me:

> That was because Don Strike, me and Robert Fripp's guitar teacher, used to have the saying, which he taught me, which was, "Five for them and one for you", and it was from the Big Band days when they had a list of songs to play. I never forgot that, and when it came to introducing new material. If you start slaughtering people with 45 minutes or an hour of completely new material they feel betrayed because they came to hear the records they know and love. You've got to balance it so that there's enough new things to keep it fresh but not so much as to become an exercise in ground-breaking discovery.

Carl's complete drum rostrum weighed in at about two and a half tons and was housed on a wheeled frame so that roadies could more easily move it in place each night. It had its own light display with Perspex drum sides in consequence. The gongs were decorated with a dragon's head on one side and its body on the other, so that when strobes shone onto the gongs it gave the dragon the appearance of movement. The whole thing had a Shinto-style frame above it which span round to add to the effect: stunning when the lights and strobes were on. The spinning, incidentally, was roadie-powered, not machine-driven. The bass drum was reputedly so heavy that it had to be moved with a forklift.

At the height of their career here, ELP now had the perfect setting to communicate the raw energy of their music.

Sadly, not too many of these extravaganzas have survived for posterity.

WEDNESDAY, 14 NOVEMBER 1973

The Hollywood Sportatorium, FL, USA.

This, the opening night, set the high standard for the rest of the tour.

They open with "Jerusalem" and, so close to the release of the album, it follows the studio version almost to the note. It doesn't have the kick of "Hoedown" but it's delivered to perfection and gets a polite ripple of applause.

"Toccata" has changed noticeably since the spring tour of Europe and now also follows the finished studio version surprisingly closely. Each time Carl plays the tubular bells he gets cheers and applause and, as he hits the drum sequencer with the recurring pattern of fourteen notes as the background for the main part of the solo, the crowd are stunned into silent admiration. All this as he revolves the full 360°, strobes going off, the works. It's powerful stuff and benefits from the quad sound system.

Keith gives Carl a well-earned credit before introducing the newer material: "We're gonna be playing some numbers which you may not be familiar with, and we're not familiar with 'em either! That was two tracks from *Brain Salad Surgery*, "Jerusalem" and "Toccata". Here's Greg Lake."

"Still ... You Turn Me On" is at the finished stage after being developed on and off the road from the beginning of the year. Some of the playing on the twelve string is totally different from the recorded version, and the overall feel of the piece is confident, romantic and plaintive – and it works incredibly well live as evidenced by the whistles and cheers as the final notes fade away.

"Hoedown" is as infectious as ever and played at a cracking pace, Keith excelling over the top of such a tight rhythm section. This oldie is superb and the next one is even better.

"Tarkus" has evolved since the Spring tour. The stop-start element of the solo in "Mass" is still there, but it's beefed-up, and the organ intro before the Moog comes in is ELP at their best (and recognized as such by the cheering crowd). The way "Manticore" sets up Greg's "Battlefield" is classic. The guitar solo is a pleasure to behold, the "Every blade is sharp" bit set up so well by Keith with a fading Moog bass note, and although he's dropped the verse from "Epitaph" (again), it comes across beautifully.

In "Aquatarkus", we've now got the template for the remainder of 1973 and 1974: a loose variation on a theme, going into a free improvised synthesizer section. Keith quotes freely from a number of pieces, including the Beatles' "Norwegian Wood", before coming back to the main theme and those grand final chords.

Greg gets into vocal character for his East End role-playing in "Benny The Bouncer". It might be another of their comedic, more light-hearted pieces, but it's lively, entertaining and a vote-winner, coming as it does between two ELP heavyweights.

Courtesy of Gudrun Friedrich.

The light, delicate work in the opening part of "Take A Pebble" is delightful and this audience know class when they hear it. Greg's simple, heartfelt performance of "Lucky Man" too draws loud and deserved applause, before Keith resumes the piano work. By now, Gulda's "Prelude and Fugue" is a standard element of his main improvisation, played fast and accurately. "Little Rock Getaway" is hard-driven and, despite the speed of the playing, is spot on. Keith's left-hand *ostinato* technique makes it sound all the heavier.

The epic that follows is one to rival "Pictures ..." in its entirety: "Karn Evil 9" is without a doubt the main event of the evening and it closely follows the recorded album version. The "1st Impression" is a thundering example of this band at their best: despair, aggression and hope both in the lyrics, and in the sheer power of the Hammond and the lead guitar.

The 'thrills and shocks' now seems an even more celebratory reaction to the initial story of a loss of humanity and Greg plays his part as circus ringmaster with aplomb. Towards the end of the "1ˢᵗ Impression", Carl is featured in a short but explosive drum solo that gets loud cheers.

The entirely instrumental "2ⁿᵈ Impression" takes us back to some precise, trio work. Keith's Moog steel drum solo, over the top of an incredibly strong, bubbling rhythm from the others, is an effective contrast to the piano and bass themes and phrases that follow.

In the final part of this "2ⁿᵈ Impression", it's nice to hear Greg's bass in such deliberate detail as he duets with Keith before Carl comes in for the jazz-like section that takes us into the "3ʳᵈ Impression". The vocals tell us of man's efforts to win back his identity but it's the computer that wins in the end – metaphorically and literally. This piece crowns a superb performance in every sense: Hammond and Moog swing from hopeful to menacing, skilfully backed by a powerful rhythm, until the computer sprouts wings and trundles to the front of the stage as ELP leave it.

As the words "I'm perfect, are you?" echo around the arena, smoke floods Keith's side of the stage, and the final repeating notes accelerate and reverberate quadraphonically. No sudden, crashing explosion as yet but the impact is immediate: this crowd go wild and bring the band back for a majestic "Pictures ..." as an encore.

How many bands could get away with something as ambitious as this suite for an encore? Well ELP can and do. Some subtle changes to the drum and organ parts in "Baba Yaga" are nicely done, Carl filling well on the new kit, and "The Great Gates ..." gets this enthusiastic crowd on their feet after the huge ending.

Hollywood loves dreams and the cheers go on long after the outro music has died away.

TUESDAY, 4 DECEMBER 1973

The Cobo Hall, Detroit, MI, USA.

Not quite the full show has survived from the Cobo Hall, but still clearly a worthy performance.

By this point, the eighteenth show, they've reverted to opening with "Hoedown", infectious and exciting as it is, and played at a lick. Keith flies through the solo as Carl drives everything along. The well-oiled machine that is "Tarkus" gets under way. There's something of an echo in the Cobo Hall that adds a haunting quality to some of the Hammond-heavy sections, and most of "Tarkus" benefits from it. "Mass" is taken with confidence at some speed, Greg having to rush a bit to get the lines out. The ribbon controller solo is just as exciting and mesmerizing as ever, manic as Keith strolls around the stage. If anything, the tempo picks up and, with plenty of improvisation from Keith in "Manticore" to add some interest,

"Aquatarkus" gives the guys a chance to stretch out musically with Keith on top form. Carl sets the rhythm and the pace for a dreamy free-form Moog solo, each one of them picking up their cues as we'd expect from this band.

"Gonna give you some *Brain Salad Surgery* now, starting with 'Jerusalem', and then a piece called 'Toccata' which features Carl on his synthesized drums," Keith tells the audience.

"Jerusalem" now seems much better placed at this point in the proceedings; the opener to the *Brain Salad Surgery* material, just as it is on the album. Despite following the album template very closely, it has bags more energy and finishes magnificently, going immediately into "Toccata".

Nominally the showcase for Carl, the first half features Keith heavily on synth before the drum solo commences. It's focused on the tympani and tubular bells, dramatic throughout, and skilfully based on the original themes. There are some nice exchanges with keys and guitar, and the closing band sequence is impressive.

A strong version of the "1st Impression" of "Karn Evil 9" has survived, and it's becoming more well-honed each night, with excellent, moving Moog, organ and guitar solos. It's played with increasing confidence, Carl putting the new snare and toms through their paces.

No other tracks remain – a pity since those that do show all the hallmarks that suggest this was a show to remember.

FRIDAY, 7 DECEMBER 1973

The Maple Leaf Gardens, Toronto, Canada.

This enthusiastic audience were up for it from the word go and the guys kicked off with an accelerated "Hoedown" The powerhouse that is Carl Palmer drove it along, aided and abetted by Greg, and Keith turns in a stunning and imaginative Moog solo to wild applause.

Keith introduces "... some *Brain Salad Surgery*". Opening this section with a belting version of "Jerusalem", Greg's vocals standing out head and shoulders above the others, they then go straight into the Moog and tympani intro to "Toccata".

It's immaculately performed, at just the right pace, with not a sign of haste so that the pauses have the right effect. Keith goes to town in the best possible way on both organ and Moog and, on this version, Greg's bass is superb, holding the whole thing together. A wave of applause, whistles and cheers greets Carl's solo – full of variety, musical patterns and sheer energy as he thunders round the revolving kit above the recurring rhythm of the Moog drum. The strobes add to the visuals but it's still a showcase for tuned percussion if ever there was one.

"You can twiddle your knobs while I twiddle mine," jokes Keith, the king of the *double entendres*.

"Tarkus", the first epic of the night, is applauded from the off. Carl's new kit adds a new edge to the sound of this piece as he fills to his heart's content. The vocals are right at the top of the mix again, underpinned by some sweet melody playing from Keith. His Hammond solo in "Stones Of Years" is downright funky, slightly off the wall for ELP, but they're having fun.

"Battlefield" and "Aquatarkus" share the honours as the crowning glory of the 'oldie' section. "Epitaph" is featured tonight and gets a brief, if slightly wild, round of applause.

Back to the new material and "Benny The Bouncer" is a showcase for the newest weapon in the Emerson armoury, the prototype Polymoog. Greg's East End of London character voice is coming along nicely, the playing is apt and it's a well above average version with some lively honky tonk at the end.

"Take A Pebble" is followed by "Still … You Turn Me On". The twelve string gives it a distinctive sound and it wins plenty of applause that is still going on as he starts "Lucky Man". The cheers for this one last for the entire first verse and, perhaps lifted by the crowd, Greg, accompanied lightly by Keith on piano, gives an excellent performance.

Keith then gives the audience the low down on one of the new numbers from the just released new album:

> "Karn Evil 9" takes up most of *Brain Salad Surgery* and consists of three "Impressions" which each have a different meaning. The "1st Impression" has a statement and a reaction to this statement. The statement, you have to listen to the words to find out what it's all about. There's an interval, the "2nd Impression". The "3rd Impression" deals with the evolution of creativity, very heavy stuff there, starting with the Stone Age, going right through the Iron Age up to where we are now, with computers and things, and the answer's all up to you, rock'n'roll. "Karn Evil 9!"

The whole thing is very close to the recorded version and the organ counterpoint that opens the "1st Impression" sets the standard: loud, powerful, exciting and played perfectly. If anything, the guys have ever so slightly slowed the whole piece down to a statelier pace, giving the listener more time to catch every nuance of the vocals, every note of the instruments. There's a clear change of mood between the 'suffering in silence' bit and the 'thrills and shocks' circus part, evidenced by Keith's keyboards, and a move from plaintive to bold and brassy from Greg.

Carl's four minute solo pushes the total time for the "1st Impression" to almost eighteen minutes. He gets a fantastic reaction from the crowd as his riser spins, he tugs on the bell-rope with his mouth and races furiously round the rest of the kit.

The often quiet, thoughtful, duo and then trio work in the "2ⁿᵈ Impression" provides a stunning contrast with the action that has just been witnessed. A series of abstract pieces, it makes a nice bridge between the two longer and more dramatic sections. The steel drum solo on the Moog stands out and is well received.

Carl drives the "3ʳᵈ Impression" towards the huge climax, the final domination of man by the computer. The "boom" from the stage was as if the Moog itself had just exploded. The live production on this piece, the climax of the main show, is just magnificent and they deserve every one of the thousands of cheers and demands for more.

As a piece of stage theatre, will that moving, talking computer, 'arms' flapping, smoke bellowing, ever be beaten?

"Pictures ..." as an encore is powerful stuff. "The Great Gates ..." has expanded to nearly ten minutes in its own right as the organ-throwing bit gets longer and more involved, and is worth every second, still as full of drama and weightiness as it was in the early days of 1970.

The crowd love it. Only ten shows left now.

MONDAY, 10 DECEMBER 1973

Boston Gardens, Boston, MA, USA.

Show 23. ELP were well into their stride, and the tour was going down a storm across North America. There's no doubt that the band's approach to introducing new material, integrating it carefully with time-honoured classics that people wanted to hear, was the right approach.

Some all-round tuning, a quick intro from an MC, and they're into "Hoedown". Not quite as fast as some recent renditions but spot on, lively, exciting and it certainly gets the audience going.

An astounding improvised Moog solo, complete with Scottish jig, and Keith's already earned his money for the night.

The first slice of *Brain Salad Surgery* material is introduced by Greg and "Jerusalem" seems to sound more and more majestic as the tour progresses. The vocals are even higher in the mix than usual, clear, precise and rich baritone sound wonderful on the old English hymn.

The coupling of "Jerusalem" and Ginastera's "Toccata" works well, the slight eeriness of the latter's intro in clever contrast to the full-on trio effort of the hymn. The instrumental works well, full of drama in both synth and drum parts, and with Greg proving just how good a bass player he is as he provides the bridge between some of the elements.

More Moog tuning, then "Tarkus" and it's a very solid-sounding version. "Battlefield" still sounds fresh and sharp, with its powerful but delicate organ, and Greg is on fire in the first solo. The "Every blade is sharp" part is delivered with real soulful emotion,

Keith introduces "Benny The Bouncer" as being in the cockney vernacular and Greg gets into character straight away. Keith even adds an extra honky tonk piano break, as might be heard in an East End boozer, after a false ending, and the crowd love it.

"Take A Pebble" is crisp, rich and full of poise. The first verses are textbook, Keith's break is imaginative, and Greg plays a moving version of "Still ... You Turn Me On", the song now well established in the set. "Lucky Man" receives its customary wild welcome.

Everything is just right in Keith's long solo, and the jazz trio bit shows a good time being had by all three; Carl filling in everywhere, with Greg keeping it all together. Keith ventures off into "Jingle Bells" at one point, before giving a few bars of "Daisy Daisy" and some silent cinema music. The ending is stirring, emotional stuff, Greg sustaining some dramatic notes in the final verse.

"Pebble" now stretches to almost 27 minutes and it's worth every penny as the applause from this audience demonstrates.

The 36 minutes of "Karn Evil 9", the closing epic, is still a touch slower than earlier on the tour and features top notch soloing and melody work from all three. Keith's Hammond and Greg's electric six string work in the 2nd Part are particularly impressive preceding, as they do, a short furious, thunderous solo from Carl. The new kit really comes into its own here with its tonal qualities, and he wins still more applause with the gongs and bells.

Barely has this died down before they launch the "2nd Impression", the instrumental intermission before the climax of the piece. The steel drum solo on the Moog really stands out, as does the abstract, moody duet between bass and grand piano.

The running battle between man and computer in the "3rd Impression" is well represented musically, with plenty of imagery in the ballsy Hammond, driven along by martial drumming from Carl and fuzz pedal bass from Greg, whose vocals sit so well above the melody of the organ. The computer has the last word, the sound echoing and reverberating around the arena as smoke fills the stage, ELP disappear, and there's the beginnings of the explosion that marked later versions.

Shouts of "Oh wow!" greet "Promenade", the opening to a storming and thundering "Pictures ...". "Great Gates ..." includes one of the longest, most off-the-wall organ throwing bits Keith has ever done, topped off with a weird and wonderful free-form synth solo before returning to the main theme. It gets them lengthy, loud and well-deserved applause.

Another audience go home, clinging to their souvenirs and mementos of the evening.

THURSDAY, 13 DECEMBER 1973

Nassau Coliseum, Uniondale, NY, USA.

Nearing the tour's end, but with this band everything was just as lively, with 100% effort every night.

After a minute of organ and Moog tuning, the simple words "Emerson, Lake and Palmer!" from the MC see them tear into "Hoedown", a version that's faster than of late with Keith very high in the mix. The echo in the hall adds to the feel of the Moog solo and not surprisingly, ecstatic cries signal the crowd's approval.

Likewise, an up-tempo "Jerusalem" is still very together, a serious moment after the levity of the opener. Greg's rich vocals are just the job for this hymn and when the full band charge in, they seem in danger of bringing the house down.

"Toccata" kicks off while the crowd are still applauding and remains very textbook, the one piece of the evening where they seem reluctant to stray too far from the script. It's clearly a big favourite of this crowd though, as the applause is generous.

More brief tuning for Keith prior to "Tarkus". This prog masterpiece is different, yet the same, every night. "Aquatarkus" hits the ground running with real pace, then slows a little as the rhythm section go into that bubbling pattern over which Keith lays down a creative improvised solo, complete with "Norwegian Wood" and all his other references.

From the sublime to the ridiculous as Greg gets into character to tell the story of "Benny The Bouncer" and Savage Sid. It's funny, lively and there's some first-rate honky tonk from Keith, enthusiastically matched as ever by Carl on the brushes.

In contrast to "Take A Pebble" on earlier American tours, when the guys played it close to the script, these gigs have seen it overflow with adventurous improvisations around a framework. The bass work is full of flair and Keith solos in no-holds-barred style.

"Still ... You Turn Me On" has been a standard on this tour but for some reason no record of it exists at this show – but "Lucky Man" more than compensates for that. The roar of applause that greets the opening chords and vocals is deafening, subsiding almost immediately as this crowd are transfixed by Greg's story of the rich man gone to war.

"Karn Evil 9" is a quality version, with "2nd Impression" tonight's highlight: the close acoustic work has developed so well and the various abstract pieces fit perfectly together. Almost for the first time on this tour, there are cheers throughout the "2nd Impression" and they're well deserved.

"3rd Impression" is a powerhouse starting, as it does, with that swirling Hammond, distorted bass and fast martial snare. Vocals are a bit low in the mix but the overall mood, driven fiercely along by Carl, is unmistakeable. The ending may be the same each night, but it's inspired, full of drama and one of the most stunning finales in rock.

As the crowd go wild, Greg apologizes for the organ breaking down. When normal service is resumed, it's with an encore of "Pictures...". Maybe Keith wants to put the Hammond through its paces after the breakdown as this version is controlled – but only just – to the point where it's as if everything is about to explode with energy. The heavy, distorted bass on "Baba Yaga" makes a welcome return and gives everything a more sinister feel.

The majesty of "The Great Gates ..." never lessens, and they pull off a pretty dramatic ending: the second in a row.

A very good show with a lively, enthusiastic audience.

MONDAY 17 DECEMBER 1973

Madison Square Garden, New York, NY, USA.

Tickets: $6.50 – 7.50

The first of two nights at the Garden, known as the "Silent Night Show", and the penultimate one of an amazingly successful tour. This one has gone down in ELP folklore as a truly magical gig, reputedly the first time that Keith ever played the so-called spinning piano.

Introduced on stage by the legendary Ahmet Ertegun, the Head of Atlantic Records, as "Emerson, Lake and Mr Palmer", "Hoedown" starts with a slightly different sound to the *portamento*. Several bars in, this crowd are still cheering wildly and are definitely up for it tonight. Keith throws in a jig during the Moog solo – what the heck, it's the last venue of the tour and everyone's enjoying themselves.

The feedback they're getting from the audience inspires superb versions of "Jerusalem" and "Toccata". Carl takes the honours on the latter: his solo is full of variety, changing moods and superb rhythms as he decorates the pattern laid down on the drum synthesizer. First tympani, then tubular bells and then a blur of hands as he works the snare and the toms. The gongs, highlighted by the strobes, look fantastic as the whole drum riser slowly revolves 360°.

25 minutes of "Tarkus" follows, and Keith's on fire for the instrumentals throughout the first half of the piece. His stop-start solo in "Stones Of Years" is well improvised, but still the band are tight as hell, everyone's on cue and they all power their way through "Iconoclast" and into "Mass". The vocals sit well alongside the Moog here and, before we know it, the first of the big improvisations takes us into a rip-roaring ribbon controller solo, driven along at a furious pace by Greg and Carl.

Greg's acoustic/vocal solo is spot on, brimming with emotion as his voice resonates round the Garden. Alas, no "Epitaph" tonight but he still deserves more than the polite ripple of applause he receives. They pick up the pace nicely into "Aquatarkus", Keith turning in a belting, improvised Moog section before the bass pedals come in to signal the main solo.

Another slice of *Brain Salad Surgery* follows in the form of "Benny The Bouncer". There's no record of "Still ... You Turn Me" on, but "Take A Pebble" gets plenty of cheers and whistles. "Lucky Man" is warmly received and loud applause also fills the gap before Keith picks up the piano solo again, precise with a perfect touch. Both "Prelude" and "Fugue" and "Little Rock Getaway" sound as they should.

It's worth mentioning the first-rate drum and bass work that underpin the piano, so responsive to Keith but also both pushing him on all the time. There's even a ripple of honky tonk before the dramatic pause and *glissando* that see in the final section of the song

Keith does his, by now, usual introduction to "Karn Evil 9", and the piece starts quietly and unassumingly with a fairly low-key two manual organ counterpoint. As the whole band come in on the theme, the echo of the hall gives it a certain eeriness and haunting quality as the Hammond swirls and the Moog bounces off the rafters. Organ and guitar solos are strong, combining well everywhere, and are taken at a cracking pace as the guys go headlong into the piece. Greg's ringmaster vocals are particularly effective and set the scene for the second half of the "1st Impression".

This band are on blistering form for the instrumental "2nd Impression" and the "3rd Impression" is a real show stopper, building lyrically and musically towards the climax.

The encore, "Pictures ...", storms its way through, with the excitement of "Baba Yaga" being such that you often feel it's about to explode with energy. The "new" touches of bass pedal effects and quieter, more haunting phrases from Keith work well and things become quite manic as they bring down "The Great Gates ..." before a more stately pace takes over.

Vocals are high in the mix and echo round the rafters, accompanied by an other-worldly Hammond and understated drums. As they reach the quiet middle section, Keith playing unaccompanied organ, Carl comes in quietly on tubular bells and there's a subtle change in the melody. Greg opens with "Silent night, Holy night" in his rich baritone and the place just erupts. As he reaches the line, "Round yon Virgin, mother and child", the choir comes in, at that point standing at the back of the stage in darkness. The audience begins to realize that something magical is unfolding, the cheers rise, and then the lights come up to reveal the choir in full flow, in Christmas robes, accompanying Greg singing his heart out: surely a fairytale of New York.

Christmas comes early as it starts to snow inside the Garden. The second verse makes the hairs on the back of the neck stand on end: Greg, choir and by now most of the audience putting their all into it, and within seconds, this crowd are on their feet, cheering and clapping. A superb piece of seasonal musical theatre.

With applause still reverberating around the Garden, Keith goes into overdrive with Hammond throwing, full of sounds so reminiscent of the Karelia Suite from his days with the Nice; a second real treat for this New York crowd who are, by now, going wild with constant applause as Keith, in his element, fills the hall with his Hammond sounds.

As if that's not enough, against the backdrop of Moog sounds, he launches into some classical phrases on the grand, excerpts from Chopin's "Revolutionary Etude" as the piano is raised in the air, spinning round and round.

As Ian Dove, writing in *The New York Times*, pithily put it: "Any rock concert that starts with 'Jerusalem', William Blake's green and pleasant piece and finishes with a large mixed choir singing a not so 'Silent Night' complete with fake falling snow on the stage, cannot be accused of being average." [67]

A Merry Christmas, ELP style.

13. *Guaranteed To Blow Your Head Apart …*

24 JANUARY – 6 APRIL 1974: SIXTH NORTH AMERICAN TOUR.
34 SHOWS.

Typical set list:	"Hoedown", "Jerusalem", "Toccata", "Tarkus", "Benny The Bouncer", "Take A Pebble", "Still … You Turn Me On", "Lucky Man", piano improvisations, "Take A Pebble" (reprise), "Jeremy Bender"/"The Sheriff", "Karn Evil 9", "Pictures At An Exhibition".
Keith:	As previous tour.
Greg:	As previous tour.
Carl:	As previous tour.
PA system:	Quadraphonic as previous tour.

This was, for many people, the second half of the previous North American tour and again, sadly, very few recordings survive.

Their participation in the California Jam at the Ontario Speedway (joint headliners with Deep Purple, with Black Sabbath also on the bill as the Brits rocked North America) was kept under wraps by the promoters and ABC until the very last minute. They were described as some of the "aristocrats of rock".

By this point, the stage show was very polished in every respect – too polished for some. They had got into a very successful 'groove': never complacent, always pushing forward but at the same time more settled and accepting that they could only do what they could do.

"Obviously there are certain things you have to play on stage in the arrangements but my attitude to playing is a lot looser. I think with the sound of the band and the attitude before we go on stage, it isn't so tense now."[68] It was during this period that the usual criticisms of ELP for being too 'flash' and more concerned with effects rather than the music, were cranked up to unprecedented levels.

Despite this criticism Stateside, by the end of the tour all three were openly talking of moving permanently to the USA because of high tax rates in the UK (83% of earnings plus a possible further 15% if it were classed as 'unearned' – in other words, royalties), and better recognition of their music.

In my opinion, most of these, and other 1974 shows, were amongst the pinnacles of their career.

3.

LIMOUSINES - Three limousines and a van are required. The van will be used for luggage pick-up and delivery between the airport and the hotel. The limousines are for the use of ELP and their personnel b-tween the hall, airport and hotel and for any other purpose related to the performance.

HOTEL ROOMS - Please supply 2 quarts of orange juice, 2 quarts of milk, 4 quarts of Perrier Water, and 1 bottle of Rose's Lime Juice to each of the individual rooms of Emerson, Lake and Palmer. Promoter will be advised of the hotel arrival time by an ELP representative.

DINNER AFTER THE SHOW - It would be appreciated if a good restaurant (or a choice of restaurants) could be arranged for Emerson, Lake and Palmer. Please investigate which restaurants will stay open. Both Indian and Japanese are favourites.

CONCESSIONS - Souvenir programs, T-Shirts and posters will be sold at the venue. The producer reserves the sole, exclusive and irrevocable rights to the sale of same. These will be sold by Brockum T-Shirts. Please contact Peter Lubin at (212) 541-5559 with any house rules, commissions etc. that may apply to the venue of the engagement. The distribution or sale of any program book or give-away other than the Producer's must be approved by the Producer or the Producer's representative, four weeks prior to the date of the engagement.

As band riders go, this one seems extremely reasonable. Courtesy of Tony Ortiz.

SATURDAY, 2 FEBRUARY 1974

The Winterland, San Francisco, CA, USA.

The eighth show of the tour was a stunner, a true testimony to the quality of ELP's sound system.

A bit of tuning and Moog fiddling from behind the curtains and then they get a formal introduction,

"Got some friends here who wanna come out and give you some *Brain Salad Surgery*! Emerson, Lake and Palmer!"

This audience go wild before they've even played a note and tonight's "Hoedown" gets big cheers all the way through and especially for Keith's solo; never the same two nights running.

Keith's introduction for "Jerusalem" and "Toccata" are still here. Unfortunately, the first verse of a beautiful rendition of the former is a little spoiled by constant calls and cheers, but the crowd settle down and the sound fills the hall, perfectly balanced as ever.

The structure of "Toccata" is such that they never seem able to venture far from the recorded version. It's predictable but oh so powerful and skilfully played. The exchanges with the bass and Moog add to the mood, as do the quieter tubular bells sections, and the overall effect is of a really symphonic piece. The theme based percussion solo is magical, controlled yet anarchic, all the time set against the fourteen note pattern of the sequencer. The effect is not lost on this lively audience and it's definitely a live favourite.

"Alright, here comes 'Tarkus'," shouts Keith. His introduction is almost lost amongst the cheering for "Toccata" but the crowd soon quieten down for a version that has a real kick at the start, full of Moog fanfares and fuzz bass. There's no passion lost even on this, an epic they've been playing every night for three years, as Keith lets rip on the ribbon controller solo in "Mass". The stop-start bit that precedes it is the fastest (to my ears anyway) they've ever played it, followed by a rip-roaring Hammond intro to the main attraction.

If anything, the piece gets faster as they head towards "Battlefield". "Epitaph" is well received, not least because the guitar coda is a pleasure to listen to. In "Aquatarkus", against a pounding beat of a backdrop, Keith is on top form.

"Benny The Bouncer" strolls in, all music hall and East End Teddy Boy. A touch faster than of late, it still sounds better than previously with Keith really going to town.

By way of contrast, it's "Take A Pebble". Keith's piano and Greg's acoustic spot dominate their respective parts of the song, with Carl's brush and cymbal work a high point from beginning to end. Vocals are so high in the mix they wash over everything just perfectly, marred only by the constant calls and whistles of this lively crowd. In this, the big piano showcase of the evening, Keith's solos are inventive and note-perfect.

After he takes a few seconds to implore some people to sit down, Greg's "Still ... You Turn Me On" and "Lucky Man" sound wonderful with the rich baritone bouncing around the hall and hanging in the air for ages in the closing reprise. The audience love it.

"Karn Evil 9", the longest epic of the night, follows without introduction but the music speaks for itself. A classic amongst a night of classics.

Whoever's in charge of balancing the sound deserves an award: Greg's vocals all the way through the "1st Impression" are right up there, carrying whole sections of the piece as he moves the message from despair to hope. Having excelled in "Toccata" earlier, Carl gives his second solo of the night, furiously fast, focusing on snare and toms, creating rhythms and patterns, with each and every sound perfectly clear.

The "3rd Impression" leaves a lasting 'impression' of musical and technical excellence. The lyrics, "Rejoice, glory is ours!", contrasting with the final "I'm perfect, are you?" As the audience are still figuring it out, the final, climactic ending with the Moog trundling across the stage, smoke bellowing forth and wings flapping, dominates everything and gets everyone making a noise.

The lights come up on ELP, opposite side of the stage to the machine, taking their well-deserved bow.

Back they come for an encore of "Pictures..." that rounds off the evening perfectly. It's big, with plenty of bottom-end Hammond and bass, and not too fast. The only slight reservation is the overly-extended Hammond throwing/Moog twiddling/organ playing solo section which goes on a little too long and detracts a bit from the overall effect of a magnificent "Great Gates ...". Still, that's nitpicking and it's still a winner, as the audience response proves.

Great show from a band who are obviously on a roll.

SATURDAY, 9 FEBRUARY 1974

The Swing Auditorium, San Bernardino, CA, USA.

After playing the Long Beach Arena the previous Sunday evening, six days before, the band had a break and this show was their fifth consecutive gig in California on this tour. If anything, the pause between shows led them to slow the tempo of most pieces, so the audience could grasp the more subtle instrumental points even more.

"Hoedown" opens and proves what you can do with a quad sound system as Keith's Moog bounces around the arena like an aural pinball.

Keith does his *Brain Salad Surgery* introduction and they kick into "Jerusalem", a majestic version of the hymn with wonderfully upfront vocals. It's taken at a statelier pace than recently, and sounds beefed-up with some lower register Moog and clever fills on the toms from Carl. "Toccata" follows the score as usual and sounds the business with a killer intro on tympani and Moog.

Whistles and whoops of admiration fill every pause before the general controlled chaos that precedes Carl's musical percussion solo. He gets the lion's share of the attention and the applause, leading nicely into the fourteen note sequencer section where he lays down pattern after pattern on the kit.

Surprisingly little applause greets "Tarkus" but they still turn in a top drawer version of the second-longest piece of the night. "Eruption" is a little laid back but as they go through "Stones Of Years" into "Mass" they up the ante. Keith plays his trump card, the organ solo in "Stones ..." being particularly noteworthy: improvised, quite slow and deliberate, and very moody. The Hammond solo in "Mass" must rank as one of the best ever, accompanied skilfully by pedalled hi-hat and toms from Carl, and Greg's nifty bass work.

After that, Keith plays a sublime Moog solo in "Aquatarkus", Greg and Carl laying down a tight, bubbling rhythm before this 29 minute epic is brought to a close.

Keith explains that the next song is usually played on the polyphonic but it's broken tonight, so it'll be on the pianos. This actually works a treat on a number like "Benny The Bouncer" as it makes it sound more authentic when played on the 'old Joanna', as they call a piano in the East End.

"Take A Pebble" is one minute short of the 30 tonight. We also get both "Still ... You Turn Me On" and "Lucky Man" but not before Greg, always thinking of the crowd, stops playing and asks the people close to the front to sit down to avoid being crushed.

A pause for tuning up, no introductions and the organ counterpoint marks the start of the penultimate epic, a stirring "Karn Evil 9". The audible intricacies of this one highlight the quality of the sound system: everything – from vocals to synth lines to drums – is an aural feast.

"2nd Impression" rolls along on a variety of patterns and rhythms, the best, in my opinion, being the steel drum solo from Keith – superbly supported by outstanding work from Carl – until a crash of drums and some tremendous fuzz bass from Greg herald the final movement.

All roads lead to *that* ending, now complete with explosion, and then sustained applause and cheers as the crowd demand more, which they get with "Pictures..." Plenty of organ heaving from Keith, some very Brian Auger-like effects on the Hammond, cheered and encouraged by this crowd, and then the grand finale is a fitting way to cap a very enjoyable evening.

The delighted audience reaction says it all really: the band could have played all night if they had wanted to.

SUNDAY, 10 FEBRUARY 1974

The Convention Center, Anaheim, CA, USA.

Tickets: $5.50

Almost all of this show has gone down in history on the Welcome Back My Friends To The Show That Never Ends *triple vinyl album, often acknowledged as one of the very best 'live' albums ever.*

Recorded by the renowned Wally Heider Studios from LA in front of 22,000 fans, this performance in California rates as one of the all time classics. Hell of a sound system, accurate recording, and Greg in the white suit – what more could you ask for?

After an upbeat, lively "Hoedown", things are slowed a touch with "Jerusalem" and "Toccata". It seems that recording pieces they know they can reproduce live, rehearsing them to the nth degree, and now playing basically the same songs every night, is certainly paying off big time. These two songs from *Brain Salad Surgery* are the textbook pieces of the evening; hardly varying at all from the script, but each in its own way is powerful and tight as a tick.

Carl's musical solo in "Toccata" – with fifteen mics on the kit – is slightly different each night. There are cheers and "Wows" as the drum podium spins around and the strobes do their work. It's a rollicking version, the crowd respond well and it bodes well for the rest of the show.

They deliver a nice attacking "Tarkus" with Keith doing the business from first to last. Things seem to have picked up pace again and this rendition is fast, not too fast, but would certainly get a ticket from a speed cop. "Mass" has what's surely one of the fastest Hammond sections ever performed live by Keith, and then they work their way onto the "Battlefield" with consummate ease. Greg's at the centre of attention here with one of his best lead solos for ages, supported well by Keith on bass pedals, but we can still tell that "the bass player's gone on holiday."

They then produce an outstanding version of "Aquatarkus": loose, free-form but always revolving around the usual theme. The bubbling rhythm, Greg's fuzzy bass at the beginning and Keith's solo that's so casual it's frightening.

Keith credits Carl and Greg, and then it's "Take A Pebble". The trio work at the beginning is so delicate, so light, that this is certainly one song that's benefited from being developed on stage every night for almost four years – to the point of quite possibly being better than the original. On the twelve string, "Still ... You Turn Me On" has a few different chords, which adds to the novelty each night, and the voice is a mixture of romantic and plaintive.

"Lucky Man" gets a surprisingly muted round of applause considering the reaction it normally receives.

Keith follows with Gulda's "Prelude and Fugue", lacking the swing but full of classical overtones, then straight into "Little Rock Getaway", another sure-fire shot from the Emerson arsenal. The whole solo is a true showcase, stuffed full of the Emerson trademark *glissandos* and *ostinatos*. Never ones to knowingly miss their cues, Greg and Carl come in bang on time and the trio jazz section is fast-paced – and fun! If they did play "Benny The Bouncer" it hasn't survived for some reason. They may not have done.

"Karn Evil 9" is instantly recognizable. Noticeable on this one is the quality of the bass work and just how bloomin' hard Carl works to provide the tempo, the rhythm and countless fills on the toms and snare. He certainly pulls out all the stops on the full-of-despair section, following it up later with an outstanding second solo of the evening. Applause is forthcoming throughout the four minutes of action-packed, musical playing. It's all there: gongs, tubular bells, bell-with-a-string, snare and tom rolls, and the crowd love it.

We know they played "Pictures …" in its usual encore slot but sadly no record of it survives. Pity: the performances tonight are first rate, from that opening *portamento* in "Hoedown" to that futuristic, crashing finale of "Karn Evil 9".

As most readers of this book will own the live Welcome Back My Friends … *you'll* have a fair idea of what a show this was.

SUNDAY, 17 FEBRUARY 1974

The Civic Auditorium, San Francisco, CA, USA.

This was the show where, in the "Mass" solo in "Tarkus", Keith grabbed the ribbon controller and was about to jump down amongst the audience when it blew up in his hand. The explosion tore off a finger nail as Greg and Carl pounded away on the rhythm behind him. He carried on for a few bars and then, clearly in some pain, with blood all over his hand, threw down the controller in disgust. The rest of the show continued with most people oblivious to the event.

By all accounts, a stunning performance from a band that really do give blood for you!

FRIDAY, 1 MARCH 1974

Louisiana State University, Baton Rouge, LA, USA.

Show 26 of the tour and no sign of any slackening or fatigue.

In fact, it's the opposite as "Hoedown" seems even more in your face than usual: faster, more of a kick to the bass and rhythm and with a keyboard solo that has a definite edge to it.

"Jerusalem" and "Toccata" largely follow the script, and magnificently so. The latter in particular never ceases to amaze as an incredibly difficult piece to reproduce on stage but yet they do it so well night after night. There's a whole section in Carl's solo that's completely different from any other version of this one: different patterns, different rhythms and it's good to see them sticking to their own forty per cent improvisation rule.

Follow that? A 30 minute "Tarkus" sees the band going with the flow along with this very receptive crowd. They give one of the best-ever renditions of "Epitaph", with echo on the vocals that fill every inch of this huge arena, which is well-applauded by the crowd. The coda is beautiful in its simplicity. "Aquatarkus" too gets riotous applause.

Greg's trilogy of "Take A Pebble", "Still ... You Turn Me On" and "Lucky Man" are all well received with the latter getting the biggest cheers and loudest applause of the night. "Greg Lake, there!" is Keith's acknowledgement of a superb solo set.

Keith gets down to business with an excellent solo, played, as Greg's was, in an almost completely silent hall, except for the occasional outburst of clapping, such is the crowd's appreciation of ELP. Keith throws in "Daisy, Daisy" and "La Marseillaise" amongst all the other improvs, all the while Greg and Carl match him at every twist. Ever ready to self parody, Keith hams it up like Les Dawson – a bit wasted on the Louisiana crowd but never mind.[69]

The reprise of "Take A Pebble" for the last verse, as Greg's voice echoes around the auditorium, is dramatic and stunning. Pausing as they do for nine full seconds before the final words, which shows confidence in themselves and in their audience.

Polyphonic light relief next, as Keith says: "This is meant to be the fun piece of the evening. It's all about a bouncer. 'Benny The Bouncer' is his name."

Greg's voice is harsh and aggressive as he gets into character. You can almost see the smiles on their faces as they play this one. This band are at the top of the tree, fans love them, critics bay for their blood, but they're not afraid to do something different. Greg forgets the words in the second verse but it doesn't alter the flow and an excellent middle eight makes up for it anyway.

At almost 37 minutes, "Karn Evil 9" is the epic of the evening. Oddly, they seem hesitant at first: it's looser and Keith's all over the place with the Moog and the Hammond. Equipment problems are dogging him,

Carl's an absolute rock and by the end of verse two, things have picked up and Keith's back on form. The quad system does wonders for the first Moog solo and, by the 'thrills and shocks' part, they're cooking with gas. Some excellent work again by Keith on bass pedals and organ to give Greg room to produce a quality solo, note-perfect and upfront. He then fluffs a vocal, only to make up for it with a more than face-saving guitar line as he now takes his turn to move back, and let Keith loose on the Hammond.

Carl's solo doesn't miss a trick: machine-gun like snare, musical toms, gongs and bells – he's got it all going on.

The mixture of styles in the "2nd Impression" shows this band's real forte, the essence of prog rock: the innate and unquestioned ability to fuse different styles and genres, proven as they move from electro-jazz to steel drum to a mesmerizing piano-bass duet, with Carl keeping time on the blocks.

"3rd Impression", the climax of the piece, is impressive from first to last.

"Rejoice, glory is ours" is in the same mould as "They were sent to the gate" from "Pictures ...", the opening line to a climactic finale. The crowd reaction to the swirling Moog as it sweeps round the sound system is clearly audible, as is their stunned amazement at the end. It's cheers, whistles and applause all round for a long time. One guy shouts out "They ought to do Lucky Man again!"; another is sure "They ain't gonna play no more!" but they do of course.

Keith has some bad news though: "Aaagh, I think your energy crisis has got us! The organ has gone off. You'll have to bear with us a second, alright?"

Carl, ever the entertainer, begins a slow martial snare beat just as Keith announces "Alright, we're gonna give you 'Pictures At An Exhibition'!"

They've had their share of the gremlins tonight, a rarity at an ELP gig, but this encore more than makes up for it. Carl plays like a man possessed, giving the piece its edge, drive and aggression. It's a gilt-edged version, with some interesting Moog and bass noises in "Baba Yaga" spicing things up a bit, right off a 50s B-movie sci-fi soundtrack.

A strong way to end a show and again they prove that the odd technical hitch can't put them off their stride.

THURSDAY, 7 MARCH 1974

The Civic Center, Tulsa, OK, USA.

One of two shows recorded by The King Biscuit Flower Hour *(the other being Wheeling, Virginia in November 1977), this is a real cracker from the word go.*

There's much audience anticipation as the band races headlong into a super-fast "Hoedown". "Jerusalem", in contrast is a model of majesty and stateliness.

It's noticeable that by this stage of the tour, the band have really got hold of the *Brain Salad Surgery* material, played it every which way, and have begun to venture off the beaten track even with pieces like "Toccata". There's a nice punchy bass line in the first half, with variations on a theme in the synthesizer-driven part before Carl's solo. This hall is huge but as quiet as a cathedral during the tympani and bell sections – testimony itself to the captivating qualities of musical percussion solos like this. The bass part to the drum sequencer section has evolved so much during the tour, now much more pulsating, giving a powerful rhythmical beat throughout. It's hard to believe that one man is doing all this.

"Tarkus" is now regularly over half an hour and this is a red-hot version, showcasing what often goes unnoticed – the superb bass work from Greg and, in places, Keith. "Epitaph" lacks some of the emotional feeling of recent shows, maybe due to a lack of echo tonight, or the fact that this crowd don't react to it at all. So often, it's been one of those songs where the audience feedback spurs Greg on to higher emotions – but not in Tulsa.

Keith introduces the next part: "We've got a few novel vibes to lay on you now. One is sung in the cockney vernacular all about a bouncer by the name of Benny. Then we move into a few other trips."

Following on the heels of a piece about an armoured armadillo, this one features a fight between two hoodlums with a switchblade and a cold meat pie. You can't say the set list isn't varied!

As if that's not enough, a real treat tonight in the comedy stakes as "Jeremy Bender" and Big Kid Josie have made a rare return to the action. It's a while since they've played "The Sheriff" but they haven't lost their touch.

We get the softer side of the band with Greg's pieces before a "Karn Evil 9" that has a pounding, pulsating bass line that drives everything along, together with some precise drumming, mostly snare.

They've getting the despair bit off to a tee: the feeling is all there in the pleading vocals and the Hammond sound. As the words "Fight tomorrow!" close that part, the Moog solos herald a change in mood and the remainder of the 1st Impression, uplifting in itself, is a classic.

The all-too-often underrated "2nd Impression" sounds even better tonight, what little echo there is in this hall adding to the atmosphere. The close of this 34 minute epic, pretty much a concert in its own right, blends everything that is ELP: musical brilliance, technical wizardry and a theatrical ending, with the guys disappearing into the darkness as the stage lights go out except for a spot on the Moog.

Then, as the final boom echoes round, up come the spots on Keith, Greg and Carl, standing at the opposite side of the stage taking their bow.

Did they do "Pictures ..."? We'll never know.

Greg once spoke of an album being a kind of "promise to deliver" when they took the music on tour. Tonight, they delivered in style.

TUESDAY, 26 MARCH 1974

The Henry Levitt Arena, Wichita, KS, USA.

The fifth show from the end of the tour and they didn't seem stir crazy yet! This one has been featured on the **Official Bootlegs** *collection and rightly so. The vocals in particular are nice and clear in the mix.*

ELP don't need time to get into their stride, they come on and open with "Hoedown", which is a test for any band with a few butterflies in their collective stomachs. Carl really does drum this fast, in places it sounds like Greg and Keith are playing all out to keep up with him, but the end result is fantastic.

The first slice of the *Brain Salad Surgery* cake is delivered to perfection and very much to the taste of this audience, who again applaud at every twist and turn. Greg is right at the top of the mix, where he needs to be, for "Jerusalem", the Hammond sounding subdued so that due emphasis is given to the words of this revered hymn.

The Moog parts are restrained too – they're still thinking very much about the mix and how the sound fits the mood of each piece. "Toccata" is a case in point: from being restrained, Keith and Carl are let loose as Greg keeps everything anchored down. The crowd love the Hammond/tympani bit and go crazy at Carl's solo, probably the most musical drum solo most of them have ever heard. With tympani, bells, snare and toms, the solo has more shades and colours than virtually any other drummer could produce: literally so as the podium spins round and the strobes highlight the dragon images on the gongs. Lucky this gig was in the days when there were no warnings about strobe lights and flash photography!

This audience get a thunderous version of "Tarkus", well decorated with some new Hammond licks in "Stones Of Years". Periodic outbursts of applause as the audience recognize the sheer quality of "Iconoclast" and "Mass", which has some interesting 'whooping' on the Moog. Keith runs up the Hammond keyboard as the intro to the machine-gun solo, the ending of which is messed up by both Keith and Greg as they miss their respective cues, and it takes them a second to work out just where they are. Never mind – Carl tidies up like a sweeper in a football team.

"Battlefield" and "Aquatarkus" save the day: Carl, the one-man rhythm section, is right on top of his game again, Keith provides melodic organ and powerful bass pedal work, and the lyrics are delivered with a ton and a half of feeling. Greg actually extends the guitar intro to "Every blade is sharp", sings his heart out, and "Epitaph" sounds out of this world with the words bouncing around the hall as the quad system works its magic. A slightly faster than usual final movement soon settles into the free-form Moog solo, the crowd whistling and calling out their approval. Never the same two nights running, it's mystical, eerie and archetypal Moog, embellished by sound drums and ear-shattering distorted bass effects. A few lines reminiscent of early Nice from Keith, "Norwegian Wood" is still there, and some classical phrases as the piece slowly gets faster with Carl's drumming steering everything. As in so many ELP pieces, the way the solo and the rhythm section knit together is amazing. Loud? You bet; but if it's too loud you're too old as we said in the 1970s.

After one of the all-time heavyweights of prog, Keith and Greg almost do a Chas and Dave [a British duo specializing in being professional cockneys] on "Benny The Bouncer". Again, "Jeremy Bender" and "The Sheriff" are rolled out, both solid versions.

Once they've overcome constant shouts for people to sit down, be quiet and listen, they give a version of "Take A Pebble", which is nearly thirty minutes long. The fact that the tiniest, quietest cymbal can also be clearly heard is another testimony to the sound system.

Greg gently ushers in the love song "Still ... You Turn Me On" before riding the applause into the opening chords of "Lucky Man". This seems to provide the spark for Keith's longer solo, and a jazz trio section that really sets things alight.

The bass and cymbal work here puts other rhythm sections to shame, highlighting the dexterity of this band. Keith deliberately plays a whole section off-key, runs through a Scottish jig, 'Daisy Daisy' and endless other ditties. When the tag comes for the final verse there's cheers, whistles and applause galore before we get a closing section with some very innovative piano.

At thirty seven minutes, Karn Evil 9 is now vying with "Pictures ..." as the longest piece they've played and as the nights and shows go by, it doesn't lose its edge. It may lose a few of the right notes on the keyboards here and there, but not its edge.

With "1st Impression" you can pretty much sense the grimacing on Keith's face as the wrong notes keep on coming. He recovers well though and Greg and Keith work together especially well on the first solo, guitar going into keyboard, before they throw the baton over to Carl, who catches it without hesitation. He gives us a solo to be proud of, his second of the night, ending with Keith asking for applause for "Bodger Palmer, Bodger Palmer!". Oh well ...

The finale to "Impression" does indeed make a big impression. The gremlins in the keys are back with Keith throwing in a couple of noticeable mistakes in one solo, but the sheer power of the piece carries everything along and he more than makes up for it in the next. Improv rules the day in the main organ solo, mostly first rate but again some technical glitches. Maybe the machines really are fighting back in this one?

The final words of "Cheers, goodnight!" from Keith as the guys take their bows leave them wanting more, but there's no record of them playing an encore.

Lots of cheering and applause and another happy crowd make their way home.

SATURDAY, 6 APRIL 1974

The Motor Speedway, Ontario, CA, USA.

They played more shows on the main part of the tour, one in Los Angeles and two in Memphis, before taking a five day break to prepare for the California Jam, a show that has gone down in rock folklore. Their name was only revealed at the last minute, allegedly to boost ticket sales. The partial, surviving clips from ELP's set have only just been released on DVD and it's worth every second of the wait.

The band are so determined to deliver on this one that they bring IES (International Entertainment Systems) technicians all the way out to California just to set up the right and left rear stacks of the quad system. It's a shrewd move as the sound quality is superb.

Deep Purple win the toss for when they play and elect to go in to bat before ELP, giving them the atmospheric dusk slot. There are wrangles after Purple's set, as Ritchie Blackmore smashes his axe into a TV camera and sets fire to his amps (well, their latest album is called *Burn*!) so the stage area has be 'tidied' before ELP can play. Purple don't stay to see their rivals – they are whisked away in private helicopters.

ELP do the full *Brain Salad Surgery* set, going on stage at about 9p.m. just as it is getting dark.

Of some tracks, no record has survived at all, audio or video. Others are simply amazing. They open with "Hoedown", and the sheer power of the sound system hits people and many are just gobsmacked at the quality of what they are hearing. The Moog solo trips round the stacks to best effect and there's a tremendous roar of applause as the final chords come crashing in. Every time the wind blows, there's a whooshing effect on the sound, a sort of natural phasing, which adds to the overall effect.

Nothing survives of "Jerusalem" but "Toccata" lives up to its hype. Carl, dressed in a black silk kimono trimmed with white, looks the part and the concentration on his face says it all. The rhythms and patterns are faultless and after the others come in for the final section, the crowd go wild.

There is no record either of "Tarkus" or "Jeremy Bender" although we know they played them both.

"Still ..." and "Lucky Man" are the only excerpts surviving from the "Take A Pebble" section. "Still ..." sounds fulsome on the twelve string with Greg sitting on the stool, resplendent in the wide-lapelled, white leather suit, happily chewing gum as he sings.

With the opening line and chords to "Lucky Man" still hanging in the air, a mighty ripple of applause works its way forward towards the stage and Greg smiles, nodding in appreciation as he sings. This is one happy minstrel. He looks so at home in front of those 350,000 people he could be playing to each one of them individually. The pause before the final "... and he died" words is drama itself, the crowd already clapping and cheering as he gives it the big strum finish. It's over to Keith, looking trim in a high-necked white shirt – a bit like a dentist – and the close camera work shows his skill at speed on the Steinway. We get to witness close up the incredible left hand trademark *ostinato*, as he moves from the Gulda classic to "Little Rock Getaway".

The *glissandos* are all there just before the tag for the start of the jazz trio part and again it goes down so well. Greg plays this section seated on a stool, grooving along with Carl, a beaming smile on his face as Keith runs through his string of snippets, all three of them right on their cues and enjoying every second. These guys must have iced water in their veins they're so cool in the face of so many punters.

Before the final reprise of "Pebble", Keith takes a bow stage front and Greg credits him. This closing section is amazing, the others still taking their cues from Keith, his hands working the piano manically. More applause as Greg comes in with the last verse, majestic in the way his voice just takes over and fills the air. The seven second pause before the last words fits the mood of the piece beautifully.

Just awesome!

The second part of the "1st Impression" is tight, upbeat and a joy to behold. Greg riffs away like mad, ably backed by Carl, as Keith takes off with the main Hammond solo of the piece. One of the biggest names in the world they may be, but the same system of little looks, glances and nods as cues are still just as much in evidence as they were in the heady days of 1970. Greg at one point almost bends double in his efforts to see Keith reaching the end of a solo – nothing is left to chance.

Carl's solo is dynamic, entertaining and a real feat of skill and endurance. The lights and strobes flash, the podium spins, the crowd cheers madly. The gongs, the bass drum, the cymbal played with his mouth, all wonderful stuff and it goes down exceptionally well. He cues Keith and Greg back in, the camera highlighting the speed and accuracy of the keyboard work as they come to the big ending of the "1st Impression".

In terms of its structure, the "3rd Impression" is the simplest, the music leading inexorably to the tale of final showdown.

"Pictures ..." as an encore is still an inspired choice, more grand and less of the archetypal encore than something like "Rondo", and in front of this crowd it goes down a storm – especially the famous (or should that be infamous?) spinning piano sequence during what would otherwise would have been the Hammond throwing bit in "The Great Gates..." He may have been playing the *Revolutionary Etude* again but to me it's indecipherable. Is anyone listening to the music anyway?

At one point, the lid comes down on his fingers, but he survives. The spectacle is memorable enough, more so as Keith darts back to his position stage left as a cacophony of noise comes from the modular Moog and Keith counts Greg and Carl back into the closing section of the piece.

It's a powerful way to end the festival. As Greg sings "They were sent to the gates", the reaction from this enormous crowd is deafening, a roar of applause sweeps forward like a tidal wave, fireworks explode and Carl crashes the cymbals with one hand and the gong with the other. On the final crashing chord, there's an even bigger firework explosion and the initials "ELP" are lit up in neon lights, Hollywood style, Keith's initial in red and the others in blue.

The guys are out front taking a well-deserved bow, the crowd going wild at the end of a fantastic set, itself the end of an historic festival, culminating in the end of an amazingly successful tour.

Just as well that Deep Purple, with new boys David Coverdale and Glenn Hughes on board, elected to go on first, as it would have been a big ask to follow ELP in this mood.

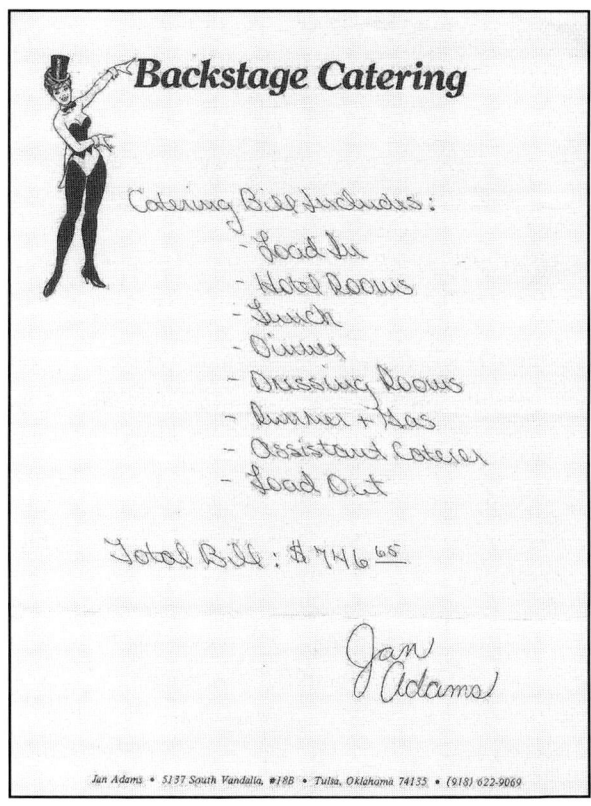

A band and its crew, like an army, marches on its stomach.
Here's a catering bill. Courtesy of Tony Ortiz.

14. *You Gotta See The Show ...*

18 APRIL – 1 MAY 1974: FIFTH UK TOUR
8 SHOWS

Typical set list:	"Hoedown", "Jerusalem", "Toccata", "Tarkus", "Benny The Bouncer", "Take A Pebble", "Still ... You Turn Me On", "Lucky Man", piano improvisations, "Take A Pebble" (reprise), "Karn Evil 9", "Pictures At An Exhibition".
Keith:	As previous tour.
Greg:	As previous tour.
Carl:	As previous tour.
PA system:	Quadraphonic as previous tour.

After the CalJam, ELP had just eleven days off – if you could call them 'days off' – before hitting a stage again, this time at London's Empire Pool, Wembley. The show was the same as for the North American dates, the tour a brief jaunt back on home soil before they set off round Europe again in early May.

These were their first UK dates since December 1972, sixteen months earlier, and the expectation among fans was sky high. Only eight shows in total, four at Wembley, one at Stoke Trentham Gardens, and a final three at the Empire Theatre, Liverpool. There was talk of a fourth show in Liverpool but it never materialized.

There was a huge demand for these tickets, the group's reputation now going before them in a massive way. Fans loved them; critics, in the main, hated them. By this point, ELP had decided as a band and as individuals to keep out of the arguments about musical or theatrical excess, and get on with doing what they did best – playing the greatest music around.

The band had the same quad sound system as on the North American dates, where they used it in much larger venues. Consequently, there were a number of complaints from fans, and criticisms from the media, that the volume at the UK shows was too high.

Recordings of only a handful of these shows have survived, surprising really when you think of the rarity of ELP shows in the UK at that time. These eight dates were the only ones they played in the UK between December 1972 and October 1992; an enormous gap.

SATURDAY, 20 APRIL 1974

The Empire Pool, Wembley, London, UK.

Tickets:£1.65 - £2.20

The third of four nights at this aircraft hangar of a venue, only the second recording of the gigs to have surfaced so far, and another typical inspired ELP performance

The band is introduced on stage by über-supporter Alan Freeman. Alan walks on to the strains of his own theme music and gets a huge cheer from a crowd that recognizes him immediately as he introduces the boys:

"Good evening! Are you ready? Welcome Back My Friends To The Show That Never Ends, Ladies and Gentlemen … Emerson, Lake and Palmer!"

Out of the gentle background noise of whoops from the Moog, comes the unmistakeable and eardrum shatteringly loud *portamento* of "Hoedown". As all three kick in, it's clear that no prisoners will be taken, and they pile into one of the fastest ever versions, which is saying something. It never loses its magic of working up an audience from the word go.

As the applause still echoes, Keith cheekily says to Greg, "Still got the carpet then?". He then announces: "Thank you!, Yeah, it's good to be back, it really is!! Gonna give you some *Brain Salad Surgery*! Start off with our smash-hit single, 'Jerusalem', and then going into a thing by Alberto Ginastera, his first piano concerto. It's called 'Toccata' and features Carl Palmer and his percussion synthesizer."

"Jerusalem" is dominated by the Hammond and Greg's vocals and then, as on the previous tour, they go straight into "Toccata". Everything bounces around the quad system against the backdrop of this big, silent audience. This piece in particular benefits from the 40% improvisation rule every night, Carl's long solo section is orchestrated, structured, musical mayhem and goes down so well.

Keith tunes the Moog and tumultuous applause greets his announcement of "Tarkus". As he says – it's changed a lot since they last played London almost eighteen months earlier. There's a real echo on the Hammond and vocals in particular tonight due to the venue's acoustics, and it gives a haunting feel to some of the sections.

However, add to that the effects of the sound system, and all just a little too often it sounds like Carl has a phased echo effect on the drums, taking something away from their impact in a few places. There's a few "Wows" and comments from the crowd as Keith vaults over the rails in front of the stage, does his 'off-the-stage' antics with the ribbon controller, touching the faithful as if he is giving a Papal blessing, and Carl knocks seven bells out of a cowbell.

The first "Battlefield" on home turf since 1972 is a cracker in every sense: the drum intro has so much echo it sounds like it's phased, and Greg kicks in with storming guitar from the off. Not a sound from anyone during "Epitaph", but the audience reaction at the end is ecstatic. The guys are well in gear for an amazing fourteen minute "Aquatarkus". The final fifteen chords have barely begun before the applause takes over, only dying down as Keith introduces the comedy interlude.

"Benny The Bouncer" is faultlessly delivered, and earns the cheers from a home crowd who understand it perfectly. On this tour, it gets all the attention as the light-hearted piece since they've dropped "Jeremy Bender" and "The Sheriff".

"Take A Pebble", providing the framework for the Lake and Emerson solo spots, is excellent and never sounds hackneyed or wearisome. Keith tears into his first piano solo before handing over to Greg on the twelve string.

"Still ... You Turn Me On" gets instant recognition and is cheered. The introduction to "Lucky Man" is played in an almost country style but fools no one, and the applause is deafening. Keith credits Greg and then leaps once more into his long solo. This audience is enthralled by Keith's smoking fingers as he charges through the pieces by Gulda and Joe Sullivan, with the others coming in bang on cue for a delightfully restrained jazz trio section: nice!

The last verse of "Pebble", still announced by a huge trademark *glissando*, is wonderful to listen to, Greg pulling out all the stops – and succeeding.

Two epics down, one to go and it can only be "Karn Evil 9"; 37 minutes of magic that is played here for the first time to a home audience. Keith races into the Hammond part, leaving the others trailing and, for once, he seems to set the pace. The whole "1st Impression" is faster than of late, and sounding all the better for it. There's an awful jarring chord on the Hammond at the end of the first 'roll up, roll up, roll up' part, but Greg soon rescues things with a killer guitar solo, closely followed in the quality stakes by Carl's solo, all seven minutes of it.

Some nice understated piano marks the opening to the "2nd Impression", soon moving into a variety of patterns as the tension builds towards that electric and now faster Moog 'steel pan' solo from Keith, who even now injects a little humour with the melody from "Popcorn", Hot Butter's instrumental electronic hit from 1972. The recurrent theme is one they come back to in the final "Impression" and so provides a bridge between the two action movements of the epic.

"3rd Impression" gets underway with a wall of sound and never lets up. They all sound like they enjoy playing this and it really shows, with Keith and Carl pulling the strings. Classy work from Keith, with the Greg/Carl engine room pumping away in the background, as he turns in a stunningly simple Moog fanfare solo set against a backdrop of melody on the Hammond. "Rejoice, glory is ours!" sings Greg at the start of the majestic, fatalistic last verse, before the Moog takes over, sprouting wings, trundling across the stage in a cloud of dry ice.

It's greeted with huge cheers and applause and, after a while, back they come for a storming version of "Pictures..." which shakes Wembley to its very foundations. Impressive in its sheer energy at the end of a long set. It gets a massive cheer and the crowd are with them all the way.

Everyone goes home happy. A touch deafened, perhaps, but happy.

SUNDAY, 21 APRIL 1974

The Empire Pool, Wembley, London, UK.

Tickets: £1.65 - £2.20

"Fluff" Freeman gives them the same build-up on this, their final night at a London venue for over eighteen years, and they open with a blistering version of "Hoedown" that has the crowd rocking in the aisles from the first bars of the *portamento*. The guys are still handling this long set well, with a confidence that never fails to improve.

After Keith's introductions for the first offerings from *Brain Salad Surgery*, "Jerusalem" goes down deservedly well. Greg's really got the hang of delivering beautifully mellow vocals, accompanied by celestial organ and understated tubular bells.

"Toccata" keeps the momentum going. Following the crashing ending of "Jerusalem" it's mystical and measured in its opening. From start to finish Carl, excels on everything: first the tympani, then the whole kit, and finally the inventive way he produces rhythms on the drum sequencer, against which he builds and embroiders pattern after pattern as he flies around the kit. In the quiet tympani/bell sections, you can literally hear a pin drop in this huge arena, followed by the weird and wonderful 'listen-to-all-these-noises-I-can-make' section. There's not a sound from the audience until the very end when they cheer like there's no tomorrow.

What sounds like Keith practising one chord to get it right, is actually the tuning up for "Tarkus" which tonight runs for a mammoth 32 minutes. The combination of Carl's driving drums, Greg's fuzz bass and that echo again on the Hammond give it an edge that isn't always there, and it's all the better for it.

"Aquatarkus" is stretched still further to almost fifteen minutes. Keith takes control with a Moog solo ranging from spooky droning to some nifty spaced-out lines. They all do it with consummate ease as the hall's acoustics and the quad system work together to produce some timely effects

"Benny The Bouncer" is greeted warmly by the home crowd. The false ending gets its usual laugh and then Keith strums the intro to "Take A Pebble" to applause and cheers. Keith's textbook solo paves the way for Greg's solo acoustic spot, first on the twelve string for "Still ...", then switching to six strings for "Lucky Man".

Keith's second, main, solo is the stuff dreams are made of, especially here in front of a home crowd. From Gulda's "Fugue", through "Little Rock Getaway", calling all points he can think of, the *ostinato* works overtime and he wins applause throughout. A spurt of racing *glissandos*, up and down the keys, impress still further and the audience go bonkers as Greg and Carl come back in.

They then proceed to show what jazz trio work is *really* all about as Carl drives them relentlessly through an amazingly powerful improvisation, but Keith still can't resist "Daisy, Daisy", the Laurel and Hardy theme and hints of things from his Nice days. Cheers, shouts and calls of "Great stuff!" raise the roof and it's an unbelievable 21 seconds before they resume for the finale of the song. The pause and then the climactic "of our lives" line is sheer drama, and recognized as such by this appreciative crowd.

The tuning gives away what's up next, and yes, they kick into "Karn Evil 9" without any further ado. It starts off more than a bit ragged, a touch too fast, with Carl for once trying to bring the others back into line. By the beginning of verse three, he's succeeded and everything sounds much more like classic ELP. The highlight of "1st Impression, Part 2", is undoubtedly Carl's solo – although Keith's organ outing runs him a close second. In fact, overall throughout this prog rock-length 34 minute version, Carl very nearly takes the spotlight away from the others altogether with an endless barrage of incredible drumming, every fill just perfect and he's never once overbearing or pushy. The drum riser spins round, the strobes flash, he pulls the bell with the rope between his teeth – and the crowd go absolutely ape.

"2nd Impression" is, as ever, wonderfully understated. They pick up speed, and volume, careering into the "3rd Impression" as if they mean business – which they do.

For the last time in London until 1992 at the Royal Albert Hall, amid the smoke and reverberating noises, the set draws to a close, they take their bows and Keith wishes a fantastic audience goodnight.

We, with the gift of hindsight, know how long it will be before the next ELP London gig. The audience don't, of course, but had they known they would probably have kidnapped the band until they agreed to play at least once a year.

They may have come back for an encore of "Pictures ..." but we'll never know. What we do know is that ELP gave their all and everyone went home with memories to treasure for the next twenty years.

TUESDAY, 30 APRIL 1974

The Empire Theatre, Liverpool, UK.

Tickets: £1 - £2.20

Second of a three night stint at the Empire, not exactly renowned for its acoustics, but to a large degree the sound system made up for that.

Pity though that the only surviving record of this one is cut off at the start of "Karn Evil 9: 3rd Impression", meaning we also lose out on the encore – which we know they did play.

They walk on to massive applause during the 'Welcome Back' introduction, and get straight into a rocking version of "Hoedown". A seriously heavy final three chords are followed by a ton of applause, showing the audience are well up for this show.

As Keith says, "Yeah, it's good to be back in Liverpool! Gonna give you a little *Brain Salad Surgery*, starting off with our smash-hit single "Jerusalem", and then we're gonna feature Carl over there on a piece by Ginastera, "Toccata"."

It's a heavy version of the old English hymn but still some nice other-worldly organ from Keith, coupled with rich, mellow vocals from Greg. Carl's drums give it some drive.

"Toccata" has always been tightly-structured and, at the same time, open to the development that comes from being played night after night. The Hammond and bass work are impressive, but it's Carl's inventiveness that carries this one. He fits in new variations on patterns with each performance, and his desire to push things onwards and upwards gets stronger all the time. This is a musical percussion solo of the first order, where keyboards and bass are the back-up, with skilful use of the sequencer framework within which he builds his mosaic of sound. Awesome!

More applause, then a brief introduction to 30 minutes of prog magic in the shape of "Tarkus". After "Mass", where Keith blitzes the ribbon controller with ease, they move inexorably to Greg's real showcase in the piece, "Battlefield", with a thundering opening from Carl. Vocals are consistently strong, with a real solid feeling to the lead guitar. It's noticeable that the bass player is playing lead on this, but there's still some powerful supporting bass lines from Keith. Tonight's final verse has a longer, more delicate guitar intro from Greg before he launches into "Epitaph", his voice filling the hall.

As the applause for Greg dies down, there's a call of "Emerson!" from somewhere, an apt precursor for a sterling solo in "Aquatarkus". Almost fourteen minutes of trio teamwork follow, all kinds of weird and wonderful noise emanating from Keith's side of the stage before he playfully introduces Greg's solo spot with: "This one features Greg Lake on Persian carpet, yeah ... bit of applause there! [Indecipherable comments]... yeah, this is Greg singing in the cockney vernacular about "Benny The Bouncer."

The strummed piano chords to "Take A Pebble" elicit a short burst of applause, followed by a respectful silence for the elder statesman of the set. The juxtaposition of "Still ..." and "Lucky Man" in Greg's solo is now well-established and provides him with a substantial acoustic showcase halfway through the show.

"Karn Evil 9" sounds like someone has told them "This is Liverpool, guys, they like their music in these parts!" The opening is aggressive, harsh-sounding and fits the mood of despair they're trying to convey. And that's all we have from this gig.

We can only imagine what the rest of the show was actually like. One thing's for sure – they must have sent the Scousers home very, very happy.

WEDNESDAY, 1 MAY 1974

The Empire Theatre, Liverpool, UK.

Tickets: £1 – £2.20

This was to be their last show in the UK for over eighteen years.

Perfectionists they may have been, but the playing and singing at this show is of a quality that not even ELP could match night after night as they so obviously put everything they had into it.

Last of three nights at the venue and, after an American-voiced introduction, on they come and tear into a red hot "Hoedown". The crowd responds well – looks like we're in for another entertaining evening.

The announcement of *Brain Salad Surgery* material is greeted warmly and without further ado, they launch into "Jerusalem" with some stylish synth work from Keith.

In mid-applause, Keith begins "Toccata". This is a really heavy version, so intricate and precise and yet flawlessly played. The bass riff underpins everything so well, giving Carl a chance to strut his stuff as only he can. A cacophony of Moog fanfares leads to probably one of the best drum solos Carl has ever produced, brimming with ever-changing colours and moods.

"Here's one that seems to have changed every time we do it and that's why we keep doing it. Basically a fantasy based on an armadillo by the name of 'Tarkus'," says Keith.

Keith's solos just get better as he moves from "Stones Of Years", through "Mass" and into an "Aquatarkus" that is so loose, it's tight, if you get my drift. "Battlefield" opens majestically as Greg steps forward for his showcase. As everything falls quiet, there's some amazing phased echo on the guitar for "Every blade is sharp" and "Epitaph", instantly recognized by this knowledgeable crowd.

"Benny The Bouncer." is faster than recent versions and so well received that more of the same is demanded and so the guys play the 'Benny' coda twice more – then, amid calls and stamps for yet more, go into the entire honky tonk closing section from "The Sheriff"! Riotous cheering follows and they've so obviously got the audience on their side.

As Keith says, "We're gonna relax a bit now and play 'Take A Pebble'!" This is full of richness and feeling, with such precise, delicate work from all three. Keith's piano playing, the left hand *ostinato* working overtime as the right hand races up and down the octaves, is sheer delight. Greg matches him with his twelve string for 'Still … You Turn Me On", and then again extending and developing the intro to a stirring "Lucky Man".

Keith winds Carl up as he needs to "get his skins right" before announcing, to huge applause, that they're doing "Karn Evil 9".

The organ counterpoint intro sounds beefier than usual, and the whole thing again sounds less hurried and more emphatic in the phrasing of the lyrics and keyboards. It all adds to the difference in feel between the two parts of the "1st Impression". The guys on the sound desk are working overtime to send organ and Moog fanfares round the quad system and, boy, it's a treat for the ears! To a drummer like me, the whole "1st Impression" is like Carl giving a drum class, being everywhere, on top form, but never overpowering. The drum solo has everyone enthralled: he uses the whole kit, hi-hat never stopping, the sequencer firing away, goings and cymbals crashing – no wonder this crowd show how much they love it.

After a "2nd Impression" that moves from relatively slow-burner to kick-ass steel pan solo, and back again (via a groovy taste of "Popcorn"), the last movement becomes more and more dramatic as we move towards that final apocalyptic showdown.

The end comes all too quickly with the crowd clapping as the Moog still races round the sound system, ending with the now familiar explosion and a shout of "Goodnight!" from Keith as they take their bows.

However many times they do this, it's still an inspired way to finish a show – and a tour.

Thank you guys, see you in eighteen years!

15. *It's A Dynamo ...*

Typical set list:	"Hoedown", "Jerusalem", "Toccata", "Tarkus", "Benny The Bouncer", "Take A Pebble", "Still ... You Turn Me On", "Lucky Man", piano improvisations, "Take A Pebble" (reprise), "Karn Evil 9", "Pictures At An Exhibition".
Keith:	As previous tour.
Greg:	As previous tour.
Carl:	As previous tour.
PA system:	Quadraphonic as previous tour.

Having got a North American tour under their belt that went back to the autumn of the previous year, followed by a short, intense UK tour, the guys now embarked on 21 shows in 27 days all around Europe.

It was the same show they'd played since 14 November and it was still going down a storm. Nonetheless only a handful of these recordings have survived the test of time, but those that have are testament to the skills of a band at the very top of their game.

The show, every aspect of it, was by now so well-honed that it was a performance in the truest sense. They had got the sound, the lights and the visuals honed to perfection, and the shows just seemed to get better.

TUESDAY, 7 MAY 1974

Palacio Municipal de Deportes, Barcelona, Spain.

Tickets: Ptas 350

Their first ever gigs in Spain, and the first of two nights at a stadium in Barcelona.

Well, it is the first ever taste of ELP for a Spanish audience and they get fair warning of what's to follow with "Hoedown". Keith going all out in the Moog solo. Carl is so fast he's almost invisible and Greg's pounding bass shakes the arena to its foundations. The applause suggests the Spaniards have had the date of this gig in their diaries for a while.

"Jerusalem" and "Toccata" still work well as a double act, although it isn't too clear if the audience can follow Keith's introduction because they don't react until the opening bars of the old hymn. Greg's vocals are sweetness itself, at the very top of the mix. The segue into "Toccata" goes down well, again with the crowd.

It's a vintage version, not a note out of place. The crowd are impressed by Carl's playing as he takes them on a journey round the kit from gongs, tympani and tubular bells to sequencer, snare and hi-hat. Like something from a sci-fi movie, he fills the air with weird, wonderful yet musical sounds.

"Tarkus", now always over half an hour, requires some tweaking of the Moog before they start and again the announcement of the piece gets almost no crowd reaction at all. However, as it progresses and the cheers grow, the audience give the game away: they're definitely up for this gig. "Manticore" and the opening bars of "Battlefield" are just so fast, powered by strong drumming and a martial beat, that it sounds like they're in a hurry to get there. As with so many of the larger venues, the natural echo of the arena adds to the atmosphere of Greg's solo vocal/guitar spot, and "Epitaph" is instantly recognized by a sizeable proportion of this audience.

After an "Aquatarkus" that is right on the button – full of mystical, surreal sounds, where time and again Keith returns to the "Tarkus" theme interspersed with phrases ranging from Lennon & McCartney to the classics, which the crowd appreciate.

Carl and Keith jazz their way through "Benny The Bouncer", Keith switching from the Polymoog to the grand piano, turns on his mellow switch, and off they go without further ado into an excellent, beautifully-played "Take A Pebble", which goes down a treat.

The warmth and emotion of "Still ..." and "Lucky Man" shine through, set as they are against a backdrop of church-like reverence from the crowd, and there's a particularly tasty extended acoustic introduction to the latter.

The "Karn Evil 9: 1st Impression", as it so often does, starts off fast, almost hurried, until Carl restrains the others a little. Tension builds well before verse four restores hope to the world with the circus section, and Ringmaster Greg advertises his 'thrills and shocks'.

The opening to Part 2 is a real powerhouse, only to be 'out-powered' by Carl's solo, his high point of the evening. Arms flailing, his snare and tom work must be without equal. He then moves to the cymbals and gongs, creating patterns from nowhere, and wins tumultuous applause. Aspiring drummers take note: this is an example of how to play musically, playing rhythms and lead simultaneously on the kit (but don't try the string pulling with the mouth routine at home!).

The "2nd Impression" has a lot to live up to but does so with room to spare. The playing in general, and the steel drum solo in particular, is so hot it's blistering. Then, in an instant, the pace is slowed, the volume cut as Keith and Greg produce a delicately balanced duet with Carl keeping time on the blocks. Now, as throughout this show, the huge crowd are almost silent as they listen amazed at it all. A final burst of energy from the "2nd Impression", with yet again some wildly impressive trio work, leads us into the finale of the whole piece.

The final quandary of "Rejoice! Glory is ours!" in the "3rd Impression" is left up to the punters to resolve. They're clearly and audibly impressed by the Moog reverberating round the sound system, the climactic cacophony giving a split second's lull before Keith, Greg and Carl take their bow and retire.

This fantastic audience are not going to let them get away from their first show in Spain without an encore and so, with tons of applause, cheers, whistles and calls for "more", ELP come out.

Keith does the honours: "Yeah, it's been wonderful playing to you! We hope to see you very soon. We're gonna give you 'Pictures At An Exhibition'!"

What follows is a highly impressive, very weighty 25 minute version of the epic. "Promenade" must be the slowest they've ever played it, each note so measured. That's then all forgotten as they tear into a roaring "Baba Yaga". Keith delivers some top class, spooky, *Twilight Zone*-style keyboard sounds, but it's Carl and Greg who are very much in the driving seat once the trio section gets underway.

Greg continues to soar above everything as Keith drives the melody on the trusty Hammond before letting rip with the Hammond throwing, much to the amazement of this crowd.

They go wild at his every move, cheering as he cajoles all manner of noise from the old L100, and going downright potty as he switches to the synth to produce some nice symphonic playing. Right on cue, after a full seven minutes, the others come back in and the climax to the evening is as wonderful as any on this tour.

"There's no end to my life, no beginning to my death. Death is Life!" marks a strong way to close a great performance. Buenas Noches!

SATURDAY, 11 MAY 1974

The Hallenstadion, Zurich, Switzerland.

The fourth gig of the tour saw the band well into its stride

An ecstatic crowd greets ELP, who indulge in more than the usual tuning and messing around before the *Welcome Back My Friends* intro. "Hoedown" bounces along, as do most of the audience, and the guys sound confident.

Keith does his usual introductions of "Hello! Alright! Nice to be back in Zurich, nice to see you again!" before announcing the first pieces from *Brain Salad Surgery*. They turn in a really heavenly "Jerusalem" that wouldn't sound out of place in St Paul's Cathedral.

"Toccata" is excellent from start to finish and the main percussion solo is worth waiting for. Carl takes his time with the tubular bells and tympani, everything at once but still right on the nail, and wins frequent applause from this good-natured audience.

They turn up the gas still further with "Tarkus". The acoustics of the arena, coupled with the quad system, give the drums a delayed echo, and at times Carl's 'kick' sounds as if he's playing double bass drum all the time. It sounds so apt in "Manticore" and "Iconoclast", both pieces that are heavy on the rhythm.

The acoustics also add to the sound of "Aquatarkus", and by the time the guys reach the climax the crowd are already on their feet clapping and cheering. There are even calls of "Yeah!" during this one from Greg, which, as we have seen, means he is having a ball.

"Take A Pebble" follows "Benny" and is a classic 28 minutes. Greg's "Still …" gets applause as soon as he starts the intro and, together with "Lucky Man", is clearly liked by this foot-stomping, cheering crowd. So much so that he has to wait a while before the crowd calms down before he can actually start "Lucky Man".

There is, again, no introduction for the longest piece of the night, "Karn Evil 9". It's undoubtedly the star of the show though and, at 36 minutes, wins on every level as the crowd clap along to the "Welcome Back My Friends" section.

The drum solo is as white-hot as you're ever likely to hear, a five minute extravaganza of musical percussion, followed by an equally credit-worthy "2nd Impression". Against the tight rhythm, Keith lays down a sharp Moog solo, with a hint of "Popcorn" still, leading inexorably to that piano/bass duet, Carl keeping the beat as if time itself is ticking away.

Tonight's "3rd Impression" is a killer, lifting the noise and energy levels with a forceful beat and loud, aggressive bass, as they take the piece to its conclusion until ELP disappear in a cloud of dry ice, the computer dominating the stage with the final explosion.

The fans crowd stomp, cheer and just won't let up until ELP come back on for an encore – and it has to be "Pictures …"

The second Keith introduces this one, and hits the keys, the place erupts and stays that way for most of the suite, from a stately "Promenade" via a hectic, near demonic "Baba Yaga", through to a majestic, measured "Great Gates …".

The band crashes in on each verse, building skilfully to a superb climax to an evening – a typically Emersonian Hammond throwing session, forcing all manner of sounds and noises from the L100, and going down a storm with this ecstatic Swiss crowd. There's plenty of gut-wrenching bass effects during this and he even gets them clapping along in time.

A pretty much faultless performance in front of a superbly responsive audience. Who says the Swiss are reserved?

FRIDAY, 17 MAY 1974

The Stadthalle, Vienna, Austria.

Some sources say this gig was at the Bundesstation Liebenau in Graz.

Show eight on the tour and their reception in Vienna virtually drowns out the *portamento* at the start of "Hoedown", pushing the band on to play louder and faster to be heard.

Act 1 of *Brain Salad Surgery*, "Jerusalem" and "Toccata", get their standard intro from Keith and both are well received. "Jerusalem" especially, is heavy, pounding, full of gong crashes from Carl, all of which contrasts so effectively with Greg's rich vocals and that church-like organ.

"Toccata" basically follows the script except where Carl ventures off into the unknown during his solo, creating patterns and rhythms that vary slightly every night. The supporting keyboard and bass work deserve a mention for the way they provide melody, and the occasional lead line, but always allow the percussion the starring role. As he moves from the quiet tympani/bell section to the sequencer bit, Carl shows just how to create shades of light and dark, highs and lows on a kit. Snare, toms, bass drum and drum Moog are all integrated to stunning effect.

"Tarkus", at very nearly 36 minutes, is the longest piece of the night, and is a marvel as they attack the opening "Eruption" with glee, something they maintain through all the instrumental sections of this one. The beat is driving, forceful and very hard, softening only as they go into a moving "Stones Of Years" that really shows what ELP are all about: on the ball Hammond, measured rich baritone and a drummer who knows how to use all the kit to perfection.

"Battlefield" and "Aquatarkus" take the honours equally tonight, cantering into the former after taking "Manticore" at full pelt. The "Every blade is sharp" section really benefits tonight from a guitar *arpeggio* played ever so quietly and delicately, emphasizing the vocals – and the feelings behind them – still more as Greg tugs at the heart strings. At this point he jumps ship completely, playing a new, improvised line on the guitar before a short "Epitaph" brings the house down.

"Aquatarkus" is exciting, colourful, a shining example of the improvised trio work this band can produce, with some neat Moog solo work over the top of a bubbly beat.

"Yeah, this is a thing about a bouncer. Yeah, him over there! It features Greg Lake on Persian carpet and me on influenza," larks Keith. Well if this is how he plays with the 'flu, it is a real sign of his professionalism. What follows is a clap-along version of "Benny ..." that really rocks along, right to the mickey-taking honky tonk false ending.

Applause is still ringing and people are still chattering as they kick off "Take A Pebble" and it takes a fair while before the crowd recognize it enough to cheer.

We go into the first piano solo, teeming with influences and never the same two nights running, and then into a "Still ...", where the twelve string adds texture to the song. Everything tonight is crystal clear, the vocals in particular are right up there – so important in a love song.

"Lucky Man" is lifted by the applause that precedes it. There's no doubt that by this stage of their live career, this whole acoustic spot, mid-"Take A Pebble", is Greg's trump card. Crowd reaction tonight is incredible; there's applause all the way through "Lucky Man" and some excited singalongs on the choruses.

Keith follows that in top gear, conjuring up a seemingly effortless masterclass piano solo and sails through the improvised jazz trio part with Carl and Greg snapping at his heels, delivering a quality solo as only he can. Plenty of nice syncopation and an increasing pace from the rhythm section who don't put a foot wrong. It's powered up well by Carl on the toms and cymbals, expertly complementing Greg's bass and vocals.

ELP move from an acoustic-based 30 minute epic to an apocalyptic, sci-fi 35 minute one with ease. No introductions are necessary for "Karn Evil 9, which is full of atmosphere, eerie Hammond, vocals full of despair and very sharp drumming. After a frantic synth solo, Greg dons his ringmaster's uniform and they move into the 'thrills and shocks' section with ease. They really do play this one with fire in their hearts and things shift up several gears with Greg's superb guitar solo, backed by heavy bass Moog from Keith, adding more feeling to an already highly-charged number.

Carl's solo is a short but tight six minutes before the others rejoin the party and the finale to the "1st Impression" is huge. After that, the "2nd Impression" is blistering, Greg and Keith are on fire for the steel drum solo with Carl providing first class backing and a strong rhythm built around the toms.

The quietest and most thoughtful part of the whole epic, the piano/bass duet, is just stunning, not least because they continue playing despite the constant vocal interruptions from some sections of this crowd. The final "Impression" marches inexorably towards the climax of the main show, driven by Carl, topped by Greg's ace vocals and some of the best, and most evocative, keyboard work of the whole evening.

A slightly shorter rendition of "Pictures ..." is tonight's encore. Noisy crowd or no noisy crowd, they're clearly loving it and although this is the final number of a very long evening, the band ask no quarter. It's a classic performance, winning sustained applause that fills every lull. "The Great Gates..." is an unbeatable way to end an evening, moving from soaring Hammond, through all manner of weird sounds from the L100, to a majestic, stately crescendo that threatens to lift the roof and fly off into the night.

You can see why the guys like playing Vienna again, the audience are so enthusiastic.

SATURDAY, 25 MAY 1974

The Ahoy-Hallen, Rotterdam, Netherlands.

Another very good performance from a band who were so obviously on a roll by this stage of the tour, at show fifteen.

You can almost feel the crowd jumping up and down to "Hoedown", by the end of which ELP are strutting their stuff and flying high.

Hot on the heels of our favourite hymn is a textbook "Toccata", Moog fanfares all over the place, heavy bass lines and an exemplary musical percussion solo from the man at the back. It seems harsh to call it a drum solo, with the emphasis as it is on creating patterns and rhythms on tympani, bells and the sequencer. It's all here, even a new rock steady 4/4 section set against the Moog.

Keith invites this lively crowd to sing along to "Tarkus", a marathon 35 minute version. It's a little subdued in places, "Stones Of Years" being a prime example, but seems the better for it. The ribbon controller extravaganza in "Mass" is completely off the wall. It's preceded by a ton of lightning fast, solid Hammond, Carl filling for all he's worth, taking every opportunity to roll on the toms. It's easy to visualize him and Greg pounding out the rhythm and watching Keith charge around the front few rows of the audience, machine-gunning anyone within reach. Musical theatre at its best!

The echo in the Ahoy-Hallen add to the effects and "Epitaph" is scintillating, much to the appreciation of this crowd. The final sixteen minutes of the piece, close to half of its entire length, is a quality version of "Aquatarkus".

When it comes to "Benny ..." it seems that Greg's more or less given up on the London accent, replacing it with a harsher lilt. It gets a polite ripple of applause after an extra honky tonk ending that seems to get shorter each time.

"This next number is called an embarrassing silence," jokes Keith, after which they turn in a dignified, unhurried and ever-so-precise "Take A Pebble", a real highlight of the evening. In so many ways it harks back to the versions from the early tours.

Keith jumps off for a piano solo that's heavy on the bass lines as the right hand wanders off and does its own thing – and very well too. The acoustic numbers, "Still ..." and "Lucky Man", have a 'twangier-than-normal' sound on the twelve string.

"Prelude" and "Fugue" kick off a cracking solo piano effort from Keith, joined powerfully by the others, right on cue, for an exciting and lively trio improvisation, tinged in places with the usual humour that ELP can never resist.

"Karn Evil 9", at 36 minutes, beats "Tarkus" for the longest marathon of the night by a minute! It's delivered with a zeal that most bands reserve for the newer numbers, not something they've been playing almost nightly for nearly half a year.

The plaintive words "Can't you see? Can't you see?" stand out as they appeal to the crowd to realize the mess that man has got himself into.

The rest of "1st Impression" is thrilling stuff, complete with that unique run of seventeen consecutive *glissandos*. The remaining not-to-be-forgotten bits are the piano/bass duet in the "2nd Impression", played with such patience and precision as an abstract bridge leading the way to the finale.

Sustained shouts of "We want more!" are finally rewarded with a, relatively short, sixteen minute "Pictures …", which compensates for its brevity by being succinct and powerful. Through all the changes in mood, tempo and pace, this Dutch crowd are right there with them, joining in the fun and humour during a unique improvised section in "Baba Yaga". Greg does a bass solo quoting from a few classical pieces and then, egged on by Carl, even swings into "When the Saints Go Marching In", ably accompanied by this up-for-anything audience.

A strong way to end a concert from a band that isn't above taking a few liberties with their classic numbers.

TUESDAY, 28 MAY 1974

Palais des Sports, Paris, France.

The fourth show from the end of the tour, the second of a two-nighter in Paris, and only their fifth show in France.

The audience starts to get impatient as the guys take their time tuning – mostly down to Keith, who doesn't seem best pleased with one of the Moogs.

As if to compensate, "Hoedown" gets under way at the speed of light, with Keith stealing the show with a Moog solo that quotes heavily from Scottish jigs and folk ditties.

The crowd's reaction to "Jerusalem" and "Toccata", although more than polite, has a feeling of anti-climax about it after that rip-roaring start.

Keith does the honours: "This next one has one of those catchy, irresistible sort of tunes that you can't really help singing to yourself, so if you wanna go ahead and sing along it's quite easy. It's in 5/4 so you should have no trouble then [laughs]. This is a fantasy based on an armadillo-type creature, and it's got a name … 'Tarkus'!".

Slowed by one of those rare technical hitches (Keith says of Carl, "Sorry, he's just changing a valve on his bass drum."), they then tear into "Tarkus", the smoking-fingered keyboard wizard leading the way. It doesn't sound as heavy as some recent versions, but it's still top-drawer stuff. You can visualize Keith maniacally stabbing at the keys with both hands, before being restrained by Carl and Greg going into the last verse of "Stones Of Years".

There's a nice touch of improvisation in "Manticore" before "Battlefield" kicks in with the force of a battalion. There's one of those guitar solos that's made to sound deceptively easy by the skill of the player and then Greg steps up, holds forth beautifully on guitar and voice, captivating the crowd with a reverb-driven coda that is, quite simply, astonishing.

Keith introduces our favourite East End character: "Ok, this next one features Greg singing in the cockney vernacular all about a guy called 'Benny The Bouncer'!" The Polymoog is right up in the mix and sounds spot on as Keith decorates that shuffle rhythm.

Tonight, Paris gets *deux* false honky tonk endings to "Benny ..." but "Take A Pebble" follows so quickly that they detract from what is an epic song. Even after a superb opening and those rich-as-ever vocals, there's still no sign of applause in recognition of this one. Never ones to be put off, ELP carry on and go into acoustic overdrive for Greg's solo parts.

Keith entertains admirably, building up a head of steam as he weighs in with a stunning solo, full of quotes and phrases and with a touch of humour here and there. Things catch fire in a particularly percussive jazz trio work-out and build nicely to that classic ending. 32 minutes of sheer magic and worth every penny.

The unmistakeable organ counterpoint introduction to "Karn Evil 9" is surprisingly subdued tonight, but as Greg and Carl kick in, it becomes exciting listening. It's like an updated "Pictures..." in the sense that the musical tableaux conjure up images of first despair and then hope.

The abstract qualities of the "2nd Impression" shine here: it's clever, a mix of time signatures designed to disorientate, ranging from the steel drum solo with an "Aquatarkus" style bubbling rhythm, to the piano/bass duet with Carl time-keeping on the blocks.

Amid a crash of fuzz bass, deafening Hammond chords and machine-gun snare, the "3rd Impression" enters the fray. An excellent organ solo from Keith has some nice stabbing staccato effect, another Emerson trademark. These guys earn their final bow!

"Pictures ..." is vintage ELP from the word go, almost half an hour long, and it's still the so called short version! They steam through the textbook bits, tearing through solos as if someone said "Light the blue touch paper and retire", and the fairly new improvisation in "Baba Yaga" is riveting. Greg starts it on the fuzz pedal, Keith plays the Moog like the soundtrack from *The Forbidden Planet*. It's almost a Floyd meets Soft Machine crossed with Crimson scenario. There's sound effects galore, all courtesy of the man on the keys, leading back into the vocals, a superb "Great Gates ...", including an eleven minute Hammond and Moog solo spot for Keith – and that's it.

It rightly brings the house down, a fitting end to an excellent night.

16. *Loaded Down With Your Talents ...*

26 JULY – 21 AUGUST 1974: SEVENTH NORTH AMERICAN TOUR.
18 SHOWS.

Typical set list:	"Hoedown", "Jerusalem", "Toccata", "Tarkus", "Take A Pebble", "Still ... You Turn Me On", "Lucky Man", piano improvisations, "Take A Pebble" (reprise), "Karn Evil 9", "Pictures At An Exhibition".
Keith:	As previous tour.
Greg:	As previous tour.
Carl:	As previous tour.
PA system:	Quadraphonic as previous tour.

These were the final dates before the three year lay-off and the band were back in North America.

The set list was basically the same as it had been for the previous four tours. This made sense as it went down a storm every time with audiences who marvelled at the quality of what they were seeing and hearing. The exception was "Benny The Bouncer" who had been sacked! The set revolved around the trio of epics, namely "Tarkus", "Take A Pebble" and "Karn Evil 9" – plus the old warhorse "Pictures ..."

The light show in particular was well-noticed by both fans and reporters for being simple yet so very effective in that every shade and nuance was skilfully co-ordinated with the music.

The tour included the famous Roosevelt Stadium show, postponed because of a thunderstorm and re-arranged for three days later.

Sadly, again, not too many of these recordings are still around but those that have survived are testimony to ELP as masters of stagecraft.

FRIDAY, 26 JULY 1974

The Rich Stadium, Buffalo, NY, USA.

Tickets: $7.00 in advance

The opening night after a break of little more than three weeks, a gig that has gone down as one of their all-time greats. It bode well for the rest of the tour as ELP set out their stall.

In spite of some out of tune *portamento*, "Hoedown" features a wacky Moog solo from Keith and heavy bass lines from both Greg and Keith. The applause starts before they finish playing and the first two *Brain Salad Surgery* songs get a strong welcome from an anticipatory audience.

The first smash of the gong for "Jerusalem" gets a ripple of applause and from then on they can't put a foot wrong.

After the eerie Moog opening of "Toccata", the drums kick in giving a sense of real driving power as Carl charges through the piece. From the crowd's reaction, the percussion solo is stunning, topped with a spinning podium as those hard-working roadies earn their corn. He's clearly built in some creative changes, focused on the sequencer patterns, since they last played this one in Europe.

They follow the "Tarkus" template right up to the furious organ solo in "Stones Of Years", aggressively played with drum fills everywhere to give it a hell of a kick. A serendipitous effect of the venue's acoustics as the echo on Greg's vocals adds a touch of eeriness.

"Battlefield" is a classic: swirling intro, strong vocals, excellent emotive guitar solo from the man in the white suit, and an "Every blade is sharp..." spotlight that's definitely worth remembering. Add to that, some of the best Moog-based melody lines Keith's ever played in this number.

"Epitaph" gets a warm welcome, before the military beat of "Aquatarkus" takes over. That bubbling rhythm – never really changed in three years of "Tarkus" – is tighter than ever.

The crowd are a bit slow to recognize "Take A Pebble" but appreciate it when they do. This is a pure old school version right up to Keith's first break, so 1970 it's unbelievable: every note on the grand, every beat on the kit, every nuance of vocal is from the textbook of the first tour.

Despite the constant audience chatter, Greg gets rapturous applause for "Still ..." and "Lucky Man". Then King Keith reigns supreme for twelve minutes of outstanding solo piano that dovetails smoothly into the free jazz section. On his own he quotes from everything – from classics, to film music, sing-along and beyond.

The intro to "Karn Evil 9" is quiet, to the point of laid back, but when Greg weighs in with the vocals, everything else is cranked up. The uplifting circus ringmaster section is carried with aplomb, Keith working hard to produce superb Moog and organ runs. Greg comes in late for his first lead solo, against a background of a rhythm that's a bit rushed, but having fluffed the first couple of bars, he soon gets a grip and plays like only he can. The whole second part of the "1st Impression" really rocks; Greg especially almost moving into the heavy metal league.

"2nd Impression" is a quiet interlude after all that, at once abstract and dynamic, with some excellent trio work on piano, bass and blocks, and a steel pan solo that simply swirls around this huge stadium. The final section is played faster than is often the case, creating a feeling of impending doom and tension as the last verse kicks in. The climactic sequence begins very slowly, reverberating quadraphonically until the crowd applaud in admiration as the show climaxes with the explosion.

"Pictures ..." at 24 minutes, is up there with any version they've ever done. The audience applaud at every opportunity and, seeing as ELP are in superb form, that means a heck of a lot of sore hands.

It never fails to raise the roof, and if this stadium had one, it would be blown clean off.

MONDAY, 29 JULY 1974

The Civic Center, Providence, RI, USA.

Four dates into the tour, and for once the "Welcome Back My Friends" intro was mistimed, ELP were not quite ready and the tuning continued unabashed.

Greg shouts "Hello!" and there's still a few seconds delay before the *portamento* marks the beginning of "Hoedown", the show proper.

A stately, hard-driven "Jerusalem", competently done, and then a spirited "Toccata" starts with the usual mix of Moog and tympani, before they all pile in and Carl engages the whole kit.

"Tarkus" is introduced, as usual, by Keith. "This next one sort of tells a story but you can make your own one up if you want to. It's basically a fantasy piece based on an armadillo-type creature by the name of Tarkus." The Hammond stands out in this one, both in the melody and the solos.

Through the solos and the vocal sections in "Stones" and "Mass", it's easy to tell that they're enjoying themselves with Keith recognizably testing the others' ability to hit their cues during the improvisations.

In complete contrast to the sci-fi fantasy world of "Tarkus", "Take A Pebble" is a classic return to acoustic majesty, this time Carl's hi-hat and cymbals really hit the button. "Still ...", always on the twelve string, isn't immediately recognized by this crowd, but once they do they lct you know. As one astute member of the audience says, "He's gonna do 'Lucky Man' now". He's right – he does, and it gets an even bigger reception than the previous one.

Keith's well-paced and nicely varied solo casts its spell over the audience, then the jazz-inspired free-form section, built around themes and cues is a heady brew of classical, boogie-woogie, touches of silent music and days of the Nice, all played by one of the tightest jazz combos on the planet. Back to the script – in a manner of speaking – as the final verse of the "Pebble" reprise sees Greg's voice resounding around the system, dramatic pauses there as ever, ending beautifully as the vocals fade away and Keith strums on the piano one last time. This crowd love it.

Unfortunately, all that survives of the rest of this show is the first part of "Karn Evil 9: 1ˢᵗ Impression".

What was the rest of the show like? We can only imagine – but, hell, it must have been worth seeing!

SATURDAY, 10 AUGUST 1974

The "August Jam" at The Motor Speedway, Charlotte, NC, USA.

Their second big U.S. festival, very much like the Ontario Speedway but this time in the Deep South. The bill, apart from ELP, had a distinctive southern rock flavour with the Allman Brothers, Black Oak Arkansas and the Ozark Mountain Daredevils all playing. Mr Lake in particular just couldn't win the discussion with the promoters over who should headline. The Allman Brothers won the battle of the Gregs and topped the bill.

It rained for a whole week before the event and, even though the sun shone in North Carolina that day, it couldn't stop everyone being knee deep in red mud. Sadly, no record of the show-opening "Hoedown" they must have played, but "Jerusalem" sounds grand, with Greg singing this most English of songs like his life depended on it.

Keith goes straight into "Toccata" with those piercing Moog fanfares before Greg and Carl pile in, and he leads the charge to the first percussion break. Whoops of delight signal how much this southern crowd love the bells, the tymps and the amazing sequencer patterns.

As with everything so far tonight, "Tarkus" is heavy on bass rhythms, courtesy of both Greg and Keith. "Mass" is brimful of that stabbing Moog, backed by Hammond, going into a lightning organ and ribbon controller solo. The crowd egg Keith on, cheering every musical gunshot as he races around the stage – and off it – like a man possessed. They all hit their cues at the end of the solo, amazing when we consider that Keith has to climb back on stage as well as do everything else, and the lead in to "Battlefield" is together and tight. The opening drum break is dramatic, as are the Hammond chords, but it's a pity that Keith's bass pedals have got too harsh, too brittle a sound to suit the mood of this one. Never mind, it's soon corrected and all's well by the time Greg fires off a nice lead solo.

"Aquatarkus" tonight is shorter, based on a chugging rather than a bubbling rhythm, but carries the day as Keith goes off on a tangent, swishing Moog notes everywhere which wash over everything.

"Take A Pebble" has a ton of crashing, rippling cymbals and it goes down well from the word go. There's a relaxed solo on the Steinway from Keith, before handing over to Greg. After "Still ..." the punters are calling for "Lucky Man" and collectively the songs get a roar of applause.

Keith's second solo, and the jazz improvisations, now seem to be truncated every night, but still sound relaxed and are played with aplomb.

A subdued Keith opens "Karn Evil 9" with the organ counterpoint, but loses any inhibitions once the others weigh in. Keyboards are high in the mix and, if anything, Greg's vocals suffer a little because of it, but at least we can make out some nice little bass touches on the Moog. The "Fight tomorrow!" line now has more emphasis each night as the beginning to the brasher, uplifting, hopeful section focused on Greg's ringmaster act. A breakneck six minute solo from Carl never fails to impress: 'accuracy at speed' seems to be his trademark.

The crowd get a little restless during the "2nd Impression", but an intense "3rd Impression", as intended, steals the show hands down. It starts amazingly fast, accompanied by long cheers, whistles and whoops from these lively southerners, and maintains the pace through each verse and solo.

The climax, smoke, wings and explosion appear to be long-anticipated by this festival crowd, the audience even clapping along to the start of the final Moog sequence. The band deserve every cheer they get as they take their bow.

A twenty minute "Pictures ..." is the encore, so full of energy that it could have been played at the top of the show. Keith attacks the L100 as if there's no tomorrow and before we know it, another superb performance is over.

The audience laps it up. ELP have set the bar high for the Allman Brothers.

TUESDAY, 20 AUGUST 1974

The Roosevelt Stadium, Jersey City, NJ, USA.

In an old ball park that had seen better days, this was the gig re-scheduled from August 17 after an horrendous thunderstorm had put paid to any hope of a show that day. Part of the stage had blown away and the Moogs, temperamental at the best of times, got a real soaking.

Speaking of the original date three days earlier: "My other favourite memory of this night. Carl showed up for the sound check with permed hair! He said someone told him it would help keep the sweat out of his eyes. Carl with a 'fro ... that was funny, " chuckles Linda Heath, a long-time friend of the band.

It's the penultimate show before what turned out to be the three year break and it's a killer of a performance. Maybe it's the previous cancellation but the crowd are so up for this one they get incredibly impatient, whistling at the preparations on stage and almost reaching the point of slow hand-clapping and jeering. Nonetheless, after several minutes it's clear that the band are ready and, before the usual MC intro is even half way through, the crowd go absolutely bananas.

The *portamento* signals a tight, very fast, head-shaking version of "Hoedown" that lifts everything and everyone from the off. The applause, not surprisingly, is ecstatic.

Keith introduces the show with "Alright, we finally made it! ...OK, we're gonna give you some *Brain Salad Surgery*, starting off with "Jerusalem" and moving into our adaptation of Ginastera's "First Piano Concerto", featuring Carl Palmer there on percussion synthesizer".

It seems that tonight ELP are determined to make amends for that postponed show and the soaking the crowd got. After a stirring "Jerusalem", there's some mesmerizing, atmospheric Moog, intricate keyboard/drum/guitar interplay, and an all-powerful solo from Carl on the revolving podium. They've upped the pace a bit and as a consequence it seems more aggressive and the faithful lap it up.

At the start of "Tarkus", both Greg and Carl miss their cue and Keith's played a full bar before the others crash in. After that, this one's just consistent, fast-paced and note-perfect. Lots of bass lines and very strong vocals in "Stones Of Years", topped off with a manic organ solo before a "Mass" that has a similar ribbon controller outing as the highlight.

Almost the whole second half of "Tarkus" is reserved for "Aquatarkus", creeping in quietly after Greg's spotlight solo, then taking off at the gallop as the rhythm section comes in. The whole Moog solo travels through so many mood changes, highs and lows, sitting on top of that bubbling bass and drum sound, that this one has become an epic in its own right.

"Take A Pebble", with cymbals everywhere, faultless *glissandos* and those lovely rich tones in the vocals, wins a wave of applause at the end of the first verse, and this seems to egg Keith and Carl on.

Keith excels with two entertaining solos, the first pretty much by the book, the second, longer one, his opportunity to indulge himself, throwing in touches of Nice, classical, jazz, and most other things he can think of, including a full rendition of "Maple Leaf Rag"; its first outing for a long time.

In between, Greg offers up a "Still ..." and "Lucky Man" that see his voice loud and clear; really necessary tonight with this incredibly raucous crowd.

The delicate acoustic intro to "Lucky Man" is new, drawn out and just isn't appreciated in the same way that the vocal sections are. The seven minute jazz trio part is livelier than usual, all of them straining at the leash. They go so far as to throw in a couple of brand new sections, including a hilarious take on "The Stripper". The fairly loose structure of "Pebble" is in stark contrast to the

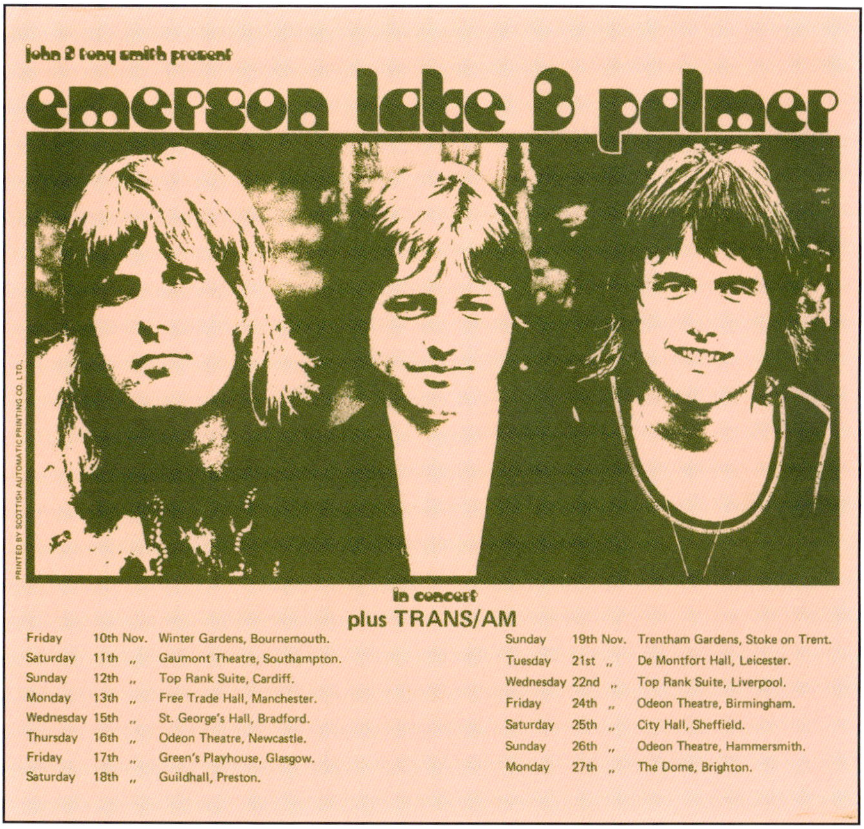
john & tony smith present
emerson lake & palmer
PRINTED BY SCOTTISH AUTOMATIC PRINTING CO. LTD.
in concert
plus TRANS/AM
Friday 10th Nov. Winter Gardens, Bournemouth.
Saturday 11th „ Gaumont Theatre, Southampton.
Sunday 12th „ Top Rank Suite, Cardiff.
Monday 13th „ Free Trade Hall, Manchester.
Wednesday 15th „ St. George's Hall, Bradford.
Thursday 16th „ Odeon Theatre, Newcastle.
Friday 17th „ Green's Playhouse, Glasgow.
Saturday 18th „ Guildhall, Preston.
Sunday 19th Nov. Trentham Gardens, Stoke on Trent.
Tuesday 21st „ De Montfort Hall, Leicester.
Wednesday 22nd „ Top Rank Suite, Liverpool.
Friday 24th „ Odeon Theatre, Birmingham.
Saturday 25th „ City Hall, Sheffield.
Sunday 26th „ Odeon Theatre, Hammersmith.
Monday 27th „ The Dome, Brighton.

WELCOME BACK MY FRIENDS TO
THE SHOW THAT NEVER ENDS
CLEVELAND STADIUM
SUN., AUG. 4th—5 P.M.
(DOORS OPEN 3:30 P.M.)
KEITH
EMERSON
EMERSON
LAKE &
PALMER
SPECIAL GUESTS!
JAMES GANG
CLIMAX BLUES BAND
CARL
PALMER
GREG
LAKE
TICKETS:
$7 ADVANCE, $8 AT GATE
TICKETS ON SALE NOW AT THESE OUTLETS: PUBLIC HALL BOX OFFICE, ALL CLEVELAND TUX SHOPS, WARD'S FOLLY— • AKRON, Mayflower Ticket Agency, Akron Tux Shop • CANTON, Cleveland Tux Shop • ELYRIA • The Men's Shop, ASHTABULA, Schaffer & Sons — ERIE, Boston Store • YOUNGSTOWN • NILES, National Record Marts • KENT, Community Store
FOR MAIL ORDERS: Send money order only to Belkin Productions, 3101 Euclid Ave., Cleveland 44115. Enclose self-addressed, stamped envelope.
Manticore
NO BOTTLES OR CANS ALLOWED IN STADIUM. FOR INFO CALL (216) 696-1066

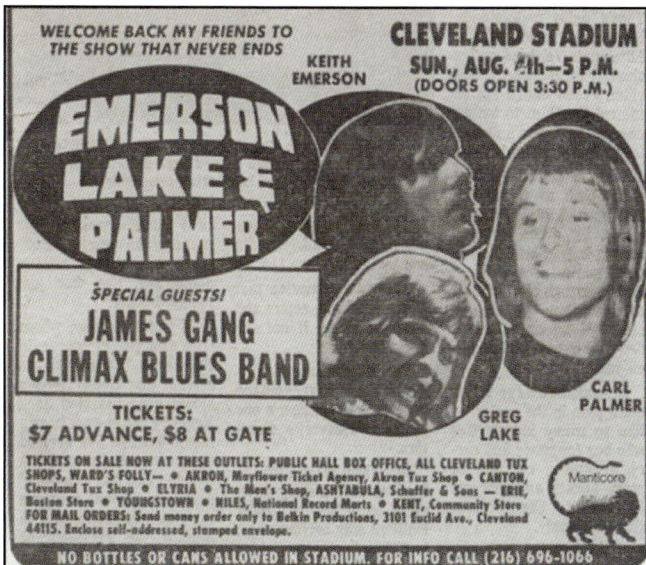

Above: Rare pink flyer from UK autumn tour, 1972. Were you at any of these dates?

Left: Looks like a good line-up. Courtesy of Neil Corsatea/Air C Images.

Left: Video screens that showed images whilst "Abaddon's Bolero" was playing.
© Graham Kennedy.

Below: Quality of this shot isn't great, but it shows Greg and choir singing "Silent Night" at Madison Square Garden December 1973.

Top left and right: Two photos of the Tarkus models, Dundee 1972.
© both photos, Graham Kennedy.

Above: Keith: "Do you know there's a tiger on the set?"
Carl: "You play the melody, I'll fill in." Courtesy of Gudrun Friedrich.

Top: Who says rock stars are unapproachable? Keith with fan Linda Heath at a Jersey City gig where rain stopped play. © Linda Heath.

Above: It's Carl "Permer". Linda Heath says he got this perm to keep the sweat out of his eyes. Courtesy of Neil Corsatea/Air C Images.

Greg and Keith in classic poses. Courtesy of Neil Corsatea/Air C Images.

Lest we forget, there were reunion tours. These shots are from 1992.
Courtesy of Neil Corsatea/Air C Images.

Keith and Greg's rigs at Lakewood, OH, 2010. Only trouble is, the gig was cancelled
… and it really was on April Fools' Day. © Neil Corsatea/Air C Images.

Top: Windcheaters were popular back in the day. This one is worth a bob or two. Courtesy of Tony Ortiz.

Above: Patches were popular too. Your mum would have sewn it over a hole in your jeans. Courtesy of Tony Ortiz.

comparative rigidity of "Karn Evil 9", on the face of it not easy bedfellows, but both excellent examples of how ELP develop material on stage.

The start of "Karn Evil 9" almost takes the audience by surprise and it takes them a few seconds to realize what the guys are playing. Tonight, it's very in-your-face, loud, aggressive and tight as could be.

It's organized mayhem towards the end of "Part 1", the "Next upon the bill" section, followed immediately by the fastest drum intro (to the guitar solo) that this listener can ever recall. Part 2, and the snare/tom driven drum solo, maintain the standard, the pace and the effect. You can feel the excitement in this one, the band carried along on a wave of their own making.

The "2nd Impression" is, tonight, a calming session before the onslaught of the final showdown. Some nifty work from the three here, especially Keith as he flies through the steel drum Moog solo, slowing to the abstract duet and trio pieces, full of poise and skill.

After that, it's bows, a brief trip backstage, and then the encore – a 25 minute "Pictures ..." – which sticks to the template of the new version, building the tension well through "Promenade" to "Baba Yaga", before the psychedelic synth takes over.

In the middle of this showcase bit, Greg, for some reason, starts playing the unmistakeable bass line to "When the red, red robin comes bop-bop-bopping along"!

"The Great Gates ..." is dominated by a way-out ten minute organ-throwing, Moog-fiddling solo from Keith, prior to the others re-joining him on stage. As the closing piece to another marvellous show, this movement is unbeatable. Power, edge, majesty and splendour are all in abundance, the final words seem to hang in the air for a lifetime, and it's another top-notch show in the bag.

The audience go totally crazy for more, but that's it and only one more gig for three long years.

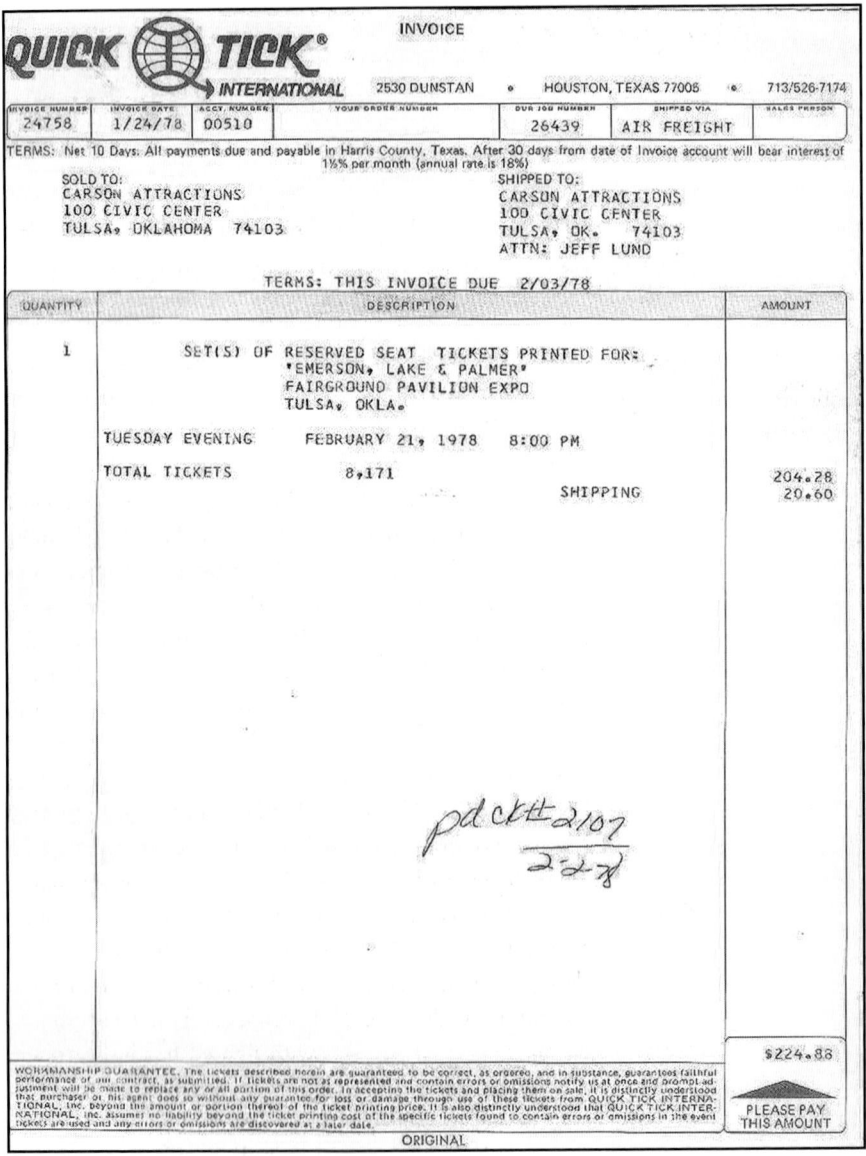

Before the internet, this is how you got your tickets. Courtesy of Tony Ortiz.

17. *If You've The Stomach For A Broadside ...*

24 MAY – 30 NOVEMBER 1977: EIGHTH NORTH AMERICAN TOUR.
85 SHOWS.

Typical set list:	**With orchestra:** "Abaddon's Bolero", "Hoedown", "Karn Evil 9 1st Impression Part 2", "The Enemy God Dances With The Black Spirits", "Tarkus", "From The Beginning", "Piano Concerto No. 1" (1st and 3rd movements), "Closer To Believing", "Knife Edge", "Pictures At An Exhibition", "C'est La Vie", "Lucky Man", "Tank", "Nutrocker", "Pirates", "Fanfare For The Common Man"/"America"/"Rondo"/"Fanfare". **As a trio:** "Karn Evil 9 1st Impression Part 2", "Hoedown", "Tarkus", "Take A Pebble"/Extracts from "Piano Concerto No. 1"/"Take A Pebble" reprise, "Still ... You Turn Me On", "Knife Edge", "Pictures At An Exhibition", "C'est La Vie", "Lucky Man", "Tank", "Nutrocker", "Pirates", "Fanfare For The Common Man"/"Rondo"/"Fanfare" (Some set changes from October onwards), "Show Me The Way To Go Home"
Keith:	9 ft Steinway Grand, Upright 'Honky Tonk' piano, Yamaha GX-1 polysynthesizer with a computer-based tuning system. Custom built Moog console, Mini Moog, Hammond C-3 and L-100 organs, and an accordion.
Greg:	Alembic eight string bass with lighted fret indicators, a Travis Bean electric guitar, Zemaitis acoustic, and three Martin vintage acoustic guitars. Echoplex unit.
Carl:	The revolving kit on the podium plus xylophone, glockenspiel, congas, tympani, chimes, gongs, castanets and crotales.
PA System:	Known as the S-4 system: 35,000 watts indoor system, 72,000 watts outside set-up, with a Yamaha PM 1000 main mixing board, mixers and submixers (including one under the stage to mix just the orchestra), designed by the same company, JBL, that had designed a smaller

system for the 1976 Montreal Olympics. 311 1,000
watt coloured computer-tape controlled lights. All
sound speakers were suspended from hanging gantries
above an uncluttered stage. Monitors were fed from a
completely separate mixer system.

"We have to make that step forward to a musical maturity,"[70] states Greg. Three
years out of circulation as a band and punk was taking hold fast, but, to quote
Alan Freeman in 1974, "The big ones are back". With a vengeance, Alan. Keith
has an interesting view on punk: "Every so often you have to introduce a freshness
to music and that was what punk set out to do. The irony was that they targeted
us as representing everything that was wrong with rock. I say it was ironic. We
were the band in prog that refused to play by the rules ... By turning on us, the
punks were almost turning on one of their own".[71]

As journalist Chris Welch put it, they had a "Genuine desire to re-think a
musical form that had been milked dry."[72]

Greg believed the band had to "... move on from wailing guitars and 'my baby's
left me'. You can only do that so long before it becomes utterly meaningless. That's
the reason we took three years off, to think of how to move the band forward."[73]

This was the tour that redefined the nature of Emerson, Lake and Palmer's live
performance. The story of the orchestra, its recruitment from 5,000 hopefuls, and
demise are fairly well-documented, as is the fact that apparently it was Keith's idea
initially, his life-long dream, to go the whole hog and take a 70 piece orchestra out
on the road night after night.

The plan was to tour the States in the early summer of 1977, then, having
sought out suitably large venues in the UK and Europe, take it to the other side of
the Atlantic by September of that year. Part of the reason given for delaying the
UK shows was the band's tax situation.

"We have a format worked out which involves pieces from all of us and pieces
of past material we want to keep in. It'll be quite a long show but we won't be
playing all night,"[74] Carl explained. The team spirit amongst band and orchestra,
none of whom were over 35, was solid. Band and orchestra rehearsed separately
at first, then together. ELP rented a small hockey arena for two months in March
and April 1977 to complete rehearsals begun in December 1976 in the Olympic
Stadium in Montreal.

Undoubtedly, the orchestral shows were well-received by fans but something
the size of this enterprise just couldn't last. Seven 45-feet long articulated trucks,
plus an extra three for the open air dates, carried the tour equipment; three buses
transported the orchestra and choir. Their entourage, in addition to the orchestra,
was 63 roadies, various road crews, personal assistants, secretaries, accountants,
a doctor and more.

Everything about the set-up was innovative: ELP were on a black-carpeted, aluminium triangular stage. Carl's podium was raised two feet higher than Keith and Greg; the orchestra (all wearing white) were behind them on five modular platforms, all with fold-back monitors so everyone could hear everyone else.

Each instrument was individually equipped with the new Frapp pick-ups – even the $66,000 Stradivarius of one violinist – with six engineers employed just to monitor the orchestra in the live mix. This was one reason for the top sound quality.

Godfrey Salmon, the conductor, towered above everyone else on his own hydraulic lift. The aim of all this, the key concept of the live show, was to provide the best possible sight lines for the audience, with absolutely nothing other than instruments on the stage itself.

Monitors were suspended below the stage on grids, with the sound projected upwards at the performers. Keith and Greg actually stood on grids when playing. Four tons of equipment were hanging from the stage ceiling: lighting, sound and light cables all concealed in thirteen huge pods that effectively formed a roof over the production, creating an environment for the band and orchestra. If some of that rig had come tumbling down it would have added a new meaning to the musical term 'flat'.

The orchestral escapade did not work for three main reasons:
- An average audience of only 85% of capacity when nearer to 100% was needed.
- The subsequent cancellation of three large, open air shows that cost over $2 million in lost revenue
- The sheer number of paid employees that meant the salary bill soared, whether the band played or not.

There was a joke doing the rounds at the time which summed things up rather well:
Q: How many ELP road crew does it take to change a light bulb?
A: All of them – one to hold the bulb and the rest to rotate the lighting rig!

The last date with the orchestra, apart from three big shows at Madison Square Garden in early July and the Olympic Stadium in Montreal in August, was in Des Moines, Iowa, on 12 June. As Greg said, "They were crying while they played."[75] "Certainly it was too much financially but it worked musically, artistically and visually without a question of a doubt,"[76] he added.

After that, the band rehearsed intensely for three days to hone their trio show, and it was this that apparently saved the financial bacon. As a trio, there are some quite significant changes to the set list, both in structure and score. Further amendments were made for the second half of the 1977 tour, from October 15 onwards to include some of the songs from the new album, *Works Volume II*.

TUESDAY, 31 MAY, 1977

The Cobo Hall, Detroit, MI, USA.

Having kicked off the tour with two nights at The Freedom Hall, Louisville, Kentucky on 24 and 25 May, this was night five of the orchestral tour, things having bedded in nicely and it showed.

Some doubt exists as to whether the recording that has survived is from the 31 May or from the following evening of this two-nighter. Either way, it's the earliest surviving recording from the orchestral tour and is 35,000 watts of pure gold.

And it was loud – very loud. "The volume never reached the threshold of pain (130 decibels), but it was, in Salmon's words 'enough to peel an apple at ten feet'."[77]

"Abbadon's Bolero" sounds impressive: these orchestral musicians are no time-servers. Everything is full of energy and life, driven on all the time by that incessant snare beat. It harks back to the days of 1972 when ELP opened shows with a taped version – but it sure wipes the floor with all that. Every note, each nuance, is 100% clear, a real testimony to the sound system.

With applause still ringing, Keith, Greg and Carl tear into a "Hoedown" that can't fail. It's a rip-roaring, bubbling version and these guys are obviously enjoying themselves.

The Moog intro to "Karn Evil 9" signals another uplifting piece followed by one of the most famous opening lines in rock, Greg's vocals filling the hall, despite the fact that he sounds as if he's got a lousy cold.

The main organ solo is now completely different, much more low key in the first instance with new phrases and sounds better. After an incredibly fluid but strong drum break from Carl, the finale of the piece brings back fond memories of the 1974 tour, ear-splitting, roof-lifting stuff complete with the flying Moog ending and explosion.

They dive straight into "The Enemy God Dances With The Black Spirits" [an arrangement of the second movement of Prokofiev's *Scythian Suite*], the first of Carl's showcases, and the orchestra makes all the difference with some strong rhythms. For the first time in the set, Godfrey and the players prove that they're not just an add-on but a vital, integral element of the show. Keith says his first words of the show, "Good to see you again, hey!! A track off *Works Volume 1*, [For the newcomer to ELP, *Works Volume 1* was a 1977 double album where each band member took the lead for one side with the remaining side being a genuine group effort] featuring Carl there, originally by Prokofiev called 'The Enemy God'. We're gonna do something now which was on a previous album, *Trilogy*, I believe, a thing called 'From The Beginning'."

Keith gives it a Moog fanfare intro, a sort of cross between sci-fi and a cinema advert, and the song itself opens with Greg singing the title before going into the melody with Carl on congas, and Keith doing some nice touches on the synth. This number has been totally re-worked, barely recognizable as the soft, moody piece it is on the album. The choirs adds some strong backing harmonies, Greg turns in a very competent lead solo, and the coda is long, powerful, with nice balance between band and orchestra.

Keith's "Piano Concerto" is, predictably with such a piece, textbook, sticking exactly to the recorded version. In contrast to many live numbers, that, however, is its strength. It's such a departure from the usual rock band thing, but the crowd lap it up, proving that there are plenty of punters who want to listen to something a little different. It's played to perfection and, if anything, is a fantastic credit to the sound balance guys who make it all work for the entire sixteen minutes. The finale is magnificent and the applause, both during and after, is loud, long and thoroughly deserved.

Greg, still clearly full of cold, credits Keith, who then returns the favour and introduces the first of Greg's solo pieces, "Closer To Believing", a stunning number with him and the orchestra winning gold stars. It's a love song, sung with heartfelt emotion and set against an immense orchestral melody. It was allegedly first performed at one of the German dates in April 1973 although according to Stewart Young, it took Greg and Pete Sinfield at least two years to complete it.

Is Greg doing the whole Charles Aznavour thing? It works (no pun intended). The richness and textures of this song mark it out as a winner.

"The first album came out about 1970 and we've re-arranged something off of that particular album. This is 'Knife Edge'," Keith tells everyone. Band and orchestra pile in for the opening chords and then the crowd really get behind the bass line from Greg and Carl's hi-hat – shades of 1970/1971 all over again. It's possibly the only number in the show where at first the band and orchestra sound a little discordant, not quite as effective as on other songs.

The trio element is still full of that harsh, aggressive edge from long ago, still sung with the same sense of urgency. The orchestra come back in for the middle section and sound as if they've always been there – by the time the last verse comes around, it all gels and sounds so together.

Introduced by Keith, "C'est La Vie" gets the biggest cheer of the evening so far. Keith, complete with accordion, steps up for the middle eight and carries all before him in a note-perfect solo straight from the Left Bank of the Seine, all he needs is a beret. The final verse, supported by choral harmonies and a wonderful string section, is as good as anything they play, and gets a huge wave of applause and cheers.

With barely a pause for breath, Greg strums the intro chords to "Lucky Man", instantly recognized by many in the crowd with cheers aplenty for this oldie but goldie.

Greg does the MC honours next, sounding audibly weary between songs but never once showing it during an actual performance, "We'd like to do something off our latest album. This is the longest piece on the ELP side, it's called 'Pirates'." Yet again, this crowd goes ballistic, but then Keith intercedes, "That's the one after this!"

There then follows some banter between him and Greg that has the audience in stitches until Keith decides, "We're gonna feature Carl over there! This is 'Tank'!"

The sheer power behind this one is almost tangible as Carl launches into the number, with the beginning very much as it was back on the first album in 1970. Moog and orchestra are all well-placed and sit comfortably alongside each other to provide both melody and rhythm for the man on the podium. Keith zips through a Moog solo, from which the orchestra picks out and repeats the main phrases. Then the spotlight's on Carl for a torrent of a three minute solo. As everyone else comes back in, they prove what an uplifting, exhilarating number this piece is. The big ending, especially, has a real jazzy feel to it, as Keith and the brass section try to 'out-brass' each other.

"Pirates" finally gets underway and sticks closely to the recorded version. The imagery is magnificent from the off, with the GX-1, percussion and strings working well together to set the opening scene with the series of repeated chords. The frequent changes of pace are well-handled, changes that match the twists and turns of the narrative from Greg. The trio section, after the tag "This town is ours, tonight!" is fast and features some excellent instrumental work from all three.

Unannounced, "Fanfare For The Common Man" starts with the tympani notes we've come to know and love. As soon as the trumpets sound, the crowd know what's afoot. The bit up to the improvisation is lively, hard-driven and stays close to the original. The long improvised solo gets off to a bit of a lame start as Keith fluffs a few notes, but he soon picks up, as does the whole piece.

It's got much of the R&B feel of the album version, with a punchy rhythm from Greg and Carl, and then, seven minutes in, they do the unexpected and go into a thunderous "Rondo". Keith goes off on one with the Hammond, so fast that it seems the others have difficulty keeping up. Keith's antics with the L100 are a delight, you can almost feel him throwing the thing around the stage.

The coda for "Fanfare ..." goes back to the original, a glorious match between band and orchestra, and a superb way to end an amazing night.

It's not hard to see why the orchestral tour lost money. Courtesy of Gudrun Friedrich.

SUNDAY, 5 JUNE 1977

The Milwaukee Arena, Milwaukee, WI, USA.

Sadly, only some of this show has survived.

"Knife Edge" is strong, full of mood and menace, but slower than in the past. Band and orchestra are working well on this one and it's got a full-sounding rhythm.

The "Piano Concerto" catches most of the crowd by surprise and they seem unsure of how to take it. Once settled, it is however played to a virtually silent audience, genuinely stunned at the quality of what they're hearing at a rock show. There are whole sections of this for which Godfrey Salmon and his orchestra take all the credit, and so they should. It's played with a verve that flows from musicians enjoying what they're doing, not the least of whom is Keith himself.

"We'd like to do something off the same album, this time featuring Greg, Greg Lake's side. This is 'Closer To Believing'," Keith tells the faithful. The combination of orchestra and Greg's rich vocals, with him right at the top of the mix, is simply wonderful. It's an impassioned version, heart-wrenching, spine-tingling stuff, beautifully delivered. The choir are very noticeable on this one, especially on the chorus, and the whole song is a treat for the senses. With the final words, "You are windblown, but you are mine!" still hanging in the air, the strings play out a brief coda and the audience go crazy.

Keith credits Greg's performance and then, always to the point, utters those words harking right back to the early, heady days of 1970, "Alright, We're gonna give you 'Pictures At An Exhibition'!".

Surprisingly little applause here, and what follows is a touch disappointing bearing in mind the "Pictures ..." of old. At fifteen minutes, it's the abbreviated version, not that far removed from the tours of 1972 and 1973, but although it's played to perfection and feels gutsy, it lacks drive, energy, pace and sheer power.

Even Keith's Moog solo in "Baba Yaga" sounds restrained, as if he's pulling his punches. Apart from some shining moments in the second "Promenade" – dominated by Greg's vocals – and the "Great Gates..." the band and orchestra never really gel as they do in other numbers. The final, spectacular verse of the "Great Gates ..." is, however, the crescendo we've come to expect, with Greg's powerful voice leading the way for everyone to unite in a magnificent finale. That "Death is life" line, backed by the choir, carries the day. The sound is just massive and wins generous applause.

Applause still ringing, Keith announces that they're going to bring things down again with another Greg Lake song, "C'est La Vie". Close to the original throughout, this is arguably *the* song of the whole show that proves beyond doubt the value and worth of the orchestra. It's sumptuous, clear, sparkling and *tres*-Gallic. Three years ago Greg was a cockney bouncer called Benny; now he's a Parisian crooner – *C'est la vie* indeed! Keith offers up a cracking accordion solo against the backdrop of acoustic guitar and subdued strings. In the coda, the aforementioned strings surge forth and lift the ending to glorious heights.

Greg keeps up the strong performance on acoustic guitar for "Lucky Man", still such an emotionally-delivered number, now with some nice new touches in the melody. From there on, the crowd are right behind them.

It's onward and upward into "Tank", a piece full of driving jazzy, rhythm, delicate synth solos and tons of imaginative drumming from Carl. Patterns and fills on the toms are stunning, as is the unbelievably fast cymbal work. Overall, this is one of those pieces that until this tour, ELP have never really been able to capture live but now they make up for that with an incredible version time after time.

The drama of "Pirates", the last of the surviving Milwaukee tracks, and the closer for the main set, is both enchanting and gripping. The long introductory series of chords from orchestra and synth works well. Greg delivers the vocals with perfection and poise, skilfully narrating the story of adventure on the high seas, as the orchestra and band together superbly recapture the textures of the original. The climax is breathtaking, picking up some pace as they come to the final verse.

That's all we have from Milwaukee.

THURSDAY, 9 JUNE 1977

Dane County Coliseum, Madison, WI, USA.

Two weeks into the tour and this one was a belter of a performance. Not all the show has made it to the present for posterity though.

"Abaddon's Bolero", the curtain-raiser, does just what it should: it whips up the crowd as the music gets louder, the full orchestra coming in on the main theme. The applause and cheers are a giveaway for when ELP take to the stage and join the players for the final, thunderous statement of the main theme. You can sense the smiles on the band's faces with a reception like this.

From one vivid, enthusiastic piece to another as Keith, Greg and Carl launch into a speedy, head-shaking but totally accurate "Hoedown". Applause is ecstatic and seems to galvanize everyone on stage to perform even better.

"Welcome Back My Friends" (as "Karn Evil 9: 1st Impression", Part 2 seems to have become known) is bass heavy, which gives it the kick it needs, the vocals are spot-on and the drum break is typical Carl. The applause is deafening as they plunge headlong into "The Enemy God ...". The orchestra provides excellent detail here, working so closely with Carl and the synth in particular and it's another number with a rabble-rousing ending.

Greg shouts, "Good to see you all!", and then the man at the keys announces a touching "From The Beginning". The strings work overtime, there's a light touch from the woodwind section, and some nifty, melodic synth. The choir makes the whole thing sound even more magnificent.

"C'est La Vie", also introduced by Keith, kicks off with some lovely acoustic. It faithfully reproduces the original, albeit with a bit more power, and Greg sounds impressive. The chorus itself is just spellbinding, Greg, choir and orchestra in perfect harmony. To cap it all, that accordion solo never fails, with some audible gasps of "Oh" and "Wow" as Keith shines.

After some lengthy and boring Moog tuning, "Pictures ..." brings everyone back to attention. Band and orchestra seem to really gel as brass and strings give "Promenade" a swinging, punchy feel. There some strong 'unison' moments in both "The Gnome" and "Baba Yaga", the sound effects on the Moog sitting well alongside woodwind, and all the time Carl's working his socks off.

Perhaps the most beautiful part, the most poignant, is Greg's vocal "Promenade" as he starts with "Lead me from tortured dreams ..." and Godfrey gently brings in the players behind him. This contrasts nicely with the anarchy in the USA that is "Baba Yaga", featuring full-blooded Hammond and Moog solos.

"Great Gates ..." wins applause in its own right. They build towards a massive crescendo and, as Keith does his bells impersonation with the Hammond stops, one of his female fans shouts out, "Emerson is God!" Makes a change from Clapton, I suppose.

The brass section earn their money with a first-rate contribution to that big ending, applause from this crowd overlapping the final chords by at least fifteen seconds.

The "Piano Concerto" is excellent, Keith's dream has come true as every twist and turn wins applause. Plenty of delicate work here from woodwind and strings in particular, all played with enthusiasm and verve. Keith's piano work is world-class: it's no wonder that the orchestral musicians so admired ELP's musical abilities throughout this tour.

That audiences, on a nightly basis, sit through almost eighteen minutes of what some might construe as 'boring' is testimony itself to the qualities of Keith's composition. The Third Movement is dramatic stuff, building the forward drive motion right to the very end. The balance between piano and orchestra is just right and applause, whistles and cheers are long and loud.

"Closer To Believing" is sung with passion and conviction, faithful to the original, but still lifted to new heights by excellent choral and string work. Smooth, rich vocals fill the hall as the final verse sweeps all before it, orchestra taking something of a back seat to highlight Greg. It's well appreciated by the crowd.

"Tank" has it all: a tight, belting rhythm, an incredible feeling of improvised jazz, understated Moog soloing and world class drumming. The call and response section between orchestra and drums leads into Carl's solo; unrelenting in its drive, variation and well-constructed patterns. Hands a blur as he hammers the toms amid waves of applause and calls of "Carl Palmer!", though nobody seems to hail him as the Supreme Deity as that female fan did for Keith.

The choice of "Pirates" to close the set is an inspired one: The opening conjures up images of a ship riding the waves in its search for conquest, after which Keith throws in a radically changed short Moog solo before Greg comes in on the vocals. These are handled with consummate ease, as is the dynamic trio middle section that has a rollicking, sweep-all-before-it GX-1 solo.

It's quite possibly the best number of the evening, leaving them calling for more.

Did they get it? Again, we'll never really know.

SATURDAY, 11 JUNE 1977

St Paul Civic Center Arena, Minneapolis, MN, USA.

Tickets: $8.50 in advance; $10.00 on the door

This was one of those shows where they could simply do no wrong. This was the penultimate orchestral show (apart from the reunions in New York and Montreal) and arguably one of their very finest moments.

There are welcomes and whistles from the word go in Minneapolis, the crowd going crazy with each re-statement of the "Abaddon's Bolero" theme as the sound builds and builds. This sure sounds better than it ever did on record, with the addition of a choir being a real strength. Keith, Greg and Carl take the stage to tumultuous applause.

Tonight's "Bolero" is even more powerful than normal, the climax is just huge and before we know where we are, Keith hits the *portamento* and "Hoedown" is off. As an audience-lifter, it works every time: it's pacey, tight, raucous, keeps the crowd at fever pitch and generates applause, cheers and whistles all the way through.

It's clap-along-a "Karn Evil 9" night as they go straight into "2nd Impression, Part 2", like a tank driving through the side of a house. Keith's Moog solo is white hot, decorating a powerhouse of a rhythm and Greg matches him star for star with a hot lead guitar solo. Carl's brief drum break fills the Civic Center in its own right and the finale is wonderfully explosive as the synth reverberates around the hall.

As if that's not enough, they segue immediately into Prokofiev's "The Enemy God ...", a showcase in many respects for the orchestra and the touches they bring to such a fiery number. Far from detracting from the flavour of the original piece, Carl's massive drum onslaught greatly enhances it, and it's played each night with scarcely any alteration to the detail of the classical version. It's heavy, punchy and goes down well with this electrically-charged crowd.

Keith shouts, "Carl Palmer there! Cheers! We're gonna do something off the *Trilogy* album. It's called 'From The Beginning'."

The sound balance on this one is just perfect as everything from congas and guitar, through delicate strings and woodwind, to that superb rich voice, is clearly audible. The overall live guitar sound is not as languid as the original, a touch more trebly, but it sits so well alongside the orchestration, the choir and a beautifully restrained Moog solo from Keith. Towards the end of this, there's an incredibly King Crimsonish moment, so much so that it could easily be Mr Fripp himself up on stage.

"C'est La Vie" is magical, with again the choir reproducing live the original multi-tracking of Greg's voice. Tons of lush strings, a discordant-sounding group and orchestra creating a very moving effect. The sad accordion solo is a winner.

The fifteen minute version of "Pictures..." opens in a suitably dramatic way, with the brass bringing the house down towards the end of "Promenade".

Nothing dampens this crowd's spirits and, having proven they're up for the electric side of things, they take warmly to the "Piano Concerto" too. It's evocative, it's descriptive and above all it's a perfect rendition played to a silent, appreciative audience. Keith's piano solos are creatively executed, the one in the 1st Movement noticeably swinging along with a real boogie feel to it. In contrast, the anger and frustration of the 3rd Movement come through well, leading inexorably to a triumphant conclusion.

Greg credits Keith, Godfrey and the whole orchestra, as the crowd go wild for several minutes after the concerto, followed by Keith introducing a wonderful "Closer To Believing".

Even as he strums the opening chords, applause starts for "Lucky Man", the only truly solo number of the evening for Greg, and he does it faultlessly. His cold of earlier shows seems to have cleared up, his vocals are spot-on, rich, measured, tugging at the heart strings. The energy of this crowd is limitless and amid the noise, Keith announces, "We're gonna give Carl a go now! This is 'Tank'!"

The jazz feel is stronger tonight, with an absolutely steaming soprano sax solo over the top of a very on-the-ball rhythm from the band and orchestra. Once the tit-for-tat section is over, full as always of frenetic rolls and fills, Carl takes charge and his solo is dramatic, furiously entertaining and still full of phrases that hark right back to the album original. Toms, tympani and gongs dominate, the podium spins, the dragons move, and the audience are besides themselves.

"Knife Edge" is a sharp re-working. The edge, the hint of menace, that Hammond hanging in the air are all present, with the orchestra really only coming into their own for the middle break.

As so often tonight, they start the next one, "Pirates", before the applause has died down and it's a classic version of a song that is already so well established and well-received every night. Never straying far from the original, it's totally clear, captivating the mind as first the strings, then Greg, tell the story. When band and orchestra play together on this one, the result is musical swashbuckling at its best. There's not a sound from this lively crowd during what's perhaps the brightest moment of the evening, the trio break and GX-1 solo mid-song, and the final climax is awesome.

As an encore, "Fanfare for the Common Man" works well. It's politely received at first – that is until the trumpet fanfare sounds – and then it's everyone-go-berserk time. Most of the crowd clap along to the first section, providing a second rhythm to back up Keith's solo, before the band charge into the semi-scripted improvisation. It's over the top, hard-driven, and makes excellent use of the bold voicings of the Yamaha.

There's frequently an aggressive edge to the playing, combined with a solid bluesy feel in the rhythm but then as they gallop into "Rondo", complete with the Emerson Express sounds of old, it's heads down and rock till you drop. Swirling Hammond takes over, Keith runs up and down the manuals, throws and stabs the L100, and finally plays it on his back with the organ on top of him. The result is the "Rondo" of old: stirring stuff that has them rocking and screaming in the aisles, prepping the way perfectly for a return to "Fanfare" and the only way to end a show as the orchestra join ELP for the closing chords.

An electric show from start to finish.

SUNDAY, 12 JUNE 1977

Veterans' Memorial Auditorium, Des Moines, Iowa, USA.

Tickets: $6.50

The last orchestral show from the initial part of the tour. The recording that survives kicks in part way through a strong, gutsy rendition of "Karn Evil 9".

Applause starts long before Greg is even halfway through the closing line and the Moog outro from "3rd Impression" echoes round the hall to wondrous effect.

With barely a pause for breath, everyone drives powerfully into a superb version of "The Enemy God ..." Carl right up there in the mix and pushing onwards and upwards. Every detail from the orchestra stands out, particularly from the string and percussion sections, adding so much to the fire of the piece itself. The usual dramatic ending elicits wild applause, followed by Keith's introduction of the 'arranged version' of "From The Beginning"

The Moog intro is deceptive and they've obviously re-worked this one. It's embellished with new layers of strings, woodwind and Keith's keyboards. Even the melody and Greg's phrasing change in the second verse – both to excellent effect. It's almost as if because they know it's the final orchestral show, they pull out all the stops on this number – and boy does it work.

Keith sets the scene for a version of "C'est La Vie" that lives up in every way to the audience's expectations. The vocals are rich but the orchestra very nearly steals the show, sounding emotional, dramatic and evocative. Keith never fails with *that* accordion solo: the mix between him and Greg's acoustic guitar is perfect, and it's spine-tingling time when the choir comes in before the final verse. This is wonderful stuff and the crowd know it.

The standard "We're gonna give you 'Pictures At An Exhibition'!" from Keith gets the usual wild applause and they launch into a thundering version. The drum-bass duet at the close of "The Gnome" seems to last forever and sounds fantastic.

The final movement of the mini-classic is itself awe-inspiring, with brass right at the top of the mix alongside the vocals, lifting the roof clean off. "There's no end to my life ..." crowns the piece, choir singing for all they're worth.

Having shown their appreciation of all things so far, the audience take warmly to the "Piano Concerto". Tonight it's just the first and last movements that get an outing, and if anything this adds to the lively overall feeling of the music. The climax is just amazing.

Greg credits Keith, Keith credits Godfrey Salmon and the orchestra, and the crowd show their genuine appreciation in this love-in. "Closer To Believing" starts hesitantly with everyone for some reason almost feeling their way into the song. Once settled, it's stirring stuff, sung with real feeling and conviction, ably backed by orchestra and choir.

Not wasting any time, and to deafening applause, Greg launches with gusto into "Lucky Man". It's definitely one of the best received pieces of the evening and sets the scene for, as Keith says, "One of the things from Carl's side of the album. This is 'Tank'!"

They never play a less-than-perfect version of this and tonight is no exception. It's incredibly tight, jazzy and ever-so-driven by the man on the drums. The call and response offers a taste of what is to come as Carl fills in the gaps with snare work at the speed of light, before offering up yet another world-class solo. The loudest applause is reserved for the delicate cymbal solo where his dexterity really shines. This man is a genius.

Keith, Greg and the orchestra come back in, the crowd cheer, shout and whistle as loudly as ever and the number builds to a majestic crescendo.

The haunting start of "Knife Edge", a touch of echo on Greg's vocals and that eerie Hammond sound, is played to a silent crowd entranced by what they see and hear.

Instantly recognizable, "Pirates" is a powerful version that's rewarded with spontaneous applause at every turn. The swirling strings are full of imagery from the off, pushed forward by Carl and Greg's tight rhythm. The middle trio section, Keith laying down an incredible, toe-tapping GX-1 solo over that solid beat, is the highlight. Greg belts out the closing verses as if he's personally leading the assault on the Spanish Main and this raises everyone else's game to new heights.

"Fanfare" is the much-demanded encore. The tympani very nearly does the impossible – silencing the crowd before the trumpet sounds send them haywire and keep them there throughout the fourteen minute piece. The opening band section is fast and Keith embellishes it nicely with some vibrato on the GX-1. The rhythm never lets up for a second as Greg and Carl seem to enjoy trying to out-rock each other. Keith's long solo and the underlying beat is full of R&B, sticking surprisingly close to the album original for several minutes before they all go off on one. It's adventurous, bold and none of them misses a cue or a note as they segue perfectly into "Rondo". Those classic train noises send the audience into ecstasy and what follows is an unrestrained, dynamic version. Keith's organ antics delight and tease the crowd, not least the "watch me lay on my back with this thing and play it backwards" section, before the guys return to the "Fanfare" beat and wind up a stunning performance.

How to send a crowd home deliriously happy? Call for Emerson, Lake and Palmer.

Courtesy of Gudrun Friedrich

MONDAY, 20 JUNE 1977

The Spectrum, Philadelphia, PA, USA.

After a significant re-working of the set sans *orchestra, this is only their second show as a trio on this tour and it's full of life from the opening bars of "Karn Evil 9". The mix helps with a strong feeling of drive and power to compensate for the loss of the orchestra.*

With applause still ringing in their ears, "Hoedown" is undertaken at full pelt. "This one needs no introduction, so I'm not gonna give you one," teases Keith, after which it's a tight version of "Tarkus", still very fast with Greg and Carl providing a thundering, booming rhythm. Keith uses the drawbars in "Stones Of Years" and "Mass" to add some nice effects to the Hammond sound. Carl in particular makes good use of the bottom end toms and bass drum.

"Mass" is cut short, no solo from Keith. Then, surprise, surprise, it's straight into "Aquatarkus". It starts at a slow pace, building on Carl's martial beat, before launching into the lively improvisation of old. The bubbling rhythm is strong as Keith coaxes all manner of sounds from the Moog and Yamaha. The ending is dramatic but it seems odd: a "Tarkus" with no manic ribbon controller solo and strangest of all, no "Battlefield". But what the heck? The audience seem happy enough.

"C'est La Vie" is hit hard by the loss of the orchestra, though vocally and acoustically Greg doesn't put a foot wrong. The lyrics still send a lump to the throat, with added poignancy from a masterfully understated accordion solo from Keith. The most noticeable difference is the loss of the choir for the final verses but it's still well rewarded by the Philly crowd.

The archetypal orchestral number, "Pirates", with its sweeping strings evoking images of adventurers sweeping all before them, works really well in its new format. Yamaha and Moog work overtime to create a superb musical backdrop for the tale of intrepid, devil-may-care men. The GX-1 solo before "Landlord, wine, make it the finest, make it a cup for a seadog's thirst" is precise and enthralling as Keith's fingers race up and down the manual.

"Take A Pebble" gets one of its first outings in three years. Keith's lost nothing in the short piano solo, ably accompanied by Greg's smooth bass and Carl's jazzy brushes. He moves from the familiar break into an excerpt from the 1st movement of the "Concerto", periodically winning loud applause, and sounding superb despite the absence of the prerequisite orchestral backing.

The reprise, resplendent with heavy rolls and cymbals from Carl, is exciting to hear. Greg's baritone vocals are rich and strong, hanging in there as this audience express their appreciation ...

"Still ..." gets a very warm welcome but it sounds unusual and discordant, the latter often being one of the strengths of ELP, but not tonight. The accordion is present throughout, overpowering Greg's acoustic, and dampening the effects of a touching and heartfelt love song.

By contrast," Lucky Man" is a true solo piece, instantly recognizable, greeted ecstatically, and beautifully delivered.

Over to the upright, a strong bluesy intro from Keith conjuring up images of another solo, and then from nowhere they charge into a roaring take of "Nutrocker". Keith takes solo honours in excellent style, and Carl and Greg find themselves back in 1971 providing that tight, punchy, heavy jazz rhythm. The crowd are baying for more and, eventually, ELP succumb. The opening of the encore is marked by those trademark tympani notes and the brass fanfare. Carl takes over, setting the tempo and this one rocks hard from the off. It sounds like most of the audience are clapping along with them for the first few bars as they explode in a wave of applause.

"Fanfare" has the same effect as "Hoedown": it's uplifting and guaranteed to get toes tapping and heads shaking. You can sense the "air keyboard" players getting down as Keith launches into his handiwork on the GX-1. Some of it is textbook, most is improvised in true ELP style, and it all adds up to fourteen minutes of pure prog.

Just past the midway point, they go into "Rondo" like a runaway train, solo honours going again to Keith as he lavishly decorates that solid rhythm. The L100 is given the heave-ho workout as Greg and Carl go about their business unabashed, Keith jumping over, around and under it judging from what he's playing.

The climactic return to "Fanfare" is just that, a true climax, and it's a wonder the crowd don't stamp their way through the floor in their continued demands for more.

THURSDAY, 7 JULY 1977

Madison Square Garden, New York, NY, USA.

Tickets: $9 – $11 for each show.

Barely a month since they last played with the orchestra, they can't wait to get back to the Garden, for the first time since December 1973. The enthusiasm and the sheer energy are almost tangible as they kick off the opening night of a three night stint.

From the barely audible beginning of "Bolero", the ever-so-quiet piccolo and snare, the orchestra prove themselves yet again. Playing with zest and precision, they build this piece to a thunderous climax, well-received by the capacity crowd, who break into spontaneous applause as the heroes of the evening, ELP themselves, take to the stage as the number progresses.

Moving stuff this and, no sooner have the last chords sounded and the audience lift the roof, than the "Hoedown" *portamento* bursts forth. It takes several bars before everyone realizes what they're playing and when they do, it's more deafening applause.

Part 2 of "Karn Evil 9: 1st Impression" goes down well, dominated by Carl's solo, superbly backed by guitar and organ. From there, it's a swift move into "The Enemy God ..." as Carl, backed by the orchestra's two percussionists, thrashes away to drive the whole thing along. The Moog also stars in this one, with plenty of flash and fireworks as it goes up in 'flames' towards the end of the number.

"Tarkus" remodelled is still a hit with everyone: the first half powers along, featuring some splendid Hammond and Moog work – melody and solo – from Keith, as Greg and Carl carve their own niche and make their mark on this legend'.

"Still ..." is a tribute to the sound engineer's art; the detail of every nuance clearly heard. It's another perfect performance vocally and acoustically from Greg, leading inexorably to "Lucky Man", an ELP standard but one that feels fresh and inspiring.

"Pictures ..." with the orchestra has grown so much on this tour, a true high point of the evening, full of highs and lows, lights and darks and all shades in between courtesy of Godfrey Salmon and the players. The differences in mood and tempo between elements such as "The Gnome" and "The Great Gates ..." are alone worth the ticket price. The honours are shared equally as they travel from the delicate touches of the vocal "Promenade", through the manic rock interlude of "Baba Yaga", arriving at the stately "The Great Gates ..." via a ton of Hammond throwing and abuse which could knock the gates down. The odd thing is, despite ELP's best efforts, it never quite gets the due recognition and applause.

The real gem of the evening, the "Concerto" from Keith, is worth the wait. There's some annoying audience chatter during the quieter passages, but it's clear that most fans appreciate the complexities and the achievement the piece represents. Played with both power and subtlety, Keith gets a standing ovation at the end with thunderous applause.

Things calm down a bit with two excellent acoustic numbers from Greg, "Closer To Believing" and "C'est La Vie", both built so much on orchestral strings.

Another one that's grown this time round is undoubtedly "Knife Edge", band and orchestra working in perfect harmony. The strings and brass give it a real edge in the more menacing, sinister moments of the song, and the middle eight is a nice relief with Keith handling the solo well. Overall, the added sound beefs it up, gives it an element of muscle.

"Tank" is the cavalry charge of the prog world: Godfrey leads the orchestra as they blast through, very much taking the lead in melody with more than a hint of jazz. Continuing the 'whipping-up' of the crowd, the band launch straight into

"Nutrocker", Keith getting down to some honky tonk boogie-woogie, rocking for all he's worth. It goes down so well that he asks the crowd if they want some more, they say "Yeah!", and ELP play it again as they used to do on previous tours earlier in the decade. How can they fail? They don't!

"Pirates" is the show-closer, complete with swirling strings, superb synth solos and a pair of cannons at the end. It's a complex piece but everyone on stage manages to shine, handling the tempo and key changes in style. Greg's narrative vocals are the icing on the cake.

Carl's crowd-pleaser went down well and so it's Keith's turn in the encore, "Fanfare ...". A simple, but at the same time intricate, re-working of the Copland piece, it's the vehicle for Keith's showcase electric solo of the evening when they go into "Rondo". He gives the L100 what for, throwing and assaulting it gleefully to give the crowd some added visual spectacle that suits the feel of the music. Thankfully, Hammonds are not an endangered species. He loves it, they love it, and throughout it all, Greg and Carl keep up the simple, but stadium-rocking rhythm.

A night to remember – definitely! The boys are back in town.

FRIDAY, 8 JULY 1977

Madison Square Garden, New York, NY, USA.

Night two of their stint and things just kept getting better.

The creeping martial beat of "Bolero" gets the crowd toe-tapping, and the orchestra are red-hot. The tension and the atmosphere build steadily, the volume grows and the fans go absolutely loco as ELP take the stage. For all three of them, it must be spine-tingling to walk on as the orchestra nears the end and the adoring crowd are applauding like that. Almost before anyone can clap further, "Hoedown" is up and away. It's a snappy upbeat version with plenty of punch, tons of drum fills, and a cracking Moog solo

"Karn Evil 9: 2nd Impression Part 2" is next and straight away gets one of the biggest cheers of the night – it's obvious that this one is fast becoming a live highlight.

Still without a pause for breath, it's "The Enemy God ...", the orchestra showing how much they add to the melody and the lead.

"Good to see you all again, Yeah," shouts Keith. "That was a number from *Works* actually, featuring Carl Palmer there on "The Enemy God ...", a Prokofiev number. We're gonna carry on with something else you can also sing along to if you want to. This is called 'Tarkus'."

The shortened version is now much tighter and gets the thumbs up. It's very much a trio number full of pounding beats and luscious Hammond. "Mass" has a real kick to it, the Greg/Carl engine room really driving things along, and by now the direct jump into verse three straight after the very short Moog solo sounds so natural, as if it's always been that way.

Ribbon controller? What ribbon controller? Nearly half of the total sixteen minutes is taken up by "Aquatarkus", Keith conjuring up a ton of neat phrases and touches on the synth. Between his bass pedals and Greg's guitar, they fair shake the Garden to its foundations.

An interesting and rare error from Mr Emerson shows he is only human after all. "This next one is off the *Trilogy* [should be *Brain Salad Surgery*, of course] album. It's a re-arranged version of 'Still ... You Turn Me On'," he states. Greg gets rapturous applause as soon as he opens his mouth. A fascinating one this: Keith adds some light touches on the Steinway, echoing Greg's acoustic lines, and the string section does everyone proud. The feel of the climax is so plaintive, so heart breaking that it can't fail. Perhaps the one thing that's missing is the acoustic coda – the ending if anything is a little too sudden.

Everyone but Greg bows out for "Lucky Man" and his voice and playing fill the Garden – until someone decides to let off a firework and Greg, as he's done before on earlier tours, stops and tells the miscreant where to get off: "Gotta tell you man, that's very dangerous! Very dangerous! We don't wanna have to stop the concert because of just one cat. That would be dreadful! Don't do it!" The cheers for him are literally deafening as he picks up the song exactly where he left off. Sections of the crowd singalong to the last verse and again, there's no shortage of encouragement and whistles.

"Pictures ..." is strong, together, with Godfrey in control of everyone on stage. The arrangement is first-rate, strings and brass sounding particularly pleasing, the whole thing played with real panache. The first "Promenade" sounds like a symphony in its own right, the second one a soothing, calm interlude from Greg.

The orchestra are just wonderful in the finale, brass section reigning supreme as they lead the way to the crescendo, choir and Greg in full voice. They don't make 'em like this anymore and these ecstatic fans know it!!

Keith announces a twenty minute break, after which the "Concerto" knocks 'em for six. The intricacies of the piece are well handled under Godfrey Salmon's guidance, it's intense, it's ambitious and it's a winner.

Almost two minutes of a standing ovation precede Keith's introduction of Greg's "Closer To Believing", with its beautifully delicate picked acoustic intro. He barely gets through the first line before the crowd erupt into wild applause, the rich, smooth, heart-warming sensations of the song winning through. Vocals are perfect, immaculately backed by the choir.

"C'est La Vie" has another wonderfully picked opening and really benefits from the choir on the chorus. Atmosphere builds as they go through this one and, as a love song, it works on all levels.

Next up, Keith introduces another number: "This is something we had a lot of requests to do so we dug it up again and re-arranged it. This is off the first album we ever did, it's called 'Knife Edge'!"

From the orchestral opening, this is magnificent. Greg's vocals have just the right hint of menace about them. The stop-start nature of this one comes across well, leading nicely into the middle section with its laid back, underplayed Hammond solo, immediately followed by the strings in full flow, only to be spoiled in places by some maniac with a klaxon. Still, the ending more than makes up for it.

Compared to "Knife Edge", "Tank" is taken at the gallop, everyone having to keep up with Carl as he brings the entire kit into play. Two things he does so well: the sustained snare drum beat whilst at the same time picking out a tune on the concert toms; and whipping up the crowd as he beats the hell out of the gongs, drum riser spinning, strobes flashing. The snare work, both on the drum and the rim, is frighteningly good and so intense. As the others come back in for the reprise and the climax, the crowd clap along perfectly in time with the orchestra. Unbelievable!

Keith tunes in the clavinet voice, messes around for a few bars and then "Nutrocker" hits the ground running, the Carl/Greg engine pumping out that hypnotic rhythm and Keith flies through a killer of a solo, crowning it with that superb boogie-woogie ending.

It sends the crowd berserk and Keith shouts, through all the noise, "Did you like it? Did you really like it? Did you really, really like it? Do you want it again?" Well, who can say no to an offer like that? An instant encore from the masters of the prog epic! Keith takes it from the middle section, absolutely rampant on the keyboard, improvising all over the place, Carl and Greg never missing a trick as they latch onto each and every twist and turn.

They follow him through all the time-honoured phrases and licks from "Take A Pebble" and "Rondo" down the years, and nothing sounds out of place. The whole thing whips the audience up still more and, with applause still deafening everyone, "Pirates" gets under way.

Even the most animated of fans keeps quiet as Greg weaves his spell. The "anchored in an indigo moonlit bay …" bit is fantastic in both simplicity and complexity, if you catch my drift, and gets a round of applause. The GX-1 solo in the trio section sees Keith soaring above everything, Carl and Greg pounding a solid rhythm. The finale is unbeatable, the relentless orchestral rhythm going down a storm.

During tumultuous applause, the tympani introduction to "Fanfare For The Common Man" isn't recognized at all, and it's not until the brass fanfare that the crowd go wild, again clapping along in time with that infectious, bubbling beat.

There's a wonderful solo from Keith, eliciting yet more applause as he strays from the script to improvise and go off on all kinds of tangents – most of them with a nice jazzy feel.

The way that Carl and Greg embellish a very simple rhythm is amazing. "Rondo" is the last crowd-pleaser of the evening: train sounds, fast keyboard runs, Hammond throwing, it's all here in a typically dramatic ending.

Prog rock at its best!

SATURDAY, 9 JULY 1977

Madison Square Garden, New York, NY, USA.

The final night of the three at the Garden and both band and fans were up for it! It was their penultimate show with the orchestra and it was obvious that everyone on stage wanted it to be a winner.

Tonight's performance of "Bolero" hasn't survived for us but it clearly warmed things up because "Karn Evil 9: 1st Impression" gets a wild reaction from the crowd.

Tactically, it is a smart move to start "The Enemy God ..." whilst the applause is still ringing, because each and every night the crowd are tempted to continue clapping in time with the beat as Carl drives band and orchestra through the piece.

After a brief "Hello" from Keith and a credit for Carl, he again introduces "Tarkus" as a song "you can all sing along to", then it's rest time for the orchestra as the trio make this their own. The armadillo's grown slightly at eighteen minutes: maybe they just can't resist throwing in slightly longer solos with this one – old habits die hard.

"Aquatarkus" rocks along at a fair old pace and the approval starts long before the end; Keith has some difficulty calming the assembled down.

Again, he makes the mistake of attributing "Still ..." to the *Trilogy* album but who really cares? The moment Greg starts singing, the place erupts. It's a sterling effort from all concerned with, if anything, Keith a little lower in the mix than last night but sounding more effective and touching because of it. The discordant effect on the strings has now been mastered to perfection and the effect adds to the overall emotions of the love song. "Lucky Man" resonates loudly around the Garden, with some beautiful chord and *arpeggio* work from Greg on the acoustic.

The second, reinvigorated mini epic of the evening is greeted as loudly and as warmly as everything else by this excitable crowd. "Promenade" sets the scene for this one: heavy, pounding rhythm, Carl's drums right up there, with the orchestra right behind. Amazing that every note of Greg's bass and the Hammond can be picked out through the wall of sound, a credit to the mixing desk. "The Gnome" is menacing, creepy, just as it should be, and then we get the immediate softening effect of the vocal "Promenade", with Greg's rich tones and the orchestral backing sounding fantastic. As with everything tonight, this crowd go crazy at the first line. "Baba Yaga" is rampant as both band and orchestra rock out,

One short interval later, back they come for the classical spectacular of the evening, the "Concerto". Plenty of tuning from the orchestra, no announcement, and it's straight into the first movement. The complex mixture of styles is handled superlatively, the formal structure adding to the overall effect. Hints of Copland and others, with some nice dramatic touches in the first movement. It's extremely well-received by these NY rockers, perhaps enlivened by some of the shorter jazzier interludes. The percussive tone of the third movement comes across just as in the original, building to the final flourish of orchestra and pianist, and the consequent adulation.

Calm restored, "Closer To Believing" soon works them up again with the swirling strings and Greg's soft, powerful baritones. Greg introduces "C'est La Vie", which goes down very well. The strings are sultry, the effect of the choir stunning and it's no surprise that the piece comes across so strongly live.

"Knife Edge" goes from strength to strength on this tour; it's strong on percussion, heavy on bass, and the acoustics of the Garden make the vocals even more eerie.

Then Keith announces. "Ok, stand by for Carl Palmer! This is 'Tank'!"

A steaming version follows, the two pre-drum solo highlights being the soprano sax solo and call and response section between Carl and the strings. You can almost sense the orchestra thinking "Anything you can do, we can do better!" Carl's spotlight seven minute solo is precision itself, incredible the way he builds the patterns and rhythms: snare triplets with the left hand and tom-tom tunes with the right being a perfect example.

From the sublime to ... "Nutrocker", the fun piece of the evening with Keith going off on a tangent all over the place.

The drawn-out intro to "Pirates" has everyone on tenterhooks, the brass fanfares decorating the strings-and-synth rhythm, and as soon as Greg opens the vocals, the applause starts again. It's still very much textbook in performance but the energy of the piece, through all the time changes, is impressive as Carl and the orchestral percussionists work overtime.

After the tympani opening calms everyone down, the brass fanfare to "Fanfare" sends the audience into overdrive. This number is so tight, so uplifting, so infectious, that if it weren't an encore it could have been the opener; a latter-day "Hoedown".

As if that weren't enough, they round it all off with "Rondo", complete with all the trimmings.

Great audience, great show.

SUNDAY, 10 JULY 1977

Hartford Civic Center, Hartford, CT, USA.

Never before did such a simple synth intro get such a tumultuous round of applause as "Karn Evil 9: 1ˢᵗ Impression" kicked things off in Connecticut. No orchestra here, just the trio.

"Hoedown" picks up where "Karn Evil 9" leaves off, toe-tapping, uplifting and exciting. Not the fastest they've ever played it but still at a cracking pace, before Keith says, "Thank you! Hello! It's good to see you all! Here's a number you can all sing along to. It's called 'Tarkus'." This is a solid performance, not inspiring by ELP standards, but they never put a foot wrong. It gets the cheers and excites in all the right places, especially with some more of the extra Hammond flourishes from Keith, but just seems to lack that 'Wow' factor.

"Norwegian Wood" is still there, as are the many variations on the "Tarkus" theme.

No need to introduce "Take A Pebble". The piano is well down in the mix and Greg has some trouble reaching the high notes. Possibly he's not in the best of health? Cymbal and brush work from Carl is faultless, preparing the way for Keith to go into the excerpt from the "Piano Concerto" as his solo.

Carl earns his keep on the glockenspiel with delightfully light touches that embellish Keith's playing just so. Keith handles the complexities and intricacies of the piece so well he gets several spontaneous bursts of applause.

There's still a roughness and edge to Greg's voice that signals all is not well. For the last two minutes, he even sings in a lower octave to enable him to reach the notes. Without further ado though, he opens the *arpeggio* from "Still ..." only to have one of those ELP rarities, a false start. He's joined cautiously by Keith and Carl, only to grind to a halt as they realize they're not in synch. "One more time!" is how Greg re-starts it, with all three pouring their heart into getting it right second time round. This one now sounds ace, full of light, under-stated piano and xylophone, complementing that lush voice. Problems forgotten, they deliver a stunner, a totally re-arranged song for the trio.

"Knife Edge" is bigged up by Keith, counted in by Carl, and sung by Greg with as much feeling and menace as ever. They seem to really enjoy playing this revitalized one: it's got plenty of dynamism, energy and power, driven along by drums and a heavy bass. The middle solo is excellent on the Moog, underscored by strong drums; one of the highlights of the evening.

There's no doubt it lifts and inspires them, and a blistering version of "Pictures ..." follows. It's full of strong bass, seriously kick-ass drumming, and strange, atmospheric, bubbling Moog. A lovely vocal in "Promenade" suggest whatever problems Greg had earlier in the set are now well and truly behind him.

Greg introduces "C'est La Vie", trying hard to make up for what's missing instrumentally without the orchestra. It's a heavenly rendition, and the effect of just voice and acoustic guitar serves to heighten the emotion. The accordion solo from Keith, so evocative in its own right, deservedly earns spontaneous applause.

With a female admirer calling out "Greg!" he starts "Lucky Man" (which he may well be if he plays his cards right with the adoring fan, after the show!). The last verse, with a slightly changed *arpeggio*, sets up a fantastic response from the audience.

"Tank" is marked by a strong synth intro from Keith, admirably, and some would say bravely, taking the role of the orchestra. He single-handedly does the call and response bit with Carl, setting up the man at the back for an incredibly fast, precise and just awe-inspiring solo. The juxtaposition of concert toms and snare drum triplets, one building a pattern over the rhythm of the other, is appreciated and generates loud cheers. All his tricks are there, including the super-fast cymbal work that audiences love. The crowd-pleaser of gongs, bass drum and revolving podium, followed expertly by a crescendo of tympani rolls and more gong crashes, never fails.

Keith gives Carl a deserved credit as the trio return to the "Tank" theme in all its jazziness. Overall, it's a stout effort but this ending more than any other number suffers from the lack of Godfrey Salmon and his team.

"Nutrocker" can't suffer from a lack of what it never had and, to prove it, this is a cracker of a version, reminiscent of the heady days of 1971. Carl and Greg keep time, Keith lets rip all over the shop and the cheers and shouts of "yeah!" from them prove how much they're enjoying this.

The last surviving track is the show-closer, a first rate "Pirates". The opening section sounds more menacing, more evocative of piracy on the high seas than it ever did with the orchestra in there. Maybe the loss of the strings in particular gives it just an edge, a hint of aggression that wasn't there before. Captain Greg's opening lines receive the same warm welcome they have every night on this tour as he tells his tale.

They've re-vamped the last verse, extending slightly the break between each line and Greg forgets and sings the last lines the way he did in New York the previous three nights. A true pro, he finds his cue again and they all finish together – and what a finish!

Not one of their best ever gigs, but a solid performance despite some problems with Greg's vocal chords.

TUESDAY, 12 JULY 1977

Boston Gardens, Boston, MA, USA.

Tickets: $8.50

This crowd were going mad before a note was even played and, as Greg opened the batting with "Karn Evil 9", they just freaked out.

Carl comes in as a powerhouse on the bass drum and snare, Keith lets rip on the Hammond with a superb solo, closely followed by Greg on lead, and the hiccups of Hartford are well and truly behind them.

"Hoedown" is taken at full charge; fast and furious, ELP as they should be! There's a background of constant cheers and whistles throughout Keith's solo, played over a barrage of percussive brilliance. A hint of the ribbon controller solos of old? "Not 'arf" as Fluff Freeman would have said.

"Tarkus" sounds fresh, driven, powerful, with some hard bass Moog playing from Keith to give it extra 'ooomph'. After a much mellower "Stones Of Years", in terms of both organ and vocals, with a really tasteful, gentle solo on the synth, "Iconoclast" and "Mass" sound faster and with a sharper, percussive edge.

"Aquatarkus" fills the last ten minutes of the piece and an excellent version it is too. What the Moog fanfare at the end lacks in power, Carl makes up for with the gong smash, and the crowd aren't slow to show their appreciation.

"Take A Pebble" is taken patiently, measured and sounds perfect. Greg's bass work on this one is top quality, as are the vocals and Carl's precise cymbals. The whole middle section, now the jumping-off point not only for the usual piano solo but also for an excerpt from the "Concerto", is truly amazing.

After a standing ovation, Keith introduces "Still ...", and the mistaken attribution to the *Trilogy* album is now so much a nightly occurrence, it must be deliberate.

Vocals full of emotion, nice xylophone and a light magical touch on the Steinway to heaven, all add up to a copper-bottomed rendition with none of the problems they had in Hartford

For atmosphere, "Knife Edge" is unbeatable. It's lost the raw quality of the earliest tours, but Hammond and vocals that hang in the air give it an unmistakeable air of menace. As with everything, it's powered along by Carl who shines. The middle solo is a little light relief but then they power their way back in, driven by that unmistakeable Hammond sound to a strong ending.

"Pictures ..." shows them all on top form: tight, full of energy and enjoying themselves. "The Curse" section is magical in the way Keith in particular conjures up images of an evil, tip-toeing hobgoblin with some eerie Moog.

Keith throws the baton over to Greg for "C'est La Vie" who has the crowd in his palm of his hand. Keith's accordion solo gets the usual cheers and whistles –

not surprising as it seems to get better as the tour progresses, more laid back, less in your face, with much more of a feel of romantic Paris about it.

Straight into a classic "Lucky Man", before "Tank", another highlight of the evening. From start to finish, there's a distinctive jazz feeling to the Moog lines, giving the piece a truly uplifting feeling.

"Nutrocker", is a bit slow to start before picking up steam. Keith does his Madison Square Garden act again, "Did you like it? Did you really like it? Did you really, really like it? Do you wanna hear it again?!!" Sure enough the reprise lifts everyone still more, not that they need it.

That distinctive opening to "Pirates" quietens people down. It's never that different from the album but sounds fresh as a daisy every night. Keith conjures up those unbelievable sounds for the intro, then fills the place with swirling GX-1 and Moog, and that's it.

A GX-1 dominated "Fanfare" lulls everyone with its quiet beginning, before taking off like a jet plane when the brass fanfare sounds. The Yamaha undoubtedly suits this number so well, it gives Keith's long solo a whole new feel and texture – if anything a little understated compared to the brashness of what comes next.

The jazziness just reaches its height as they lead into "Rondo", the last crowd-pleaser of the night, with the Emerson express taking over, complete with knives, Hammond throwing, the full kit and caboodle. Unashamedly over the top, but it's all good clean fun.

The cheers, screams and whistles say it all as the noise continues throughout the outro of Respighi's "Church Windows".

31 nights in on the tour and ELP seem to be enjoying it more than ever.

FRIDAY, 22 JULY 1977

The Cobo Hall, Detroit, MI, USA.

Tickets: from $7.50

There was an echo to the Cobo Hall that really added to the effect of the music, especially with the Moog intro to "Karn Evil 9". It bounced around, off the roof and back again, before Greg entered with those rich vocals.

"Hoedown", a classic vehicle for Keith to decorate a rhythm with Hammond and ribbon controller, is memorable for Carl's drumming. The guy just never stops being inventive, and clearly everyone digs it. Two loud, up-tempo numbers in the bag, they're already taking Detroit by storm, and all is right with the world.

"Tarkus" sounds as if it had only been written yesterday, again driven by that inventive drumming and some thundering bass.

One of the main ELP strengths has always been contrast, and a classic "Take A Pebble" proves the point. The opening wins rapturous applause. It's classic stuff – despite the awful feedback – taken at just the right pace, and the crowd spontaneously erupt into wild applause several more times. Carl's snare brushwork is compelling and toe-tapping, Keith's treatment of the excerpts from the "Concerto" is perfection. He's chosen wonderfully uplifting, resonant pieces, much appreciated by the crowd, and his playing is simply faultless.

Somebody's obviously had a word in Keith's ear: "We're gonna carry on with one from the *Brain Salad Surgery* album. This is one that applies to you. It's called 'Still ... You Turn Me On'." That acoustic *arpeggio* intro is tastefully and very delicately supported by Keith on the keys. Keith's announcement of the reworked "Knife Edge" surprisingly gets hardly any reaction from this audience, and despite the band's best efforts it stays that way at the end. Greg livens it up with a few "Yeahs!", but it makes no difference. Applause is polite: Detroit doesn't take to the reworking of the old Janacek classic.

In complete contrast, "Pictures ..." goes down a storm, with all three guys getting a fair crack of the whip. Greg and Carl play light and dark with the rhythm, and Keith is egged on continuously by the fans every time he goes anywhere near the Moog. "Great Gates..." is the stand out piece here. Played out to a silent audience, it's room-shakingly loud, definitely one of their best endings. The other-worldly tubular bells/Hammond drawbars bit, followed by some nice innovative Moog, is stunning and the crowd love it. What Keith does is transplant their usual ending from "Karn Evil 9", the synth swirling round the arena leading to a mighty explosion, to the moment just before Greg sings the last verse. The effect is musical theatre of the highest order.

"C'est La Vie", once everyone has calmed down, is wonderfully executed by Greg on the twelve string. Following the usual format, he goes straight into "Lucky Man", the opening chords a dead giveaway despite the twiddling about at the start. There's a Mexican wave of applause as he sings the first line. Razor sharp guitar and wonderfully rich vocals make this another classic, with the dramatic final verse and short coda adding to the atmosphere.

"We're gonna give Carl the chance to bash around now, otherwise we'll never hear the last of it! This is "Tank"," jokes Keith. As you'd expect, Carl takes the honours but there's some powerful and inventive bass from Greg and a ton of nifty, nimble synth from Keith with a hint of the jazz feel about it

A ton of messing around from all three precedes "Nutrocker", the opening bars of which elicit tons of clapping. Keith goes overboard with the Little Richard-style rock'n'roll *glissandos* but the crowd love it – which opens the way for the by now standard reprise from the middle section. There's an almost tangible air of a band enjoying themselves, playing to an audience that can't get enough. "La Marseillaise" even gets a brief workout during the reprised solo.

The opening to "Pirates" is stunning when we bear in mind there are only three of them on stage. Pounding bass, ubiquitous, soaring synth, and a drummer that keeps it all going are the essential elements in this tale. Some nice touches from Carl on the fills, and from Keith with the laid back melody on the GX-1.

Long, loud demands for more bring them back for "Fanfare ...". It's fast becoming an epic in its own lifetime, and this crowd clap along for the first minute or so. After a nimbly-played jazzy solo on the Yamaha, Keith takes off on the L100 when they charge into "Rondo", winning still more ecstatic applause. This version is surely the fastest on this tour so far, with for once a raw feel to it that harks back to the days when they first set foot on stage together. Keith's antics stun most of the crowd into an amazed silence, only to release their pent-up excitement at the very end.

A very, very good show before an enthusiastic audience in Motor City.

SUNDAY, 24 JULY 1977

The CNE (Canadian National Exhibition) Stadium, Toronto, Canada.

Tickets: $11 – 12.50 Canadian

The first show in Canada on the tour and the punters benefitted from ELP being well into their swing.

A powerful, and much applauded, "Karn Evil 9: 1st Impression" opens the outing. A loud, very upfront Hammond solo from Keith is followed, and matched, by a corresponding lead solo from Greg. This version has so much clout behind it that it builds superbly to the usual climax and works up the crowd nicely.

"Hoedown" is taken at breakneck speed, embellished to perfection by Carl on the toms throughout. Keith's in overdrive for the main solo, ribbon controller gone out of control. It goes down a treat.

Slightly shorter tonight, "Tarkus" is a killer.

"Take A Pebble", another classic version, definitely works as the vehicle for the "Concerto". Greg and Carl shine in the beginning and the reprise, although Keith's *glissandos* are always a force to be reckoned with. As soon as the others bow out for five minutes, he goes off into his own classical world and turns in a performance to be proud of. In those few short moments, he captures perfectly the changing moods, emotions and tempos of the entire "Concerto".

"Still ... You Turn Me On" is politely received. Greg's acoustic is still uppermost, subtly backed by piano and xylophone, and it's a strong, emotion-packed rendition.

Equally emotional, but now aggressively so, is "Knife Edge", a hard, cracking number, full of driving rhythm, pounding bass and upfront organ. There's even a "Yee-hah!" from one fan as Keith plays the chorus with gusto but then gets ahead of himself at one point and has to audibly slow down for a split second so the others can catch up. Not surprisingly, it gets loud applause.

Working the crowd up still more, "Pictures ..." picks up where "Knife Edge" left off: there's a noticeable "ooomph!" to each beat in "Promenade", and the second "Promenade" features Greg's best vocal performance of the night – and that's saying something.

The acoustic double bill puts the spotlight on Greg again. "C'est La Vie" gets hardly any applause as Keith announces it or as Greg starts playing. It's so fulsome, you can hardly tell the strings have long since gone. "Lucky Man" is a more subdued number, strong nevertheless and gets a warm reception. He throws in a dramatic pause before the penultimate verse, the effects of which are enhanced by the acoustics of the hall: it sounds sublime.

"Tank", at almost ten minutes, is without a doubt one of the strengths of the set. It might be the jumping off point for an amazing solo on a nightly basis from the guy on the podium, but Keith and Greg get credit for best supporting roles.

The light relief of "Nutrocker", tonight without the Keith-driven reprise, is value for money, guaranteed to excite anyone who isn't already well hyped-up, and sets things up a treat for the two remaining mammoths of the show.

"Pirates" is deceptively laid-back to start with, only to impress everyone once the pace hots up. As with everything tonight, the instrumental sections stand out the most, but that's not to say that there's any weakness with the vocals, there just isn't.

For once, and ironically from this Toronto crowd who have been slow to applaud all evening, "Fanfare" gets an enormous greeting from the very first notes and the guys respond well with a thunderous version. Some annoying firecrackers, a worrying feature of several dates on this tour, don't put the trio off their stride as they deliver a formidable "Rondo", the last crowd-pleaser of the night. It's a touch of prog-meets-hard-rock and it goes down oh so well, Hammond throwing, upside down playing and all.

"Fanfare ..." finally gets Toronto rocking and sets the seal on an evening of superb ELP.

FRIDAY, 29 JULY 1977

The PNE (Pacific National Exhibition) Coliseum (or National Pacific University Center, Vancouver, Canada).

Show 42, almost exactly half way through this giant of a tour, with still no sign of wear and tear.

Led all the way by stunningly clear vocals, driving Hammond and lead guitar, "Karn Evil 9" is a clever choice of opener. It's short, punchy, uplifting and gets the expected response from the crowd. "Hoedown", taken at a slower pace than some recent versions, keeps up the good-natured feel of things and never fails to excite. The tempo and the beat change for the solo, with Keith into all sorts of knob-twiddling and ribbon controller antics, the first crowd-pleaser of the evening.

"Tarkus" is driven by Carl, especially on that famously fast kick pedal, and it produces a version with a much more percussive feel to it. Even now, this band are not ones to sit back on their laurels and play it by the book.

"Aquatarkus" has the slow beginning that sets up an excellent synth solo from the man in the waistcoat as the pace, volume and anticipation build during a solo that occupies over half of the entire piece, which the assembled lap up.

Applause is still ringing in their ears as "Take A Pebble" kicks in gently, accompanied by some new, and highly inventive, cymbal work from Carl. Vocals are rich, lush even but for some reason they don't sound as confident as usual with this one tonight. If these ears are correct, there's a problem with Greg's bass: it just isn't there in the mix at all and the others work overtime to compensate and pad out the bottom end.

The piano solo, built around the "Concerto", allows time for the problem to be sorted, and it is, although Greg's bass never features that highly in the mix for the rest of the show. This is one of the few gigs when the "Concerto" excerpt in "Pebble" wins its own applause as soon as Keith plays the first few notes. Contrary to most audiences, the people of Vancouver seem to recognize it instantly and that, if anything, spurs on Keith.

Lacking the orchestra, the light piano and xylophone work their magic on "Still ...". The king of the intros, Keith, steps up to the mic again, and it's a whopping version of the new "Knife Edge". After some initial confusion over the tempo, lasting barely a second or two, Carl and Greg groove into the rhythm and that brash Hammond sound kicks in.

"Pictures ..." is Carl giving a drum masterclass: he's everywhere, but never overpowering. The across-the-toms rolls towards the end of each phrase in "Promenade" get better and better. After a spine-tingling, manic "Baba Yaga", where they all outshine each other and share the honours, it's onwards through the "Great Gates ...", into a version that's the equal of anything in the entire show.

Carl is so forceful he helps push those sustained Hammond notes and Greg's vocals out into the hall, again the tom rolls are wonderfully done, and Keith repeats the Moog crescendo and explosion *à la* "Karn Evil 9".

No "C'est La Vie" tonight: Greg goes straight into the strummed intro to "Lucky Man", accompanied by cheers and calls of recognition, probably eliciting that famed nod of acknowledgement. This one really sounds full now he uses the twelve string and in some of the choruses there's a large section of the crowd joining in. Sing-along-a-Lake!

Carl's "chance to bash around" is how Keith introduces "Tank", and undoubtedly it's one of the stars of the evening. Keith goes all freelance on the Moog, and the call and response section between him and Carl – that originally involved the orchestra – is a marvel. This is one of those "This-is-how-you-should-use-every-bit-of-the-kit" solos that Carl excels at. So many parts of it are crowd-pleasers, from the kick rhythm through the gong rolls, to the terrifically fast snare, tom and cymbal work. The spinning of the riser, complete with strobes, is the icing on the cake.

The reprise of the theme is dominated by Keith's piccolo-effect Moog solo, with the whole crowd going wild at the end, leading nicely into an upbeat, up-tempo "Nutrocker" that goes down a storm. They're rocking away to their hearts' content, and enjoying every bit of it.

"Pirates" is instantly recognized and loudly applauded. Sticking to the template, except for those musical fills, amazing kick rolls, and the middle GX-1 solo, it's a measured, perfect offering. Vocals are at the top of the mix and Greg sure can tell a tale.

Somehow, either they didn't encore tonight, it escaped the recording, or it hasn't stood the test of time.

We can only imagine how good "Fanfare ..." must have been – everything else tonight certainly was.

SATURDAY, 6 AUGUST 1977

The Alameda Coliseum, Oakland, CA, USA.

This was due to be the first of two nights at the Coliseum but we believe they cancelled the second show. Perhaps they were still worried about sales after the financial problems with the orchestra tour. Or maybe they had performed too many shows in California? They had scheduled nine in just ten days.

Judging from the crowd reaction at the start of this one, you'd think ELP had already been playing for an hour or more! It's almost possible to sense the huge grin on Greg's face as he launches into "Karn Evil 9". The sound mix is spot-on too.

"Hoedown" is the liveliest it's been for ages: fast, accurate, brimming with percussion, pounding bass and that glorious Hammond. Each time Keith produces the *portamento* effect, it encourages the fans to go even wilder than they were. The cheers, whistles, and whooping are deafening.

Lifted by all that, "Tarkus" is so very, very good and longer than the norm. Improvisation rules, particularly in "Mass" – where the focus is now on the song rather than the machine gun solo from Keith as in years gone by. Not better, or worse – just different.

Now the main star of the piece, "Aquatarkus", is an excellent vehicle for Keith's solo to replicate in the first instance the snort of the defeated armadillo. Carl's martial drumming pushes everything along, allowing Keith to move from Moog to GX-1 to decorate a top-notch rhythm section.

There's enormous applause at the start to "Take A Pebble", and also as soon as Greg sings the opening line. The Emerson touch – based on those wonderful right hand *glissandos* – is everywhere, as is Carl with his cymbals. In between "Pebble" and its reprise there's that astonishing solo built around the "Concerto". The audience recognize it instantly, encouraging Keith to perform to perfection. It's beginning to be a classic in its own right.

"We're gonna do, right now, a song off Greg's side [of *Works*]. A Greg Lake composition called 'C'est La Vie'," Keith announces. This is a strong version, the chorus in particular resounding round the hall and back again, filling every corner. To cap it all, the slight natural echo in the Coliseum gives the vocals a nice touch.

For some reason, only the first half of "Knife Edge" has survived. It's rhythmically strong, driven by Carl's hi-hat and bass drum, with both vocals and Hammond full of dark menace.

"Pictures …" sounds like they've taken an overdose of energy pills, and at times it's hard to believe there are only three of them on stage. There's almost mass hysteria after that, as if this audience need an excuse to yell, cheer and whistle, and after both Greg and Keith thank them, Keith comments, "This applies to you, this is 'Still … You Turn Me On'!"

Greg wastes no time, going straight into "Lucky Man" after "Still …", but for once there's barely a whisper of recognition from the assembled multitude. The sudden, emphatic ending though arouses the audience and, at last, they show their appreciation in full.

Keith then tells the faithful, "Ok, this is Carl's interpretation of the *Gong Show*. Carl Palmer! 'Tank'!" This is everyone's chance to crank it up and rock out for eleven minutes or so. Keith's work is so clear and sounds fantastic as he fires off solo section after solo section, with the call and response bit head-and-shoulders above many other things tonight. Carl's solo is one of his best for a long time, and that's saying something by his standards.

The honky tonk piano false intro to "Nutrocker", coupled with a few seconds of jazz bass and cymbal, leads into a hard-rocking version with all three of them on fire. Keith flies through the solo, charging up and down the keys, carrying all before him. The crowd love it to bits, and show their appreciation as ELP kick into "Pirates".

Unfortunately the only surviving part of this one is the intro. "Fanfare", the encore, is here in part and it's very well-played and received with deafening applause and cheers. It's an amazing version, so full of energy, with solos from Keith that kick some serious ass, always tinged with more than a touch of humour in the playing. Yet again, however, the full version has been lost somewhere in the ether.

A seriously excellent show, much loved by a lively audience.

WEDNESDAY, 10 AUGUST 1977

The Sports Arena, San Diego, CA, USA.

In came the Moog intro, in came Greg with one of the most famous opening lines in rock, Keith and Carl weigh in, and we got an opening number which just couldn't fail to take the place by storm as an opener.

"Hoedown" takes off without a pause, this crowd love it, and it's played to perfection at full speed. One of the fastest intros Keith has given in a long time gives the crowd another excuse to raise the roof; this time it's "Tarkus", a full-on, percussion-driven version. It sounds excellent because the whole piece has a strong percussive edge to it, and they are just so together in every sense.

A thoughtful, rich-sounding and very melodic "Stones Of Years", with a really dreamy solo on the GX-1, is followed by brash takes on "Iconoclast" and "Mass", the latter winning applause as soon as the cowbell/Moog intro kicks in.

Keith has free rein in "Aquatarkus" and uses it well, to produce a creative, imaginative but still recognizable solo. The bass and snare work are faultless to a tee, providing the backdrop against which Keith launches into the trebly GX-1 part with a ton of accompanying whooshes from the Moog. Time and again he returns to variations on the "Tarkus" theme, always the same but always different, and at the end the crowd show their appreciation in no uncertain manner.

No intro for the next one but someone can clearly be heard assuring his friends that it's "Take A Pebble", and of course he's right. Keith goes from the first part of his solo, which could in all honestly be lifted straight from the 1970 album – it's so close to the original – to a stunning rendition of the "Concerto" excerpt, ably supported by Carl again on the xylophone.

The closing section of "Pebble", in contrast, is now such a free-form improvisation, with a distinctive jazz feel to it, that apart from the *glissandos* and the vocals that mark it out, parts of it are unrecognizable as the piece they first put under the spotlight seven years earlier. Greg gives Keith his due credit, a favour returned by Keith introducing "C'est La Vie".

One piece that's never really fails to go down well is "Knife Edge", and tonight is no exception. It's heavy, intense, evocative and Greg gets an immediate ripple of applause when he comes in with the vocals. The trademark Hammond is eerie in the verses, driving in the chorus, and just crazy in the solo. Hardly surprising that it wins some of the best applause of the evening, and, while the crowd are in such welcoming mood, Keith announces a blockbuster "Pictures ...".

Plenty of attacking, hobgoblin-type synth in "The Gnome", accompanied by Keith doing his 'watch-how-high-I-can-jump' visual cues, pounding drums and then Greg turns in a wonderfully evocative vocal "Promenade".

"Still ..." gets an upbeat intro from Keith, and then it's a bit of a let down for this rocking crowd as it settles into its romantic, thoughtful, and evocative self.

They're a buoyant bunch of fans tonight and we can imagine how ELP must have whipped them up with the remaining numbers. Sadly, none of those songs have survived.

THURSDAY, 11 AUGUST 1977

Long Beach Arena, Long Beach, CA, USA.

Tickets: up to $8.75

The opening show of a three night stint (the original follow-up show on the 12 August and an extra one squeezed in two nights later) at this famous venue where ELP had traditionally gone down well. Tonight would be no exception.

It's wild, crazy applause and cheers as soon as the Moog gets "Karn Evil 9" underway. Even as Greg sings the final "See the show!", the crowd are off their seats, applauding manically and are still on their feet as the guys charge into "Hoedown", a rip-roaring version.

ELP all seem to shift up a gear for "Tarkus", and the playing is as tight and as energetic as ever. Carl offers up timely fills and cymbal work in "Stones Of Years". Carl's in the driving seat all the way through "Iconoclast" and "Mass" too, battling with the Moog for attention – and winning as he segues seamlessly into "Aquatarkus". This one is full of textures from the Moog and GX-1 as Keith decorates that expertly-laid down rhythm. This audience are quick to applaud as the solo progresses, a classic example of the full-on improvisation from ELP, nothing held back, each of them spot-on their cues, and each of them with an uncanny sixth sense for when the others are going to do something that needs a response.

"Take A Pebble" is still relatively short at eleven minutes and the re-working of this one too continues unabated. The instrumental opening is deceptively laid-back and understated – until Greg's powerful vocals come in, and Carl in particular goes for broke with the cymbals, bass drum and fills. The first part of the piano solo, lifted straight from the original, is note-perfect and goes beautifully into the "Concerto" excerpt. Keith by now handles the rhythmic complexities perfectly, the sweeping patterns sounding so majestic and it earns a long ovation.

After a quick apology from Keith for not being able to do more of the "Concerto" without the orchestra, he paves the way for a solid, impressive take on "C'est La Vie". The second of Greg's songs, "Lucky Man", has some nice changes to the guitar parts in the verses that add dramatic effect to the phrasing of the lyrics. A touch of Echoplex during the final verse and it ends on a high, much to the obvious delight of this California crowd.

Keith tells everyone: "Actually I knew it wasn't my day today. I went water-skiing and about three boats broke down on me. Now the Moog synthesizers broken down! What we'd like to do is take a short break of about two minutes so we can get it mended and then we can play on a bit more. Is that alright with you? [huge applause]. Thanks a lot. We'll get it fixed as soon as we can."

When ELP resume, there's audible calls from some fans for "Welcome Back My Friends!", Keith gives "Knife Edge" the usual nostalgic intro, Carl counts it in on the sticks, and we're off. What a version: inventive, hard, more raw than of late, with a distinct edge to the vocals and the Hammond. The middle section sees Keith adding a few frills, Carl a few fills, Greg a fitting bass line as well as a very loud "Yeah!" and the outcome is ELP at their best.

The abbreviated "Pictures ..." goes from strength to strength, with Carl's drumming during the opening proving his credentials as the engine room driver. The band really hit the spot when they all crash in on "Baba Yaga". Keith makes this one all his own with the Hammond and synth leads over the top of first-rate playing from the others. It's furiously fast and exciting, paving the way just right into the "Great Gates ...", and many of the audience join in the first line along with Greg. Now it's sing-along-a Pictures!

"Still ..." is sublime, but the audience reaction, however, seems to suggest it could be positioned better in the set list, coming as it does after the mini epic and before the rocked up classic of "Nutrocker". It's as lovely as ever but just doesn't seem to get the appreciation at this point in the set when they've striven so hard to work up the crowd.

"This next one features Carl Palmer and his own version of the *Gong Show*. This is a number called 'Tank'," Keith states.

They take this one with gusto: soaring synth, driving percussion and a real underlying jazz feel to the whole thing all combine to make it work on every level. It's played at a brisk pace and as well as Carl shining as usual – especially on the call and response part – there's some exceptional bass from Greg. The solo, all seven minutes of it, is masterclass combined with crowd pleasers. That spinning podium and the strobes sends the crowd crazy and every ounce of applause is so well earned.

It sounds like the start to a free-form jazz improvisation but after they've teased everyone for a minute or so, they go careering into a rocking version of "Nutrocker" that takes no prisoners. Carl is irrepressible, Greg lets rip and Keith's solo is one of his best on the tour – all played at incredible speed and accuracy.

We then have half an hour of pure ELP magic: a wonderful "Pirates", bested only by a show-stopper of a "Fanfare ...". On paper, "Pirates" is the one piece in the trio set that could have suffered irreparably without the orchestra – but that is to overlook the inventiveness of these guys. They all play their part like men possessed: in parts, noticeably with the soaring GX-1 that conjures up images of a sailing ship on the high seas, it's so often like there are twice as many of them on stage.

With ELP dragged back by this appreciative audience, "Fanfare ..." gets the welcome it deserves. There is simply no better way to end a gig than this: Greg and Carl with heads bobbing and Keith taking the solo wherever he fancies. All the influences are there: classical phrases, jazz, throwaway lines, all wonderful stuff, mostly improvised – and nobody misses a cue. And as for "Rondo", this one's as rough and as inspiring as ever, a helluva crowd-pleaser.

Endless applause, cheers and whistles prove how popular the band are in this State.

SATURDAY, 13 AUGUST 1977

The Swing Auditorium, San Bernardino, CA, USA.

Their sixth show in the Bear State in nine days, a run broken only by a trip out to Phoenix, Arizona, four days before this gig. It proves yet again that ELP can't put a foot wrong on the west coast; the welcome is huge before they even play a note.

The opener is a faultlessly-played, hard-driven "Karn Evil 9: 1st Impression" Part 2 that sets the standard for the rest of the show. Funny how the tempo of this one seems to vary on a nightly basis more than any other piece; this version is more stately, less hurried than some recent renditions. Instrumentally and vocally it's uplifting, effervescent and guaranteed to get any crowd going.

With a blistering "Hoedown", full of charged-up power, Greg and Carl pound out the beat while Keith stabs the Hammond, and then the ribbon controller, into life. The beat during the solo has an almost funky groove to it, quite different to the last tour, and it kicks extra life into an already vivacious number.

The prominence of the rhythm section is clearly a feature of the sound tonight: in "Tarkus" they get distinction for drumming and bass work, complemented with several calls of "Yeah!" from Greg. To excellent effect, "Stones Of Years" has been slowed right down to the point of being pretty near soulful.

As "Mass" thunders in, it gets a huge wave of applause in its own right, and then the same happens when it thunders out into "Aquatarkus". From a martial-driven beat and a fairly laid-back opening, Keith goes into the *Star Wars* theme, the film having been released in May 1977.

The opening of "Take A Pebble" calms things down before Keith, playing a stunningly evocative six minutes of excerpts from the "Concerto", silences the fans – a silence broken only by cheers of admiration for Carl's xylophone accompaniment.

"C'est La Vie" gets better and better and "Lucky Man" receives a positive reaction too. Keith credits Greg, as do the crowd with long, loud applause, during which Carl audibly counts them in for "Knife Edge", the opening loud, heavy and aggressive with the bass drum, hi-hat and vocals so prominent.

The mini epic that is "Pictures..." is delivered in real style and audience reaction is wild throughout, all the more so for the big finale of "The Great Gates ...". From that, they bring us down again in one sense, up in another, to a classic "Still ..."

Carl's big number, "Tank" by name and by nature, is hard-driven, with an incredibly fast and flowing GX-1 solo from Keith to complement that tight, grooving rhythm. Nice touch from Carl to use the temple blocks in the call and response section. There are so many rhythmic patterns and colours to this musical solo it's easy to see why there are spontaneous outbursts of wild applause and cheering throughout. His skill at keeping a rhythm with the left hand whilst belting out a tune on the toms with the right just gets better. A wall of sound marks the end of the solo, that famous beat on the snare provides the tag, and in come Keith and Greg for the well jazzed-up ending.

With the road crew still metaphorically nailing the roof back on, Keith tinkles on the keys, Greg rumbles away, Carl teases on the toms, blocks and cymbals – then they all pile into a wonderfully jazzy, free-form "Nutrocker". The solo is a *pot pourri* of jazz, rock and Little Richard-style rock'n'roll all packed into a storming three minutes.

From an epic mini to a mini epic as the story of "Pirates" is unfolded. This elicits hardly any crowd reaction until the brass fanfare kicks in, Carl gets to work on the tympani and Keith thunders in on the Yamaha. Then it's lets-go-crazy time for this excited audience as ELP launch into fifteen minutes of rock as only they can serve it.

"Rondo", when it comes, has a stonking intro and an incredibly fast break from Carl. The crowd never let up in their audible appreciation of Keith's visuals and the amazing rhythm from the engine room.

The tag, the cue, the "Fanfare ..." reprise, the finale to a memorable show.

SUNDAY, 21 AUGUST 1977

The Assembly Center, Tulsa, OK, USA.

Tickets: from $7.00

Show 57 of 85 and there's no let up for this band who seem to be enjoying every moment on stage.

The greeting from the Tulsa devoted sounds like ELP have already done their full set, it's so loud. What it does do is to encourage the band to deliver a fast, driving opener of "Karn Evil 9", Keith turning in a corking Hammond solo to the backdrop of Greg's riffs and Carl's time-keeping on the cowbell. The drum break sends everyone crazy: whoever thought of opening with this abbreviated number certainly knows which buttons to press to get things cooking.

As if that weren't enough, the band barely pause for breath before producing a "Hoedown" so fast and intricate it harks back to the heady days of 1974.

25 seconds later, time for them to catch their breath and for Keith to introduce "Tarkus", and they're off again. The stamina of these guys is unbelievable.

As so often with this shortened version, it's this movement that allows all three of them to shine: Keith produces just the right amount of light and shade, Carl just the right pace for the mood, Greg just the right feeling behind the lyrics.

"Aquatarkus" marches in to give us a feel for the ELP improvisation early in the show. The opening of "Take A Pebble" is quite dreamy, more so than usual, and gets a huge cheer as soon as Greg sings the first line. After the technical wizardry of "Tarkus", it's an effective contrast and highlights the 'unplugged' virtuosity of this band, years before the term was even coined.

It takes the Okie audience a while to realize that Keith is playing his excerpts from the "Concerto", but they make up for it with the applause. The jazzy reprise is well-handled, complete with dramatic pauses from Greg and is admirably received.

"C'est La Vie" continues the thread of evocative acoustic numbers, the vocals and twelve string combining so well and, like "Lucky Man", it gets an enthusiastic reaction.

Introduced by Keith as "a bit of nostalgia", "Knife Edge" has a hint of rawness and menace in the vocals and the Hammond, especially in the quieter moments from Keith. The instrumental sections take everyone back to 1970/1971 with the forcefulness, power and intricacy of the middle solo.

Again, after a pause that's hardly long enough to catch breath, they take "Pictures ..." at full pelt, with Keith seeming to play "Promenade" an octave higher than normal; it sounds very cathedral-like. The stop-start music and antics of "The Gnome" get everyone cheering and out of their seat, only to be calmed down by a first-rate vocal "Promenade" from Greg.

The "They were sent to the Gates" bit of "The Great Gates ..." is majesty exemplified, the audience stunned into silence for once as both Keith and Carl emulate the church bells of old Kiev.

The old "We're gonna give you some *Brain Salad Surgery*" patter works, as the welcome for "Still ..." shows. It's sung with true confidence, a love song aimed – according to Keith anyway – at their fans.

"Tank" kicks off with Carl in real "Let me at 'em!" mode, the opening solo from Keith played out over a tight, fast backing which demolishes everything in its path. Carl arrives at the solo in full flow and never lets up, turning in a classic performance as he creates pattern after pattern, rhythm after rhythm, a one-man band in many respects.

Continuing the theme, there's the jazz night-club/honky tonk false start to "Nutrocker" and, when the real thing gets going, it's a funky little number with a killer rhythm. Parts of it are a cross between Little Richard and Jerry Lee Lewis with only a faint nod in the direction of Bee Bumble and his Stingers. The crowd love it.

"Pirates", the icing on the cake of the main set, follows without introduction. He's on top form for the solos that feature so heavily in this one, Greg and Carl always in close attendance, the story-telling vocals nicely up in the mix. It wins a standing ovation, the handclaps and cheers bringing them back quite quickly.

"Fanfare ..." is everything an encore should be, a thriller from start to finish, with a large part of this crowd frantically clapping along with them for the first minute or so. It's a strong version, a superb mix of the bold, brassy sounds and thrilling solo voicings of the Yamaha. In parts it touches on the studio original – which was, after all, a taped soundcheck – with its 'dirty' R & B, almost bluesy sound, especially in the brassy chords middle section. The work throughout from Greg and Carl is nothing short of impressive, even more noticeably so when they go headlong into a storming "Rondo", introduced with a cracker of a drum break and a ton of distorted bass.

It leaves them wanting more, as an encore should, as ELP notch up another excellent show.

FRIDAY, 26 AUGUST 1977

The Olympic Stadium, Montreal, Canada.

Arguably the most famous show they ever did, certainly the one from which most film clips are shown. The final gig with the orchestra, literally a show to end all shows, the video recording gives an interesting perspective on the nature and feel of an ELP orchestral event. It was reputedly filmed to offset the losses from the orchestra.

224

The lights dim, the spot picks out the lone piccolo playing, along with a snare drum, the opening of the "Bolero". This one is pure magic: chorus after chorus introduces each new section of the orchestra, the lights doing the same, and the tension building among everyone – especially the audience.

As we approach the grand finale, out walk Keith, Greg and Carl to add their weight to the last chorus and we get a truly magnificent ending. Batting barely an eyelid, ELP charge straight into a cracking trio version of "Hoedown". It's high-energy, high-speed, whipping up this audience into a fervour.

The stadium erupts and the sequenced Moog intro to "Welcome Back My Friends" bursts forth. Carl plays like a man possessed, Greg and Keith having to match him at every turn. From that, it's the Moog reverberating around the stadium, faster and faster with audible gasps from this amazed crowd, as they are stunned with sound-effects explosions. Back come the orchestra, joining the band for a blinding version of "The Enemy God ...". Prokofiev would have been proud. Carl, standing out in white T-shirt and jeans, is undeniably the main attraction here.

The orchestra picks out so much light and shade in this piece, perfectly complemented by the trio. It thoroughly deserves all the wild applause. From a Russian classic to an ELP one, and "Tarkus" is next up. It's, not surprisingly, played as a trio piece, with a constant undercurrent of cheering, applauding fans. Some nice, extra flourishes from Keith, added to the power of the drums, that thumping bass and the sheer excitement of this huge arena, make it a killer of version, much more upbeat and edgy than some recent renditions.

Greg's first feature spot, with "C'est La Vie", is greeted with a level of applause that must set a decibel record. Having the orchestra adds so much to the finesse and quality of this one, setting off his voice just as it should be. Interesting that the backing vocalists can be heard clearly on the chorus, followed by Keith's accordion solo that wins another huge round of applause.

Through all the cheering, "Lucky Man" is just about discernible and Greg again acknowledges the reception from the crowd. A light touch of Echoplex and the natural acoustics of the venue make this a dramatic-sounding version that goes down a treat.

"Pictures ..." is greeted in the usual way and quickly gets going with the orchestra making all the difference to a piece that sounds full even when played by the trio. Powerful, wild in places in "The Gnome" and "Baba Yaga", yet remarkably symphonic in texture and feel elsewhere. Greg's vocal "Promenade" is beautifully played, with the stadium's echo again adding a certain *je ne sais quoi* as the sweeping strings of the orchestra kick in. The spotlight picks out Greg, resplendent in white collarless shirt open to the waist and off-white trousers.

"The Great Gates ..." is the real *piece de resistance*, a mighty movement with the orchestra proving its worth, everyone right on the button – a fantastic way to

Above: $3.50 a ticket. It makes you weep doesn't it?
Courtesy of Neil Corsatea/Air C Images
Below: However, in the space of 4 years, the ticket price has doubled.
That's 1970s inflation for you. © Richard Galbraith

end such a mini epic. Greg and the choir are in perfect unison with those famous closing lines in the crescendo to beat them all.

Amid the rapturous applause, Keith credits Godfrey Salmon and the orchestral players, before the "Concerto" is unleashed on the Montreal crowd. With Keith looking neo-classical in dark jeans, white shirt and striped waistcoat, it's listened to in virtually silent admiration. It kicks off with Keith playing the percussive left-hand *ostinato* as the orchestra play the melody above him. The delicate intricacies, the ups and downs, the changes and variations in tempo, are all skilfully and expertly handled under Godfrey Salmon's guidance. Always ambitious in a concert environment, this is a winner.

The piece, the band, the orchestra, all get a standing ovation and long applause, after which Keith humbly offers a quietly spoken "Merci". He introduces Greg again with "Closer To Believing", with the choristers in particular blending so well with Greg's voice; all go together to make a version that surely ranks alongside that of Madison Square Garden the previous month as one of the most moving.

There's a delayed reaction to Keith's announcement of the Janacek piece, "Knife Edge", but then a wave of cheers hits the stage just as Carl counts everyone in. It's got a plaintive and sinister feel about it at the same time, the Hammond working its usual magic in the way it gives the number a solid classical air. Mid-way, the orchestra come in with their equivalent of a solo, closely followed by Keith and Carl driving forwards.

Carl's bash, as "Tank" is introduced by Keith, is a masterpiece of what is almost a percussion concerto. It's taken at breakneck pace, an immaculately played oboe solo dominating the first part. By the time his solo comes, the others apparently exhausted from trying to keep up with him, we get typical Palmer-esque rock theatre. The audience go wild at the tricks, the spinning riser, flashing lights, the gong rolls, the tympani rhythms, the pounding bass drum; it's hard to believe that one man is so skilfully entertaining a crowd larger than for some of the Olympic events held here the previous summer.

Seven minutes of "Nutrocker" starts, unbelievably, with a pounding bass line from Greg, a fast drum roll, and a quick take on the keyboard intro to Queen's "Seven Seas Of Rye" from Keith. A boogie-woogie blues section moves nicely into the song proper, the floor-shakingly loud bass almost overpowering everyone else. Funky syncopation from Carl underpins a breathtakingly fast solo, laden with all its usual tags and cues, but well decorated with some off-the-wall improvisation. The closing section in particular is ELP at their rock-the-classics best, and it wins heartfelt applause. Keith does the "Did you like it?" bit, much to the delight of the excitable crowd, and they tear into a reprise that's even faster than the first time round.

A shout of "Pirates!" greets the dramatic intro to the next mini epic. This one, with its imagery of high-seas adventure, really is tailor-made for the orchestra and this version is virtually an exact carbon copy of the original. The echo of the stadium complements Greg's voice, set so well against the orchestra and Carl's razor-sharp drumming. The instrumental section just before "Who'll drink a toast with me?" is sheer delight, orchestra and rock band in perfect unison, wonderfully balanced through the stunning sound system.

The brass intro to "Fanfare …" wakes everyone up – not that they needed it – and the reaction it gets is amazing. Once settled into that tireless beat, sections of the audience clap along, holler, whistle and generally groove on down.

One fan's shout of "Here we go!" greets "Rondo", a demonically fast, raw take with an extended intro. Keith flies through the solo, assailing the L100 and coaxing all manner of sounds from the instrument as the rhythm section doesn't miss a beat. It actually gets faster as Keith throws the knives and leaps around the organ, before moving back into "Fanfare..." for that unmistakeable Copland coda. The ever more appreciative audience aren't slow to show their gratitude for an amazing performance.

A showpiece of a concert and what a night!

MONDAY, 17 OCTOBER 1977

Madison Square Garden, New York, NY, USA.

WNEW-FM Benefit show.

Tickets: up to $10

Day 2 of the post-interval dates (begun in Athens, Ohio on the 15 October) was in reality the second half of the long tour of the summer and autumn of 1977. From the Olympic Stadium show to the one on 15 October, ELP had taken a break, during which time a lot of thought and hard work had gone into the setlist. Newly featured tracks included several from the band's about-to-be released album, **Works Volume II,** *as well as a stunning take on "Show Me The Way To Go Home".*

After a grandiose intro from the MC of "Ladies and Gentlemen, Emerson ... Lake ... and Palmer!", the opener is now a completely new number, a gutsy reworking of Henry Mancini's "Peter Gunn" that goes down a treat. It's lively, bouncy and presents an ideal opportunity for Keith to turn in a prime solo with a truckload of pitch-bend on the Yamaha as Greg and Carl build up a solid rhythm. It gives a whole new feel to the opening of an Emerson, Lake and Palmer show and it goes down predictably well.

With almost no discernible gap, they tear straight into the old rabble-rouser "Hoedown"; fast but very, very precise, with if anything a cleaner, crisper Hammond sound.

A typically short intro from Keith – and it's a big up for "Tarkus". ELP have always been a tight band, but this is tight as tight can be, but still with room for some nice flourishes from Keith and Carl in particular.

"Aquatarkus" flies by in a hail of Yamaha over the top of a cracking rhythm. Opening with a touch of the *Star Wars* theme, a blanket of bass Moog always there in the background, Keith produces some really fluid fingerwork and a solo that takes the honours.

"Take A Pebble" gets a warm welcome despite Keith making a bit of a dog's dinner of the piano strings strumming at the start. The whole first section and solo are an emphatically faithful reproduction of the original, in stark contrast to the "Concerto" excerpts that now stand out even more. The audience applaud at every twist and turn, every change of tempo, and then to everyone's surprise and delight, Keith launches into a true bar-piano version of "Maple Leaf Rag", another new one from *Works Volume II*. Greg gives him a quick credit, and then the reprise is wonderful: intricate, jazzy and light.

"C'est La Vie" and "Lucky Man" provide the calm before the storm that is "Pictures ...". "The Great Gates ..." fills almost half the entire piece and is worth every moment. The swirling Hammond, kick-ass drums, powerful bass and voice all combine as well as ever to produce a magnificent ending, reverberating synth and all, that threatens to bring the house down.

Moved back down the running order, "Karn Evil 9: 1ˢᵗ Impression" Part 2 has exactly the same effect on the crowd as it used to. It never lets up. There's a very Hank Marvin-esque solo from Greg, and a powerhouse of a drum break from the man at the back. Greg does the ringmaster thing to perfection, exciting this lively crowd still further, and the finale is deafeningly good.

Another new one is played without any intro as Keith chugs out the bass chords to "Tiger In A Spotlight" on the Yamaha, and Greg gives it an overdose of "Ooooooh!" and "Yeah!" as Carl comes in with that deceptively easy beat. This one is a testimony to ELP as a performing band: the live rendition has far more get-up-and-go about it, more of an edge, than the studio version.

"Thank you! That was a number, a new one, which is gonna be featured on *Works Volume II*, and we're gonna feature another one of those tracks that's gonna be on the forthcoming album. It's another Greg Lake classic. It's called 'Watching Over You'," Keith tells the audience.

A brief false start for him to get the tuning just right, Greg turns in only the second ever live version of this one. It's a touching lullaby, benefiting tremendously from the simple acoustic guitar/vocal treatment. Keith adds a synth solo, mimicking a harmonica voice, which really tugs on the heart strings.

Greg's voice fills the arena and the number is well received.

Then Keith says "It's Carl's turn for a bash around now, we'll never hear the end of it otherwise! This is 'Tank'!"

This one sounds more jazzed up every time they play it, mainly due to the synth voices from Keith. His solo is nicely improvised with shades of "Pirates" creeping in every now and again. After a strong call and response duel between him and Carl, the latter takes off on a classic, musical percussion solo, the epitome of which is the tune he plays on the toms while keeping the beat going on the snare.

229

Emerson, Lake and Palmer, impressionnant avec tout son fourbi: sono de 75 000 watts, une multitude de musiciens, techniciens, éclairagistes...

The scale of the orchestral gigs is overwhelming. This is ELP's
happy hunting ground of Montreal. Courtesy of Gudrun Friedrich.

Just as everyone expects a reprise of "Tank", the guys launch into a heavy, solid version of the opening section of "The Enemy God ...". It's superbly played with keyboard contributions nicely balanced between the Moog and the GX-1. They bring it off well, losing a bit of the depth that only the orchestra could provide, but it goes down a treat.

The false start to "Nutrocker" is becoming bluesier every night, providing a nice contrast to the main item that shows them on blistering form. The main improvised solo sees Keith throwing in bits of anything and everything he can think of, with Greg and Carl in close attendance. There's even a touch of rock'n'roll style de-tuned piano that sounds just crazy.

Keith does his "Did you like it? Did you really like it? Did you really, really, really, really like it? You want it again?" party piece. We all know the crowd's answer: they take it again from the middle of the solo, complete with "Daisy, Daisy" and tunes from the rock'n'roll hall of fame, not the least of which are the plethora of Jerry Lee Lewis-style *glissandos*.

Keith's opening bass chords for "Pirates" echoes around the venue, and the music is immediately transformed from rock'n'roll cliché to pseudo-classical high seas adventure. It feels slowed down a little, more weighty, especially the rhythm section with Carl in particular running the show. Everything is right with this one, a perfect show-closer.

The encore, "Fanfare ...", at almost twenty minutes grows in strength and stature. Keith decorates the driving rhythm with a stunning, smooth-voiced solo on the GX-1 and the whole thing still sounds as fresh as a daisy.

A furious break from Carl opens the gates for the "Rondo" express, the voice on the Hammond sounding more Nice-like than for many a moon. Pounding beat, organ-throwing crowd-pleaser – you can almost see Keith as he throws the thing around. Back to "Fanfare...", they close with that magnificent dramatic coda.

Do you wanna play some magic? ELP did.

SATURDAY, 22 OCTOBER 1977

Cole Field House, University of Maryland, College Park, MD, USA.

Tickets: $7.00, $7.50 and $8.00

This crowd have already gone bonkers before ELP have played a note, and "Peter Gunn" excites them even more. It gets better each night, the rhythm more solid and driving, the solos more improvised and free-form with Keith exploring some unusual voices on the Yamaha.

Picking up speed towards the end, they literally go straight into overdrive with a dynamic, toe-tapping, head-shaking "Hoedown". Carl uncharacteristically makes a *faux pas* at one point but soon realizes the mistake and gets back into the steady rhythm.

As with "Peter Gunn", Keith's soloing is spot-on, this time on the Hammond. It's got a real percussive feel to it, Carl's hi-hat, snare and kick standing out well. He and Greg let rip during the ribbon controller solo: there are fills galore and some strong bass as Keith mows down everyone in sight.

It's a night for hard drums and snappy bass playing: "Tarkus" being a case in point, with Keith stabbing at the organ. Actually, he is on top form, providing so many textures on Moog, Yamaha and organ, at times sounding as if he's playing all three at once.

"Aquatarkus" marches out, making a grand entrance. The standard of playing here is unbeatable: Carl is everywhere on snare, toms, kick, cowbell, hi-hat – you name it, he works it in. Greg's bass stands out nicely during the long solo; Keith's Moog sounds menacing and dark one moment, uplifting and light the next. Keith throws in a new section on the Moog just before the reprise of the theme – which receives a hero's welcome – and it works well. The whole piece is testimony to the excellent quality of the sound system.

"Take A Pebble" is hardly recognized until Greg sings the opening line. The first part is dominated by terrific piano from Keith, perfectly complemented by top-notch bass and percussion. The "Concerto" excerpt is given instant recognition, and Keith handles it expertly, delighting the crowd with the shifts in tempo and mood. Carl, as always, provides some nice, understated backing.

Greeted at the end with huge applause, Keith pauses, then launches into his honky tonk bar-room piece, "Maple Leaf Rag". It's popular with the crowd, most of whom join in with a clap-along, and he gets an enormous cheer at the final chords.

After that, the reprise of "Take A Pebble" is quite disjointed. The whole thing now lasts only about twelve minutes and, although played perfectly, just sounds a little too disparate now that the four elements of it are so distinct. From opener to classical to honky tonk to reprise – all sounds well, but they've lost the flow that was there previously.

Keith again introduces "C'est La Vie", the title that was once translated for him in a Montreal cab as meaning "What the fuck!" in French Canadian. Much too lovely a song for that. No introduction is necessary for "Lucky Man", of course.

After almost twenty minutes of mostly acoustic pieces, "Pictures ..." charges in with a vengeance,

Playing with renewed confidence after their re-examination of the set list, the band offer a rendition of this one that gives them each the spotlight but still features some cracking trio work.

"Karn Evil 9" is another that needs, and gets, no introduction. There are exciting, sterling solos from Keith and Greg, a superlative and incredibly musical drum break from Carl. Greg does the ringmaster bit in a way that's guaranteed to get toes tapping.

"Tiger In A Spotlight" starts quite differently with some laid-back, detuned Hammond. It settles quickly into a textbook version unbelievably close to the original with the addition of a skilfully improvised solo from Keith on the GX-1.

"Watching Over You", according to Keith, is "another one that you won't be familiar with". Greg's playing on this one is worth its weight in gold. Starting very slowly, the delicate guitar builds nicely accompanied by soft, lullaby vocals. It's a simple song, decorated by a few cymbal strokes and a touching synth solo from Keith. It's becoming a firm live favourite if the audience reaction tonight is anything to go by.

"We're now gonna feature Carl the cripple in a medley of numbers, 'Tank' followed by 'The Enemy God', Keith says cryptically. Quite what the 'crippling' affliction was we shall never know, but it doesn't affect his stalwart performance in any way.

On the reprise, Keith drives them into "The Enemy God..." with the bass lines on the Moog, and once again it's a clap-along. Even on this one, the solo synth voices sound more jazzed-up than previously, with touches of "Karn Evil 9" creeping in now and again.

The guys send the crowd crazy with a bluesy intro to "Nutrocker" that is just so "Little Red Rooster" it's unbelievable. It's a fun number, the rhythm section pulling out all the stops, Keith playing in true rock'n'roll style, ever so slightly out of sync with the others, and it works. The ending goes on forever and works the audience up nicely for the sea-saga that is "Pirates".

An astonishing "Fanfare ..." which has everyone bobbing along, heads shaking, a real crowd-pleaser if ever there was one. To build the tension and expectancy, the pauses between the tympani strokes at the beginning are ever longer. Keith charges off all over the place with the solo, both here and in "Rondo", supported to perfection by an engine room so tight it's sandstorm-proof.

The distorted bass and train whistles that sound the entry of "Rondo" whip the audience up further, and by the time the Hammond throwing comes around, followed by the return to the theme and those rapid organ glissandos, everyone is bound to go home pleased. And they do.

MONDAY, 8 NOVEMBER 1977

Dane County Coliseum, Madison, WI, USA.

On a high from the off, the band take "Peter Gunn" at a lick; the crowd clapping along and cheering for most of it.

Tempo quickens even more towards the end and barely has Carl hit the final crash than Keith's off with the *portamento*, and it's a raring-to-go version of "Hoedown". Plenty of harsh-sounding, attacking snare gives this one a real edge.

"Thank you! Hello again! Good to see you! We're gonna carry on now with a fantasy piece about an armadillo, name of 'Tarkus'," Keith tells 'em.

The engine room gets hold of this one from the off: driving bass and drums make this one the most powerful-sounding rendition for some time. Some almost church-like Hammond chords dominate the opening verses to "Mass". From there, it's the now standard segue into "Aquatarkus", which tonight gets underway at a faster pace than normal, charges through the *Star Wars* theme, then settles into a steady bubbling, whooshing rhythm over which Keith lays down a note-perfect solo, amazing when we consider the speed of the playing.

"Take A Pebble" starts ever so quietly with no introduction. Greg plays some beautiful bass lines throughout the opening verses, as well as winning recognition for inspired vocals. Keith and Carl are both understated, it's more what they don't play than what they do. Keith's textbook piano break seamlessly becomes the "Concerto" excerpts, the audience seeming to recognize it immediately.

The closing section virtually swings along, aptly so as Keith pauses for effect and applause, and then launches into a laid-back but toe-tapping "Maple Leaf Rag", one of the few things tonight that quietens this audience for a while.

Keith runs through, retrospectively, the last few numbers and plugs *Works Volume II*. "Right now, we're gonna feature Greg Lake on one of his songs, 'C'est La Vie!'". That gets tumultuous applause, and Greg delivers a strong, heart-felt version. A touch of tuning and "Lucky Man" is up next, quietly at first, and then Greg really gets into his stride.

"Pictures ..." eases in with a quiet organ intro before Greg and Carl weigh in to give it real clout. Excellent tom rolls really complement the Hammond, underpinned always by solid bass. Tonight's "Pictures ..." is the best in a long time.

Amid the tumult, the M.C.'s announcement that "Ladies and Gentlemen, there will now be an interval of fifteen minutes. Thank you" takes everyone by surprise.

The second half of the show kicks off with a storming "Karn Evil 9: 1st Impression" Part 2, that has wonderful vocals, and blistering solos from Keith and Greg. The drum break sounds as if there are at least two drummers up there, such is the power, volume and speed of Carl's playing.

They go straight into a bouncy "Tiger In A Spotlight" with the audience helping to keep time. The enjoyment of playing this one comes through well and we can visualize Keith bobbing his head up and down as he takes the GX-1 through a cracking solo.

Keith talks up Greg's "Watching Over You", in essence a simple lullaby to his daughter. Tonight's version is perfection: rich, emotional vocals complemented by an evocative guitar, and a touching Moog solo. It's interesting that this lively crowd are in submission during this one: it's played against an almost silent backdrop.

It's M.C. Emerson time: "Now we're gonna feature something that really needs no introduction, so we're not gonna give it one." They all pile into "Tank" as Carl gets things moving. Complete with excellent Moog contributions and a solid bass line, this is a fast, top-notch rendition that pulls no punches.

Longer than of late, at over thirteen minutes, it's packed with inventive synth lines, dynamic drumming and a call and response section that shows how it should be done. The eight minute solo spot itself is a masterclass: he shows a real intuitive feel for the toms and snare as he conjures up pattern after pattern, sending the audience wild with expectation. The crowd-pleasers of gongs, cymbals and bass drum draw the inevitable praise, and by the end of the outing everyone is suitably wowed.

"The Enemy God ..." is short, moody and inspired.

The nightly bluesy false intro to "Nutrocker" just gets better and better. Pity that tonight Keith and Carl are both all over the place in the intro proper; but never mind, they make up for it with a red-hot, rocking version that gallops along and is full of inventiveness.

The first of the two mini epics, "Pirates", is a stunner in every sense. It's a powerful one that gets the crowd going. Where the earlier versions of this orchestra-less number sounded relatively empty, more recently it's sounding fuller and fuller, more rounded, richer, as ELP in general, and Keith in particular, have added to the textures of the piece. There's now a warmth about this one that grabs you from the off.

As a show-closer, "Fanfare ..." works a treat. The opening tympani beats are held just a few extra seconds for dramatic effect, and as soon as Keith starts up the bass riff on the Yamaha everyone is up for it. It's reassuringly familiar and builds well to the segue into "Rondo". GX-1 gives way to Hammond and it's a superb performance from all concerned. Keith gets that harsh, aggressive sound from the C3, knocks seven bells out of the L100 as he throws it around, and the crowd go crazy. The reprise of "Fanfare ..." is awesome, building effectively to that storming climax with all three in perfect harmony.

After all that, the encore slows everyone down, with two minutes of world-class blues in "Show Me The Way To Go Home". The piano is unbelievable, with a stack of amazing runs. Is this really the same guy who ten minutes earlier was throwing the Hammond around, assaulting it and everyone's senses?

What a show. What an ending.

MONDAY, 15 NOVEMBER 1977

Michigan State University, Lansing, MI, USA.

If it's Monday it must be Michigan as we approach night 77 of the odyssey.

The hard, driving rhythm from Greg and Carl opens "Peter Gunn", then Keith launches into an excellent solo on the Yamaha. Maybe not as fast as some versions, but if this is just the start there's a night ahead.

Speaking of which, "Hoedown" is confident, driven by Carl, with Keith playing like a man possessed. The middle ribbon controller solo is ferocious, manic and typically Keith. Great stuff!

There's definitely no sign of wear and tear on this tour and "Tarkus" proves it. They take the world by storm from the very start.

"Aquatarkus" marches in along the usual measured lines, picking up speed as Keith starts another smoking run on the keyboard. The trio of bass Moog, Greg's bass and Carl's rumbling fills all combine to provide the ideal backdrop to another enthralling solo.

Keith's on top form tonight: "Now we're gonna feature Carl Palmer tap dancing. Oh! What? He isn't there? Well, he does it downstairs in the shower. We're gonna pass on to a Greg Lake number called 'C'est La Vie'".

It's followed by "Take A Pebble", which gets a round of applause as soon as Keith touches the piano strings, rather than having to wait for Greg's vocals. The sheer quality of their sound system favours this delicate acoustic number as every piano note, each touch of the cymbals, is perfectly clear.

Understated as ever, the bass lines are impressive in texture and delivery. The classical excerpt from Keith's "Concerto" is well appreciated by a crowd who listen attentively before periodically bursting into applause: although they just erupt at the end. Wasting no time, Keith charges into "Maple Leaf Rag", the shortest number of the evening but without doubt one of the highlights.

After the "Pebble" reprise, which gets sustained applause, the vocal and guitar strains of "Lucky Man" fill the hall.

The return of the trio with "Pictures ...", organ-packed and under the total control of the engine room, is a powerful one. None of them are put off one jot by the feedback problems during "The Great Gates...". The majesty of the finale with crashing gongs, soaring Hammond, thumping bass and vocals that say it all, is fantastic.

Post interval, the reverberating Moog of "Karn Evil 9" rings out and as they all come in it becomes a highly impressive version. No worries here about a band losing momentum. Keith livens up the Hammond solo with some underlying, eerie-sounding Moog, pursued by Greg with a distinctly cool guitar solo. Carl's lively drum break precedes Greg's closing ringmaster verses that roll along in breathtaking manner, all rewarded with some generous applause as the guys go straight into "Tiger In a Spotlight". Tonight, this one's got a real boogie feel to it as Carl and Greg groove along in that tight rhythm, and Keith goes off at a tangent, albeit at a very stately pace.

As the mood changes again, proving beyond all doubt that this band are masters of their craft, "Watching Over You" is Greg's last solo number of the evening. He's saved the best, the most beautifully poignant, till last. The guitar is so precise, so deceptively simple, complementing the mood of the lyrics as befits someone at the top of his game. Keith's solo is perfection.

"And now... [fanfare of organ, bass and drum roll] ... take it away Carl," exhorts Keith.

This version of "Tank" is the liveliest, the most upbeat, the most uplifting for ages – and that's saying something for a number that is normally in-your-face anyway. The call and response sounds downright impish with Carl's tom rolls and splash cymbals. The same is true of the solo itself: every part of the kit is used to construct tunes and rolls, often at the same time. The snare work is incredible, coupled as always with bass drum patterns and the throwing-sticks-from-behind-over-my-shoulder trick. The shirt comes off, deafening gong rolls abound and this audience go crazy. Eight minutes of world-class percussion work take things expertly into "The Enemy God ...".

The imitation of a late-night jazz jam session is so realistic it's uncanny. It's heavier than of late, with Carl looning around on the small concert toms at the end, before Keith picks up the "Nutrocker" theme, opening the way for a rockin' version that combines boogie and rock'n'roll.

Keith puts a touch of synth pitch-bend on the intro to "Pirates" but overall it's still very close to the original. The nearly four minutes of instrumental intro creates the mood and the context of the song perfectly: soaring, swirling organ and Moog, given that bit of an edge by the bass and drums, sound spot on. Greg's on top form vocally, Keith excels in the solos, Carl is everywhere.

The middle solo in particular is devastating, with soaring, up-front bass lines. This crowd have been lively all night; now they're cowed into submission by sheer musicianship and listen in virtual silence.

Sadly, only a partial "Fanfare For The Common Man" remains. It gets a rapturous welcome as it literally fills the air with sound. Intro out of the way, ELP steam into the long improvised solo section with a speedy Keith being pursued by a hard-driving Carl and Greg. Innovative, imaginative playing is the order of the day all round as Keith really goes to town full steam ahead on the GX-1.

The solo in this one is drastically different to recent versions and excites the crowd even more with its highs and lows. After a powerful drum break, "Rondo" kicks in at full volume and full pelt, driving hard as Keith doesn't slur a single note in the incredibly fast organ solo.

We can only imagine how well the rest of it went down, and sing the usual encore, "Show Me The Way To Go Home".

SATURDAY, 27 NOVEMBER 1977

The Bayfront Theater, St Petersburg, FL, USA.

Show 83 of 85, the finishing line is in sight on this gruelling tour that began with the orchestra in Louisville, Kentucky many moons ago, and these guys sound as fresh as ever.

A driving, bouncing "Peter Gunn" features a nicely different solo from Keith, before they go into a solid, highly enjoyable "Hoedown" at full speed. The ribbon controller solo, as usual, is frantic, manic and as loved by the crowds as it was in the early days of "Tarkus".

All three are playing at 100 mph, Keith right on form with the melody and the solos, Greg solid on the bass, and Carl's razor-sharp fills showing how much energy he has.

"Aquatarkus" is a highlight, a slow-burner that soon gets going, and then some. Built on a rock solid foundation of bubbling toe-tapping drums, bass and Moog, Keith lets rip with a particularly quirky solo on the Yamaha that goes onwards and upwards to a reprise of the theme and that spectacular coda. It's thunderous, just like the applause it receives.

A delicate "Take A Pebble" leads into a "Concerto" excerpt that shows how entertaining a classical piece can be for a rock audience, played as it is to a virtually silent crowd. "Maple Leaf Rag" hits the speakers and excites everyone again with the bar-room piano. The reprise of "Pebble" is rich, seductive and full of poise; the *glissandos* and hints of jazz as spectacular as ever.

"C'est La Vie" is as much a well established part of Greg's solo spots as "Benny The Bouncer" was three years ago. Always one to tease the audience a little, Greg plays around a little before strumming the opening chords to "Lucky Man", offering a strong, resonant version that's fully appreciated by this crowd. The vocal performance in these two songs is priceless. The closing section has a delightful country feel about it, and they are well south of the Mason Dixon line after all, so it's no surprise that Greg wins the approval of the onlookers.

No intro for "Pictures ..." tonight, but it's a top notch performance, played at an above average tempo for this mini epic, but it lacks that extra sparkle that it so often has.

The M.C. announces, "Ladies and Gentlemen, there will now be an interval of fifteen minutes, so don't go away because the second half is even better!"

They open after the break with the now standard "Karn Evil 9: 1st Impression" Part 2, and a killer it is. A wave of applause greets Greg's opening lines and as Keith flies off into the Hammond solo, Carl drives everything along superbly. The whole "Soon a gypsy Queen ..." section is exciting, dynamic, with masterly playing from all concerned and the audience roar their approval.

"Tiger In A Spotlight", the first of two numbers from *Works Volume II*, is a real rocker, Greg calling out "Oooh Yeah!" as Keith plays the intro. The middle eight solo on this one always sounds better on the GX-1 than the original piano version.

Greg swiftly moves to the solo guitar again and offers up "Watching Over You". The delicate guitar lines are beautifully played, the vocals sung with genuine feeling, as if he was really singing to his own daughter. As one of the crowd can clearly be heard commenting, "I could fall asleep now. Goodnight!"

Had he done so, "Tank" would have woken him up quickly enough. "We're gonna feature Carl Palmer, taking off his T-shirt to show us his definition. This is 'Tank'," jokes Keith.

For many the highlight of the show, "Tank" is prog/electronic jazz at its best. The Moog solo is outstanding, the drums in the call and response section get faster every night, and Carl's solo itself is pure technique and entertainment.

"The Enemy God ..." comes out of the speakers hard and fast, driven by Carl, the man who never lets up. This new version, shortened and more powerful for it, sounds right coming just after the main percussion solo.

The jazz blues intro to "Nutrocker", by now an attraction in itself, gets more authoritative with each show, leading into a rocked-up version of the Tchaikovsky classic that has the crowd up on its feet. Plenty of free-form bass and drumming underpin Keith blitzing the solo with consummate ease, and it goes down a treat – complete with extended false endings.

"Pirates" is pure bombastic cinema, and it's done superbly well. A dramatic opening that if anything they're now taking more slowly than of late to add to the effect. The majestic themes are so rich, the textures so vivid, you can almost see and feel the sea splashing against the ship's bows – especially in the long instrumental intro section. As Greg tells his tale and the colours are added by Keith and Carl, it's as if the pirates are right there, slaughtering the screaming souls and drinking their toast to the devil in stolen gold goblets.

The opening tympani beats of "Fanfare ..." have the same effect as the synth at the start of "Pirates": they work up the audience into a frenzy of expectation that ELP meet with no holds barred. This crowd, as so many others, clap along with the rhythm for a while, before being subdued by the sheer power and force of these three guys.

Just as "Pirates" began more slowly, they tear into this one with 100% effort. Nice staccato touches on the solo from Keith as he puts many of the usual tags in the bottom drawer for the night and produces a highly inventive, jazzy and very different solo on the GX-1. These ears haven't heard the like of this before.

Exciting stuff, becoming more so when "Rondo" kicks in to cap a superb evening in true ELP style: showmanship, hard-driving prog and musicianship of the highest order, all very much to the delight of this noisy and appreciative crowd.

If they came back for an encore it must have been a belter.

TUESDAY, 30 NOVEMBER 1977

The Civic Center, New Haven, CT, USA.

Tickets:

And finally ... Welcome Back My Friends To The Tour That Eventually Ends. Show 85 of 85 at the end of a long haul that began over six months earlier. One of the most famous of ELP gigs and deservedly so.

"Peter Gunn" gets things underway and it's immediately obvious that – relatively speaking – they're demob happy as Keith elaborately decorates that pounding rhythm laid down by Greg and Carl. From there, scarcely is a breath taken and they charge into "Hoedown".

A joint "Hello!" from Keith and Greg is swamped with applause, and hardly has the former introduced "Tarkus" than they launch into the fantasy piece full of confidence, power and aggression. Noticeable again are the bass lines played by Greg, supporting and fitting perfectly with Carl's every beat and the bass Moog lines from keyboard corner.

The combination of power and delicacy from Carl sets off that unmistakeable Hammond sound in the solo, before Keith closes his effort with an evocative run on the Yamaha. Crowning a superlative "Mass" comes a downright off-the-wall "Aquatarkus". As with other pieces in the set, they've played it so many times but still it seems fresh and inspiring.

Keith builds not-so-slowly but very surely towards the final climax, and Greg and Carl join in with abandon. At one point, it sounds like Carl is about to throw himself into a frenzied drum solo, but then hauls himself back to make way for another run on the Moog from the demonic player stage left as Keith lets rip. This is sterling stuff! Overall, it's one of the longest versions of "Tarkus" for some time and head and shoulders above some.

The first, short, piano solo in "Take A Pebble" proves the quality of the sound system as each and every one of Carl's brush strokes and cymbal beats is crystal clear and perfectly weighted. Keith progresses into the "Concerto" excerpts as if he's playing in an empty auditorium, such is the appreciation of this audience. His skill is amazing, his performance scary in its accuracy, the driving left-hand *ostinatos* being a case in point. From classical to bar-room, "Maple Leaf Rag" is short and a real crowd-pleaser. He plays it like he's sat at the upright, sleeves rolled up, entertaining the drinkers at his local. The return to "Pebble" is the best example of the night of how well this band improvise, instinctively picking up on cues and tags in the free-form jazz section before the verse.

Keith reminds the crowd that *Works Volume II* was released just yesterday before linking into Greg's "C'est La Vie". We get an excellent rendition, not a note or word out of place, and so clearly a favourite of the crowd. Even tonight's accordion solo sees Keith adding a few light touches to vary the feel of the piece.

There's a really nice moment when Greg strums a few bars folksy-country style through the Echoplex, before he launches without warning into a cracking, surprisingly lively and edgy "Lucky Man".

Either no "Pictures ..." tonight, or it hasn't survived the test of time, but the next one up, the "Karn Evil 9" excerpt, causes much excitement. That Hammond is right up there leading the way, well supported by the omnipresent Carl and

Greg with some cool, gutsy guitar in the melody and the solo. The last "See the show!" hangs in the air for an age, and then they charge straight into "Tiger In A Spotlight" that features some excellent syncopated drumming, energetic vocals and tight, jazzy Yamaha.

"Gonna feature Greg Lake with a number off his new record, 'Watching Under You'. Sorry, 'Watching Over You'," laughs Keith, and then Greg chips in "Watching With You!". We get a slowed down, very deliberate version of the song he wrote for his daughter, all the more poignant for being played at a slower tempo. No doubt he is looking forward to seeing her soon. The pauses are more dramatic, the words seem to be given more meaning, the GX-1 solo more evocative.

"Nutrocker" goes down a treat with all three guys letting rip with some exceptional free-form playing. Greg gives Carl a credit for his powerful work, after which the opening, stirring notes to "Pirates" come in without any warning. By this stage of the proceedings – and the tour – the band are so relaxed that although this song live never strays far from the original, each of them throws in a plethora of improvised touches that make this a rollicking version

A mighty "Fanfare ..." is followed by an even mightier "Rondo" as Keith turns it up to eleven with the distorted Hammond sound, Greg and Carl crank up the pace with skilful playing, and the crowd are overawed by it all. All manner of noise is squeezed from the L100 as Keith gives the crowd one of the main things they've all come to see. "The Fanfare ..." reprise causes more drama.

No record of any encore but we have to assume they played "Show Me The Way To Go Home".

That's all folks: a memorable ending to a wonderful tour.

18. *On The Flood Of The Morning Tide ...*

16 JANUARY – 13 MARCH 1978: NINTH NORTH AMERICAN TOUR.
47 SHOWS.

Typical set list:	"Peter Gunn", "Hoedown", "Tarkus", "Take A Pebble"/ extracts from "Piano Concerto No.1"/"Maple Leaf Rag"/ "Take A Pebble" reprise, "C'est La Vie", "Lucky Man", "Pictures At An Exhibition", "Karn Evil 9: 1st Impression" Part 2, "Tiger In A Spotlight", "Watching Over You", "Tank"/"The Enemy God Dances With The Black Spirits", "Nutrocker", "Pirates", "Fanfare For The Common Man"/"Rondo"/"Fanfare", "Show Me The Way To Go Home".
Keith:	9 ft Steinway Grand, Upright 'Honky Tonk' piano, Yamaha GX-1 polysynthesizer with a computer-based tuning system. Custom built Moog console, Mini Moog, Hammond C-3 and L-100 organs, and an accordion.
Greg:	Alembic 8 string bass with lighted fret indicators, a Travis Bean electric guitar, Zemaitis acoustic, and three Martin vintage acoustic guitars. Echoplex unit.
Carl:	The revolving kit on the podium plus xylophone, glockenspiel, congas, tympani, chimes, gongs, castanets and crotales.
PA System:	Known as the S-4 system: 35,000 watts indoor system, 72,000 watts outside set-up, with a Yamaha PM 1000 main mixing board.

The final tour before the break-up.

Works Volume II was one of those ELP rarities, a record that just didn't sell, and as such did not do as much as hoped to alleviate their previous financial difficulties left over from the orchestral tour. They continued to plug several numbers from the new album on the tour, perpetuating the eclectic set list from the previous outing.

The shows went down well but Keith still apologized on a nightly basis for not having the orchestra with them. Surprisingly and yet again, very few of these have survived, barely a handful of the 47 they played.

Ironically, to my ears, their playing, togetherness and improvisation on this last tour was among the best ever. Humour in abundance, ingenuity and a determination to entertain as ever they had done: the mid-way interval was still there with a spectacular opening to the second half of each show, as the guys rose up through the middle of the stage on a hydraulic platform to the accompaniment of the sequenced Moog of "Welcome Back My Friends".

They opened with a two-nighter at the Forum in Montreal, Canada.

WEDNESDAY, 18 JANUARY 1978

The Ontario Memorial Auditorium, Kitchener, Canada.

What's survived from this show is often mistakenly said to be from the previous night at the Forum in Montreal.

Kitchener is only the third show on the tour and a celebration of Emerson, Lake and Palmer live. This Canadian audience are definitely in the mood; not surprising since the show is two hours late starting due to a snowstorm and some of the entourage losing their way. Greg apologizes profusely when they hit the stage

A simple intro, and it's "Peter Gunn", a solid version, at a rock steady tempo, not too fast. The more measured pace gives more focus to Keith's solo, now quite different from the earlier renditions of this piece back in October and November.

From one rouser to another and "Hoedown" is fast, exciting, precise and shows them all in fine fettle. Some nice use of the Chinese crash cymbals, the hi-hat and the kick gives the kit a stronger sound and Keith flies through a wild ribbon controller solo with consummate ease. Roars of approval from the crowd egg him on as Greg and Carl keep that beat going.

"Tarkus" is well received and it's an impressive performance. The mix is just perfect, the Hammond soaring above everything, ideally complemented by the bass and toms in particular. The sheer power of "Eruption" never loses its magic, gliding seamlessly into "Stones Of Years", tonight edgier, harder and with an aggression reminiscent of old. The dreamy synth sound is gone; back has come the Hammond with a vengeance.

From "Iconoclast" into "Mass", they sound all there. They've kept the segue into "Aquatarkus", which occupies half of the entire piece, as Carl and Greg settle into a rhythm that allows things to really take off. Keith is rampant, whizzing up and down the manuals, still with that beefy, fuzzy Moog sound underneath everything. This solo is so full in places it sounds as if the orchestra's crept back on stage.

The appreciation from the punters is obvious. From that, in comes the delicate intro to "Take A Pebble"; it takes everyone a full twenty seconds to realize what

243

they're playing and reward the band accordingly. Keith's foray into the classics in the form of the "Concerto" is well received by a crowd who listen in almost total silence.

The applause lifts the roof off as Keith hits the ground running with "Maple Leaf Rag", a crowd pleaser if ever there was one. It's fun, bouncy and has them all clapping along. A short piece, from a much-maligned album, it gets an unbelievably wild reaction from this appreciative crowd.

A confident Greg is truly on form for "C'est La Vie". "Lucky Man" again features the Echoplex and is a stirring version with a ton of feeling and emotion in the vocals.

Then it's time for "Pictures ..." all expertly performed, going majestically into "Great Gates..." with Keith flying through the lead lines. There's that wonderful tubular bells sound courtesy of Carl and the Hammond stops, the reverberating Moog, and the explosion that paves the way for the grand finale.

No record of any "Welcome Back" after the break although we know they played it on this tour. They seem to enjoy "Tiger In A Spotlight" more each night: Greg contributes more than a few shouts of "Yeah!, with Carl setting the upbeat rhythm and the tempo.

"That was 'Tiger In A Spotlight'. When Greg adjusts his underwear, we're into another one from *Works Volume II*. This is 'Watching Over You'," Keith tells us. The trademark sound of Greg Lake doing one of his acoustic numbers hits the speakers and is much appreciated by this lively crowd.

"The Tank"/"The Enemy God ..." medley – now officially referred to as that in Keith's intro – livens everything up and never relents for almost thirteen minutes. All the ingredients are there: power rhythms, keyboard flurries, jazzy solo, terrific call and response and a percussion solo that's unbelievably fast, dynamic and entertaining. The trio work on "The Enemy God..." is longer than for "Tank" and is a stirring way to end Carl's solo effort, drawing prolonged applause from this up-for-it crowd.

Nice touch as ELP let the cheers die, the atmosphere calms down, and then they ease into a light bluesy jam, shorter and less jazzy than usual, before lighting the blue touch paper and firing the rocket that is "Nutrocker". Now less structured than ever, this one smacks of a piece that's at least 90% improvised with a ton of imaginative playing from Keith. Full of energy, the occasional mistake, but what a rabble rouser.

"Pirates", the film music that never was, is a winner. The synth intro, complete with its varied attack and decay time, stuns the crowd into submission. Everyone plays their trump card from the start, almost too keenly at one point as, in a most un-ELP fashion, all three guys lose the plot for about a second getting a bit ahead of themselves – and then, realizing it, get a grip again.

The closing number, "Fanfare ...", never needs an intro and gets a huge audience response the moment the brass fanfares sound. From start to finish this one's played with real conviction and everyone's on top form. There's some powerful kick drum from Carl, and Keith achieves the perfect balance between heavy chords on one hand, and scuttling up and down the manuals on the other to produce an amazing solo, laid back and very, very Nice-ish in tone. He leans on the Hammond, turning in an incredible 1960s-sounding section, and then charges into "Rondo". Definitely a retro feel about Keith tonight: most of the Hammond solo harks back to early versions, not only with ELP, but also with the Nice.

Arguably the slowest encore in rock, "Show Me The Way To Go Home", a classic version, slow, measured, oozing with feeling and sung from the heart. This Canadian crowd clearly enjoy their blues as they clap along eagerly to the rhythm. Carl then joins in with glee, Greg gets into the swing of it, and Keith hammers away on the melody.

Undoubtedly a very good night.

FRIDAY, 20 JANUARY 1978

The Universal Amphitheater, Chicago, USA.

Tickets: $9.50

The build up with the intro music is by now an example of showmanship: It's slow, built on heavy, floor-shaking bass Moog and the slow, deliberate name-check from the M.C. raises the expectations of this typically enthusiastic Chicago crowd. They applaud at every opportunity and, with ELP on top form, this means frequently.

"Peter Gunn" does its job well, a slightly shortened version compared to the 1977 takes. This band really does take no time at all to warm up, and by the time "Hoedown" struts its stuff, ELP are flying high with Keith turning in some wonderful work on Hammond and synth. There's a constant barrage of sound from the fans that shows their appreciation of these two opening pieces.

"Tarkus", in all its glory, sweeps by at full pelt with "Eruption" having lost none of its aggression and drive since the first performances back in 1971.

Another wonderful "Mass" soon becomes an even more wonderful "Aquatarkus", awash with bubbling rhythm and a red-hot solo, with a spacey feel to it, from Keith as he overlays some fantastic tom and bass work from Carl and Greg. The atmosphere builds so convincingly towards the climax as the chords become more powerful, edgy and aggressive. The crowd love it.

Keith's work for "Take A Pebble" is pretty near drowned out by the cheers for "Tarkus" that are still ringing round the arena. No sooner do the audience recognize it than they let off a mighty cheer, and we get a strong, exemplary version. The main feature of Keith's first solo is how prominent the bass line is – just as on the original 1970 album – and how well it's played.

Moving swiftly into the "Concerto" excerpt, Keith, delicately supported by Carl on the xylophone, turns in a truly stunning performance. The livelier section is a fine way to end it and it's hardly surprising that, with cheering this loud, "Maple Leaf Rag" creeps in barely noticed.

"C'est La Vie" wins instant recognition. The natural echo of this hall adds a nice feel to the song but maybe the crowd are just a touch too restless and noisy for Greg to weave his magic with the usual effect. The vocals are rich and warm, and wash over everything, giving a tingly feeling that lingers. Unfortunately Keith's accordion solo is so low in the mix that Greg's accompaniment sounds more like the solo itself.

A tidal wave of applause greets "Lucky Man" and a stirringly emotional rendition it is. At the end, the appreciation is such that Keith can barely get a word in edgeways but still manages to shout, "Alright! We're gonna give you 'Pictures At An Exhibition'!"

We get a heavy, driving version, full of bass and kick, that nonetheless casts its spell over this lively crowd. "The Gnome" and "Baba Yaga" in particular get everyone more excited, with sporadic outbursts of applause. Technically, the playing is superb, with all of them on top form. The Hammond and Moog sound enormous throughout.

Post-interval, "Welcome Back" is the ideal opener. ELP come on stage on a hydraulic lift through a hole in the floor, all playing tambourines in time with the sequenced Moog. Greg's voice has the same effect as the *portamento* in "Hoedown" or Keith's lead in "Peter Gunn". This five minute excerpt from "Karn Evil 9" has everything: killer organ and guitar solos, a drum break that gets a fantastic response, a vocal delivery that excites and lifts, and an unstoppable rhythm. What a way to start the second half!

Keeping the mood and tempo is a rocking "Tiger In A Spotlight" that conjures up every image of Keith bobbing away at the keys as Greg and Carl provide the drive power. He rings a few changes with some discordant notes just before an off-the-wall main solo and the whole thing goes down a storm.

"Watching Over You", surely one of the most evocative pieces ever penned by Greg, calms everything and everyone down so that we can appreciate this beautiful lullaby. And appreciated it is.

Carl's turn, and "Tank" is a corker, the whole band playing at speed as it builds to one of the most musical percussion solos in rock. It may be the drummer's showcase, but Keith shines both in the initial synth solo and then again in the call and response.

After a tearaway "Nutrocker", delivered at incredible speed, "Pirates", with its measured, deliberate, thoughtful intro, is a relief and a chance to catch breath. This one already has the status of a classic, paired as it is at the end of every show with "Fanfare For The Common Man", and it deserves all the praise it receives. The climax, complete with cannon shots, is simply breathtaking.

"Fanfare ..." itself arrives to wild applause and never lets up. The tympani beats shake the foundations of the place, Carl and Greg set the pace, the crowd go all clap-along and a fun time is had by all.

Keith lets rip with a stunner of a solo, giving the crowd a chorus of "My Kind Of Town Chicago Is!", then charging forcefully into "Rondo" with a full head of steam. Again, he's throwing in a segment of late 1960s-style blues, which sounds cool and fades like a passing storm leaving chaos in its wake.

Follow that! ELP finish them off with a swinging "Show Me The Way To Go Home", an amazing choice bearing in mind what's gone before. It never seems to fail. Greg carries the opening on vocals before the rhythm proper kicks in.

Emerson, Lake and Palmer Unplugged for a show-stopping encore?

Yep!

SUNDAY, 22 JANUARY 1978

The Universal Amphitheater, Chicago, IL, USA.

Tickets: $9.50

A noisy, excited crowd greet ELP as they step out after what must have been, from the foot-stomping and whistles, a delayed start.

The intro music builds the tension nicely and the people of Chicago go mad when they hear "Peter Gunn". This must be one of the few occasions when the audience clap along with an opener!

It's straight into a "Hoedown" that's greeted with wild cheers and shouts of "Yeah!". Carl fills well with some tuneful work on the toms but again it's Keith's Moog and Hammond that shine way above everything. The total change of rhythm that sets up Keith for the ribbon controller solo is superb: it's manically fast, takes no prisoners and must have been spectacular to watch.

The whole epic that is "Tarkus" is built on a series of changing rhythms that tonight fly out of the stacks and hit you right in the face. This is powerful stuff as all three seem to be vying with each other for the title of fastest instrumentalist of the year.

Carl's drumming is faultless; he isn't just keeping time; he's adding colour and texture to every part of the long solo, tearing round the toms and delicately making full use of the range of cymbals. The Hammond solo is measured and full of soul. Through a rip-roaring "Iconoclast" into "Mass", they never let up, the latter razor-sharp and moving smoothly into a particularly strong "Aquatarkus" that entertains us solidly for nine minutes. Over that infectious, toe-tapping rhythm, Keith builds a solo that gains steadily in volume, pace and edge, using both the Yamaha and the Hammond.

The decision not to announce "Take A Pebble" but just to launch into the acoustic, almost jazzy opening, is a masterstroke that works each night without fail, with the audience playing "I'll name that tune in ..." The "Concerto" excerpt is uplifting as Keith meets his own high standards again and again, a faultless and inspiring performance. He then switches effortlessly to "Maple Leaf Rag", the musical bouncy castle of the show, a wonderfully happy and lively piece from one of the most unloved ELP albums, *Works Volume II* [though not as unloved as its follow up *Love Beach*!].

The "Pebble" reprise is excellent jazz-rock: bass heavy, accentuated skilfully, lightly by Carl on cymbals and toms, and teeming with stunning piano glissandos. Wild applause starts as Greg's final line is still hanging in the air, and Greg himself credits Keith's work.

A huge cheer lifts the roof as Keith repays the compliment and we're treated to "C'est La Vie", which wins the loudest and longest cheers so far tonight as Greg launches into "Lucky Man" to yet more applause. This Chicago audience sure like their Lake acoustics!

Greg starts singing "Promenade" over the applause and does a sterling job of holding and keeping the crowd in the palm of his hand before handing over to Keith to introduce a downright wild "Baba Yaga". The Moog-driven finale sends the audience crazy: the ending is pure musical splendour with all three of them shining. The applause goes on for ages, well into the fifteen minute intermission.

A rousing "Welcome Back My Friends" picks up where "Pictures ..." left off with Greg in particularly good form on the vocals. Their entry for the second half on the hydraulic lift is pure theatre that befits the stature of the "Karn Evil 9" excerpt.

They charge straight into a fast and very lively "Tiger In A Spotlight", Keith offering up a different intro solo that's well received. Heads-a-bobbing, this one's a winner – even though Greg totally misses his cue for the penultimate verse, as Keith and Carl take it round one more time before they get it right.

From two uplifting numbers, Greg takes the spotlight with "Watching Over You" and thoroughly deserves the sincere applause he gets. This one seems to get more poignant each night, more heartfelt. A simply beautiful song played with style. How many prog rock bands can perform a lullaby and be taken seriously?

Greg gets a standing ovation and ironically sets the scene perfectly for Carl's showcase of "Tank"/"The Enemy God ...". In keeping with the pace of tonight's show, Carl's main solo is fast – very fast – but he doesn't miss a trick or a stroke. Hands a blur, never tiring, he builds patterns and rhythms that never let up and this excitable, noisy crowd go wild at the spinning riser, the gong crashes, the flicking of the drum sticks over his shoulder.

The spectacular theatre matches the music perfectly and the people of Chicago are quick to show their appreciation. "The Enemy God ...", features stunning playing and the whole thing reaches a shattering climax.

"Nutrocker" has a different false start every night: tonight it's 'Keith plays the blues with a vengeance' – before tearing into the riff at light speed. Everyone's trying to play faster than everyone else, and not a note or a cue is missed. The boogie-woogie is terrific as Keith goes off on one big style.

Having worked up this crowd to a fever pitch, Keith can't resist his "Did you really, really, really, really like it?!!!" routine and off they launch again into a fantastically improvised two minutes of magic.

After that, "Pirates" slows things down but it's a captivating version to close the main part of the show. The long middle solo in particular is fast and furious – Keith at his best. Carl is everywhere and the pounding bass lines are almost a feature in themselves. It's obvious that the band are having a whale of a time.

Fireworks and a loud "Goodnight!" from Greg elicit a level of thunderous applause, whistles and cheers that ELP can't resist and, after barely two minutes, back they come. More fireworks, the intro to "Fanfare ...", and the crowd go berserk. Keith's bass line gets some of the loudest applause of the night and then it's off into that killer rhythm. "My Kind Of Town (Chicago Is)" is an obvious home crowd pleaser, but why not? Some nice "Nice" touches fill the arena as he moves from GX-1 to Hammond and back again with very nifty playing.

"Rondo" is everything it should be: fast and furious with a belting rhythm. The organ-throwing drives the crowd wild. The almost seamless, skilful return to "Fanfare" features a few powerful bars of "America" before a crescendo that blows the roof off. Greg comments, "You've been very kind, we've got one more tune" and Keith goes into night club mode with the measured, tasteful intro to "Show Me The Way To Go Home".

What a superb show-closer!

TUESDAY, 24 JANUARY 1978

The Hulman Civic Center, Indiana State University, Terre Haute, IN, USA.

Tickets: $7.00 (advance purchase)

As seemed to be a feature on this tour, the crowd were vocal from the off and not backward in coming forward.

"Peter Gunn" is dominated by bass and drums, decorated in an almost understated, laid-back way by Keith in a superbly-played solo. An uneasy start to "Hoedown" – with the *portamento* not quite in tune – can't put these guys off and within seconds they've picked it up and thrown it out of the speakers bigtime.

Keith does the professional thing and acknowledges the out of tune Moog that's dogged them so far tonight. "We had a bit of bother but we got there! We're gonna carry on with a fantasy piece about an animal that's a bit like an armadillo. It's called 'Tarkus'" The sound system tonight favours the power of the bass, so again it's Greg together with Keith's lower manuals that provide the force behind this one.

A mighty "Aquatarkus" closes the epic. Keith lets fly on the GX-1, floor-shaking Moog and the engine room bubbling away below him. The mix is just right: synth nice and clear right at the top, every beat of the toms, cymbals and hi-hat there for all to hear, Greg's bass lines strong and powerful.

Loud calls of "Alright!!" greet the refined intro to "Take A Pebble" and the audience soon settle down to listen attentively.

The bridge into the "Concerto" excerpt signals the start of a wonderful six minutes that highlight Keith's forte. The tempo of "Maple Leaf Rag" is unbelievable. That huge *glissando* marks the reprise of "Pebble", and a mighty one it is too: a fusion of jazz and rock, improvisation abounds and it's just so obvious that these guys can almost read each others' musical minds.

"Gonna feature Gregory now, Gregory Lake on a song called 'C'est La Vie'," says Keith. The double act of "C'est La Vie" and "Lucky Man", back-to-back, is a well-thought out move and still carries all before it every night. Other than the accordion solo from Keith, both are simple vocal-guitar pieces and hit an emotional, romantic nerve each time.

The band take their interval after "Pictures ..." and you can't really blame them. It's a bit shorter than of late but it sounds huge!

With no record of "Welcome Back My Friends" being played, "Tiger In A Spotlight" gets the toes tapping. A solid bass line accompanies accurate syncopated drumming from Carl, over which Keith lays down a lively, well-improvised solo on the Yamaha. As Keith admits, "My goodness what a lot of fun that was! 'Tiger In A Spotlight' from *Works Volume II*. Something in a mellower mood, Greg Lake with 'Watching Over You'."

Direct, simple and heart-rending, this one is classic Greg, played to a silent audience who are not slow to show their appreciation. And then it's Carl's turn: Keith introduces the percussive medley, "Gonna feature Carl Frederick Kendall 'I'm a dojo' Palmer thrashing away at his assortment of hardware in a variety of numbers, one of which is called 'Tank' and the other one is by Prokofiev and it's called 'The Enemy God'. Take it away Carl!" [The 'dojo' reference is to Carl's karate skills].

The number is dominated by Carl, building and embellishing pattern after pattern, rhythm upon rhythm, starting at the call and response, and driving all the way through the Prokofiev piece. The faultless intricacies of this one are a delight to behold as it crashes to a halt, literally, with a huge gong smash.

Boogie-woogie bass, followed by honky tonk piano and a jazz rhythm from Carl, introduces "Nutrocker" and off they go, hell for leather. The solo's light-hearted, bouncy, and fun-loving. It's almost possible to see the broad grin on Keith's face as he improvises to his heart's delight, underpinned by a rampant Greg and 'let's-see-how-cheeky-I-can-be-on-these-toms' Carl.

"Pirates" is good. Seriously good. No longer sounding so empty, it's full of highs and lows, richness and depth, a lot of which is due to Carl filling for all he's worth, using those toms to astounding effect. In these pre-MIDI days, Keith's work is a pleasure as is the resonance and solidity of Greg's bass lines.

From "Fanfare ..." through to a hint of "Rondo" and back again, ELP turn in a closing finale that's worthy of its place in the set. Where the train whistles of "Rondo" used to blow the roof off the arenas, it's now the opening brass fanfares that do the job. The band are oh so tight, and just power their way through the eleven minutes of inventive keyboard solos.

How to follow that? Sustained calls for more see them playing the now standard encore, "Show Me The Way To Go Home", that gets a whopping reception from this excited crowd. Blues, jazz, rock, and boogie-woogie are all fused into a version that winds everything and everyone down nicely. Greg's voice wraps its warmth round the whole audience and sends them all home happy.

Top show.

WEDNESDAY, 25 JANUARY 1978

The Coliseum, Richfield, OH, USA.

Tickets: $6.50

The recording of this show featured the complete fanfare build-up as the crowd went from excitement to ecstasy when ELP hit the stage.

Rhythm is heavy with Greg high up in the mix, and Keith shines with an inventive solo that uses pitch variation and innovative licks really well in "Peter Gunn". Thing is, it still sounds as if it's only plodding along with no overt sense of direction or purpose.

"Hoedown" soon puts that right: it's fast and rocks for all it's worth. This is what an ELP show ought to be like!

Eighteen minutes of "Tarkus" follows – and what an eighteen minutes. "Eruption" does just that: it explodes through the sound system, featuring really tight playing from all the guys. The opening of "Stones Of Years" has some airy touches on the synth that fit the slowed-down first part perfectly.

By now beginning to rival "Aquatarkus" as the longest movement of the whole epic, "Stones ..." is developing cult status in its own right. "Iconoclast" is so powerful it must have been at risk of blowing the stacks clean off the stage. Carl fills everywhere he can, Keith sounds like an orchestra of Moogs and synths, and Greg holds the whole thing together with such aplomb.

"Aquatarkus" is ELP at their best: world-class instrumentalism, mesmeric solos and the ultimate infectious rhythm. The *Star Wars* theme soon settles into a steady rocking, bubbling pace that allows Keith to shine so much that the crowd must have needed sunglasses.

The applause is at best lukewarm for "Take A Pebble" until Greg's opening lines and Keith's first glissando; after that, they're home and dry with this one. The "Concerto" excerpt is deservedly well-received, with a further burst of applause for Carl's work on the xylophone.

From a light-hearted, tearaway, in-your-face and thoroughly enjoyable "Maple Leaf Rag" where it's hard to believe that just one man's playing all the piano parts, they move easily and effectively back to the "Pebble" reprise, which creates the perfect mood for Greg's first solo piece, "C'est La Vie". It may be credited as a Greg solo spot but it just wouldn't be the same song without Keith's accordion contribution.

The opening chords of "Lucky Man" get the usual reception. That ever-so-slight dramatic pause before "A bullet had found him" has just the desired effect.

"Pictures ..." is a winner from the word go, Carl in particular making this a "Promenade" to remember with strong work on the toms and cymbals to accentuate Keith's playing. Each stop-start bit of "The Gnome" gets its own round of applause as the guys expertly build the atmosphere. Set against superb playing from Greg and Carl, Keith's playing on "Baba Yaga" provides the ideal backdrop for Greg's wah-wah bass spot. As ever, the finale is stunning, majestic, with a last chord that goes on forever, leaving everyone shattered – but wanting more.

Time for a break.

Kicking off the second set with "Tiger In A Spotlight" is inspired. Possibly the simplest drum beat of the night, you can just imagine Carl's grinning face as he drives the whole thing on. Some nice jazzy bass adds to the overall effect. It goes down well.

Keith announces that they're gonna "Take it down a bit" with Greg's "Watching Over You", which is played a touch more slowly, with some nice dramatic pauses that capitalize on the sentimentality of the lyrics.

Carl gets the usual full name credit from Keith as he drives off into a strong, pounding 'Tank'. All the crowd-pleasers are there, greeted like long lost friends.

His cymbal/hi-hat section is so delicately played, so warmly received and is followed in total contrast by resounding rhythms on the gongs, tympani and percussion synth.

After that, the short, determined "The Enemy God …" provides an excellent coda to the Palmer section of the show. There's plenty of intricate, incredibly fast whole-band work that illustrates yet again just how in-tune (excuse the pun) with each other these guys really are.

"Nutrocker" is a real rabble-rouser, guaranteed to get everyone rocking. It seems to get faster each night, especially in the closing bars when Keith and Carl in particular are trying to out-do each other in the speed stakes.

The stately, dramatic opening to "Pirates" calms things down until Keith gets the main opening theme going. In fact, Keith takes most of the honours on this one, despite a couple of rare wrong notes just before Greg sings the opening lines. A word-painting on a canvas of musical imagery is what this one is all about, and it works a treat.

Back they come for an encore of "Fanfare …" that gets riotous applause, a welcome that generates a storming version from all three. Keith's solo has such a mix of everything, phrases old and new, as he frequently goes completely off at a tangent, set perfectly against Carl's fills and Greg's thumping bass. Improvisation rules tonight!

The show closer, "Show Me The Way …", is a classic, wind-down, "Goodnight and God Bless" number. The crowd seem unsure of what it is until Greg sings the opening lines and then it's surprisingly warmly received. Laid-back piano and drums do it justice as Greg belts out the lyrics with real feeling. It gathers pace nicely, ending a superb show in style as Respighi flows through the speaker cabs.

Gold stars all round for this one!

SATURDAY, 28 JANUARY 1978

The Capital Center, Largo, MD, USA.

Tickets: $7.50

The surviving recording of this show kicks in part way through "Stones Of Years" – a pity because it's a corker of a version. As one reviewer put it "ELP seemed to use enough electricity to power the city of Bethesda for a week."[78]

Vocals are strong and Carl's driving everyone forward in boisterous form. It's certainly faster on a nightly basis than it was during the orchestral phase of the tour, rockier, less soulful; in many ways harking back to the classic versions of the early 1970s.

"Take A Pebble" gets a well-deserved round of applause as soon as Greg sings the opening line. Shouts of "Alright!, Alright!" greet Keith's first solo, very much a textbook one, ably backed by the others. As they move into the excerpt from the "Concerto" there's plenty of whistles and calls from this animated crowd – who then surprisingly settle back to listen to the piece in almost total silence.

It's six minutes of classical excellence before Keith, pausing for effect, launches like a man possessed into "Maple Leaf Rag". This is the only clap-along number, and the shortest piece of the night – but it's fun, lively, toe-tapping bar-room teasing, and in complete contrast to the prog seriousness of epics such as "Tarkus" and "Pirates".

And it works! The re-entry to "Pebble" is marked by the grandest *glissando* of the evening and the jazz-oriented playing that follows is pure magnificence.

Keith hands over the baton to Greg for a graceful, thoughtful and touching "C'est La Vie". As the audience show their appreciation, amid shouts and a few klaxons, Greg comments, "Here's one you might remember". They do! "Lucky Man" is ecstatically received.

"OK, here's another old faithful! We're gonna give you 'Pictures At An Exhibition'," shouts Keith. "Promenade" has a different, trebly, less bassy sound to the organ that seems to soothe the crowd before the musical cavorting of "The Gnome" wakes and excites them again.

"The Great Gates ..." opens majestically and stays open. Tubular bells, organ stops, resonant bass, powerful Hammond and that old faithful, the reverberating synth from the glory days of "Karn Evil 9", are all there, adding up to a stunning climax to the first half.

The second half is, as the M.C. promises, even better. "Karn Evil 9: 1st Impression" is a prog powerhouse: Greg and Carl set up a strong rhythm, Keith goes off on one as only he can and Greg takes over the soloing with aplomb on the six string. There's a ton of amazing drum work from Carl in the lead-up to "Come and see the show!" and the final chords bring the house down.

This band waste no time, going straight into a nicely tight and jazzy "Tiger In A Spotlight". You can almost see Keith's head bobbing up and down as he plays the middle eight and the coda. The crowd love it.

"Gonna feature gorgeous Gregory with one of his songs, called 'Watching Over You'," is how Keith paves the way for another Lake solo spot. Richer sounding, bassier version tonight, baritone vocals crystal clear and set against a backdrop of complete silence from a very appreciative audience.

After a lengthy introduction from Keith, "Tank" kicks off at breakneck speed. Machine-gun snare work takes us straight into "The Enemy God ...", a faultless rendition with honours shared equally between all three.

The crashing final gong precedes Keith's credit for Carl, and then it's 40 seconds of cool jazz and honky tonk before they charge into "Nutrocker". Keith plays his rocks off in his attempts to keep up with Greg and Carl – and succeeds. A totally improvised ending is barely over before we hear the opening chords to one of the true masterpieces of the evening, "Pirates". Nice extra touches from Keith on the GX-1 are a delight. The hard-driven instrumental breaks are fantastic and work the crowd to an even higher fever-pitch. Simulated cannon explosions mark the end of the main set but back the guys come for two encores, the first of which – "Fanfare ..." – is out of this world.

Whistles, shouts and ecstatic applause greet the opening tympani and synth, as one over-excited fan calls "ELP!" several times – just in case anyone wasn't quite sure who was playing. This one's very fast with a driving hard rhythm that fair bubbles as Keith decorates it with, at first, a very laid-back voice on the GX-1. As the fever-pitch builds, so does the volume of Keith's solo lines. There's tons of pitch-bend and then he's off onto the organ for that retro-sounding solo, so reminiscent of the Nice. A few brief licks from "America" then its back to "Fanfare ..." and that crashing ending.

All three of them take their turn at thanking the crowd for being so wonderful, then Greg says what everyone wants to hear, "We're gonna play you one more song before we go!". "Show Me The Way To Go Home" opens in a measured, understated way with Keith on the piano and Carl on the xylophone, and then swings slowly with real taste and poise. Greg's voice is so suited to this one. The temptation at this stage of the night is to try to blow 'em away but this band are masters of the unexpected.

"ELP proved once again that they are not just your average rock and roll band"[79]

THURSDAY, 2 FEBRUARY 1978

Maple Leaf Gardens, Toronto, Canada.

Tickets: $8, $9 Canadian

Back across the border for two nights at the Maple Leaf Gardens and ELP got their usual warm reception: they really loved this band in Canada.

The introductory fanfare builds the tension as the lights go down and the M.C. announces the guys on stage. Applause lifts the roof as ELP walk on and launch into an infectious and powerful "Peter Gunn" giving Keith the opportunity to get his rocks off on the Yamaha. Not for the first time can we hear shades of the *Mission Impossible* TV theme at the start of the solo before he jumps ship and improvises his way through the rest.

No pause for breath, straight into a "Hoedown" that sounds as if he's using pitch-bend on the *portamento* again.

"Eruption" settles down and another powerful version of "Tarkus" can be logged. Oddly, without the middle solo in "Mass" and the whole of "Manticore" and "Battlefield", the re-worked epic has so many more nuances, more shades of light and dark than for a while.

"Aquatarkus" sounds better than ever, controlled yet off-the-wall. In total, almost two-thirds of the seventeen minutes is a showcase for Keith's soloing talents and the prowess of Greg and Carl in holding down a rhythm. Keith delves deep to come up with some amazing sounds.

This noisy crowd are still celebrating "Tarkus" as "Take A Pebble" quietly kicks in. The keyboard solos roll along for a classy six minutes before Keith picks up "Maple Leaf Rag" and gives it a shake-down. His playing is on fire tonight: the move from classical excerpts to bar-room boogie is faultless and wins a massive wave of applause, not to mention a spontaneous clap-along. Not to be outdone, the vocals are highlighted in the mix and the cymbal playing in particular from Carl is magical.

Greg's two song solo spotlight is clearly very popular. "C'est La Vie" goes down a storm, encouraging him to put even more va-va-voom into the delivery. The use of dramatic pauses is real musical theatre, giving the Toronto audience even more time to show their appreciation. "Lucky Man" receives the loudest response of the night for its trouble.

Keith announces "Pictures ...", a keen fan shouts "Holy shit!" and we're off with the longest piece of the night. It's a long time since "Pictures ..." took that accolade.

The echo in the hall well suits the varied moods and tempos of this one. Flitting from Moog to Hammond, onto GX-1 and then round again, Keith plays a blinder and is consistently well rewarded with applause.

With the MC promising an even better second half, this is not the show to spend too much time on the interval drinks.

The lights go down again, the spots hit centre stage and up comes the hydraulic lift bearing the boys, tambourines in hand, beating time to the sequenced Moog from "Welcome Back My Friends". Looks good, sounds good and by golly it does you good! The reaction is ecstatic.

No time to waste and they swing their way through "Tiger In A Spotlight". A note perfect solo from Keith puts the icing on this particular cake.

"Watching Over You" provides a quiet, thoughtful interlude before the maelstrom of the "Tank"/"The Enemy God ..." medley. Calls of "Wow!" and "Oh God!" are still heard as Carl power-starts "Tank" with that driving rhythm, paving the way for a fast, fluid synth solo from Keith, itself culminating in an entertaining call and response section that's different every night.

Come the solo proper, Carl takes off at breakneck speed, using every single part of the kit, and he never lets up. The riser spins, coloured spots emanating from below it, and, at the 180° mark, he turns to the gongs and tympani behind the kit. After rolls and rhythms on both, the gongs and tympani are hidden once more as the riser spins the remaining 180° for Carl to resume his solo – and again the audience raise the roof, joining in the rhythm as Greg and Keith come back in right on cue for "The Enemy God ...".

Suitably worked up, this audience clearly love the slow blues build-up to "Nutrocker", Keith and Carl in particular playing what almost amounts to a duet. The rocked-up classic itself is just the job, nicely placed in the set list after the riotous percussion pieces.

From there, ELP take us onto the twin epics of "Pirates" and "Fanfare ..." both featuring instantly recognizably dramatic openings. "Pirates" tempts some fans to sing along – way out of key. Greg's job is safe!

Keith certainly hogs the limelight in "Fanfare ...", his organ and Moog solos are fast, accurate, inventive and totally off-the-wall in places. No "Rondo" as such by this point of the tour but a rousing display of 1960s-sounding Hammond more than compensates. Typically Emersonian. Never fails.

Throughout this one, the keys and drums echo round the hall, Carl knocking hell out of the crash cymbals, with that huge ending sounding even bigger than usual. Demands for an encore are loud and incessant, paving the way for a cool "Show Me The Way ...".

At first, the crowd, as with some others, don't seem too sure of how to react, but they soon warm to it as ELP get into the swing. Inspired.

SATURDAY, 4 FEBRUARY 1978

The Boston Gardens, Boston, MA, USA.

Back over the border to a venue they've played often enough before.

"Peter Gunn" thuds along as Greg and Carl hammer out that beat and Keith delivers a solo that's totally different from any other on this tour. Pitch-bend galore with lots of varied attack and decay, it sounds excellent. The New England audience agree.

By now almost a medley with the opener, "Hoedown" asks no quarter and goes for gold. "Tarkus", at nineteen minutes, is longer than on most dates recently, mostly accounted for by the blinding solo in "Stones Of Years" and the showcase that is "Aquatarkus". But what gets the loudest cheer of the whole piece? Carl's gong smash halfway through "Eruption"!

Keith is undoubtedly top dog all the way through "Tarkus", the more so since they dropped Greg's "Battlefield" party piece.

The "Take A Pebble" intro is almost drowned out by the continuing cheers after "Tarkus", but yet again, as soon as Greg's bass and vocals kick in, the crowd recognize it. As one punter with a good line in understatement says, "Nice tune!"

Always so measured, so stately, this one is a real winner tonight. As Keith's brief solo segues perfectly into the "Concerto" excerpts, a wave of applause hits the stage and he delivers a version to savour. There's a nifty romp through "Maple Leaf Rag" that entertains this up-for-it crowd delightfully.

Greg strums away nonchalantly as Keith introduces "C'est La Vie", and then gives a superb performance, slightly slower than of late but that's the beauty of the song: it can be taken in, savoured as it should be with those beautiful, telling lyrics. A minor problem with the accordion solo (or as one of this vocal audience puts it, "I think it's out") doesn't spoil the ambience of the piece.

"Lucky Man" seems an intensely heartfelt version, the guitar and delivery spot-on as usual. After receiving the same introduction for over seven years, "Pictures ..." creeps in this time, almost apologetically with a barely audible organ picking up volume as "Promenade" proceeds and the others pile in. Whatever the beginning, this is a strong, tight, massively improvised version that does them proud as all three hold their own, yet gel so effectively as a trio when it counts.

For the second half, the lights come up, ELP appear through a hole in the stage, and "Welcome Back My Friends" wins ecstatic applause. Classic Hammond, heavy rock guitar and driving percussion all add the 'Wow' factor, topped off by some lush vocals. Carl even eclipses himself with the drums in the "Soon the Gypsy Queen" section and it builds to a forceful ending, warmly received by the fans.

"Tiger In A Spotlight" keeps the pot boiling, tonight played with an extended keyboard intro before Carl dives in – and it gives the crowd time to start clapping along. Clearly the band are having fun as Greg can barely sing at one point for laughing at something.

The keyboard solo is nimble and precise, the whole piece bouncing along with a helluva lively tempo.

Having worked everyone up, Greg does a sterling job in the face of an initially vocal audience to deliver a beautifully played "Watching Over You".

"We now feature someone who needs no introduction – so we're not gonna give him one. The first one was written for his car and that's called "Tank". We follow that one up with a thing by Prokofiev called 'The Enemy God'. Go," commands Keith like he's starting a race. Carl excels during the solo sections particularly and this whole percussion medley seems to improve with age.

Once the now much shorter jazz intro is out of the way, "Nutrocker" is supersonic in its tempo. Surely the fastest ELP have ever played it and note-perfect all the way.

"Pirates" is a symphony in its own right, magnificently played with a barrage of keyboard brilliance. The crowd are still giving it some as "Fanfare ..." gets under way.

Keith's bass line on this one is nice and clear, reminding us that the rhythm section really consists of all three of them. Greg and Carl keep up that bubbly, bouncing tempo as the backdrop for an entertaining solo spot from Keith that teems with improvisation. He throws in a few bars of "America", strolling up and down the manuals of both the Yamaha and the Hammond. It's certainly an above average performance with a mind-boggling level of dexterity as he launches into that 1960s style organ section that harks back to the days of the Nice and beyond. "Rondo" may be gone but this is great; As the climax approaches, he goes off in "Space Oddity" style, returning just perfectly for that tight finale.

"Show Me The Way ..." starts differently every night. Carl plays what sounds like a vibraphone and the bass line is wonderfully light but telling. As ever, it's very well received and this audience aren't slow in the 'let's clap along' stakes – and they're in perfect time! Through all that, they just keep on cheering and yelling.

The slow piano fade-out from Keith is the perfect vehicle for the band to take their bows as once more Boston gives heartfelt applause with more than a feeling.

THURSDAY, 9 FEBRUARY 1978

The Uniondale Coliseum, Nassau, NY, USA.

Tickets: $8.50

The first of two nights at the Coliseum in funky Nassau and the only one of the two that's survived through the years, although it's often misrepresented as February 10. The show was recorded by WLIR-FM in New York.

There's an electric atmosphere from the off with a storming "Peter Gunn". This New York audience are definitely in the mood to be entertained and, as they show their appreciation, Keith fires off the *portamento* for "Hoedown", a feature that has a distinctly different feel about it tonight. The number itself has developed well during this tour with a radically punchier rhythm during the middle ribbon controller solo as Carl goes manic on the toms.

Keith greets everyone with "Hey! Good to see you all again," before counting in "Tarkus", an epic with plenty of kick and blistering bass lines.

Carl uses virtually the whole kit for "Mass "and Keith goes to town on the Moog and GX-1. "Aquatarkus "starts with a weird and wonderful sound on the Yamaha, before Keith wanders off in *Star Wars* mode, perfectly complemented by that bubbling rhythm and a ton of fuzz bass from Greg. Loud cheers greet the famous five notes from *Close Encounters Of The Third Kind*, then Keith really takes charge, soloing off into the night as the engine room maintains the rhythm

This is one of those few shows where "Take A Pebble", a faithful representation of the original, wins instant applause, The well-practiced "Concerto" excerpt is immaculately played through all its tempo and mood changes, Keith pausing only to allow the crowd to react before cranking up everything to eleven for "Maple Leaf Rag". As an example of ragtime, this one works big time. Scott Joplin's instruction for this piece was not to play it fast, but thankfully Keith has always had a healthy disregard for orders. He plays it penny arcade style: at breakneck, downright devilish speed and doesn't fluff a single note.

The reception for "C'est La Vie" is ecstatic. The guitar playing, mostly *arpeggio*, sounds a little too sharp, has a touch too much edge to it but the effect of the strong vocal delivery more than makes up for any shortcomings. "Lucky Man", on the other hand, sounds just perfect, acoustic chords and singing both spot-on. Greg introduces it for the first time in ages with a perfunctory, "Here's one you'll remember!" They do, of course.

"Pictures ..." doesn't disappoint. In places Keith replaces organ solo breaks with some inventive Moog and it still works well.

From there, ELP get into the groove with "Tiger In A Spotlight", with all three audibly enjoying the show. Again, the main solo is radically different to other nights, always inventive, always entertaining.

"This next song is a lullaby that I wrote for my two-year-old little daughter, Natasha. This one's called 'Watching Over You'," says Greg with pride. Beautiful, heartfelt, touching – it's all of those and more, sung with genuine emotion by a loving father a long way from home and his beloved daughter.

"Tank" is launched with a barrage of percussion and never lets up for a second, with the percussion synthesizer being particularly memorable.

Although now under three minutes, "The Enemy God ..." is a first-rate adaptation, rounding off nicely Carl's showcase spot. It's rewarded in this crowd's usual exuberant way.

Unless the radio recording has missed off the free form bluesy-jazz intro, they've changed "Nutrocker" tonight and dive straight into the fast-paced rocker we've come to know and love. Some nice touches of boogie-woogie liven up things even more and a quick change of tempo in the middle works well. Keith's tongue is firmly in his cheek as he throws in a dash of the silent cinema and a huge classical-style ending. "Did you like it? Did you really like it? Did you really, really like it? Well ... I thought it was terrible," jokes Keith.

The opening to "Pirates" is itself by now a mini epic: those dramatic chords and notes on the synths echo around and fill the arena, guaranteeing the piece a generous reception. Nobody is reserved on this one, a totally convincing number, especially during the long instrumental intro that features some truly first-rate playing. Greg's on top form. The synth solos have been tweaked in a few places to add some variety and spice but they still capture the mood of the song.

No trace of "Show Me The Way ..." tonight and the gap between "Pirates" and "Fanfare ..." indicate that the latter was the encore, a fact reinforced by the almost riotous welcome it receives. The bass chords and tympani opening have some timely pauses to increase the drama and expectation, before the band launch into a superb version with tight rhythm and wonderful solo. There's precise syncopation, a ton of funky playing from Keith on both Moog and GX-1 before "America" shows its head again in style as the precursor to the 60s retro-style section that he now uses every show. The "Space Oddity" segment grows in strength, power and class each night.

Greg says, "Thank you very much! You've been a very nice audience! Thank you!"

Respighi's closing music plays them out and another good night has been had by all.

THURSDAY, 2 MARCH 1978

The Boston Gardens, Boston, MA, USA.

Some doubt here as to the exact date of this one, with some sources quoting the gig being played on the following night, but ELP were actually playing the Rupp Arena in Lexington, KY on March 3.

Either way, it's show 39 of the tour and back in Boston for the second time in a month.

"Peter Gunn" does the trick, livening up still further this lively audience. The groove set up by Carl and Greg puts every other rhythm section to shame as Keith turns in a fantastic solo. "Hoedown" gets a roof-lifting reception, swinging into action immediately with the mighty Hammond and ribbon controller against a constant background of cheering and applause as the crowd take to Keith and egg him on.

"Hello Boston, good to be back, hello! We're gonna carry on with a fantasy about a creature that looks a bit like an armadillo, name of 'Tarkus'," says Keith giving the time honoured intro. Clearly, some of this vociferous audience take a shine to this one.

With a pounding, driving bass and drums this is a strong version and is well-played. "Stones Of Years" is a nice contrast to the sometimes hard, aggressive prog of "Eruption". "Mass" moves quite naturally into "Aquatarkus". Strange, now that they've played it many times like this it seems perfectly natural without the long middle solo and as almost the preamble to the long finale. "Aquatarkus" itself begins low-key, like *Star Wars,* then develops the pulsating, bubbling rhythm that allows Keith to show what he's made of. That includes a much appreciated segment of the *Close Encounters* ... theme. A solo of its time, with a finale that defies time

The crowd show their appreciation for "Take A Pebble" immediately and in return they get a fantastic performance. Keith entertains masterfully with the "Concerto" excerpt, still in total command of its tempo and mood shifts, and it's mind-bogglingly clever. Interestingly, never at any of these shows does the crowd seem bored by Keith's classical solo effort.

Pausing for the crowd to react, he gets another wave of applause with "Maple Leaf Rag" as this huge gathering claps along in time, audibly cheering, whistling and laughing at what is very much a light-hearted piece.

Keith then, justifiably, shows some impatience with the crowd, "Someone just threw a bottle up here just now. That's not very cool and it's very distracting. Please don't do it! We're gonna carry on with Greg Lake, 'C'est La Vie'."

The song is delivered extremely well, vocals full of emotion, spot-on guitar and a more understated, less in-your-face accordion solo than of late. "Lucky Man" gets the loudest and warmest reception of the evening.

"Alright!!" is one fan's response to Keith's announcement "We're gonna give you 'Pictures At An Exhibition'!" and, after a quiet, almost unobtrusive start, "Promenade" powers its way around the hall.

Keith doesn't allow some hiccups with the Moog during "The Gnome" to put him off his stride.

"Ladies and Gentlemen, there will now be a short interval. If you wander off please make sure you're back for the second half because you must take my word, it gets even better," notes the M.C.

After the break, they return with a storming "Welcome Back My Friends", high-powered, with cracking Hammond and guitar solos. Keeping the pace going is an excellent "Tiger In A Spotlight" with Carl giving those musical toms a damn good thrashing.

According to Keith, "We're gonna take it down a bit now and Greg's gonna introduce one of his ballads", answered by Greg with "This next song is a song I wrote for my little baby daughter. It's a lullaby and it's called 'Watching Over You'."

The closing section of "The Enemy God" gives the audience time to applaud long and loud as ELP deliver another tight instrumental performance.

Cheers abound as soon as the blues start to "Nutrocker" kicks in, turning to riotous applause as soon as they start the piece proper. Even for ELP, this is fast and Keith's solo is every bit as improvised as other nights.

Barely has Keith's "Did you like it?" bit finished than the overture to "Pirates" sounds out through the speakers. One tone deaf fan asks someone, "Is it Fanfare?". Oh well!

After its powerful climax, the song gets an almighty reception, the crowd still in full flow as the fanfare of "Fanfare ..." rings out across the arena. The return to the original coda is precise and gets the applause it rightly deserves.

"Show Me The Way ..." is ELP doing just that – showing anyone who wants to listen that this is how you end a show in style.

Another notch on the speaker cabs.

MONDAY, 6 MARCH 1978

The Civic Center, New Haven, CT, USA.

Tickets: from $7.50

ELP's second visit to this venue in just over three months and another success. Their 42ⁿᵈ gig; unfortunately only a partial recording of this one has survived. But what there is ... is worth hearing!

We clearly have an up-for-it audience, determined to enjoy everything they hear. At the "Take A Pebble" reprise point of the show, all is going very well judging by the quality of the playing and the crowd reactions. There's a strong, very free-form piano intro from Keith, well-supported by resonant vocals and a whopping rhythm section. With that final line hanging in the air, it gets a fantastic reception, and Greg credits Keith for his piano work in the number.

"C'est La Vie" has a large fan club in Connecticut judging by the audience reaction. Beautifully sung, touchingly accompanied by Keith on accordion, it's one of the finest moments of the evening.

Greg strums his way thoughtfully into "Lucky Man", a song that's warmly applauded and appreciated. Vocals are strong, clear and his rich baritone gives this one extra clout. Having worked up the crowd, Greg passes the baton to Keith to announce a cracking rendition of "Pictures At An Exhibition".

This one impresses from the off. "Holy shit!" is one fan's audible reaction to the menace of "The Gnome" with that stunning Hammond sound dominating matters. The quality of the "Great Gates ..." reminds me of the heyday of 1970 and 1971: it fills the hall, it's majestic, has a wicked organ solo and rich vocals that sets it apart from other prog pieces.

After the interval, making their reappearance from centre stage to wild adulation, ELP carry all before them with an uplifting "Welcome Back My Friends". The ending is a crescendo of sound, the audience adding to the volume with deafening applause as Greg quietly takes up the strains of "Watching Over You", again dedicated to his daughter. A superb version, but it doesn't elicit the reaction it has on previous nights and passes us by almost uneventfully with a polite ripple of applause.

The same can't be said of the following piece. "Gonna give Carl Palmer a chance to have a bash around!" is how Keith introduces the percussion medley. "Tank" is incredible in terms of pace and detail: Keith's initial solo is fast enough, but when Carl gets going into his showcase he puts everything and everyone else to shame. The spectacle and the music fit together perfectly.

As a coda to the whole solo, "The Enemy God ..." fits the bill: fast, rhythmic, driving, with some excellent Moog work.

"Nutrocker" starts with some of the funkiest bass and piano duet work I have heard from ELP. Recent versions of this track have been breathtakingly fast and tonight is no exception. It's complete with extended silent cinema-type ending, just as they used to do with "The Sheriff" four years earlier.

From the intro, with floor-shaking bass, rattling cymbals and synth chords that hang in there for an eternity, "Pirates" grabs the attention and never lets go. As ever, the climactic ending generates wild applause that never really dies down as "Fanfare ..." begins in its triumphant way.

No two versions of this mini epic are ever the same and tonight's solo leans heavily on blues and 1960s influences throughout. It has a real foot-stomping groove feel to it as he undoubtedly steals the show.

It's so off-the-wall that the reprise of the theme comes as a surprise when he suddenly throws in the tag, but the others pick it up without a moment's hesitation, and the crowd show their feelings with downright manic cheering and applause.

"Thank you very much, it's been a real gas! We'll play one more song," Greg tells them. "Show Me The Way ..." is creatively played with real panache sending thousands of fans go home very happy indeed.

THURSDAY, 9 MARCH 1978

The Omni, Atlanta, GA, USA.

Tickets: $8.50

This show is often listed as the 8 March but was in fact played a day later. Night 44 on the road, three away from the end, and the last surviving recording of Emerson, Lake and Palmer before the 1992 reunion.

Loud, very loud, cheers from this southern crowd greet the opening music and the M.C.'s introduction, paving the way for a "Peter Gunn" which gets them going.

German single. Courtesy of Gudrun Friedrich

Sounding more like the *Mission Impossible* theme than ever, Keith conjures up a still jazzier, livelier sound from the GX-1, and the rhythm section excels.

The opener has now effectively become a medley, moving straight into an upbeat "Hoedown" full of impish fills and light cymbal touches from Carl.

"Tarkus" is an aggressive, percussive take, strong on the Hammond sound, heavy on bass and drums, and played at a demanding pace. As so often with this mini epic – especially since they stopped playing Battlefield – "Aquatarkus" is the highlight. Initially faithful to the original, Keith soon decorates the martial rhythm with a highly imaginative solo built around the themes from *Star Wars*, *Close Encounters* ... and other favourites. Even "Norwegian Wood" from way back when is still there, casually tossed into the mix as he wanders all over the musical world.

"C'est La Vie" continues the calmer mood of the reprise section. There's some beautifully understated guitar and accordion with vocals from the heart, a slightly different intonation in Greg's voice; a nice touch. He goes immediately into "Lucky Man" and a Mexican wave of applause hits the stage after a few seconds, repeated three minutes later at the end of this excellent version.

"Pictures ..." bursts out of the speakers in typical fashion, grabbing and holding the attention from the off. Tonight's is a stunning rendition: everything is just so. Keith taking charge on the solos as Greg and Carl prove their credentials as a rhythm section yet again. The crowd is on the band's side and they go for it, big time. The Hammond/tubular bells duet section still makes the hairs on the back of the neck stand up, followed by the sequenced Moog explosion that sends the audience crazy. After that, ELP just can't lose.

The interval, the dramatic re-appearance and a hard-driven take on "Welcome Back ..." all add to the feeling of real rock theatre at its very best with the music leading the way. An ebullient Greg throws in a few shouts of "Yeah!"; this is a version that all three are definitely enjoying. In the solos, the baton is passed almost imperceptibly from Keith to Greg, and then to Carl for a storming drum break. Ending on a high as the band go straight into "Tiger In A Spotlight" – of which we only get a few seconds – the sad thing is that this is the last track from this show that has survived.

Doubtless the rest of the evening matched or surpassed the high standards set so far by ELP ... but we'll never know.

They played 3 further shows in Johnson City, TN, Springfield, MA, and Providence, RI, before the curtain came down on the final Emerson, Lake and Palmer tour of the 1970s

Here's one for groupies and diehard fans, the coveted backstage pass.
© Richard Galbraith

Postscript: Were You There?

SUNDAY, 25 JULY 2010

Fortieth Anniversary reunion show,

High Voltage Festival, Victoria Park, London, UK.

Did it – could it – live up to expectations? Emerson, Lake and Palmer were the headline act, the final act, at the festival, on the Classic Rock *stage. Throughout the build-up and on the night, it seemed like the eyes and ears of the rock* cognoscenti *were on them and only them. Reputations were at stake here.*

ELP take to the stage at almost exactly 9p.m., just as the sun is beginning to dip over the park on a warm summer's evening. Perfect timing. The set list has been carefully crafted: "Hoedown" and "Still ... You Turn Me On", amongst others, are rehearsed but not included in the final programme, nor was "I Talk To The Wind" the King Crimson number that Greg has sung during his tenure with the band. The key feature of this show is the re-working of established classics, a refreshing approach when one considers the temptation to just go out and "play it again".

A heady mixture of nostalgia accompanied by inspirational musicianship.

The stage is set out as always – Keith, Carl and Greg (complete with Persian rug) as you look it at left to right. The show's about to start.

"London, will you please welcome on stage ... Emerson, Lake and Palmer!" The guys stride on very confidently, acknowledging from the front of the stage the wild cheers from this large crowd. Swirling synth kicks off "Karn Evil 9", the rhythm section piles in, complete with Carl's tambourine, and Greg's vocals are as powerful as ever. The band are enjoying it and it shows in the sheer quality of the playing. This is the start of a classic show and it receives tumultuous applause.

A quick hello from Keith and they launch into a fairly moderately paced but nonetheless entertaining "Barbarian". Both this and "Bitches Crystal" are intricate, cleverly updated takes which give all three guys a perfect opportunity to showcase: Carl's work on the hi-hat, the blocks and toms are just scintillating, Keith does fast runs and *glissandos* on the Hammond, and Greg's vocals are right on the money – something noticeable throughout the show.

"Knife Edge" relies more on synth than Hammond for the melody and sounds less upfront, less rocking, but every bit as haunting as ever. There's a pleasantly

The show had to end sometime – thanks for some great memories guys.
© Richard Galbraith

surprising delicate middle-break before they deliver the *coup de grace* for this one – that loud, driving final section that has the crowd going wild again.

By now, it's dark and the lighting effects are really kicking in. "From The Beginning" from *Trilogy* and "Touch And Go" (from the 1985 *Emerson, Lake And Powell* album with Cozy Powell instead of Carl Palmer), takes advantage of the mood thus created.

The former has a wonderfully melodic opening section after which it's Greg on acoustic guitar with a simple "Thank you!" before he sings the opening line. This is a real classic version, complete with a misleadingly simple solo from the man stage right.

"Touch And Go" has a new instrumental intro before the familiar rhythm takes over. Carl, arms high in the air, gets the crowd clapping along and they're definitely on a roll here. The song grabs you and takes you with it, honours shared evenly between Greg's vocals, the precisely sharp drumming from Carl, and Keith's amazing work on synths.

A beautifully melodic intro from Keith, with strings and piano, heralds a radically different but excellent version of "Take A Pebble". There's some nice syncopation again in the keyboard solo bit and then Carl and Greg bow out and leave Keith to it. The crowd immediately recognize what's going on when he launches into "Eruption" from "Tarkus", a wonderfully innovative approach to one of their classics. "Stones Of Years" is stripped down to a simple song with vocals echoing round the park, followed by a Hammond solo which is simply Keith at his best.

Have you ever heard an ELP audience singing along to the opening of "Mass"? You have now! Carl and Keith in particular hit you right between the eyes with this one and then out comes the ribbon controller. Keith wanders around left and centre stage, shooting fireworks in time with the rhythm, much to Greg's visible amusement and the audible delight of the crowd.

"Battlefield" has a slow measured start from Carl on the toms, but gaining pace. It's as majestic as ever, the "Every blade is sharp" line particularly telling and dramatic, delivered to an absolutely silent audience.

"Aquatarkus" features exact *ostinato* and Hammond from Keith and, as they reach the *crescendo*, the crowd go wild.

Keith credits both Carl and Greg as there are loud shouts of "ELP!" and before we know it, and without further ado, we're into "Farewell To Arms" from the *Black Moon* album. This is a true "goosebumps" version of a song they haven't played live since the summer of 1992. This is definitely Greg's song: there is just *so* much feeling in the words, backed as they are by stunning keyboards and crisp, powerful drum work.

Carl has a chat with the crowd and then "Lucky Man" continues the mood; the closing solo from Keith is sharp and just so right.

How else can they introduce the next track but with "Alright! We're gonna give you 'Pictures At an Exhibition'!"? "Promenade" is powerful and true to the spirit of the evening, the rest of the piece is completely re-jigged. Keith, tongue nervously on his lips, gives a quick smile in Greg's direction and then it's "The Gnome", complete with its precision-timed musical hobgoblin jumps, reliant as ever on visual cues and nods. The imagery is as evocative as ever and the Moog/synth work awesome!

"The Sage" is simply breathtaking. The sides of the stage are bathed in blue light and Greg stands – no guitar – and impresses with emotion and deep feeling in his vocals, backed by strings from Keith. It's the first time it's has been played like this and it's magnificent.

From that, it's straight into the musical mayhem that is "Baba Yaga", complete with wailing siren, just to prove that no, they haven't slowed over the years. "The Great Gates Of Kiev" is, yet again, one of those things that makes you wonder how just three musicians can produce what they do. It's fists in the air time amongst the crowd, fans visibly singing along with Greg. Carl's there as ever with the tubular bells as they build to the mighty crescendo that is "Death is Life!". The last chord is held and held as twin cannons at either side of the stage, echoing perfectly their official debut 40 years earlier at the Isle of Wight, are fired at the end of a spectacular, epic piece of music.

The crowd are totally ecstatic. Carl's at the mic again, wanting to know if they want another one, Keith and Greg are all smiles and it's obvious what's going to follow.

"Come on, we've been away for twelve years, you can make more noise than that," Carl reckons.

"Fanfare For The Common Man" is right up there with the best of them. Carl does his mighty muscle man pose on the kit, Greg's beaming on stage right and hell's teeth – we're off. This one rocks for England, as do the entire crowd.

After a tight first section, the others leave Carl to a solo that shows once and for all what a master craftsman he still is. Sticks are a blur, especially on the cymbals with reverse stick playing drawing huge applause. Not bad for a man who recently turned 60 years old.

Back come Keith and Greg, they tear into "Rondo" with that driving rhythm section and Keith's antics with the Hammond deserve the ecstatic reaction they get.

Before we know it, that's it, the guys stand stage front to take a bow and give their own applause to a very receptive, willing and appreciative crowd. The backstage crew can be seen applauding wildly and the whole atmosphere is of a performance that worked from beginning to end.

It might have been 40 years ago that ELP first took the stage together, and many of the fans weren't even born then, but tonight they delivered the goods as well as ever.

Will they reform again? Carl thinks the 2010 gig was the end of the road, sadly: "A week after that gig I told the others that was it for me. It's over. I don't want to be part of a nostalgia act. Leave people with the dream."[80] Well, we can only hope they reform. However, if they don't play again then thanks for everything and a garland of Martian fire flowers to the three of them!

Appendix

WEDNESDAY, 4 JULY 1973

Keith Emerson appearance with Cleo Laine and John Dankworth, BBC 2 TV, UK.
(The recording that survives is truncated and is cut after Gulda's Fugue).

Intro of Keith playing something (unknown) on the Moog, and then chat ensues between him, and husband and wife jazz team, John Dankworth and Cleo Laine.

JD: Wow, we've had some instruments in the house, but that's the first synthesizer we've had.

CL: I think I'd like one in my hall.

KE: Every home should have one.

JD: How much did this set up cost, all of it?

KE: Well ... it's difficult to estimate it now because a lot of things have been added to it since I first had it. I started out with this first console bit here you see, which I guess cost about £2,000.

JD: Would you sell me the lot for £5,000 here and now?

KE: Ah, I wouldn't replace this, it's irreplaceable.

CL: Do you have to be a fairly rich person to have one? To go out and perform with one? If you were starting off from scratch, you wouldn't be able to get one easily?

JD: Well ... this is a small one (referring to the mini Moog).

KE: It's like all prototypes of anything are more expensive, but since this one was invented lots more people have jumped on the bandwagon and made others, which are possibly better, but I'm used to this, used to working with this on stage.

JD: Why do you use both?

KE: Well, it's a monophonic keyboard, which means that if you go to the keyboard and you try and play a chord, you end up with just one note. The main sound source comes from an oscillator over here, and if you hear that on its own... I'll demonstrate. That's the basic sound, and you have a choice of four waves: a sine wave, a triangular wave, a pulse wave and a tooth wave. Now if you're after imitating another instrument, you have to sort of decide first which sort of wave you want.

JD: I'm so glad I've only got one wave on my instruments!

CL: What are all the numbers coming up here, Keith?

KE: That's the frequency counter, it measures the cycles of the oscillators.

CL: So, it's really like learning another language?

KE: Yes, you have to remember all the numbers.

Keith then plays a piano piece.

JD: That was a piece of music played by Keith Emerson, without Lake and Palmer. What was that piece called?

KE: It was the *Fugue* from Frederick Gulda's *Prelude and Fugue*.

JD: Oh yes, he's a great pianist and a great composer, we've played with him in Germany. Do you often pick music by other composers to play in your own repertoire?

KE: Occasionally ...

JD: Because one of your most famous albums was *Pictures From* (sic) *An Exhibition*, which was Mussorgsky, which was later arranged by Ravel for the symphony orchestra, and you brought it back to a keyboard state with Greg Lake and Carl Palmer.

(recording cut).

Endnotes

1 Forrester, Hanson and Askew, *Emerson, Lake and Palmer: The Show That Never Ends*, page 52.

2 Chris Welch, *Melody Maker*, 29 August 1970.

3 *Melody Maker*, 19 September 1970.

4 Forrester, Hanson and Askew, *Emerson, Lake and Palmer: The Show That Never Ends*, p.53.

5 *Melody Maker*, 19 September 1970.

6 Carl's view; Chris Welch, *Melody Maker*, 29 August 1970.

7 Karl Dallas *The Times* 31 August 1970.

8 Keith Emerson, *Pictures of an Exhibitionist*, page 185.

9 Chris Welch, *Melody Maker*, 29 August 1970.

10 Chris Welch, *Melody Maker*, 12 September 1970.

11 Greg Lake, The Official Greg Lake Site, *Shows I'll never forget*.

12 Michael Wale *The Times*, 28 October 1970.

13 Greg Lake, The Official Greg Lake Site, *Shows I'll never forget*.

14 Keith Emerson, *Contemporary Keyboard Magazine*, 1977.

15 Keith Emerson, *Pictures of an Exhibitionist*, 2004, p. 190.

16 Attila Sik.

17 Alan Anderson, *Melody Maker*, 10 April 1971.

18 Keith Emerson, interview with Chris Welch, *Melody Maker*, 8 May 1971.

19 As above.

20 Attila Sik.

21 Chris Welch, *Melody Maker*, 8 May 1971.

22 Dirk Uther.

23 Mike John, *The New York Times*, 2 May 1971.

24 Attila Sik.

25 Greg Lake, The Official Greg Lake Website, *Shows I'll never forget*.

26 Keith Emerson, *Pictures of an Exhibitionist*, page 210.

27 Carl Palmer, interview with Chris Welch, Melody Maker, 18 September 1971.

28 "From my perspective, I can honestly say I give 100% every time I go out there and it really hurts when you can't do that. When something is preventing you from giving everything, it really is a drag". Greg Lake, interview with the author, 21st March 2005.

29 Translation by Dirk Uther.

30 Dirk Uther.

31 Attila Sik.

32 *Melody Maker*, 15 May 1971.

33 Chris Welch, *Melody Maker*, 26 June 1971.

34 Chris Welch, *Melody Maker*, 26 June 1971.

35 *Melody Maker*, 31 July 1971.

36 Greg Lake, The Official Greg Lake website, *Memories*, Michael J.Cash .

37 Keith Emerson, *Pictures of an Exhibitionist*, page 215.

38 Keith Emerson, *Prog*, issue 27, 20 June 2012.

39 Dirk Uther.

40 Dirk Uther.

41 Don Heckman, *The New York Times*, 22 November 1971.

42 Attila Sik.

43 Dirk Uther.

44 Carl Palmer, *Melody Maker*, 22 April 1972.

45 Don Heckman, *The New York Times*, 4 April 1972

46 Dirk Uther.

47 Keith Emerson, *Pictures of an Exhibitionist*, page 238.

48 Keith Emerson, *Melody Maker*, July 1972.

49 Greg Lake, *Melody Maker*, 29 July 1972.

50 Keith Emerson, *Pictures of an Exhibitionist*, page 239.

51 As above.

52 Dirk Uther.

53 Keith Emerson, *Melody Maker*, 30 September 1972.

54 Martin Walker, *The Guardian*, 2 October 1972.

55 Carl Palmer, *Melody Maker*, 7 October 1972.

56 Keith Emerson, *Melody Maker*, 30 September 1972.

57 Dirk Uther.

58 Barbara Drillsma, *Melody Maker*, 18 November 1972.

59 Courtesy of Grant Parker, The official Greg Lake website, *Were You There?*.

60 *Melody Maker*, 17 March 1973.

61 As above.

62 Greg Lake, *Melody Maker*, 21 April 1973.

63 Greg Lake, *Melody Maker*, 31 March 1973.

64 Keith Emerson, *Melody Maker*, 21 April 1973.

65   You turn me on,
        You can sing my song
        You put me back where I belong
        You can find me when I'm gone

> You, you can see my face
> You can see my love in this place
> You can touch my hand
> You can understand
> Courtesy of Ken, <threefates1970>.

66 Penultimate verse:

> Though your flesh has crystallised,
> Though you've made me so unwise, You look me in the eyes,
> You're gonna get your prize,
> But still you turn me on yes you do, baby oh you
> Turn me on, yes you do, Oh you turn me on.

67 Ian Dove, *The New York Times*, 21 December, 1973.

68 Carl Palmer, *Melody Maker*, 26 January 1974.

69 Les Dawson was a British stand-up comedian who, despite being an able pianist, made something of a reputation for himself by deliberately playing the wrong notes and chords as part of his act.

70 Greg Lake, *Melody Maker*, 12 March 1977.

71 Keith Emerson, *Prog* issue 27, 20 June 2012.

72 Chris Welch, *Melody Maker*, 12 March 1977.

73 Robert Palmer interview, *The New York Times*, 8 July 1977.

74 Carl Palmer, *Melody Maker*, 12 March 1977.

75 Greg Lake, *Melody Maker*, 9 June 1977.

76 Greg Lake, *Melody Maker*, 9 June 1977.

77 *Time* magazine, 1977, reviewer unknown.

78 Mark Kernis, *The Washington Post*, 30 January 1978.

79 Mark Kernis, *The Washington Post*, 30 January 1978.

80 Carl Palmer, *Prog*, issue 27, 20 June 2012.

Author Biography

Garry Freeman is married and lives with his wife and two sons in Leeds, West Yorkshire. He has been listening to and collecting rock rarities since the late 1960s, notably heavy and progressive rock. His previous works include the *Discover History* series (Hodder & Stoughton) and *The Bootleg Guide* (Scarecrow Press).

Garry has worked as a teacher for 35 years, specializing in Special Needs since 1992. He is currently Director of Inclusion and Special Needs Coordinator at a high school in northwest Leeds where, since 2010, he has worked with Carl Palmer to provide enjoyable, drum-based musical experiences for hundreds of special needs children of all ages. He previously taught in Bradford, where he also worked with Carl.

Garry Freeman with Carl Palmer